Major Gen
Alexander M. McCook,
USA

Major General Alexander M. McCook, USA

A CIVIL WAR BIOGRAPHY

Wayne Fanebust

McFarland & Company, Inc., Publishers
Jefferson, North Carolina, and London

All photographs are courtesy of the Library of Congress unless otherwise noted.

LIBRARY OF CONGRESS CATALOGUING-IN-PUBLICATION DATA

Fanebust, Wayne.
    Major General Alexander M. McCook, USA : a Civil War biography / Wayne Fanebust.
       p.   cm.
    Includes bibliographical references and index.

    ISBN 978-0-7864-7241-3
    softcover : acid free paper ∞

    1. McCook, Alexander McDowell, 1831–1903. 2. Generals — United States — Biography. 3. United States — History — Civil War, 1861–1865 — Biography. 4. United States — History — Civil War, 1861–1865 — Campaigns. I. Title.
E467.1.M235F36 2013
355.0092 — dc23
[B]   2012042573

BRITISH LIBRARY CATALOGUING DATA ARE AVAILABLE

On the cover: Alexander M. McCook (National Archives and Records Administration); American flag background (iStockphoto/ Thinkstock)

Manufactured in the United States of America

McFarland & Company, Inc., Publishers
  Box 611, Jefferson, North Carolina 28640
   www.mcfarlandpub.com

Table of Contents

Preface

The Civil War began more than 150 years ago, but it continues to be a subject of great interest to Americans. We are attracted to that part of our history almost as if we have no choice in the matter. The war had a profound and lasting effect on those who fought it as well as those who experienced it through letters and newspapers. The survivors handed it off to the next generation while the embers were still white hot. The fiery mass has been passed to new generations ever since. The Civil War is the Grand Canyon of American memories; a chasm we cannot seem to cross, a dark night without end.

We remember that terrible war for the unthinkable suffering and death and because out of the struggle, there emerged a united nation, free from the chains of slavery. We remember it because of Abraham Lincoln and his wisdom and leadership, without which our great continental expanses would be broken into smaller, weaker nations. Lincoln so loved America that he saved the country the Founders created and gave it a path to the future.

My interest in the Civil War began in my college days. In recent years I have been engaged in extensive reading about the men and women of the war and the great battles they fought. I am impressed by the enormity of their sacrifice and the immense suffering they endured, in a struggle where one side sought to preserve the Union and the other to create its own country, while at the very epicenter loomed the question of slavery.

I freely confess to be more than just a little bit amazed at the North/South dichotomy that exists as to the cause of the Civil War. While it is clear to me that slavery was the proximate and actual cause of the war, I am also aware of strong opinion of others who downplay the role of human bondage. But I find myself constantly asking: why all the fuss? It seems like simple logic: had there been no slavery there would have been no reason for the South to secede, and therefore, no war.

Still we seem to be locked in an argument without an end and the debate will continue to inspire writers from both sides of the polemic. I wish to join the fray and offer my book, a biography of Major General Alexander M. McCook, the story of a dedicated soldier, a fierce fighter and a strident opponent of secession. Like other men of his time with strong, unyielding political views, McCook threw himself into the grinding wheels of the war machine, determined to fight until the South was defeated and the Union was triumphant. McCook believed a Rebel was a traitor and treason had to be punished by the sword of justice until it was soundly defeated.

The outspoken Ohio general was joined by sixteen other members from the extended McCook clan — his father, his brothers, cousins and uncles — all of whom served as soldiers, surgeons or in other capacities. General McCook's father and three brothers were shot and killed by enemy fire, while the subject of this biography survived combat without a scratch on his body. While some might call that a sign of good fortune, others will point to the number of dents in his reputation and conclude he was overly cautious or prone to making bad decisions.

They would be wrong, for Alexander M. McCook took risks. He was brash, bold, brave and reckless — very much like another young Civil War general, namely George A. Custer. General McCook had many of Custer's characteristics, as both men were well suited for life on horseback in a uniform. What McCook lacked was Custer's luck.

Custer's luck turned sour after the Civil War ended. He died with his men at Little Bighorn, but McCook, who also served on the Plains after the war, completed his military career without undue fanfare or disaster. Unlike Custer, McCook's army days came to a gradual and pleasant end. He outlived most of his contemporaries and critics. As an old soldier basking in the warmth of the California sun, he was able to look back on a long career that — despite the setbacks — provided satisfaction and reward.

Like every writer, I owe thanks to a number of people, libraries and archives. I begin by thanking my friend and fellow Civil War buff, David Swan, for his careful, patient and very useful review of several chapters. Every writer needs an editor to ask pertinent questions, clean up silly mistakes and provide direction and depth toward the final product. I am fortunate to have such a sincere friend and advisor in David.

I am also lucky to have found the McCook Family Manuscript Collection at the Library of Congress. It takes a considerable period of time to review the approximately 3,000 pieces of paper, but I enjoyed every minute of it. The people at the Library of Congress were professional and helpful, and I thank them. I also thank the people at the archives of the Ohio State Historical Society, in Columbus, where I reviewed and took notes from the unpublished biography of Anson G. McCook, cousin to General McCook. The History Center at Connecticut Landmarks in Hartford allowed me to review a large collection of McCook letters, many written from tents or around campfires, and I thank everyone who assisted me at that facility.

Researching and writing a book forces the writer to get out of the house and travel, and in addition to flying to Washington, D.C., Hartford and Columbus, I visited a number of libraries. At the library of Augustana College in Sioux Falls, I reviewed the entire set of hardcover volumes of the *Official Records of the War of the Rebellion*, without which no book on the Civil War can be written. Other Civil War books at the Center for Western Studies at Augustana College provided useful data. Research facilities include the libraries at San Diego, CA, Sioux Falls, SD, Pierre, SD, Yankton, SD, Hartford, CT, Columbus, OH, and the University of South Dakota. I wish to thank all my friends and colleagues at San Diego Independent Scholars. And of course, I would be remiss if I forgot to thank Google, the researcher's faithful tool.

My heartfelt gratitude is extended to friends, relatives and colleagues who are willing to listen to my endless Civil War harangues. They include Bruce Blake, Tom Kilian, Richard Nordstrom, David Swan, Tom Maldari, David Davis, Courtney Callahan, Jill Adams and my sister Connie Lilla. A special thank-you goes to fellow Civil War writer Mark Dunkelman who always answered my e-mails and offered valuable suggestions.

I thank my mother, brothers and sisters, all of whom seem to understand my insatiable need to be "doing something creative." Thank you for your patience, love and support and for knowing that a book is meant to be more than just a paper weight. Finally, to my wonderful daughter Danae Howell, an accomplished and educated lady in her own right, and to her daughter, my precious granddaughter Angelina, I pledge my undying love and affection, along with my thanks. No book of mine would be complete if I failed to mention their names in it.

Wayne Fanebust • Sioux Falls, South Dakota

Meet the McCook Family

The McCook presence in the United States was the result of something more than the usual arduous and boring voyage across the Atlantic Ocean. It began with the Americanization of the flamboyant and gutsy George McCook and his spouse, Mary (McCormack) McCook. The aggressive couple came from Ireland in 1790. George McCook was born in 1852 in Antrim County, Ireland. He was the son of Alexander McCook and Sarah Darrah. Mary McCormack — the woman George was destined to marry — was born December 26, 1763, in Ireland. George had been involved in a radical political movement in Ireland, and when the authorities closed in on the organization, he fled to America with his wife and nine-year-old daughter Fanny, fearing retribution from the angry English.

The McCooks settled in Canonsburg, Pennsylvania, where three more children were born, and moved to Ohio where George was a merchant. They were Presbyterians, thus setting a strong religious precedent for the next generation of McCooks. More importantly for their adopted country, they were the grandparents of the "Fighting McCooks," a Civil War family united by the desire to preserve the Union and crush the rebellion.

The aggressive nature and fighting attitude of the Civil War McCooks resided in the heart and mind of their grandfather, whose political and personal life was marked by radicalism and violence. Controversy seemed to cover George McCook like a hot blanket. In 1794 he and other western Pennsylvania men became embroiled in a major break with the authorities called the "Whisky Rebellion." Angry with the federal government and upset over having to pay a revenue tax on whisky, the westerners not only refused to pay, but fought with and occasionally tarred and feathered, the tax collectors. The fighting in the Ohio Valley got so brutal that President George Washington sent a large army out to restore peace and enforce the law. Some of the "Whisky boys" escaped; some were arrested and convicted of treason, but were later pardoned by the president. Having escaped capital punishment for treason a second time, in a second country, George McCook settled down to work and raise a family.

The first child born in America was George McCook, born June 15, 1795. He was followed by Daniel McCook, born June 20, 1798, and John James McCook, whose birthday was February 21, 1806. With this male trilogy, three distinct lines of McCooks were established in the United States, two of which produced the "Fighting McCooks" of Civil War fame.

Dr. George McCook graduated from Jefferson College in Canonsburg, Washington County, Pennsylvania, at the age of 16 in 1811. He studied medicine with a Dr. Warren and established a medical practice in Canonsburg and Pittsburgh.

He met and married Margaret Latimer and the couple moved to Ohio. In 1844, Dr. McCook held a professorship at the Lake Shore Medical College of Willoughby and in 1847 he was practicing medicine in New Lisbon. Two years later, he was in Pittsburgh where he continued his success as a physician, building an extensive practice.

During the Civil War, Dr. McCook served on a board that examined the credentials of doctors seeking appointments as army surgeons. George and Margaret McCook were the parents of seven daughters and two sons, one of whom, George Latimer, became a Civil War doctor.

Dr. John J. McCook was educated at Jefferson College and earned a reputation as an excellent doctor and surgeon. He was an outdoorsman, fond of hunting and fishing.

In 1831 he married the gifted Catherine Sheldon from Connecticut. She was a worldly woman of "rare culture" combined with literary, artistic and musical talent. Dr. McCook practiced medicine at New Lisbon and Steubenville, Ohio. He and his wife were the parents of five sons, all of whom served in the Civil War, and one daughter.

Daniel McCook, father of the subject of this book, was educated at Jefferson College. He married Martha Latimer on August 28, 1817. She was born March 8, 1802, the daughter of Abraham Latimer and Mary Greer. She was also the sister of Margaret Latimer, wife of Daniel's older brother George Jr. In 1826, Daniel and Martha moved to New Lisbon, Ohio. They also lived in Carrollton, Ohio, a town that Daniel was instrumental in creating. Daniel built the family home, in the classical style, in Carrollton, about 1840. He made a living buying and selling grain, wool and other agricultural produce.

Staunch Presbyterians, the McCooks were parents of a whole passel of children that in time became known as the "Tribe of Dan." It was said that the stern but fair Daniel McCook, Sr., "ruled his household in the fear of the Lord." It was this household that contributed the greatest number of warriors to the clan known as the "Fighting McCooks."

The Family of Daniel and Martha McCook

The first child, a boy, **Latimer A. McCook**, was born at Canonsburg, on April 20, 1820. Latimer received his higher education at Jefferson College in Canonsburg and went on to study medicine under the tutelage of his uncle, Dr. George McCook, a surgeon of great ability. When the Civil war erupted, Latimer entered the army as a contract surgeon and served through the duration of the rebellion, eventually attaining the rank of major.

On November 2, 1821, the second child of Daniel and Martha, a son named **George Wythe McCook**, was born at Canonsburg. He graduated from the University of Ohio at Athens and studied law along with Edwin M. Stanton. They went on to form a law partnership in Steubenville, Ohio. George distinguished himself in the legal profession editing the first volume of the *Ohio Reports* and later becoming the attorney general of the state. His partner, Edwin M. Stanton, went on to a high-profile and controversial political career which culminated in the office of secretary of war in the Abraham Lincoln administration.

Next came **John James McCook**, born on December 28, 1823, in Canonsburg. He received his education at the United States Naval Academy and was assigned to the United States frigate *Delaware* as a midshipman. While serving off the coast of South America, he took ill with a fever and died on March 30, 1842, and was buried in Rio de Janeiro. The first of the young McCooks to take up the military as a career, he was also the first to die in the military and the only one to die in a foreign country. But his name would live on, as shall be revealed in the pages ahead.

The fourth son was **Robert Latimer McCook**, born on December 28, 1827, in New Lisbon. Following the profession of his older brother George, Robert studied law at the office of Stanton and McCook in Steubenville. He went to Cincinnati and engaged in a large and successful law practice with Judge J. B. Stallo. This kept Robert well occupied until the outbreak of the Civil War.

The fifth son was **Alexander McDowell McCook**, born on a farm near New Lisbon on April 22, 1831. Like his older brother John James, Alexander opted for a military education, enrolling at the United States Military Academy at West Point. He graduated in 1852.

The sixth son, **Daniel McCook Jr.**, was born on July 22, 1834. He struggled through a sickly childhood, and yet he was bright, ambitious and headstrong. Dan graduated from the University of Alabama at Florence, and, with improved health, returned to Ohio. He read law at the office of McCook and Stanton and was admitted to the Ohio bar.

The seventh son, **Edwin Stanton McCook**, was born at Carrollton, Ohio, on March 26, 1837. He was admitted to the U.S. Naval Academy, but did not complete the course. In the pre-war years, he worked as a steamboat pilot on the river waterways. When the war came, Edwin, in step with his older brothers, opted for the army.

Charles Morris McCook was born at Carrollton on November 13, 1843, becoming son number eight in the most prolific branch of the McCook family. In 1861 at 17, while enrolled at Kenyon College, he answered Lincoln's call for volunteers. He entered the war as a private, unlike his brothers who started soldiering as officers.

The last son, number nine, **John James McCook**, having been given the same name as his late brother, was born at Carrollton on May 25, 1845. Along with brother Charles, he was a student at Kenyon College when the war broke out. Since he was only 16, and because all of her other sons were in uniform, Martha McCook refused to let John join them. That refusal, however, did not long hold up, for John finished his freshman year at college and enlisted in an Ohio volunteer regiment as an aide to the brigade commander.

Three girls were blended into the band of boys, starting with **Catherine McCook** who was born in Canonsburg, Pennsylvania, in 1825. Her life was brief for she died on June 18, 1847, of acute bronchitis at Carrollton. Sickly early in life, and forced to suffer over the years from the oppressive burden of disease, she was nevertheless described as beautiful, a "child of nature

Major General Alexander M. McCook (courtesy Ohio Historical Society).

without folly or affectation." Possessed of her full share of the McCook resilience, she got the most out of her short life, but she missed all the tragedy and excitement of the Civil War.

Mary Jane McCook was born in Columbiana County, Ohio, 1830. Her first husband was Timothy Guard with whom she shared a daughter, Sallie, and a son, William. Her next husband was Lewis Baldwin, a steamboat master from New York. They were parents of Martha "Mattie" Baldwin. Mary died April 15, 1902, in Mexico City, where she was buried.

Martha McCook was born in Carrollton in 1841. Her first husband was Dupont Alexander Davis, whom she married at St. Louis on November 29, 1860. He died leaving Martha a young widow. Her next husband was John Green Curtis, an eminent physician from a distinguished New England family. He was a graduate of Columbia University in New York, and enjoyed a prestigious medical career, writing and lecturing on medical topics. They were married on October 25, 1874. Martha died in 1897. She had no children.

The McCook girls were thoroughly dominated by the lives and exploits of the McCook boys. That domination, along with the mores and manners of nineteenth-century society, is why comparatively little is known of the girls. Whereas the boys are introduced over and over again in books, articles and tributes, the girls remain largely invisible to history.

Boys and girls together, the McCooks were an exceptional family living in an extraordinary time. Much has been written about brothers, fathers, uncles and cousins serving in the armies of both the North and South. But in the annals of history, no family contributed so many members and so much patriotic, single-minded dedication to the army of the North and its Herculean effort to defeat the rebellion and preserve the Union. As a family and as individuals, as warriors and advocates for a cause they deemed noble and worthy, the McCooks stand alone at the head of the line.

CHAPTER 1

Disunion and the Democratic Party

How poor is human wisdom and how weak is human strength in the presence of such an exigency?

— George W. McCook

George W. McCook from Ohio was referring to the state of the Union at the threshold of the Civil War. A terrible crisis gripped the country as North and South were bitterly divided over the great political and economic issues of the day, while at the very epicenter of the controversy loomed the subject of slavery. McCook understood the enormity of the crisis and confessed his poor power to do anything to avert a violent conflict that many saw as inevitable. The country arrived at this desperate stage after decades of disagreement between North and South that reflected two distinctly different and evolving cultures. Although both had its own hierarchy of wealth, privilege and power, one was agrarian and dependent on slavery, while the other was industrial and had rejected slavery.

By 1860 the sectional discord had reached a breaking point, and as it was a presidential election year, both sides threw themselves into the struggle, sparing neither energy nor emotion. There was a sense that the people had one last chance to save the Union and the great Constitution that the Founding Fathers created. Both sides paid homage to the grand document, but each side came up with a different meaning of the Constitution as it applied to slavery. The South believed it legitimized slavery for all time to come, and while informed Northerners agreed that it sanctioned slavery, they also believed the Founders crafted a Constitution that would eventually be used to eliminate human bondage.

The Democratic Party was scheduled to hold its national convention on April 23, 1860, in Institute Hall at Charleston, South Carolina, with two major

9

items on its plate: selection of a platform and the nomination of its candidate for president of the United States. The leading contender was Illinois senator Stephen A. Douglas, an able man and excellent orator who had debated Abraham Lincoln, a former congressman from Illinois, in 1858. They went head to head in seven debates in various Illinois cities, all on the issue of slavery. Both men were seeking the office of U.S. senator. They were friends and treated each other with respect, and yet their views of political issues were poles apart, except for both being anti-secessionist.

By 1858 Lincoln was known throughout America as a devoted and tireless opponent of slavery. His speeches and writings were firm and unequivocal in their condemnation of slavery and were difficult to refute. In an 1854 speech Lincoln declared, "I hate it [slavery] because of the monstrous injustice of slavery itself. I hate it because it deprives our republican example of its just influence in the world ... enabling outsiders to taunt us as hypocrites."[1] The ambitious Lincoln was prepared to devote his great political and oratorical skills and the rest of his life to see it abolished, or confined to the South until at some future date it would be cast aside like other failed social experiments.

Douglas was the favorite going into the Democratic National Convention. But his supporters knew the upcoming fight would be brutal, for the "Little Giant" did not endear himself to his Southern brethren when he offered the nation his "popular sovereignty" doctrine. According to Douglas, the matter of slavery should be put to a vote in the new territories. Let the people decide — let them opt in or opt out — for he didn't care one way or the other.

Lincoln saw this as a specious idea fit for simple-minded folk and argued that Douglas — a fence-sitter — lacked moral fiber. On the surface, popular sovereignty seemed plain and fair enough because it allowed slavery where the voters said "yes" to it, and disallowed it where the voters said "no." But it was open ended. It created the legal machinery to perpetuate slavery and left the door open to the enslavement of other "inferior races" or other categories of unpopular people. While only blacks were slaves, popular sovereignty exposed everyone to slavery, except the powerful.

Like a dreamer gazing at some distant utopian shore, Lincoln wanted America to see what he saw. He wanted America to accept the universal truth: slavery cannot be justified, morally or philosophically; it is wrong, and always will be wrong, for one human being to own another human being.

Lincoln firmly believed he had the moral high ground, and from that lofty precipice, he made his case with confidence and poise. His premise, simply stated, was that the Founders accepted slavery where it existed at the time of the adoption of the Constitution, but that document was unequivocal in that it prohibited the spread of slavery to other parts of the country.[2] He was willing to use this great truth as an intellectual cudgel against Douglas or any other challenger.

Old Meeting House at 188 Meeting Street in the heart of historic downtown Charleston, South Carolina. The building still stands and now serves as a Confederate museum featuring photographs, books, papers, paintings and other artifacts of the Civil War.

If Douglas thought his "popular sovereignty" policy would be accepted in the Deep South, he was disappointed. In fact it was just the opposite. The idea that new states and territories could decide whether or not they would allow slavery rankled the fire-eaters of the states where "cotton was king." The pro-slavery men had long counted on the support of Democrats in the free states. In the 1830s and 1840s, votes from soft-on-slavery Democratic senators and congressmen in Northern states prevented the passage of many anti-slavery measures. So it frustrated Southerners that Douglas — once considered one of their own — was disrupting the spreading of the "gospel."

The great Southern statesman and apostle of slavery, John C. Calhoun, who died in 1850, had indoctrinated the South with his "positive good" theory. He meant, of course, that slavery was good for both the slave and white society. His fellow Southerners took the theory to heart. They believed that Democrats like Douglas betrayed the teachings of Calhoun by advancing contrary ideas that stood in the way of the spread of slavery. Believers in the South came to understand that to bolster support for slavery they had to move it into as much of the country as possible.

They expected danger from without the Democratic Party, but counted on cooperation from within. As such there was great cause for concern. Someone must have considered the arithmetic and realized that if they did not press the issue of creating new slave territories and states, in time the pro-slavery element would be hopelessly outnumbered. Section V of the Constitution requires a three-fourths vote of the states to pass an amendment, and the Cotton States feared that unless they pursued slavery with a passion, the North might one day be able to push through an amendment outlawing slavery.

But while the "peculiar institution" was shrinking in the North, it was gathering steam in the South. All politically astute people from Lincoln on down understood that the only way slavery could lawfully and permanently be terminated was by way of an amendment to the Constitution. Southerners understood that the only way to save slavery long term was to prevent such an amendment from coming before the people, or conversely to pass an amendment to protect and enlarge slavery. The Mexican War doubled the size of the United States, and slave men were anxious to move slavery into the newly acquired western domain. Some Southern theorists — or dreamers — idealized over a vast, slaveholding confederacy that would include Cuba, Mexico and Central America.[3]

California, where gold was discovered in 1848, was wildly coveted by Southerners who flocked in to work the mines and influence politics. The new state was looked upon as fertile ground for slavery because of its rich mines and potential for agriculture. When California entered the Union in 1850 as a free state, angry, pro-slavery zealots cried foul. When statehood was being debated, Richard K. Meade, an ex-Virginian living in California, exclaimed: "To the Pacific, then I say — to the Pacific ... secure yourselves, while you can have an empire." He believed the exclusion of slaves from the Golden State threatened the Southern way of life.[4]

The solution, according to a Charleston, South Carolina, newspaper, was to ramp up the pro-slavery movement. The fiery editorial declared: "The means of defense must multiply with the means of attack," for "Slavery must spread in area and power." In other words, if new states are admitted without slavery, that action "must be counter-balanced by addition of Slave States."[5]

The more the North applied pressure, the more the South resisted, relying on leading politicians such as Calhoun who believed a state had the legal right to secede from the Union. Northern theorists considered it very strange then, that if secession from the Union was lawful for a state, why was it wrong for a black slave to undertake any act, legal or illegal, to leave his master? The Southerner's reply was, of course, that one possessed freedom and the other did not, and the Cotton States were prepared to pursue this bedrock belief with great resolve.

The slave men demanded the right to take their "property" anywhere they wanted to take it. If a man had the right to ride his horse from Missouri to Kansas, he certainly had the right to bring his slaves with him, for both horses and slaves were "property." For these men, the Douglas doctrine of popular sovereignty was an ugly sellout and almost as bad as abolitionism. Not all Democrats were warm on the "peculiar institution" of slavery, but the party was dominated by those who were in favor as well as those who were indifferent. The Democratic National Convention of 1860 promised to be very exciting.

There were among the delegates at the convention, sincere men who earnestly wanted their party to unite behind a strong, conservative candidate, but the mood was dominated by partisan anger and distrust. Early on the feeling was that unless the slave holders were granted wide-ranging concessions, the convention would splinter, and two or more candidates would emerge. The South had political muscle and was prepared to use it to get what it wanted.

This was especially troublesome to 39-year-old George Wythe McCook of Steubenville, Ohio. He was the chairman of the Ohio delegation at the National Convention. He and his younger brother Alexander M. McCook attended on behalf of Ohio. They also represented their politically astute family who, like so many others, understood that the country they loved was perilously close to a precipice, and they looked anxiously for some form of political rescue. But the shape of political things was shifting so fast that there wasn't very much to grab and hold. George W. McCook knew that it was a time for action, and he and his relatives and associates were eager to play a role in the great drama.

McCook and his colleagues also knew that a divided Democratic Party could not win against a united Republican Party. But that prospect did not deter the fire-eaters who blustered and threatened that unless they got their way, the South would take their share of the party and go home. Hinting at secession by a united South, the angry Southern delegates were only too willing to bully and overpower the moderates as there would be no more concession to anti-slavery advocates or those who were soft on slavery. Alabama senator Clement Clay warned that if the "black Republicans" get control of the federal government, "we of the South will tear the Constitution to pieces and look to our guns for justice."[6]

The Republican Party had been created in 1854 in Wisconsin, as a direct consequence of the odious institution of slavery. The new party attracted former Whigs, anti-slavery Democrats, abolitionists, northern intellectuals, immigrants, workingmen and other "free-soilers." These men and their party were determined to do what the Whig Party could not or would not do: bring about an end to slavery, or at least contain it until it died a natural death. Toward that end, the party platform featured an anti-slavery plank.

The entry of the Republican Party, a young man's party, onto the field of politics raised the level of anger and debate to a new high. It was one thing for the South to contend with anti-slavery groups and factions, but it was something quite different to oppose and defeat a movement driven by a national political party. As a political movement, the growth of the new party was fast and phenomenal. By 1858 the two parties were about equal in strength, and Republicans believed they were in a position to take control of both houses of Congress.

Some months prior to the opening of the Democratic National Convention of 1860, Mississippi senator Jefferson Davis introduced a series of radical, pro-slavery resolutions in Congress. Davis was an unbending supporter of slavery and the implacable foe of any man who opposed it. Intending that the resolutions should form the basis of the Democratic Party platform that the Southerners planned to control, Davis — a slaveholder and plantation owner — proclaimed that it was the duty of Congress to protect slavery. Congress, he insisted, had no choice but to defend and preserve slavery because it had no authority to do otherwise. It must not impede the progress of slavery in the new territories and states. (While the Constitution doesn't mention the word "slavery," Section 2 of Article I recognizes the existence of black people in that each one counted as "three-fifths" of a person for the purpose of determining the number of representatives that a state was allowed in Congress.)

Davis was unable to understand why the argument over slavery raged on with such force and fury. The Constitution protected property rights, and slaves were property: what could be more plain? And couldn't everyone see that keeping blacks in bondage was best for them and the rest of the country? He said slavery "was established by decree of Almighty God" and "sanctioned in the Bible, in both testaments." It had flourished in past civilizations and it would continue to flourish because the practice, having been carried forth over the centuries, was permanently embedded in human culture.[7]

One of the South's most articulate proponents of slavery, Davis was taking a desperate and hard line. He tossed down the gauntlet and dared an anti-slavery senator to pick it up and entertain opposition. He made it clear that unless Congress supported the preservation and spread of slavery, and enforced the Fugitive Slave Act, the next step by the Southern states, where cotton was "king," would be a triumphant — with heads held high — exit from the Union. A leading Virginia newspaper summed up the Southern position in 1856 in words most Southerners could understand: "Freedom is not possible without slavery."[8]

The Fugitive Slave Act was another point of contention. It was originally passed in 1793, and reinforced by another law in 1850 that punished anyone who intervened on behalf of slaves who were subject to official capture and return. It was extremely unpopular in the North, hard to enforce and encouraged the spread of the "Underground Railroad" system by which slaves were secreted out of the South to Canada where they lived as free people.[9] For the

South, the flow of black people moving through the Underground Railroad to Canada was like money going down the drain. Slaves were not only an important cog in the Southern economy — they were its most valuable asset.

At the 1860 Charleston convention, the committee on the platform played to Davis's resolutions when it issued both a majority and a minority report. The first plank of the majority report, directed at protecting slavery, was like a bombshell tossed out on the convention floor. It read:

> *Resolved,* That the Democracy of the United States hold these cardinal principles on the subject of slavery in the territories: First, that Congress has no power to abolish slavery in the territories. Second, That the Territorial Legislature has no power to abolish slavery in any Territory, nor to prohibit the introduction of slaves therein, nor any power to exclude slavery therefrom, nor any right to destroy or impair the right of property by any legislation whatever.[10]

In one bold stroke, Southern leaders of the Democratic Party made it clear that they were prepared to cast aside decades of compromises and statutes that were implemented to placate both sides of the slavery question. While the series of compromises had held the Union together, by 1860, the house was, as Lincoln said, "divided against itself" and needed only a good push to cause it to collapse. The release of the majority report placed the Southern states on the verge of secession and in a position to apply the final blow. Meanwhile, in the streets outside the convention hall, slaves were offered for sale. In Charleston, it was business as usual.

The minority report was much less volatile. Without mentioning the word "slavery," it conceded that slavery should be allowed if the Supreme Court ruled in favor of human bondage. As if embarrassed by the issue, the minority report referred to "rights of property," which were "judicial in their character." In other words, the decision to allow or disallow slavery would be handled on a case-by-case basis, with the Supreme Court being the final arbiter.[11] The minority report asserted that the 1857 Dred Scott case, decided by the U.S. Supreme Court, was the basis for their platform.

In that landmark case, the plaintiff Dred Scott was denied his freedom because, as a slave, he was a mere chattel, not a U.S. citizen, and not even a human being. He therefore had no standing to sue for a decree declaring him officially free. Because his owner had brought him into the free-soil states of Illinois and Wisconsin, he boldly sued for his freedom, and the case went all the way to the Supreme Court. Led by Chief Justice Roger B. Taney, who favored the South, the court by a 7 to 2 vote slapped him down.

Dred Scott — who unwittingly gave his name to history — was not made a free man, and the Missouri Compromise of 1820 that restricted the spread of slavery, and provided some level of comfort for both sides, was ruled unconstitutional. As if more harsh rhetoric was needed during the expanding sectional crisis, Taney wrote that blacks were "unfit to associate with the white race …

and so far inferior that they had no rights which the white man is bound to respect."[12]

This turn of events and Taney's mean-spirited language outraged many Northerners, including Lincoln, but emboldened the South. Its leaders looked to make further gains in their fight to preserve slavery, including the return of the African slave trade. Southern newspapers greeted the Dred Scott case with great joy, telling the world that the highest court in the land upheld slavery, while the Northern press denounced it.

Lincoln was especially caustic in his criticism of what he believed to be Taney's twisted and distorted meaning of the Constitution as it applied to slavery. If Lincoln had seen any of Taney's earlier legal writings, he might have learned that the chief justice once called slavery a "blot on our national character."[13] But with the Dred Scott decision, Taney had made a dramatic about-face. While he believed that slavery should be phased out, he also was convinced that the Constitution gave exclusive right and authority to the states to preserve or prohibit slavery. Taney may have believed that slavery would eventually disappear, but he wanted to make sure it would not end while he still lived.

The historic case gave Senator Douglas more ammunition to use in his ongoing fight with Lincoln. Douglas applauded the decision by "honest and conscientious" justices, while labeling opponents as enemies of "our whole republican system of government." Like Taney, Douglas believed that the Constitution was for whites only, and he insisted that blacks were incapable of engaging in self-government. He further inflamed angry whites by suggesting that the Republican Party wanted to make the races equal so that black men could marry white women.[14]

The thought of the mixing of the races was to contemplate the unthinkable, even though slave masters were fathering mixed-race children. Southerners lived in morbid fear of slave insurrections, with nightmarish images of murdered white men and the mass rape of their women and girls. Southerners believed that the abolitionists were covertly trying to provoke slaves to revolt.

While Lincoln did not want to see a slave revolt, he warned the promoters of slavery to beware of the consequences of their actions, once saying, "Familiarize yourself with the chains of bondage, and you are preparing your own limbs to wear them." He went on to say that men who "trample the rights of others" risk losing their own independence and "become the fit subjects of the first cunning tyrant who rises."[15]

It all seemed to come to a head at the 1860 Democratic National Convention in Charleston where delegates fought among themselves while also taking vicious hits at Republicans. Day after angry day, delegates engaged in argument and debate with sarcasm and bad behavior taking many forms. All dignity, order and purpose disintegrated as day after brutal day the antics and arguments raged on.

On the eighth day, most of the delegates from Georgia walked out, along with men from Arkansas, Virginia, Kentucky, North Carolina and Maryland. This draining away of delegates did not, however, impede the flow of speakers to the podium, and if the madhouse Convention was anything at all, it was colorful. Among the diverse makeup of the membership was T. B. Flournoy of Arkansas who spoke plainly and with pride about what it was like to be a "Southern man." He said: "All I have is the product of slave labor. I believe the institution a patriarchal one, and beneficial alike to master and slave."

Flournoy was speaking frankly. In calling his success the "product of slave labor," he proclaimed that slavery was a labor system. But implicit in his speech was another truth; slavery was a systematic form of population control. In order for the "patriarchal" system to work, the slave master had to maintain complete and absolute control over the slaves, for their benefit, of course. Lose control over the enslaved population, and the system collapses.

Following Flournoy, a slave trader, W. B. Gaulden, was given the podium, proving the Democratic Party was, indeed, a "big tent" party long before that expression became popular. Gaulden straight-facedly promoted his profession, insisting that slavery was "right, socially, politically, morally and religiously." He believed and so stated that if slavery was abolished, "civilization would go back two hundred years."[16] His speech was greeted with loud applause and laughter, and while the none-too-subtle purpose of such rhetoric was to warn the Northern Democrats not to place Senator Douglas in nomination, the senator's supporters would not be deterred. Then, in the midst of the pro-South tirade, George W. McCook — a Douglas supporter — spoke up and moved to adopt a resolution that would begin the process of naming a nominee.

The resolution failed to get any traction, however, as more angry men joined the verbal melee. McCook — who owned no slaves and wanted none — was determined, however, to get the process moving away from angry speeches and down to business. He sprang to his feet and urged that his resolution be adopted. Finally, in the afternoon session, the chair said that balloting for the nomination of a presidential candidate was in order. Through 12 ballots Douglas led a field of eight candidates, all of whom except for Senator Andrew Johnson of Tennessee were not household names. While McCook proudly voted all 23 of Ohio's delegates for Douglas, the day's session ended with no one elected.

On the tenth day a fragment of the conventioneers convened, but without any progress toward deciding on a nominee. Sensing the futility of it all, the president gaveled out a final adjournment, stating that all matters were concluded until June 18, 1860, when the delegates would meet again in Baltimore. As delegates streamed out of the hall in a frantic search for carriages and trains, the Douglas men were in good spirits.[17]

Davis and his allies, however, were despondent over the breakup of the Convention. He expressed a dire wish that the breakup would be only temporary and that the "party will reunite upon sound and acceptable principles." With the spread of the radical, anti-slavery rhetoric throughout the North tormenting him, Davis saw in his party "the only conservative element which remains in our politics."[18]

While they rushed to get out of Charleston, the Democrats and their fellow travelers were far from finished, however, and in a series of conventions, three men were nominated for president for the purpose of opposing the Republican candidate. The unity that George W. McCook hoped for and worked so hard to bring about was trampled to death as men raced to catch trains to other destinations.

Calling itself the Baltimore National Constitutional Convention and meeting in that city, a sizeable and harmonious group of delegates from the old Whig and Know Nothing parties began deliberations on May 9, 1860. This group considered itself the keeper of the Constitution. The following day the self-styled Constitutional Party — also known as the Peace Party — emerged from its work, having selected John Bell of Tennessee as its candidate for president. Bell was looked upon as the man of the hour, well liked in the North, and the man to unite the people, elevate the Constitution and save the Union. Seeing no hope coming from the Republicans or the Democrats, this party favored a middle course.

Next, the National Democratic Convention convened in Baltimore on June 18, 1860, in numbers greater than those attending the Charleston convention. Once again, Douglas supporters were in high dudgeon, touting the "Little Giant" from Illinois, once described as "a queer little man" with a "leonine head and duck legs."[19] His staunch supporter, George W. McCook of Ohio, was present at the convention, once again trying to get down to the business of fielding nominations. But dissension ruled the day as the conventioneers argued and sparred over resolutions and amendments. Fist fights broke out in the streets as each faction tried to out insult the other. The Douglas men castigated the Southern men, calling them traitors and anti–Unionist.

The Southern men retaliated by labeling the "Douglasites" as abolitionists in disguise. Finally, after five days marked by name-calling, accusations and angry and passionate speeches, including those of "slave breeders," the doomed convention blew up. But instead of adjournment following the withdrawal of Virginia and other Southern delegations, Stephen A. Douglas was nominated as the Democratic candidate for president by those who stayed.

The bolters were not the least bit subdued by the nomination of Douglas, whom they could not stomach. After bolting the National Democratic Convention, the disaffected and dyed-in-the-wool Southerners, along with a smattering of Northerners and a full slate of delegates from California and Oregon, convened in Baltimore at Institute Hall. They nominated John C. Breckinridge as their candidate for president. Breckinridge, from a prominent Kentucky family, had just concluded a term of service as President James Buchanan's vice president.

Breckinridge was pro–Union but also pro-slavery and profoundly a Southern man who was expected to carry the torch of that "peculiar institution" into the indefinite future. Breckinridge was also a moderate who had, over the years, used his considerable diplomatic skills to seek compromises that both protected slavery and placated the North.[20]

The "Seceders'" Convention, as it was called by journalist Murat Halstead, was no doubt motivated by the results of the Republican National Convention that convened in Chicago on May 16, 1860. The Republican delegates busied themselves with sifting through a large number of candidates; among them the popular William H. Seward of New York was the favorite. He had served as both a governor and U.S. senator from New York. He sincerely believed he had paid his political dues and was entitled to the nomination.

While the convivial Seward was a friend of Breckinridge and Jefferson Davis, he was one of the most vociferous and outspoken critics of slavery. His house was open for blacks escaping via the New York Underground Railroad. In a speech in 1850, Seward reminded his audience that slavery was an abomination, a weakness of character and an insult to people who believe in democratic institutions, and the sooner it was discarded the better. A fighter and an intellectual, Seward's popularity spread across the North until by 1860, he was thought of as presidential timber. His supporters at the 1860 Republican convention were in "high feather," believing his nomination was inevitable.[21]

But the debates with Douglas in 1858 prepared and inspired Abraham Lincoln, fueling his ambition and popularity. When Lincoln was declared the winner of the nomination, Seward was crestfallen and his supporters were in shock, but thousands of other delegates were overjoyed. Suddenly, a wild demonstration erupted. Weeping and hugging men rocked the convention hall, while the joyful news spread into the streets. Happy men shouted their approval of the nomination of "Honest Abe" to the sky as if their collective noise would be heard throughout the South, all the way down to the southern tip of Florida.

The Republican platform was subdued in tone compared to the fiery document put forth by the Southern Democrats. Among its planks were pledges to provide free farms in the West, government support for infrastructure including railroads and a protective tariff for the benefit of American industry. But it was the firm opposition to the spread of slavery in the new territories that made the platform radical and historic. The document called the proposed reopening of the African slave trade "a crime against humanity and burning shame to our country and age." Not surprisingly, the platform condemned all talk of disunion and praised Republican members of Congress for not making disunion threats "so often made by Democratic members."[22]

When all the conventions were concluded, it was three against Lincoln, and with so much at stake the country braced itself for a savage political battle, fearing the outcome. Alexander H. Stephens, the man destined to become the vice president of the Confederacy, understood the high stakes. He proclaimed that if Lincoln won the entire North and Breckinridge all of the Southern states, "no earthly power could prevent civil war."[23]

George W. McCook had similar forebodings. He went back to Steubenville to console his family and influence events as best he could. He was met at the train station by his cousin Anson G. McCook to whom he revealed details of the madhouse convention. Anson recalled, in his unpublished memoir, that George had seen and heard enough to be convinced that the Southerners intended to "destroy the Union if possible." But he also saw in his cousin George the unwavering personal resolve to back the United States government to the hilt even if it meant war.[24]

The presidential campaign of 1860 was super-charged with emotion, although Lincoln himself kept a low profile as he did not want to alienate any faction of his party, nor did he want to further inflame the South. Nevertheless the South did its best to make Lincoln unpalatable with personal attacks and vile political slogans, calling the Republican Party the "free love, free Nigger" party.[25] A North Carolina newspaper declared that the nomination of Lincoln meant that the Republican objective was the "ultimate extermination of slavery."[26]

Lincoln's selection of a running mate, Senator Hannibal Hamlin of Maine, was like tossing another log on the fire of secession. Hamlin was attacked by Southerners who looked at his "swarthy" appearance and dark complexion and concluded he had "nigger blood" in him. It was all the more reason to hate Lincoln.[27]

When he was 22 years old, a fortune-teller in New Orleans told Lincoln that he would one day be president of the United States.[28] In the fall of 1860, the voodoo prophecy was fulfilled as Lincoln was elected president, with Breckinridge, carrying the solid South, coming in a strong second in popular vote. Lincoln received a paltry 39.9 percent of the total vote, with almost no support in the South. In fact, he got no votes at all in ten of the Southern States where the Republicans weren't even on the ballot.[29] Therefore, to no one's great surprise, the election result precipitated the secession of the Southern states, led by South Carolina. Federal arms facilities in the seceded states were then raided for guns and ammunition.

The McCook family, led by George W. and his father Daniel Sr., was dismayed by the dramatic and sudden turn of events, but they had not given up. Four letters, one by George W. McCook, another by Anson G. McCook and two by Daniel McCook, Sr., shed some light on their views and ideas for averting war, bringing back the seceded states and saving the Union.

1. *Disunion and the Democratic Party*   21

Writing just before the election, Anson's letter confessed that the Douglas wing of the party had "abandoned the field," and for the moment everything was subdued, like a "calm" that "possibly may presage the storm." Clearly, the McCooks were very upset with Breckinridge's candidacy. Anson stated in his letter that his "Uncle George [Dr. George McCook] swears by G —— that he will vote for Lincoln if there is any danger of that state going for Breck." As for the Douglas men, Anson claimed that a "general apathy" surrounds the campaign while the "Breck's are full of zeal and spirit."[30] Judging from the tone and content of his letter, Anson G. McCook was anxious for the election although he was dreading the result, for he and other Douglas men had little hope for their candidate.

There was, of course, little for the McCooks to be optimistic about and the result of the voting was probably no surprise. Lincoln won with a large number of electoral votes. Next, Congress met in December, and in what now seems to be a strange twist of fate, John C. Breckinridge, presiding over the Senate as the outgoing vice president — who lost his bid to become president — announced to the Senate that Abraham Lincoln and Hannibal Hamlin had been elected president and vice president, in accordance with the Constitution.[31] Although Breckinridge was on good terms with Lincoln, it must have been a bitter pill to swallow.

More bitter yet for the North was the secession of South Carolina on December 20, 1860. In a succinctly worded Ordinance of Secession, the state declared that the "Union now subsisting between South Carolina and other states, under the name of the United States of America, is hereby dissolved." Emboldened by South Carolina's brazen act, a group of secessionist commissioners went to the other Cotton States, urging them to leave the Union to protect slavery.[32] The propagandists did their work well, for Mississippi, Florida, Alabama, Georgia, Louisiana and Texas all seceded, in that order. Arkansas, North Carolina, Tennessee and Virginia also eventually joined the new Confederacy.

Collectively the Confederacy owned more than 3.5 million slaves valued at 1.75 billion dollars.[33] They were in too deep. With all this at stake and believing the abolitionist North was out to destroy them, Southerners refused to accept the results of the vote and essentially hijacked a free and constitutional election by seceding from the Union. In so doing, they were quick to call Lincoln the catalyst. Among the secession lights who took this view was Jefferson Davis. He wrote: "The Election ... was the last feather ... which you know breaks the Camel's back."[34]

Davis meant that there would be no turning back. But that is exactly what he and many others wanted. Indeed, the Cotton States had, rather happily, charted a perilous course. They were embarking on an unprecedented political experiment, for the Confederacy was the first and only attempt to form a government for the purpose of preserving and perpetuating slavery.

Lincoln kept quiet following his election, staying in Springfield, Illinois, sending letters to his political allies, while trying to think things through. He told an Albany, New York, editor that no state had the right to secede without the consent of other states, and that it was "the duty of the President, and other government functionaries, to run the machine as it is." With this, Lincoln was suggesting that he would take a hard line against any seceding state.[35]

After the secession parade began, George W. McCook laid out his ideas for damage control. Clearly the McCook with the most influence and political connections, George lamented the lack of "moral obligation and the impulse of patriotism" that permeated the mood of the nation. He was angry with his fellow Democrats who were unable to "rise above the dust of the dirty arena where the factions have been struggling for party supremacy," while the government "is being destroyed before their eyes. I boil over with indignation and could talk and write unceasingly upon it." He placed blame on all sections, but "the South has so much provoked it by defection in the Democratic Party, and is so clearly and carelessly wrong in the remedies she seeks, that I have little patience remaining as to her."

After letting off some steam, George got up on another soapbox. He was expected by his family to assume a leadership role in both Ohio and national politics, and wanting to meet those expectations, he carefully laid out a plan. First, it was necessary to "strengthen the hands of the friends of the Union in Conservative states who stand by us." He was no doubt referring to border states like Kentucky, Maryland and Missouri and the necessity of keeping them in the Union even if it meant granting concessions.

Lincoln, he said, must be "peacefully inaugurated," and his inaugural address must be "conservative," for this would allow "breathing time." He wanted to avoid more hotheaded rhetoric so as not to alienate the men in the border states. The non-seceding states he said "constitute the government, *de facto and de jure*," with the "possession and prestige of the flag and the fourth of July." He insisted that there be no recognition of any form of government of a seceded state, as to do so would "assume secession as a fact." The Union should carry on as before and "leave the seats [of the seceded states] in Congress unoccupied but not *vacated* until ready for the return of representatives."

He urged that to effect the "postponement of an Evil day," the Union take no military action against the South, "unless the general government is driven to the wall," and then only take defensive action. George expressed his fear that South Carolina might take extreme measures and move against Fort Sumter in the Charleston harbor, or Fort Pickens in Florida. Should South Carolina, or any other seceded state, act with hostility toward either place, war was inevitable.

George's letter indicates his belief that the South could be shown the error of its ways and brought back into the Union with minimal military coercion. He explained that with the discontinuance of postal service and the blockading of ports, the loss of trade and the burden of debt would cool the "fever in the blood" and persuade the seceding states to rejoin the Union. While time would prove him right in many respects, he wisely conceded that "it is not given us to see the end from the beginning and this is the limit of my poor vision." Having committed his views to writing, George closed, saying, "May God help us and them & make us friends & not enemies, and keep our country in the present as he has in the past."

For George W. McCook, hoping against hope, the outlook was grim, for he was watching his party break up, and that was bad. But worse yet, his country was doing the same thing and he couldn't stop it.[36] Furthermore, understanding the aggressive nature of the men of his family, and their strong sense of patriotism, George no doubt sensed that the McCooks would be in the thick of the fighting. He could not be faulted for wondering about the probable cost to his family in blood and suffering.

The McCooks were probably satisfied with Lincoln's masterful inaugural address, for it was anything but inflammatory. Guarded by a number of carefully placed sharpshooters, Lincoln gave a thoughtful, well-crafted and eloquent address at his inauguration on March 4, 1861. He said with firmness and conviction that the Union was perpetual and that the Southern states had no right to secede, but at the same time, he called his disaffected countrymen friends, not enemies. While Lincoln made it clear he would uphold the Constitution, enforce the law and protect federal property, he also pledged that he would take no military action against the South, for in Southern hands only lay "the momentous issue of civil war."[37]

Believing Lincoln's inaugural address meant the North intended to make war, the South declined Lincoln's invitation to peaceably rejoin the Union and instead went on the offensive. After every presidential election, the losing party simply accepted the verdict of the majority and began working to win the next one. All that changed with the election of Lincoln; there was no respectful transfer of power.

Writing on April 15, 1861, from Washington, D.C., George's father, Daniel McCook, Sr., expressed the melancholy thoughts of people throughout the North when he put pen to paper and wrote, "all the evils of Civil War is [*sic*] upon us." It was the fall of Fort Sumter and the sight of the "disunion flag" floating over the battered and crumbling edifice, and "Southern Chivalry ... exulting over the greatest triumph at arms ever recorded in the history of the world" that pained him so. He went on to write: "We hear nothing but the continual hum of War, the Sound of the bugle and fife, and the heavy tramp of the troops." Washington was turning quickly to the urgent matters of protection and security; avenues and bridges were under guard, and it was expected that martial law would be announced the next day.[38]

In a letter dated May 4, 1861, Daniel McCook, Sr., once again aired his views. If George was disconsolate, his father was red hot, fighting mad. Writing from Washington, which the elder McCook described as an armed camp, he dared the "Southern traitors" to attempt to invade the federal capital city. He angrily decried those men who sabotaged the Democratic conventions at Charleston and Baltimore. These men foolishly believed that by bolting the conventions, running their own candidate for president, they could seize the upper hand. They were deluded if they thought their defection left the North a divided nation. Let them come; the North was united and the federal army would drive them back. With great and deadly emphasis, he wrote, "*Treason must be put down.*"

With more troops arriving daily, Daniel McCook, Sr., felt safe in Washington, saying, "We in this city are no longer prisoners of war." He was confident although wrong when he predicted the war would be short, as "we will soon conquer a peace." But he was right when he said that war would settle, "for all time to come," the question of secession and rebellion.[39]

It was slavery that provided the incentive to secede, and secession over slavery meant that the Union was about to self-destruct. This Lincoln could not accept for he had taken a sacred oath to preserve and protect the Union and its Constitution. The grand and glorious Union that he so revered and respected had, according to his view, been created by the Founders for perpetual, uninterrupted existence. The Constitution provided for its preservation but contained no authority for its destruction.

For a thinker like Lincoln the concept of secession from the Union was not only indefensible but illogical and would lead to lawless anarchy. If a state could secede from the Union, why then could not a county secede from the state and a town from a county? Taken to its logical extreme, a citizen who disagreed with a law could declare himself "seceded" and therefore above the law. Under the constant threat of secession, what could people count on to hold the country together? Where would it all end? Lincoln saw the secessionist standing at the brink of anarchy, unaware of, or blind to, the danger.[40]

The seceded Southerners — proud of their stance — were also looking to settle the "question" for all time to come. They were quite willing to fight the North for as long as it took to gain their independence. Slavery was thoroughly embedded in their culture, and no one knew this any better than the newly elected Confederate vice president Alexander H. Stephens. While he was a diminutive specimen — once described as having a body so small that he looked transparent — Stephens had a sharp mind and aggressive personality.[41]

In a speech delivered in Savannah, Georgia, Stephens said that Thomas Jefferson and other men who believed that slavery was a violation of natural law were wrong. He proudly declared, in Roger Taney–like language, "upon the great truth that the negro is not equal to the white man; that slavery, subordination to the superior race, is his natural and moral condition." This, Stephens insisted, had become the cornerstone of Southern culture, the "great physical, philosophical, and moral truth."[42] It remained to be seen how many men and boys would be willing to die in support of this "moral truth."

Interestingly, Daniel McCook, Sr., did not include slavery in his prophetic statement about the impending war. Although they placed the greater amount of blame on the Southerners, none of the McCooks mentioned slavery or abolition in their letters. With the exception of Henry C. McCook who was an anti-slavery Republican and a Lincoln supporter, the McCooks were conservatives, not abolitionists. They blamed the radical abolitionists for recklessly driving the South to the wall, and seeing the dire consequences of war, they probably were willing to accept slavery so long as the South rejoined the Union and peace was restored. Nevertheless, they were knowledgeable men and had to understand that human bondage was at the heart of the matter, for had slavery not existed there would have been no reason to secede. No reason to engage in a four-year war of unprecedented and massive destruction, causing widespread sorrow, suffering and the deaths of 620,000 people.

Although the hotheads were anxious to start shooting, for the more thoughtful majority of men, it wasn't so much that one or both sides decided that there must be war; it was simply that the dueling parties came to the harsh realization that they were helpless to prevent it. There existed no words, no ideas, no theories, no man or group of men with the power and ability to intervene and restore calm and peaceful co-existence. Years of accumulated anger had pushed the country beyond the reach of rescue. Slavery has been likened to the original sin of America, and Americans were about to pay the price for letting that serpent wind its deadly coils around the heart of an otherwise great nation.

CHAPTER 2

The McCooks Answer the Call for Volunteers

Friends of the Union, stand by your colors! You may suffer and you
may die, but you are making history which distant ages will be
proud even to record."
— *The Daily Times* (Cincinnati), October 14, 1861

After the fall of Fort Sumter on April 14, 1861, the nation found that it
had become a two-headed monster, with both heads about to breathe death
and destruction. The South, led by South Carolina, in another attempt to seize
federal government property, opened fire on the North, signaling a beginning
of hostilities and a temporary end to the great American experiment in feder-
alism. The Constitution was reduced to a fragile piece of paper, and the proud
beacon of light sent beaming across the world by the Founding Fathers was
dimmed. The world could only watch as it waited for war to sort it all out.
Would the future include a strong, united America or several small, weaker
countries carved out of the great continental expanses?

There was a sad and solemn sense that peace would not be given a chance
despite Abraham Lincoln's eloquent plea that Americans, in both the North
and the South, be guided "by the better angels of our nature." He was quick
to learn, however, that people would be guided by decades of accumulated
hate and anger. So Lincoln, with a heavy heart, but with fierce determination,
set out on a course of action that would result in the preservation of the Union,
the end of slavery and the creation of the role of commander in chief.

Not a man to react angrily, Lincoln gently reminded the Southern people
that if war was imminent, they had the power to stop it. "You have no oath
registered in heaven to destroy the Government; while I have the most solemn
one to preserve, protect and defend it."[1] That his message was rejected by the
South only strengthened his resolve to carry out his constitutional duties as
president.

Lincoln would need that resolve, for the guns fired at Fort Sumter hit targets far beyond Charleston Harbor, causing big chunks of the shattered country to fall on one side or the other of the great divide. Suddenly, pro–Union folks found themselves in seceded states, and in the North, large numbers of Southern sympathizers were living at odds with their anti-secessionist neighbors. There was too much anger in the air to expect another compromise, and since all previous compromises had failed, there was nothing left to do but fight. As if the hypnotic smell of blood was in the air, both sides were struck by war fever and patriotic ardor, and each began to mobilize their men at arms.

Bringing soldiers to Washington, D.C., so they could protect the Capitol would be one of Lincoln's first tasks as president, but he encountered a great deal of trouble getting there ahead of the troops so he could get to work. The District of Columbia had been carved out from a corner of Maryland, bordering Virginia. Maryland was divided into secession and anti-secessionist groups, each seething with anger and casting blame on the other.

Hounded by assassination plots and surrounded by security provided by the Pinkerton Detective Agency and other personal bodyguards, Lincoln managed to reach Washington on a special night train from Philadelphia that slipped quietly through Baltimore without stopping along the way. Lincoln and his security team had devised a clever plan that worked to perfection.

On March 4, 1861, Abraham Lincoln was inaugurated as the 16th president of the United States by Chief Justice Roger B. Taney. The aging chief justice was Lincoln's nemesis and a supporter of secession. In the presence of outgoing President James Buchanan, also sympathetic to the South, Taney performed his constitutional duty.

The day after Fort Sumter fell, President Lincoln — about to become a renowned war president — called for 75,000 volunteers to serve for three months. Northern communities responded as leading citizens organized and trained regiments, ready to fight for the Union. New York City alone turned out over 8,000 volunteers. In Rhode Island, recruiters had three times the number of men to choose from, and many potential soldiers were turned away. The governors of the northern states in short order produced about 90,000 troops.

In Ohio — where the rush to enlist was like a stampede — professional soldier Alexander McDowell McCook took up the cause and organized the 1st Ohio Infantry Regiment. His older brother George W. McCook, a veteran of the Mexican War, was called upon by the governor of Ohio to take charge of enlisting other regiments. Their cousin Captain Anson G. McCook helped to organize Company "H" of the 2nd Ohio Infantry Regiment and marched off with it toward Washington, with the sounds of the bombardment of Fort Sumter ringing in his head.

Anson and George were swept up in the excitement of the moment and reacted to Lincoln's proclamation with patriotic zeal. Their hometown of Steubenville was a veritable beehive of activity, alive with war fever. All businesses were suspended, and streets were filled with men marching to the tune and beat of martial music. Ladies were busy making uniforms for new soldiers and a flag for Anson's regiment.[2]

Anson's oldest brother Edward M. McCook suddenly found himself in the army too. He had been living in Colorado Territory and was about to leave Washington, D.C., for his mountain home when the "intelligence of that barbarous attack on Sumpter [sic] reached me." He saw no honorable choice but to join and support the Union.[3]

Anson's younger brother, Henry C. McCook, was also actively involved in raising troops for the Union. Henry was a 23-year-old student at the Western Theological Seminary in Allegheny City, Ohio, when the Civil War was in its early stage and fighting seemed imminent. He volunteered to serve, entering

the army as a private, and was later given the rank of lieutenant in the 41st Illinois Infantry Regiment. He also served as the regimental chaplain.[4] Edward noted that in Henry, the Union had a man "who could both fight and pray."[5]

Charles M. McCook, at age 17, the second-youngest brother of Alexander and a student at Kenyon College, joined the 2nd Ohio Infantry Regiment as a private, apparently with the assistance of his older sister. Martha "Mattie" McCook went to Lincoln's personal secretary, John G. Nicolay, on May 23, 1961, asking for a visit with the president in order to get her brother Charles into the army. Nicolay responded to Mattie, telling her that seeing the president was out of the question. Instead he directed her to Secretary of War Simon Cameron.[6] Mattie apparently saw the secretary, for Charles was offered a commission but turned it down, preferring to enter army life as a private.

Portrait of an Ohio soldier looking proud in his Union uniform, having answered Lincoln's call to arms. His name, rank and unit are unknown. But this soldier is not really anonymous; he was one of the more than 300,000 bold men from Ohio that served conspicuously in the Union army and navy in the Civil War.

Younger yet, at age 16, Charles' brother John J. McCook was also a student and eager to exchange his books for lessons in the art of war. But his strong-willed mother objected, for she had too many precious lives on the line. Young John stayed in school, enrolling in Kenyon College in the fall of 1861. While in school he could not help but be proud of his siblings on the war front and often in the newspapers. It would be just a matter of time before he would become a soldier and join the ranks of the "Fighting McCooks."[7]

Over time other brothers and cousins would follow suit and volunteer and wear Union blue. All served in the army except for Roderick S. McCook, who chose the navy. The family that would become known as the "Fighting McCooks" of Ohio was moving front and center, with loyalty and pride. Motivated by the desire to serve, fight and sacrifice if necessary, the McCooks, although die-hard Democrats, were staunchly pro–Union, as was their home state.

With the exception of Henry C. McCook, they were not abolitionists but were nevertheless strongly against secession, as it offended their sense of loyalty and patriotism. They did not relish seeing the strength and prestige of the United States diminished by the loss of even one state. In secession, they saw elements of both disloyalty and dishonor.

At the outset of war, the star of the McCook military entourage was Alexander McDowell McCook. At age 16, an eager Alexander, already showing signs of becoming a soldier, entered West Point Military Academy. A colleague and fellow officer described cadet McCook as "frank, generous and companionable in disposition" and a "favorite of his classmates." He was not among the top students, nor did he aspire to be the best in his class, but he did apply himself in those classes that he favored, including art and the classics of literature. As a result he "won the esteem and confidence of his preceptors and associates."[8]

Cadet McCook graduated from West Point in 1852, although it took him five years to complete the course of study. He ranked 30th in his class. He was commissioned a brevet second lieutenant in the regular army and assigned to duty with the 3rd U.S. Infantry, stationed at Newport Barracks, Kentucky. Not long afterward, he was transferred to the far western frontier and served in New Mexico Territory from 1853 to 1857. McCook's duties included scouting in Apache country and pacifying the Utes and Apaches. He also fought at the White Mountains southeast of Las Lunas, New Mexico, and at Sawatchie Pass and the headwaters of the Arkansas River. McCook learned the country well enough to be appointed "chief of guides" with the Gila Expedition of 1857. On June 27, 1857, McCook's unit engaged the Apaches on the Gila River.[9] A colleague wrote that McCook participated in "many of the exciting Indian campaigns on that wild frontier."[10]

Over time McCook became a confident, brash, and at times hotheaded young officer, imbued with excessive feelings of self-importance, who seemed oblivious to failure. His contemptuous attitude toward Indians mirrored that of many military men as well as much of the civilian population. In a letter to his father, Alex declared, "I see no possible way of subduing them [the Indians] save by a war of extermination — making no peace."[11]

McCook would not, however, have the chance to engage in such an exercise as he was granted leave following the Indian fight at Gila River, and was thereafter ordered to West Point where he would become an instructor in infantry tactics. He reported for duty on February 12, 1858. In December of that year, he was at long last given his first lieutenant bars, the first in a series of promotions and awards, most of which came at the advent of the war. He was well suited for the military.

At the Academy, one of Lieutenant McCook's students was George Armstrong Custer, a brash young cadet destined for an illustrious military career. First, however, he would have to survive four pressure-packed years learning to be a soldier. McCook was unusually hard on Custer, earning the cadet's "undying hatred." Custer made a personal vow of vengeance that upon graduation, his tormentor, McCook, "would not live to tell the tale."[12] Graduation and war, however, changed everything, and Custer put aside old animosities in favor of *esprit de corps.*

With the outbreak of the Civil War, McCook's teaching days ended, but not without one final act of respect and affection. Upon learning that he would soon leave the Academy, a group of cadets gave their lieutenant a send-off serenade at midnight.[13] The next morning, ex-Indian fighter McCook left as ordered, going back home to Ohio, to Columbus, where he organized and mustered the 1st Ohio Infantry Regiment, ten companies of volunteers who agreed to serve for 90 days. McCook was given the wartime rank of colonel as of April 16, 1861, two days after Sumter fell.

On April 19, the new regiment departed Columbus, and at Lancaster, Pennsylvania, it was mustered into the service along with Anson McCook's 2nd Ohio.[14] At Lancaster, they were visited by former president James Buchanan who was described by Anson as "a man of very quiet and gentle manners."[15] Buchanan mingled freely but was greeted coldly by the men because he was known for his lack of decisive action during the secession crisis.

Moving on, the Ohio regiments stopped at Harrisburg, Pennsylvania, and later at Philadelphia, where they camped at the fairgrounds. Accommodations were shabby at best, and Anson McCook located his headquarters in an "old horse stall." He recalled with pride that his cousin Alexander was named the "senior colonel" of the camp, "the right man in the right place." Colonel McCook took charge, and "under his teaching and vigorous methods we made fairly good progress in company and regimental drill."[16] The Ohio volunteers were joined by and drilled with Pennsylvania regiments under the command of General Robert Patterson, then an old soldier, whose service in the military dated back to the War of 1812.

Ohio senator John Sherman joined the volunteers and accompanied Colonel McCook and the 1st and 2nd Ohio Infantry regiments, consisting of approximately 2,000 men. They boarded a train to Washington, at the time blockaded by the "roughs of Baltimore." Baltimore had long maintained a reputation for street gang violence and was dubbed "Mobtown." For decades preceding the Civil War, the name stuck, and if a man said he was going to Mobtown, everyone assumed he meant Baltimore.[17]

After they arrived at Baltimore, Colonel McCook gathered his officers together and informed them that the Ohio volunteers would have to march through the dangerous streets of Baltimore. Some weeks before, the 6th Massachusetts Infantry regiment had been attacked by an angry secessionist mob resulting in the killing of four soldiers and a dozen civilians. McCook ordered 20 rounds of ammunition to the man, with instructions that they were to march with the muskets loaded but "not capped." The men were to ignore any insulting remarks from the citizens, and "no possible pretext was to be given for an attack upon us." But if a shot was fired at them or if they "were assailed in any way," they were to "clear the streets," fighting their way through without waiting for an order to commence.

The procession, led by the 1st Ohio, extended a mile or more in length, and was greeted by "hisses and groans" from the anti–Union demonstrators. Anson recalled that a "burly ruffian shook his fist in my face and called me a 'damned Yankee cutthroat.'" Another man suggested that the Ohio troops would make "good manure for Virginia battlefields." Despite the barrage of insults, there were no acts of violence by either side, and, moving with steady determination, the volunteers passed safely through Baltimore.[18]

The new soldiers from the Ohio regiments arrived in Washington as if they were conquering heroes and were received by President Lincoln.[19] In contrast to the rough treatment in Baltimore, people cheered as Colonel McCook led the Ohio regiments down Pennsylvania Avenue. They joined a large encampment of troops, all "well-armed and well-fed." According to one journalist, the capitol resembled a "vast military camp," with "soldiers to be seen on every hand." Every public building, hall and hotel, "and in fact every appropriate and inappropriate place," was occupied by soldiers.

Troops were arriving at the rate of about 1,000 each day, answering Lincoln's May 3 call for 43,034 volunteers to serve for three years. Lincoln made this second call for volunteers after he came to realize that troops would be needed to serve longer than 90 days.[20] The proud regiments marched in the streets, visited public places, and guarded bridges and railroads. Bayonets gleamed in the sunlight and big guns were perched on every hilltop. The mood was one of confidence, almost as if daring Jefferson Davis, head of the "so-called Confederate States" to attempt an attack on the city.[21]

Colonel Alexander M. McCook left Washington with the Ohio regiments and reported to Brigadier General Robert C. Schenck at Four Mile Run in Arlington County, Virginia. The Union army had crossed the Potomac River on May 23, 1861, and took control of Alexandria and Arlington Heights, immediately after Virginia voted in favor of secession. In doing so they drove out the small Rebel detachment that had occupied the area. They raised the Stars and Stripes in the presence of people "who wept for joy."[22] The growing Union army was assembling there in anticipation of an invasion into the heart of the Old Dominion.

Colonel McCook's father, Daniel McCook, Sr., age 63, volunteered to serve the Union at the outbreak of hostilities. He was a member of the Frontier Guard that stationed itself in the White House to protect Lincoln until other regiments arrived. The Guard was essentially a band of rough frontiersmen, led by James Henry Lane, a lawyer and partisan anti-slavery man and all-around border ruffian, who had recently been elected senator from the new state of Kansas. The Frontier Guard set up camp inside the White House, loaded their guns, and guarded the presidential residence with a fierce determination.[23]

After the Guard disbanded, Daniel McCook, Sr., stayed in Washington with his wife, daughter Martha and son Edwin. When the Ohio troops crossed into Virginia, the elder McCook and his family members maintained regular contact with the regiments so as to be close to Alexander, Charles and Anson as they prepared for battle.[24]

The plan of attack was focused on Manassas Gap, or Manassas Junction as it was also called, considered by both sides to be of vital importance because it was a railroad hub. If the Federals could take Manassas, they would be in a position to move by train to Richmond, the new Confederate capital. First, however, the army had to be organized and trained to become battle ready.

With a sense of urgency, Lincoln turned to a military icon, Lieutenant General Winfield Scott, from Virginia. General Scott was a living legend, having led and fought with distinction in the War of 1812 and the Mexican War. At age 74, Scott was older than the Constitution and the republic he served. He had been general in chief of the U.S. Army since 1841. His popularity with the people and vaunted leadership skills earned him a spot on the top of the Whig Party's presidential ticket in 1852. While he lost the presidency to Franklin Pierce, he remained politically active, and his loyalty to the Union went unquestioned.

By 1861, however, Scott was overweight, afflicted with gout, unable to ride a horse and too far advanced in years to actively lead troops into battle.

It was, however, his mind and field experience that interested Lincoln, and Scott, nicknamed "Old Fuss and Feathers," went about concocting a plan to defeat the rebellion. While his master plan included naval blockades of major southern ports and the conquest of the Mississippi River, his first priority was to defend Washington, and it was for this reason that troops gathered in and near the Union capital city.

Scott's immediate strategy did not include a major offensive against the South.[25] He concluded, however, that even a green, untested army could be compelled to march on Manassas, a short 25 miles south of the Potomac River. And although not in accord with members of the press and public who were anxious to make a major assault, Scott continued to mobilize his forces.

General Scott chose a friend and ardent Unionist to lead the Union forces in the field. That man was Brigadier General Irvin McDowell, who in May of 1861 was a 42-year-old native of Ohio and a graduate of West Point. He was a large man with military bearing, neat in appearance, intelligent and well mannered, but given to gluttonous eating habits that left his fellow officers aghast. While he was an energetic man, he was strangely prone to falling asleep, even while on horseback. McDowell — who liked music and fishing — was also thin skinned, preachy and prudish, and a dyed-in-the-wool non-drinker. On one occasion, when he was rendered senseless after his horse fell on him, his surgeon was unable to administer a sip of brandy through his tightly clenched teeth. While he was courageous and a man of his word, McDowell was also ill fated, burdened by bad luck and destined for an earnest but disappointing Civil War record.[26]

McDowell had been a classmate of Confederate general Pierre Gustave Toutant Beauregard, of French/Creole ancestry from Louisiana. Beauregard was placed in command of the Rebel army gathering at Manassas, or the "Disunion" camp, as it was called by the *New York Tribune*. Beauregard was a straight-faced, intelligent man of few words and fewer smiles. Although thin skinned, irritable, humorless and egotistical, he was thoroughly military with a good record in the U.S. Army. He once claimed he was not a "disunion man," but was equally adamant in stating that the South need not humble itself to the North, nor make concessions.

"Old Bory," as he was called by admiring soldiers, spent most of his time deeply involved in all things military, but was given to spurts of patriotic zeal, and on once such occasion designed the Confederate battle flag. The South eagerly embraced the flag, making it the symbol of everything Southern, and to this day, it is an object of adoration in some circles, a relic of the past that refuses to be confined to books and museums.

The battle flag that unified the South only added to Beauregard's soaring stature. He was lionized throughout the South after he commanded the Confederates who shelled Fort Sumter into surrender. He was mobbed and cheered wherever he went; admirers screamed for speeches (which he declined to give), and women waved hankies, cried and swooned. And despite this sudden, heroic vault into Southern stardom, and prior to taking command of the Rebels at Manassas, Beauregard was mistakenly arrested in Memphis by the pro–Confederate vigilance committee. He was charged with being a spy for the Union. Fortunately General Gideon Pillow recognized his fellow officer and Beauregard was released with appropriate apologies.[27]

Despite this embarrassing incident, Beauregard was a committed Southerner, with pro–South leanings that dated back well before the start of the war. He declared in a letter to Jefferson Davis dated February 13, 1858, "For us the question of slavery is one of life or death."[28] Three years later he was dedicating his military expertise to the Southern cause, believing that the answer to the vexing question would be answered by men like himself. A self-anointed savior of the South, he was one of 313 regular army officers who opted for the Confederacy out of a total of 1,098.[29] For Beauregard, secession was the natural consequence of the divisive politics and unreasonable tactics of the Northern radicals.

On May 14, 1861, the Department of Northeastern Virginia was created by the United States War Department with McDowell in command. The department was bestowed with the honor of leading an invasion into the heart of Virginia, which most people believed would result in the speedy demolition of the secessionists. To accomplish this goal, McDowell had to defeat his former friend Beauregard.

By early June, McDowell's army was taking shape, looking at least somewhat like a fighting force. Throughout the month, volunteer regiments flowed into northern Virginia allowing McDowell to create four brigades. Among the new units was the brigade of General Robert C. Schenck, consisting of a mere two infantry regiments: the 1st Ohio organized and commanded by Colonel Alexander M. McCook, and the 2nd Ohio, Lieutenant Colonel David Mason commanding.

Schenck — an Ohio lawyer with a good education — was a "political general," among the first of many who would make their appearance during the war. He was a good physical specimen but was lacking in military experience, a shortcoming that was not lost on the men who were about to serve under him. Many men angrily protested his appointment, as opposed to McCook, "in whom they placed all their confidence."[30] It was the timely intervention by the respected Colonel McCook and other officers that quieted the minor mutiny.[31]

Schenck received his appointment because of his two decades of public service, which included a vigorous campaign for Lincoln in the 1860 presidential race. Schenck's pre-war service included four terms in Congress as a Whig, after which he was designated the minister to Brazil by President Millard

Fillmore, a job he held until 1853. It was his support of Lincoln's campaign, however, that earned him the onerous job of commanding a brigade of volunteers.[32]

While most "political generals" were viewed with suspicion or outright contempt by the West Point officers — and Lincoln was often dubious of their military skills — the president nevertheless understood their importance to the overall war effort. Understanding the politics of war was as important as the art of command. A well-connected and loyal congressman from a key state came to the table with the ability to solidify support for the war and could be a useful recruiter. Such a man was often given a commission as a matter of national strategy. It is significant that so many inexperienced men were willing to serve, give up lucrative political or business careers and risk their lives in battle. Their belief in the Union cause was just as sincere as that of the West Point men.

Furthermore, there was the American belief in the "citizen soldier," dating back to the Revolutionary War, from whom both patriotism and leadership would emerge during an emergency. People looked for heroes when heroes were needed and believed that innate abilities to lead resided in ordinary men, waiting to be unleashed in a time of crisis. There was faith that many a talented and brave man would naturally develop the skills needed to lead men in battle and win the fight. Honestly analyzed, the contribution of the political generals to the overall war effort was significant.

Although McDowell despised the non–West Pointers, he was depending on Schenck and his other brigade and division commanders, having hurriedly devised a plan of attack. The Union army would march in four columns on Manassas Gap to face Beauregard's Rebels waiting on the opposite side of Bull Run Creek. This creek, about to become a permanent and well-remembered part of Civil War history, was a formidable barrier to the Union advance. Its densely timbered banks were about five feet high, so crossing it would be a challenge. Still there were seven fords and at least one bridge big and strong enough for an army to cross.

McDowell's army would have to cross Bull Run Creek in order to take advantage of his numerical odds and win the coming battle. His army would outnumber that of Beauregard as long as Rebel General Joseph E. Johnston in the Shenandoah Valley could be kept busy by Major General Robert Patterson, and thereby prevented from joining the main Rebel force at Manassas.

At a strategy meeting with the president and his generals, McDowell insisted that he could not defeat the combined forces of Johnston and Beauregard, but he was encouraged when Scott said, "If Johnston joins Beauregard, he shall have Patterson on his heels."[33] McDowell was counting on Patterson to keep Johnston well occupied.

General Scott had confidence in Patterson, an old soldier like himself, and a man the country could depend on. Scott was a thoughtful military man and a careful planner who preferred deliberation to hot haste. Once when pressured, the old general bluntly stated that he had no fear of General Beauregard but he was afraid of "General Impatience!"[34]

While both Scott and McDowell urged patience, Lincoln was feeling the heat of public pressure on top of the constant nagging of the newspapers, and he wanted to strike a blow at the South — just enough to convince it to secede from secession. A jingoistic journalist for the *New York Tribune* came up with the catch phrase "Forward to Richmond!" This ill-timed phrase was picked up by the public and press and used to fan the flames of a pro-war populace. The North was infected with the naive belief that Southern resistance would be weak and easily overcome. It was widely believed that the Rebels would run rather than fight. It was reported falsely that 23,000 Southern troops at Manassas were living under conditions "bordering on starvation."[35]

Both sides used bombast and posturing to bolster their respective positions at the expense of the other. Fist-shaking bravado was thick in the air as newspaper reporters on both sides bragged of inevitable victories against a weak opponent. Cries of "On to Richmond!" were countered by shouts of "On to Washington!" At a celebration in Richmond, one orator boasted that within "less than sixty days the flag of the Confederacy will be waving over the White House."[36]

The legislature of South Carolina made an audacious statement when it voted to eliminate the Fourth of July from among its official holidays, thus further irritating the Unionists. Pressure from one side was countered by pressure from the other. The war of words was a fitting prelude to the terrible bloodletting that would follow.

Not unaffected by the noise, Lincoln felt the ungentle nudge, and knowing it would be impossible to fight a bloodless war, he was not overly anxious to strike a blow. A man of compassion and peaceful instincts, he held some slim hope that the matter could be settled peacefully. Still, he couldn't afford to wait too long. The enlistments of many of his three-month volunteer regiments were about to expire, and if he wanted to get some fighting out of them, the shooting would have to start before July ended. In a speech on the Fourth of July, Lincoln's premier political skills came to the fore when he put forth his belief that the impending war was a "peoples' contest" rather than a war of conquest.

When McDowell complained that his men were too green for battle, Lincoln calmly agreed but added that the South was just as green, so make the best of it. To paraphrase a more recent politician, Lincoln was willing, however reluctantly, to go to war "with the army he had" rather than the army he wished for.

CHAPTER 3

<hr>

The Inevitable Conflict

> No matter in what shape it comes, whether from the mouth of a king ... or from one race of men as an apology for enslaving another race, it is the same tyrannical principle.
>
> — Abraham Lincoln

<hr>

Anticipation for battle ran strong on both sides of the impending conflict. With eagerness and grim determination, the editor of the *Daily Times* of Cincinnati growled: "No compromise with the agents of the devil, but *war*, stern, unrelenting war, to the knife." Driving the blade in further, the editor declared that the word "compromise" is "an invention of cowardice and crime" and it is "not in our dictionary."[1]

Extreme religiosity pushed itself to the front. In Charleston, South Carolina, a newspaper article urged ministers to "hold a season of prayer" in support of secession and to thank God for "his sensible interposition in our favor at the battle of Fort Sumter." The Charleston Bible Society was busy buying and distributing Bibles to the faithful. The *Cincinnati Weekly Gazette* mocked this effort in a little piece called "Secession Religion."[2]

The anger flowed like hot lava into the streets and countryside where tempers flared, guns were fired and ropes put to deadly purpose. In New York, a secessionist man was shot and killed by a pro–Union man after the former had made a strident pro-Confederate remark. A man described as a "rabid secessionist" was hung from a third-story window in the county courthouse at Lane, Illinois. F. D. Burke was accused of starting fires, causing angry citizens to lynch him.[3] At Manassas Junction, a pro–Union man was "outed" and hung following a mock trial. He had busied himself shoeing horses for cavalrymen, and apparently this activity was enough to deem him a spy.

General Pierre G. T. Beauregard published a "proclamation" that further stirred the cauldron of hate and rage. To the people of northern Virginia, the "Creole," as he was called, declared that Abraham Lincoln, "a reckless and unprincipled tyrant has invaded your soil" and "has thrown his abolition hosts among you." Raising the level of alarm even higher, Beauregard warned that Union soldiers were actively engaging in diabolical and savage attacks on helpless people, "committing acts of violence and outrage too shocking and revolting to humanity to be enumerated." Aside from saying that the bellowing and brawling Yankees were after "beauty and booty," he would let the Southern people fill in the blanks.[4] As if any further inflammatory messages were needed, the prospect of Yankee men raping Southern women was seen as unthinkable in the extreme and worthy of God-inspired retribution.

Both sides of the great quarrel were mired in stubbornness that resulted from a lack of understanding of their cultural differences. An indignant Southern man complained that people from the South "don't understand the people of the North. You don't fight duels, nor do various other things which Southern education holds to be indispensable to a reputation for courage." According to this man's logic, Northerners were cowards, unworthy of respect, thus deserving all manner of insults.[5]

Technology in the form of the telegraph facilitated the heated exchanges. The telegraph was revolutionizing communications and was destined to be used extensively by both sides of the great conflict. Some men found the upsurge in telegrams an alarming and undesirable trend with the potential for mass mischief by spreading false rumors. Failing to see the obvious benefit offered by the telegraph, one newspaper editor warned against the new "curse to the country," proving that when something new and dramatic is injected into the public life there will always be some people who are against it.[6]

Most people, however, just wrote letters — angry letters that added to the vitriolic mix — as folks on both edges of the deadly chasm imparted their opinions and feelings in the columns of newspapers. While both armies were mobilizing for the first major clash, a fire-breathing woman from New Orleans unleashed her partisan fury in a letter to a friend in Newark, New Jersey. Declaring that "God is on our side," she condemned the "Northern Black Republicans" and their leader, Abraham Lincoln. Though she conceded that she was just a woman, she relished the chance to confront Lincoln, swearing that she would "cut his ears so close no one could see where they grew — the horrid old wretch!" She insisted that the South had nothing to fear from the North. Let the soldiers come and die in southern swamps. As if heartfelt hate and bitterness had a conquering power, she released, in one furious retort, a blast intended to bring on the fiery destruction of all northern "bigots, fanatics, negro-lovers, and thieves."[7]

This letter made its way to the New York Tribune, perhaps the most influential newspaper in America at a time when it and two other New York dailies — the Times and Herald— dominated the world of news. The Tribune was eager to publish anything that would prick the sensibilities of its readers.

In order to succeed, support for the war had to come from an aroused public. What better way to get support than through letters that were intentionally hostile, provocative and insulting?

A provocative letter dated April 25, 1861, from former president John Tyler to South Carolina governor Francis Pickens, was published in the *Tribune* under the caption: "John Tyler's Treason." Tyler's short letter, made public in the *Charleston Courier*, lauded the Virginia legislature for passing a secession ordinance, thus adopting the "provisional constitution of the Confederate states."[8] It was a time for choosing one side or the other, and Tyler had made his choice.

Another man from a distinguished American family also chose the South. George Wythe Randolph of Virginia, grandson of former president Thomas Jefferson, was an ardent secessionist and was picked by Jefferson Davis to be the secretary of war for the Confederacy.[9] While the grandfather dedicated much of his life and intellect toward the creation of a "more perfect Union," the grandson was prepared to devote his mental energy toward its destruction.

The same could be said for John Bell of Tennessee, one of four presidential candidates in the 1860 election. Bell was admonished by northern critics because he came out publicly for secession after waffling for a short time. Now in full feather, he wanted to raise a volunteer regiment to "march in defense of the South against the Federal Government" and the Constitution he so recently campaigned to uphold, preserve and protect.[10]

Turncoats like Randolph, Tyler and Bell were the targets of scathing attacks by northern newspapers that lashed out with accusations of treason. Among them, Horace Greeley's *New York Tribune* wasn't just blowing smoke to puff up a pro-war stance in order to sell a few more newspapers. The *Tribune* was dedicated and ready for the long haul, although there would be times when the Lincoln administration would question the quality of its support.

Greeley's reputation was already mythic when war fever brought him even more prominence. A founding member of the Republican Party, his rags-to-riches story and the literary content of his newspaper made Greeley a hero to his readers. But secession was hard on "Uncle Horace," a self-styled moralist and constant, and at times quixotic, crusader. It was a challenge like no other he had ever confronted.

Greeley was pacifistic and fell into bouts of depression over the prospect of all-out war, but lucky for him his newspaper was primarily in the control of Charles A. Dana, the managing editor. A brilliant journalist and advocate for abolition, the cold and pragmatic Dana was more militaristic and optimistic than Greeley, although he did admit, prophetically, "We do not expect a great rebellion, which has been thirty years ripening, to be crushed out in thirty days."[11] While he had no crystal ball, Dana provided an accurate forecast of the bloody spectacle that was to come. He was among those who saw destruction, suffering and an avalanche of bleeding and dead bodies of boys and men, served up for the world to see.

Not every journalist shared Dana's gloom. A writer for the *Daily Times* of Cincinnati, a different kind of prophet, waxed almost poetic while he contemplated the wisdom and woe of warfare. If the thing must come, then let it come, he wrote, for "there is some consolation in the anticipation that good will ultimately flow from this evil."[12]

The army officers charged with the responsibility of fighting and winning the war that lay ahead probably had less lofty ideals in mind. Among them, General Irwin McDowell was a thoughtful and capable leader, seriously devoted to duty. However the soldiers he led were a flabby mixture of inexperienced, undisciplined eastern and western boys, dressed up in a colorful and odd blend of uniforms, especially many of the New York regiments. The federal army lacked uniformity in more ways than one.

McDowell's regimental commanders were largely inexperienced and incompetent, and the boys they commanded — mere civilians in uniforms — were as overconfident as they were undisciplined. They treated the coming battle as if it were a lark, expecting the Rebels to be defeated with ease so they could march home as heroes and go back to being just boys again. When the army was drilling or on the move, anxious but uninspired soldiers would cast away "excess" gear at will, including blankets, haversacks and ammunition. Without any sense of discipline, they would stop and drink creek water, pick and eat berries or take a nap whenever it pleased them.

The volunteers would often treat their officers with casual disrespect and sometimes with insolent disregard for rank and authority. For example, Colonel Alexander M. McCook was once greeted with a "Hello, Guts," possibly a reference to his chubby shape.[13] While some officers were shocked by this remark, "Guts" was McCook's nickname at West Point, so he may not have been offended.[14]

On June 17, 1861, while the army was taking shape, McDowell sent General Robert C. Schenck with 700 men from the 1st Ohio, including Colonel McCook, out to conduct reconnaissance in the vicinity of Vienna, a small town in Fairfax County, about 15 miles west of Alexandria. The day before, the train to Vienna had been fired upon and one man was killed, hence the reconnaissance.

The Ohio troops traveled on the Loundoun and Hampshire Railroad, dropping off two companies when the train reached a crossroads south of Falls Church. Later, two other companies were disembarked, leaving just 271 men relaxing aboard the train as it moved slowly toward Vienna.

About a quarter of a mile from Vienna, the train rounded a curve and approached the entrance to the town. Suddenly, without warning, the train was fired upon by two "field guns." The artillery was well concealed, and as a result the term "masked batteries" was coined. The Ohio soldiers were relaxed and some were laughing when the blasts from the "masked batteries" hit the train as it rounded a curve. Schenck and McCook were sitting together in a passenger car when the firing started that killed eight men and wounded six. In a panic, the inexperienced troops abandoned the train.

McCook sprang into action, quickly forming his men in a line of battle as best as could be done under the circumstances, directing them into a wooded area. Rebel fire continued in the direction of McCook's men, causing him to "quietly march them over to another clump of trees," where he re-formed his men into another line of battle. Wild enemy cannon fire continued, striking and toppling trees and tearing up the ground, but it failed to hit a human target. McCook understood that he was greatly outnumbered, so he gathered his wounded and led his men away. A reporter for the *New York Tribune* commended McCook and his brave Ohio men, who by "manly defiance ... preserved themselves."[15]

To make matters worse, however, the panic-stricken engineer detached the engine and one car and sped away, ignoring the Union soldiers. But fortune favored the foolish. Skirmishers from the 1st South Carolina Infantry, also on a reconnaissance mission, did not pursue the retreating federal soldiers, thereby enabling them to escape. An angry McDowell wanted to send a larger force to Vienna, but Scott vetoed the idea.[16]

The *New York Tribune* trumpeted the story under a headline, "The Masked Attack at Vienna," blasting the Rebel gunners that fired from ambush. The newspaper also praised the bravery of Union soldiers who were killed and wounded, noting that one of the dying Ohio boys said, "Stand up for the Union, boys." While blaming Rebel treachery for the casualties, the *Tribune* questioned Schenck's deployment of troops along the way to Vienna. It was considered unsound, in a military sense, to weaken his force while traveling in enemy country, especially when he had no skirmishers in front of the main body of troops and had taken no other precautions to prevent a surprise attack.[17]

The *New York Times* was strident in its critique of the incident. First it printed an article from the *Washington Star* that resulted from the "wild rumors" circulating in Alexandria after news of the attack reached that city. The *Star* claimed that as the train was entering Vienna, a man "stepped out upon the road and waved his hand," as if trying to stop the train. He yelled out to warn them to stop for if they did not they "were dead men," because the Rebels had a battery and a "strong force ahead." The officer in charge (not named in the article) received the warning and, "as if turning the matter over in his mind," decided to ignore it. A short distance later, the Confederate guns on high ground opened up on the Ohio soldiers.[18]

A correspondent for the *Times* picked up the story and asked, rhetorically,

"Is it not something like madness to send troops by railroad through an enemy's country?" The better practice would be to go in on foot with skirmishers in the lead. Then leaning on McCook, the article called him a "brave but impulsive" officer who, on this occasion, "acted wholly on his own discretion in going so far as Vienna," when his orders were to "guard railroad bridges within two or three miles of that city."[19]

A *Times* editorial called the incident an example of "rash" behavior "if not criminal negligence." While praising "every gallant and skillful act of officer or private in the Army," and without naming names, the *Times* concluded it was at the very least, poor judgment to take a small command into enemy country, "penned up inside the cars," where they were at a distinct disadvantage. The editorial refused to believe the *Star* story about the man who frantically attempted to warn the Union soldiers, but it came down emphatically against the careless use of a train to transport troops into hostile country.[20]

The Confederate ambush at Vienna produced very few casualties when compared with other, day-long battles that waited in the future, but the mangled bodies of the dead soldiers — so suddenly and unexpectedly blasted to pieces — brought the survivors face to face with the horrors of war. The dead men were wrapped in blankets and buried by their comrades in the woods near their place of death. The 1st Ohio had shed its first blood.

The "disaster at Vienna" was brought to the attention of President Lincoln, as there was apparently some concern about who was responsible for the affair that was seen as preventable. It came to light that Schenck was not actually ordered to go in person, but was told to send a regiment. The colonels of both of his regiments being absent, he went with the troops. McCook caught up with the regiment and was essentially placed in charge because he was a "regularly educated military man."

Lincoln, no doubt, read the newspaper accounts of the incident. It was brought to his attention that both Schenck and McCook were warned of the possibility of Rebel troops waiting for their arrival. The informant, however, was considered unreliable because he personally had not seen the enemy, but rather simply had "seen a man who had heard there were troops there." Lincoln saw no cause for concern, and in a memorandum, both Schenck and McCook were cleared of any lapse in judgment. It was also noted that no other officer or enlisted man at the scene of the disaster "ever cast a word of blame upon either Gen. Schenck or Col. McCook." Instead they expressed their willingness to "have another trial under the same officers."[21] Schenck praised McCook for acting "coolly under this galling fire."[22]

Not long after McCook and Schenck returned to their encampment, they found themselves embroiled in another uncomfortable diversion. This one was caused by a Maryland woman, Caroline F. Noland, who claimed she was seeking a runaway slave that had taken refuge with the two Ohio regiments. The indignant daughter of the Confederacy sent a letter to General Scott claiming that the "the interference of the soldiery" denied her the opportunity to reclaim her property, a "servant named George."[23]

This prompted sharp responses from both McDowell and Schenck, the latter stating that he was absent when the parties came to capture the slave, but "Colonel McCook ... the senior officer present gave his immediate attention to the matter." He hotly denied that the slave catchers were "harshly dealt with," as was claimed by Noland. Schenck further denied that any slave was being concealed by his troops, and resented the accusation that his regiments were "practicing on the abolition system of protecting runaway negroes."[24]

Next McCook laid out his written explanation of the affair in a letter dated July 6, 1861, to Schenck's assistant adjutant. He asserted that it was "absolutely and unqualifiedly false" that the representatives of the aggrieved slaveholder were badly treated or denied the opportunity to find their human contraband. McCook accused Mrs. Noland's slave catchers of having "lying propensities," and further doubted that she ever owned a slave.[25] It is clear that both officers found the slavery issue unpleasant to deal with.

As a result of this minor flurry of sectionalist strife, the House of Representatives, by resolution in a special session on July 9, 1861, declared that it "is no part of the duty of the soldiers of the United States to capture and return fugitive slaves."[26] Clearly, the federal government wanted to put its foot down and with great emphasis stamp out the controversy. Union soldiers were solely responsible for fighting the South and would not engage in any activity that sustained the South.

For Colonel McCook, camp life was humming with military routine. His cousin Edward came to Virginia, found brother Anson, and the two of them rode the lines together. The McCook boys were growing weary of camp life, and pumped by youthful bravado, were eager to engage the Rebels. But when would the fighting start? Anson complained that he knew nothing unless he read about it in the New York newspapers.[27]

Then one day in early July, the Ohio regiments received a guest from their state in the person of Dayton congressman Clement L. Vallandigham. The congressman was a boyhood companion of Alexander McCook. He was a fellow Democrat and a friend of the McCook family. But that is where the similarity ended, for Vallandigham was an outspoken opponent of any hostile action toward the South and soon emerged as a leader of the opposition to the Lincoln administration, commonly called "Copperheads."

With Colonel McCook as his guide, Vallandigham walked among the Ohio troops seeking out friends who were now serving in the two regiments. Seeing Captain Anson McCook, Vallandigham greeted him kindly, but made an anti-war reference while pointing to Anson's uniform. As he was proud to serve, Anson said that he and the other men were disappointed at the congressman's stance and that they were "loyally supporting the president and his efforts to preserve the Union."[28]

Vallandigham was spotted by some Cleveland troops who, being familiar with his anti-war views, taunted him, calling him a traitor and a southern sympathizer. Amid the many insults cast at Vallandigham was a threat to run him out of the camp. Vallandigham was rankled by the taunts and returned the insults, measure for measure, calling the troops' conduct dishonorable. A soldier replied that it was the congressman who was shameful, for "we are here fighting for our country," while "you have meanly and traitorously tried to prevent it." A writer for the *Daily Times* of Cincinnati reported hearing a band strike up the "Rogue March" as Vallandigham passed through, while onions were tossed at his head.[29]

Still the stubborn congressman refused to depart. Finally a fight broke out between the opposing parties, but Colonel McCook and other officers quickly broke it up. The story was picked up by Republican newspapers that could not resist the chance to jab at a vocal, dissenting Democrat, and as a result, exaggerated reports of the incident emerged from the presses.[30]

The excitement was of short duration, however, for Vallandigham left the camp safely and Colonel McCook, along with other officers, turned their attention to the military crisis at hand. It was essential that the focus remain on Manassas Gap, and toward that end, the Union army continued to receive volunteer regiments. Among them Colonel William T. Sherman, an Ohio man with whom the McCooks were already familiar, reported for duty on June 29, 1861. By that time McDowell's Army of Northeastern Virginia consisted of 13,666 men present for duty.[31]

As more and more regiments reported for duty, the growing army was organized into five divisions that McDowell was preparing to lead in a flank attack against Beauregard's Army of the Potomac. From 1st through the 5th, the divisions were placed under Brigadier General Daniel Tyler, Colonel David Hunter, Colonel Samuel P. Heintzelman, Brigadier General Theodore Runyon, and Colonel Dixon S. Miles.

The McCooks — Alexander, Charles and cousin Anson — and their regiments were assigned to the division of Brigadier General Tyler, by then considered to be an old soldier of 62 years of age. He was a member of the West Point class of 1819, but never had any combat experience. He left the army in 1834, only to return, as did so many other officers, after the Civil War began. Tyler was successful as a civilian and brought his high opinion of himself into the army where he ruled over his division with a hard hand. His division — the largest in McDowell's command — consisted of the brigades commanded by Schenck, Sherman, Colonel Erasmus D. Keyes and Colonel Israel B.

Richardson. Under McDowell's plan, Tyler would march toward the Rebels by way of Vienna.

On July 16, 1861, the army that McDowell described as "good, bad and indifferent" began its slow, irregular march toward battle, after many postponements.[32] Runyon's division was held in reserve and would not participate in the fighting. The remaining divisions moved out after allowing the emboldened troops the chance to write an "if I should die" letter home to their folks and sweethearts. Traveling with the motivated group was a gaggle of reporters from some of the leading newspapers of the northeast, all eager to write about a Union victory. Singing as they marched, the columns moved slowly that first day, through thickly wooded terrain. The movement proved to be largely uneventful, impeded by fallen trees and firing from Rebel pickets.

The next day, Tyler's division moved south from Vienna, between Centreville and the Fairfax Courthouse. He sent one brigade marching from each location and held the remainder of his division for "discretionary use." On the 18th, Tyler was ordered to "make a show of force," for the purpose of giving the impression that the Union army was "moving on Manassas." Acting upon these orders, Tyler's division moved toward Centreville, cautiously, with pickets leading the way.

Upon reaching Fairfax Courthouse, they found evidence of a Rebel occupation in the form of trenches and other works, but no enemy soldiers there to fight. The Rebels had apparently abandoned that position the night before in haste, leaving behind a bewildering variety of provisions and personal items. In one tent, an uneaten breakfast was sitting on a table. Elsewhere sick soldiers were found abandoned with no food. Among the many letters picked up and read was a missive from a girl to her brother, asking that he "kill a Yankee for me."[33]

A reporter for the *New York Times* took note of the deserted food, supplies and equipment, and watched as excited Union troops helped themselves to the unexpected largess. He wrote, "They rushed to the plunder with a degree of enthusiasm which I only hope will be equaled when they come to fight." The reporter was uncomfortable with the glee displayed by the looting soldiers, who then began to burn houses. Still he was satisfied that an army on the march could not be kept from excesses and concluded that this behavior is "due to the spirit of frolic."[34]

Tyler learned from civilian sources that the Rebels had retreated to Blackburn's Ford at Bull Run Creek, a stream that was referred to by northern newspapers as "Bull's Run Creek." He continued his cautious advance, meeting with no resistance, which led him to believe that the Rebels would continue to retreat so long as he moved forward.

Since he disliked McDowell, a confident and scheming Tyler envisioned a mighty conquest of the Rebels, led by his division. He believed he was in a position to pull off a win that would bolster his career at the expense of McDowell.[35] However, after floundering around in disarray, Tyler's division moved out slowly in the pre-dawn darkness, with Schenck's brigade in front, towing a cumbersome, 30-pounder rifled Parrot gun that weighed approximately 6,000 pounds.

Schenck was every bit as cautious as Tyler, and this combined with the bulk of the big gun slowed down the progress of his brigade. On July 18, Richardson's brigade of Tyler's division encountered Rebel resistance at Blackburn's Ford, and after a hot skirmish, the Union troops were repulsed. Richardson suffered about 40 killed, wounded and missing.[36] Daniel McCook, Sr., and John Logan, an Illinois congressman, were among those who took the dead and wounded from the field.

An over-anxious Richardson had exceeded his orders but Tyler got the blame, and his conduct drew an emphatic rebuke from Daniel McCook, Sr. Tyler's setback had a demoralizing effect on the Union troops and civilians who were forced to accept the bad news. For the next two days, McDowell was compelled to deal with one delay after another, allowing Beauregard to receive reinforcements and supplies by rail from Richmond. A *Times* editorial sounded anything but optimistic, noting that "in the event of a collision at Manassas Junction, our Army may not obtain that victory which is popularly regarded as certain."[37]

Meanwhile in Washington — crawling with Southern sympathizers and spies — anxious rumors ruled the day. A *Times* reporter observed, "The air has been pregnant with rumors of battle and carnage." Reports that a well-armed Rebel force at Bull Run was "more formidable than was at first supposed" were circulated.[38] The Rebels were indeed waiting in force, for Beauregard was told of the Union advance by one of his notorious and dependable spies in Washington, the widowed socialite Rose O'Neal Greenhow.[39] Beauregard would be more than ready to meet McDowell's semi-organized army that moved toward Bull Run Creek with some degree of uncertainty in the pre-dawn of Sunday, the 21st of July.

Greenhow was a pivotal figure in the battle that was about to begin, as the intelligence she gathered in Washington, while visiting among politicians and officers, was very useful to Beauregard. Greenhow was smart, clever, charming and tough-minded. She was fiercely loyal to the budding Confederacy and hated the Yankee abolitionists. The "secesh" lady was well acquainted with leading political figures of the time, including Edwin M. Stanton, William H. Seward and former president James Buchanan. She was reputed to have been the lover of Massachusetts senator Henry Wilson.[40]

Being a *grande dame* of the social whirl, she had easy access to those who possessed military intelligence and was willing to risk her life to learn as much as she could and send it, in cipher, to Richmond. Having obtained a copy of

McDowell's orders indicates she had contacts with Union officers who were part of her spy network.[41]

A Washington insider who knew Greenhow and visited her at the Old Capitol Prison after she was arrested for her spy work believed that she was full of excessive feelings of self-importance. She so loved the South that her sole purpose in life was to become a martyr for the Southern cause.

Greenhow was released from prison and escorted beyond Union lines. She went to Richmond and received a heroine's welcome. Not long after, a grateful Jefferson Davis sent her to England on a secret mission where she wrote a book about the battle of Bull Run, claiming her intelligence was the key to victory. Upon on her return to America, Rose Greenhow met her death by drowning in Wilmington Harbor, a casualty to the cause she believed in so fiercely.[42]

CHAPTER 4

The Battle of Bull Run

It is indeed quite within the range of possibility that, in the event of collision at Manassas Junction, our Army may not obtain that victory which is popularly regarded as certain.

—*New York Times*, July 21, 1861

The *New York Times*, under the tutelage of President Lincoln's supporter, Henry J. Raymond, was sounding a cautionary note, while trying not to come across as pessimistic. A voice of reason, however, was not what angry Unionists wanted to hear, and when the citizens of Washington, D.C., were convinced that a major clash was imminent, dozens of the curious and anxious made preparations to experience the fight firsthand. Mathew Brady, who gained fame as a Civil War photographer, ventured forth with his camera equipment loaded into a wagon. He was lucky to have transportation, as every available horse, wagon and carriage in the city was rented. Members of Congress and their spouses, other ladies and gentlemen from Washington society, all dressed for the occasion, packed expensive linens, wines and gourmet food in their baskets, and set out to make a day of it. Merchants were equally giddy, charging exorbitant prices for the luxury items the observers just had to take along to enjoy the spectacle.[1]

Daniel McCook, Sr., wanted to be near the action too, but not as a spectator. Since he was not accepted into the army due to his age, he volunteered to serve as a nurse. In a letter to his son Robert, then serving in the Union army in western Virginia, McCook acknowledged that he had the "consent of your dear Mother" to go to the front. He loaded a carriage with three days' supply of provisions and with son Edwin, Illinois congressman John Logan and one other man, headed out in the direction of the Ohio regiments camped near Centreville.

The Union camp was so close to enemy lines that Daniel McCook, Sr., could hear the Rebel pickets talking. With enemy soldiers "within talking distance," he was not in the mood to sleep, and about midnight he was asked to bring his son Colonel Alexander M. McCook a cup of coffee. The elder McCook delivered the coffee to his son, and not long after the cup was empty, the order came to move out.[2] Although for many of the men, their three-month enlistments were expiring, not a single man in either Ohio regiment opted to go to the rear.[3]

If Major General Irwin McDowell was aware of the gathering sightseers, he paid it no mind, for his thoughts were set on more serious matters. He left the division of Colonel Dixon S. Miles in Centreville and, taking the remaining three divisions consisting of about 15,000 men, struck out toward Manassas with the intent to hit the Confederate left. It was to be a surprise attack. Unknown to McDowell, however, General Joseph E. Johnston was busy bringing his division to reinforce General Pierre G. T. Beauregard, thus increasing the Confederate force to about 30,000 men. Nevertheless, the battle started with the South on the defensive.

According to Brigadier General Robert C. Schenck's official report, his brigade moved out at 2:30 A.M. on July 21, pursuant to orders, from their camp one mile south of Centreville. His brigade was spearheading Brigadier General Daniel Tyler's division, with the 1st Ohio in front followed by the 2nd Ohio and the 2nd New York State Militia. A battery of light artillery, consisting of six brass guns and the huge 30-pounder, under the guidance of Captain J. Howard Carlisle, followed.

Marching alongside the men of the 1st Ohio was a soldier named Louisa Hoffman, a young woman who cut her hair, donned a uniform and enlisted. Her disguise must have been very convincing for it can be assumed that had Colonel McCook known that one of his troopers was female, she would have been summarily discharged and sent home. As unusual as it may seem, Hoffman and other women on both sides fit in and performed as well as men on that Virginia battlefield.[4]

The brigade proceeded cautiously, feeling its way through the darkness, with five companies of skirmishers from the Ohio regiments leading the way. When they reached the Stone Bridge at Bull Run Creek, Schenck discovered the presence of the enemy forming a line on a hillside on the opposite side of the creek. Schenck then deployed his three infantry regiments in a line of battle by the Warrenton Turnpike, a road that ran west from Centreville and crossed Bull Run Creek at the Stone Bridge. Schenck formed the left wing of Tyler's division. To its right was Sherman's brigade.

Schenck woke up anyone on either side who may have been asleep by unleashing a round from the big Parrott gun. There was no response from the other side, so after a few minutes of silence, the metal monster was fired again. And again, there was no answer from the other side. Therefore, according to his orders, Schenck's regiments took up positions in a wooded hollow, "covered by a ridge." They remained there for "two and a half or three hours with no evidence of our nearness to the enemy," except for some musket firing by his pickets.[5]

According to Anson McCook's memoir, Generals Hunter and Heintzelman were to cross Bull Run at Sudley Springs and start the battle by attacking the Confederate left. Meanwhile Tyler's division was ordered to wait in readiness at the Stone Bridge, and when the shooting started, it was to cross the creek and join the attack. Anson recalled, however, that attack by Hunter and Heintzelman occurred three hours later than was expected.[6]

When it was certain that the divisions of Hunter and Heintzelman had engaged the enemy on the opposite side of Bull Run, Schenck's orders were to stay alert for any "sign of a stampede by the enemy." The overall strategy was for the larger force of the combined divisions of Heintzelman and Hunter to strike the Rebel left flank and turn the enemy toward Tyler, who was to cut off its retreat. Schenck's brigade was ordered to be prepared to cross Bull Run Creek after the enemy had been pushed back. Since it was believed that the Stone Bridge was mined with explosives, engineers were ready to erect a prefabricated bridge for the crossing.[7]

Schenck ordered McCook's regiment forward to "feel the battery of the enemy" which was believed to be on a hill from which the Rebels could cover the creek crossing. Supported by the 2nd Ohio and 2nd New York, McCook advanced his regiment as ordered, moving cautiously along a narrow road through a thick wood. When he reached the point where the road met the stream, McCook discovered a well-entrenched battery, supported by four Rebel regiments in rifle pits. While Schenck and McCook were maneuvering their men into position, the Rebel artillery opened up "with shells and round and grape shot," the deadly effect of which was felt primarily by the 2nd New York regiment. The Southerners had the advantage of higher ground from which to fire their artillery.

Seemingly undismayed, Schenck ordered his artillery to return fire, and a lively exchange took place. It was, however, an unequal exchange due to the superior firepower of the Rebels. Schenck, nevertheless, stayed with his big guns, satisfied that he was at least keeping a small portion of the Rebel force occupied.

A reporter following Schenck's brigade said the soldiers "endured the storm of balls with the greatest fortitude, and returned fire for fire." In addition to troops who fell under the intense barrage, the reporter recalled that the "favorite drummer-boy" of the 2nd Ohio was struck and blown in half by cannon shot. The reporter remembered hearing a "childish shriek of pain mingling with the whistle of the rifled shot as his little life went with it down the wind."[8]

With the death of the boy, the onslaught from the entrenched Rebels seemed to increase. Feeling he was out-gunned and out-positioned, Schenck drew his guns back into the cover of the woods, thus joining the rest of the brigade. Later in the day, about 1:00 P.M., Schenck got Carlisle's battery in position to fire upon what he believed to be masses of the enemy in retreat. He was encouraged by "cheering reports" of the Union success on the other side of Bull Run Creek. Soon after, however, he learned of a "reverse of fortune" which essentially ended his brigade's involvement in the battle.

While he did not attempt another advance, Schenck was successful in getting his artillery in position to fire, with some effect, into the Confederate ranks that crossed the creek as if to attempt a flanking movement. This, too, ended when, according to Schenck, it was learned from "unpleasant intelligence" that the entire army was withdrawing back to Centreville.[9]

The early-morning blast from Tyler's big Parrott gun, in the vicinity of the Stone Bridge on Bull Run Creek, signaled the beginning of the fight that would continue throughout the day. The Rebel army had formed itself in a broken line, about six miles long, from Union Mills Ford to the Stone Bridge. McDowell hoped to strike the left flank of the Confederates by surprise, but his troops were detected and the Rebels had time to react. Despite losing the element of surprise, McDowell proceeded to out-maneuver Beauregard, and by late in the afternoon, he believed that he had victory within his grasp.

The brunt of the battle was born by the divisions of Hunter and Heintzelman on the Union right. They succeeded in driving the Rebels back according to plan. Tyler's division was in the thick of it too, with the exception of Schenck's brigade. When the fighting was furious, Tyler was ordered to move forward to support Hunter, who was badly wounded in the throat and had to be carried from the field. Still, Hunter's division, aided by a charge from Sherman's fresh brigade, was successful in driving the Rebels back. By mid-day, Union expectations were soaring and McDowell was riding up and down the lines shouting "Victory!" He was winning with sizable reserves to spare. In contrast, a worried Jefferson Davis rode among the stragglers urging the Rebels get back into the fight, shouting, "I'm President Davis! Follow me back to the field!"[10]

Late that afternoon, excited reporters rushed back to Washington so they could send word to their newspapers proclaiming that the Union had won a great victory. Noting the intensity of the fighting and the terrible slaughter on both sides, the *New York Times* called it "the greatest battle ever fought on this continent." A reporter for the *New York Herald* sent a wire from Fairfax, saying, "We have carried the day. The rebels accepted battle in strength, but are totally routed."[11]

The *Herald* got it wrong. Yet McDowell may have actually won the historic battle had he sent his entire force into the fight. But his two large reserve divisions were not called into action. Also Schenck's brigade never crossed Bull

Run Creek; instead it stayed on the Warrenton Turnpike, close to the Stone Bridge.[12] A war correspondent from the *Tribune* said Schenck was clueless most of the time, and was seen riding his horse across his lines as if oblivious to the musket fire.[13] Anson McCook recalled that he *heard* much more of the fighting than he *saw* while waiting at the Stone Bridge.[14]

As Tyler's division did not present a well-organized offensive, Schenck found his brigade cut off and vulnerable to a Rebel assault. Schenck, an authority on draw poker, needed a game-saving wild card. Fortunately the general had Alexander M. McCook as his ace in the hole. The *Tribune* correspondent gave Colonel McCook full credit for saving the brigade. He wrote, "I am inclined to believe that the coolness and precision of Col. McCook of the 1st Ohio Regiment saved us from disaster." McCook, he said, displayed leadership and soldierly resolve in the face of the Rebel charge.[15]

A correspondent with the *Cleveland Herald* said McCook's unit, the 1st Ohio Infantry, "covered itself with glory." The regimental commander was described as "cool and collected" in battle "as when drilling his men upon the parade ground." McCook "issued his orders with bullets and cannon balls whistling about his ears as thick as hailstones, without any apparent excitement whatever." He was commanded by the enemy to surrender not once but twice, but managed to escape capture on both occasions, and "the ball had not been molded yet to take his life!"[16] Colonel McCook emerged from the battle a winner, having stood tall when the fighting was fierce.

His father later recalled that Alexander fought the battle of Bull Run in his "shirt and pantaloons." Because he did not wear a jacket, the enemy could not identify him as an officer, and therefore he "did not become an object for the sharp shooters." Since Alexander was on foot and lacked the gaudy attire of other brass-decked officers, many of them on horseback, his father believed his life was spared.[17]

Back in Steubenville, Ohio, family and friends learned by way of a telegram that Alexander and Anson were both killed. Dr. John McCook said the town was "in a ferment" over the tragic news. Relief came with a message from a soldier who informed the McCook family that the boys were safe and unhurt.[18]

The Civil War careers of both Alexander and Anson McCook were off to a historic beginning, as were the lives of many others who fought in that furious, noisy and dirty battle, the likes of which had never been seen on the continent. Clouds of smoke from the battleground could be seen from the highest points in Washington, where people anxiously awaited news from the front. The secretary of war, Simon Cameron — whose son was killed that day — received a dispatch telling him that the Union troops had "engaged the enemy with a large force, silenced their batteries, and drove the Secessionists to the Junction." This caused the city and its inhabitants to engage in wild celebration.[19] Unfortunately, however, the Confederate reinforcements turned the tide of battle against the Union. Seemingly overwhelmed and succumbing to a collective defeatist mentality, the Northern forces began to retreat without waiting for orders to do so.

Suddenly it was Beauregard's turn to celebrate. He personally rode among his troops and rallied them when all seemed lost. Throughout the fight, the weak and disjointed structure of the Confederate command led to miscommunications and missed connections. But the Union managed to out-bungle the Rebels, proving that the fortunes of war are fickle indeed. On that hot July afternoon in 1861, the fates smiled on Beauregard's game but awkward army. He had luck to thank for his victory, more so than his military skills or those of his field commanders.

The luckless McDowell valiantly tried to rally his troops and showed great personal courage at all phases of the battle. But his efforts were unavailing because his men were over-heated, without water, hungry, tired and beaten, and his officers, for the most part, lacked the experience and desire to step up and lead. Sherman, whose career would flower later in the war, was forced to watch his brigade as it was used up, after which the remnants were scattered like dry leaves in the wind. When all looked lost, Tyler decided he would save the army by leading a charge of all of his men that he could rally. But instead of charging forward, he was forced to watch men swarm in the opposite direction.[20]

Portrait of Major General Irwin McDowell, field commander of the Union forces at the battle of Bull Run. The dignified-looking McDowell was a professional soldier with an impressive resume. He was selected by General Winfield Scott to lead the Union army in its first major battle. While McDowell was a qualified and loyal soldier, he seemed plagued by bad luck and following the defeat at Bull Run went on to a mostly undistinguished record in the Civil War.

At first the withdrawal was orderly, but as shells from Confederate big guns raked across the retreating federal ranks, panic set in and soon thousands of Yankees were on the run back toward Washington, scattering haversacks, guns, coats, and musical instruments. The commanding officer of the 12th New York Infantry tried to rally his men around the regimental colors but was forced to confess that he was knocked down and some of his men "actually ran over me."[21]

Senator Lyman Trumbull of Illinois, who came out to harm's way as an observer, was packing up after finishing lunch with some friends when he "heard a great noise, and looking up toward the road saw it filled with wagons, horsemen and footmen, in full run towards Centreville." He and his friends mounted up and galloped in the same direction.[22]

Others had a tougher time retreating. Hundreds of wounded men limped along as best they could. Adding a tragic-comedy effect to the rout, the troops were impeded in their retreat by the presence of a large number of newspapermen, civilians and political figures who had driven out in carriages — with their fancies and dainties — to watch what they were certain would be a glorious Union victory. Fully caught up in the mass fear and panic, the frightened gentlemen and screaming ladies from Washington discarded their champagne glasses and joined in the humiliating stampede toward safety. Those on horseback or in carriages or wagons were beset upon by those on foot, begging to be allowed to ride to safety. But it was essentially every man and woman for himself or herself, and the panic-stricken pedestrians on the run were turned away with shouts of anger or threats of violence.

A correspondent for the *London Times* roamed the area on horseback in the midst of the chaos and clouds of dust, taking mental notes of the terrible panic. He actually tried to convince some of the fleeing men to calm down and come to their senses, but he confessed later that he "might as well have talked to the stones." The English journalist described the extraordinary experience as one where people acted "as if driven by some unknown terror."[23]

The daughter of Thurlow Weed, a prominent New York journalist, politician and friend of the president, forgot all sense of dignity as she made her escape clinging to the back and neck of a mule, denuded of all harness except for a rope around its head. Worse yet, perhaps, was the dilemma of Senator Henry Wilson of Massachusetts, who desperately sought a way out of the frightful mess. He attempted in vain to use his high status in order to convince a teamster to give him a ride. Hearing shouts of "I am Henry Wilson, United States Senator!" the teamster replied, "I don't give a _____ who you are," and drove off, whacking the backs of his mules.[24] Like other spectators, Wilson was desperate to exit the mad theater of war.

All vehicles competed for the limited space on the bumpy roads back to Washington. Collisions and turnovers added to the debris. A bottleneck at the crossing of Cub Run Creek — a tributary to Bull Run Creek — slowed down the mad retreat, making matters worse. Exaggerated rumors of casualties also made their way back to the Capitol, including the false report that Schenck had been killed. It was not a good start for the Union. On the plus side, heavy rains the next day rendered impossible any Confederate plans to advance on Washington.

The stampede from the Stone Bridge on Bull Run Creek toward Centreville included a fully animated Schenck, along with Colonel Erasmus D. Keyes and remnants from Sherman's brigade. Schenck may have ordered his troops to retreat to safety without getting orders to do so. He did, however, deploy two companies of the 2nd Ohio to slow down the Confederate onslaught while the rest of his men left the field of battle.[25] Bringing up the rear of Tyler's division, Schenck reported that his regiments retreated in good order, "sharing comparatively little in the panic which characterized so painfully that retreat." He blamed the unmilitary behavior on "the fears of frightened teamsters" and civilians who had no business being at the edge of the battleground in harm's way.

A reporter for *The Philadelphia Inquirer*, who claimed eyewitness status, said that Schenck "failed to rally his column in any order." Instead men from the Ohio and New York regiments "scattered through the woods in pursuit of shelter and water."[26]

Tyler appeared to be satisfied with Schenck's management of the crisis. When the retreat was in progress, Tyler sought out Schenck for the purpose of covering the flow of soldiers to the rear. When he finally found Schenck, Tyler acknowledged that his brigade commander "appeared active in rallying his own or some other regiments."[27]

Schenck's official report to Tyler soft-pedals the disgraceful nature of the rout. He makes it clear that his regiments played no part in the panic. He was also careful to note that he acted strictly on orders throughout the day, and rationalized the return to Washington as necessary because his Ohio regiments were to be mustered out and sent home, their "term of service having expired."[28] A soldier in the 1st Michigan Infantry Regiment summed it up succinctly and without apology: "We had fought incessantly for four or five hours, without food or drink, almost exhausted at the beginning, our ranks were thinned and broken, we saw no prospect of support, and we retreated in disorder; but there was little running."[29]

Anson McCook's testament was that Schenck's brigade retreated orderly and that there was "no special confusion in the brigade." But his memoir expresses some confusion about events leading up to the mad retreat. He wrote: "I do not think that any of us at the Stone bridge realized exactly when the tide turned," nor could he explain why the brigade did not cross "the Run."[30]

Reports from other officers flowed into Washington, and the long-running analysis of the battle of Bull Run was just beginning. During the lengthy process, accusing fingers were pointed in every direction, and many a man was under scrutiny; and many an officer's military career ended as the wheat was rapidly separated from the chaff. If there was any benefit from the embarrassing loss, it was in the form of eliminating unqualified officers from the army.

Anson McCook wrote about the "oceans of ink" expended in analyzing the battle and what went wrong, finding much of it "wild and absurd." He tended to think that the Union's effort failed because of bad timing. The troops were unable to get into position fast enough to be effective in carrying out what he believed was a well-planned battle.[31]

The correspondents of the *New York Tribune* were also actively engaged in trying to sort it all out as best they could. Unfortunately their reports failed to satisfy everyone and in fact riled up some men to the point of indignation. It was time for the editor to step in and attempt some clarification. In an editorial on August 1, 1861, the *Tribune* discussed Schenck's role in the "great" retreat, having previously been critical of the general. The *Tribune* acknowledged receiving "from several members of the staff of Gen. Schenck some pretty animated criticism" based on a recent article by one of its correspondents.

Members of Schenck's staff weighed in and supported their general, casting blame for the alleged "inaction of Schenck's brigade" on General Tyler. They insisted that Schenck, as stated in his official report, was responsible for the "successful resistance to the flanking movement of the enemy at the close of the fight." Credit originally attributed to Colonel McCook belonged to "the clear head and courageous heart of the General [Schenck], who took in at a glance what your correspondent fails even now to comprehend."

The *Tribune* was willing to publish these assertions and further admit that "every General or other commanding officer engaged in that deplorable battle did his entire duty as a strategist and a hero." The editorial ended with a plea and a fervent question: "Is it not possible to banish all further bickerings and personal controversies," and instead concentrate on carrying the fight to the Confederates?[32]

Unwilling to let the matter die, Daniel McCook, Sr., wrote a letter to his son George adding additional controversy and more tantalizing detail to the story of the desperate retreat from Bull Run by Schenck's brigade. The elder McCook said that neither Schenck nor Colonel McCook deserved credit for disrupting the Rebel cavalry flanking movement. "I made the discovery myself," he wrote with obvious pride, and "called the attention of the Gen'l to the fact, and desired him to send me down a section of his battery to dislodge the Enemy." Schenck honored the request, and Daniel McCook, Sr., ordered the Ohio regiments into position "to direct the throwing of the shell."

Alexander asked his father to retire from his position, saying "'*that my life was not paid for.*'" Instead of retiring, the old man continued to direct the fire "until the Enemy were dislodged and retreated." As for his son, "how much he contributed to bring off our forces from the great battle god only knows." Clearly Daniel McCook, Sr., didn't know, for had he known the extent of Alexander's role, he no doubt would have described it in detail in his letter to George. The point of his letter was to set the record straight in the mind of his family and show that the Ohio soldiers, including his sons and nephew, did something other than run away as did so many others.[33]

Colonel William T. Sherman, the soldier of misfortune, was stung and upset by the actions of the fleeing troops, feeling no doubt the way a reporter felt when he wrote, "All was lost to that American army, even its honor."[34] He was right. It was so disgraceful that Bull Run became the yardstick by which disaster on the battlefield was measured. Over the next four years, other defeats and failures of the Union army were often compared to the battle of Bull Run.

The ill-starred battle created special relationships among the men and officers, many of whom experienced the terror of gunfire and the death of comrades for the first time. Among the many friendships formed was that of Colonel McCook and Colonel Sherman. While Sherman's star ascended to the highest point of the military firmament, and McCook's did not, the two men remained steadfast friends for the rest of their lives as a result of wartime bonding.

Private Charles M. McCook of the 2nd Ohio must have been part of Schenck's "orderly retreat," for he was not among the fleeing mob. One source says he was attempting to cover the retreat of the army when he was surrounded by Confederate cavalry from the so-called "Black Horse Cavalry." This happened near a field hospital where his father, Daniel McCook, Sr., was working as a volunteer nurse. His mother, Martha McCook, was in Washington, listening anxiously to the sounds of battle, knowing that her husband, two sons and a nephew were in danger.

Moments before the encounter with the Rebels, Charles stopped briefly to assist his father, where he was surrounded and ordered to surrender. Young Charles was skillful in the use of a bayonet, and instead of surrendering, he disabled the officer in charge and succeeded in keeping the others at bay until he was shot and fatally wounded.[35]

The *New York Tribune* reported the incident with some variations. Charles McCook — who was erroneously referred to as "Capt McCook" — was inside the Sudley Church that had been converted into a hospital. Suddenly members of the "Black Horse Cavalry" descended upon the church, shooting at wounded men. Private McCook and another soldier ran out of the building in an attempt to escape. McCook was shot through the spine and killed.[36]

An Ohio newspaper, the *Cleveland Herald* romanticized the tragic incident into one of heroic proportions. Noting that McCook was just 17 years old, the *Herald* informed its readers that he bravely faced off the enemy while he was standing guard at the hospital. When ordered to surrender, he said, with "fixed bayonet, steady nerve and cool bearing ... I never surrender!" His father stopped his work on the wounded and, seeing that his son was surrounded by cavalry, begged Charles to do otherwise. "Charley," he pleaded, "surrender for God's sake or you are lost." The young soldier turned to his father, "with all the lion in his countenance," and said firmly: "Father, I will never surrender to a rebel." After that storybook line, he was shot in the spine, but as he fell, he managed to fire his musket, killing the Rebel horseman who had shot him. Other Confederates tried to drag Charles' body off, but the elder McCook intervened, securing his mortally wounded son.[37]

Romantic images and larger-than-life heroics gush from an account taken from the "Proceedings of the Scotch-Irish Society of America," in a book by Henry Howe. According to this source, young Charles was shot and while cradled in his father's arms said, "Tell her [his mother] that I refused to surrender, that I am not afraid of death, that I am glad to die for my country." Then as life was slipping away, the dying soldier, with a faint voice, repeated in Latin, "*Dulce et decorum est pro patria mori!*" which in English means: "It is sweet and glorious to die for one's country."[38]

A more recent account that quoted John G. Nicolay, Lincoln's personal secretary, called Charles McCook's death "one of the most affecting scenes" of the battle. Nicolay recalled that "one of them — [Charles] — the youngest I think, was killed while engaged in some duty about one of the hospitals, in one of the many such inhuman assaults the enemy made upon the sick and wounded." Nicolay, possibly an eyewitness to the incident, said that after Charles was shot, his brother Alexander went to him and "kissed him and said 'Good bye Charley, die like a man.'" But strangely, Nicolay puts the incident at the beginning of the battle, not the end, noting that after his noble gesture, Alexander "went to the head of his regiment which had that moment received marching orders, and led them bravely and gallantly to the fight."[39]

The varying accounts of Charles' death all contain elements of the truth, and are summarized in a letter dated July 26 from his father, describing the battle of Bull Run and the tragic end of a young soldier's life. At about noon on the 21st, the elder McCook, in the company of son Edwin, took some food to Charles. After sending Charles off to his regiment, Daniel McCook returned to the field hospital. Edwin told his brother, "Father and I will take care of ourselves."

Charles had not walked too far when he was confronted by a Confederate cavalry officer who demanded his surrender. When Charles defiantly refused, the officer shot him in the back, "severing his rectum, cutting off the bladder and cutting the intestines badly."

Daniel McCook, Sr., shocked and angry, took his badly wounded son from the Confederates and found a surgeon who examined Charles and pronounced his wounds fatal. While his father was driving him back in the direction of safety, Alexander passed by with the retreating Ohio troops. Seeing Charles in the wagon, "he patted his cheek and kissed him and returned to the head of his column." Daniel and Edwin then continued on their way over the rough trail, with Charles in great pain, but holding up bravely.

Charles tried to convince his father that he was going to die, but Daniel refused to believe he was about to lose his son and was determined to get to the hospital at Fairfax Courthouse and find a surgeon who could remove the ball. They reached the hospital and the ball was extracted, and once again the wound was declared to be fatal. It was then that a saddened father told his young son that death was imminent. Daniel sent Edwin home to Washington. He gave Charles some tea and water, washed his wound and made him as comfortable as possible. Alone with his son and a "house full of wounded soldiers," Daniel McCook, Sr., waited for the inevitable. At about 2:30 A.M., Charles breathed his last. With the aid of a servant of one of the wounded men, Daniel wrapped his son in blankets, strapped him to the lid of a musket box, and placed him in the wagon.[40]

Daniel McCook, Sr., brought his boy's body back to Washington, driving the wagon himself. News of Charles' heroics reached Washington before his body arrived. Upon reaching the Long Bridge, a company of Fire Zouves assumed duty as an honor guard and accompanied the McCook wagon for the remainder of the sad journey.[41]

Charles' body was taken to Mrs. Parris' boarding house across the street from the Brown Hotel, where the McCooks were staying. He was carried inside by sympathetic volunteers.[42] His mother was the first to see his lifeless body.

The valiant young soldier was buried in the congressional burying ground by members of the 1st Ohio regiment. Later he was disinterred, taken back home and reburied in the family plot at Spring Grove Cemetery, Cincinnati, Ohio. He would not long rest alone, for throughout the war Charles would be joined by others from among his family's honored dead.

The account of Charles' heroic death became a story for the ages, retold in the decades to come. The story was given legs in a book entitled *The Fallen Brave*, published before the year 1861 was out. In this book "Captain" Charles M. McCook, "The Boy Hero of Bull Run," was given a send-off worthy of the noblest of soldiers, promising that he and his kinsmen would long be remembered for their patriotism, sacrifice and gallantry.

Kenyon College, known for its bells, dedicated Bell Number One to the fallen youth. The bell was inscribed to state, "In memory of Charles Morris McCook, killed in battle, July 21st, 1861," followed by the Latin phrase, "*Dulce et decorum est pro patria mori.*"[43] After the war ended, Charles' younger brother

An unknown soldier lies dead on the battlefield of Bull Run, along with his equally silent comrades. Bull Run was called the battle of Manassas by the Confederates. In the first major bloodletting of the Civil War, the Union lost 491 men to death while the South tallied 387 dead soldiers. The result was a disaster for the Union and a nightmare for Abraham Lincoln. He wanted a decisive victory as a sign to everyone that the war would be short and that the restoration of the Union would follow.

John James McCook enjoyed recounting the story of his sibling's death to enraptured students at Kenyon College.

The Rebel horse soldier who killed Charles was given elevated status, even though his name is unknown. Although the "Black Horse Cavalry" was in actuality just a mounted militia company of men from the area around Warrenton, Virginia, they emerged from the battle of Bull Run with almost mythical status. Riding black or gray horses and led by Colonel R. C. W. Radford, they were seen galloping furiously among the confusion and chaos of the fighting, and someone used the name "Black Horse Cavalry" to describe them. Use of the apocalyptic appellation spread throughout the Union ranks and entered many a campfire conversation. Soon newspapers picked up and circulated the neat phrase, and a Rebel legend was born.[44]

No one would have faulted Charles for surrendering when surrounded by the enemy "Black Horse Cavalry," and many probably thought it would have been wiser to do so. And yet Charles M. McCook became the all-American boy for choosing loyalty over secession, and in his first battle, death over the dishonor of surrender.

Charles' uncle, Dr. George McCook, understood the fierce patriotic ardor that motivated his nephew and the other young family members. Long after the war ended, it was reported that Dr. McCook said at the outset of hostilities: "If this war lasts six months there will be more McCooks in the army than there are Indians in hell."[45] The brazen and mean-spirited metaphor had some prophetic import despite the popular racist tone.

The two branches of the family were commonly referred to as the "Tribe of Dan" and "Tribe of John." A total of 15 men from the two groups served in some capacity during the Civil War. Dr. George McCook and his son Dr. George L. McCook contributed some service as surgeons, bringing the grand total to 17.

While the list of dead and injured was relatively light when compared with the battles that were fought after the battle of Bull Run, the news media and the nation were shocked and horrified. Americans killing Americans: it was all too much to believe. But the battle of Bull Run was no ordinary nightmare, and its awful message of suffering was blazoned across the country from coast to coast, border to border, like fire in the sky. Americans had seen their world split apart and the pieces hurled into the dark void, forcing a confused and saddened people to weep and suffer while wandering through the wilderness of war.

While most people would not have believed the war would continue for four years, the unprecedented number of casualties gave all thoughtful people reason to hope for a speedy return to peace. McDowell's losses consisted of 491 dead, 1,072 wounded, and 1,040 missing.[46] Beauregard lost 387 killed, 1,582 wounded and just 13 listed as missing.[47] Both sides went about the grim task of what was to be the first of many mass burials. Some of the fallen were forgotten and unattended until their skeletons were found thirteen months later when the second battle of Bull Run was fought.[48]

It was reported that among the Confederate dead was the last descendant of George Washington, one of the most illustrious of all Virginians. The man who "bore his name and inherited his estates was shot from his horse and killed — a rebel spy!"[49]

The disaster was a terrible blow to Lincoln's gentle psyche, but he gathered himself and began to pick up the pieces. The country would find that adversity made Lincoln stronger and more determined. He had no time to bemoan the loss and instead set himself to making plans for ultimate victory. The day after the battle, Lincoln signed a bill passed by Congress providing for 500,000 three-year volunteers; three days later he signed another bill calling for another half million men.[50] The South would be made to know he was serious.

General Scott, on the other hand, was shocked and angered by the resounding defeat and blamed himself. Unlike Lincoln, the loss caused Scott deep anguish; he must have sensed that his army days were numbered, with retirement a viable option.

Both Scott and Lincoln had to deal with critical newspaper reports of the debacle. Dana, the managing editor for the *Tribune* called on the cabinet to resign. Dana's boss, Horace Greeley, took the embarrassing defeat to heart, fell ill and took to his bed. He was plagued by feelings of guilt because it was his newspaper that led the media charge for battle. In a letter to Lincoln, he all but sounded the death knell over the Union while urging the president to consider an armistice or another "peaceful adjustment." He closed his letter saying, "Yours in the depths of bitterness, Horace Greeley."[51]

Richmond was cast into a state of shock as the dead and wounded were brought in for burial or treatment. No one sang songs of victory; no one reveled in the glory of war. Instead a dark sense of gloom hovered over the city where so many families had suffered losses. The harsh reality of war was brought to bear upon the citizens of Richmond, unprepared but forced to mourn their losses and face the prospect of months or years of hardship and suffering. The hated Yankees may have lost the battle but they inflicted a terrible wound on the psyche of Virginians, and the pain had just begun.[52]

Despite the suffering and loss of life, many Southerners were disappointed that the victory on the field of battle was not immediately followed by a successful attack on Washington. But such expectations were unrealistic, as the Confederate army was in no way prepared for such an assignment. Armchair generals would have to be satisfied with winning the first major battle of the war.

The wobbly victory for the South meant Beauregard's star would shine even brighter, although he would prove to be an irritant to Jefferson Davis, a thin-skinned man who lacked Lincoln's ability to work with those who opposed him. After a subsequent clash of egos, Beauregard would be sent to the western theater. On the other side, McDowell, the luckless loser, was replaced by Major General George B. McClellan, whose recent but modest successes in western Virginia made him the coming man.

Among Tyler's division, Sherman's brigade had borne the brunt of battle, and his casualties were high. Keyes, Richardson and Schenck, however, suffered light losses because their involvement in the fight was minor by comparison. Schenck reported 21 dead and 21 wounded at the Stone Bridge. Of the dead, 19 were from the 2nd New York.[53] Colonel McCook's 1st Ohio suffered 1 dead, 4 wounded and 7 missing. The 2nd Ohio tallied only 1 dead soldier: Charles M. McCook.[54]

The first major battle of the Civil War left its mark on Alexander McDowell McCook. He commanded a regiment in combat operations; he suffered the loss of his brother, one of hundreds of men killed that day. The combined experiences, however, did not soften his resolve, for he was trained for the military, and he emerged from the battle dedicated to seeing the fight through. The Union's cause was his cause, and his anger at the secessionists was all McCook needed to motivate him to fight until the South was defeated.

Nowhere is this attitude better reflected than in his condemnation of his former friend, Ohio congressman Clement L. Vallandigham, whom McCook denounced in the harshest terms. While most Northerners were rattling their sabers at the South following Bull Run, Vallandigham talked openly and forcefully about seeking a peaceful resolution to their differences, blaming Lincoln and the Republicans for starting the war. To McCook, this was gross wrong-thinking and unpatriotic. The war had started, the Union was under fire and the South must be punished. In the presence of a pro–Vallandigham Dayton newspaper editor, he said, "Damn any man who is not for the Union and damn Vallandigham too! He is worse than a Judas; he is a damned traitor!"[55]

Alexander McDowell McCook was fired up, having escaped the battle of Bull Run without a scratch on his body or a dent in his military reputation. Newspapers were complimentary. In fact, McCook's leadership and bravery were seen as a bright light in an otherwise dark day.

McCook went back to Ohio and mustered out with his three-month volunteers on August 16, 1861. But he stayed in the army, recruited the 1st Ohio for three years' service, was given a brigadier's star and was sent to Kentucky for further duty.[56]

CHAPTER 5

General McCook and the Kentucky Campaign

> I think to lose Kentucky is nearly the same as to lose the whole game.
> — Abraham Lincoln

It was near the small town of Perryville, about 60 miles southwest of Louisville, that the most decisive Civil War battle in Kentucky took place. The bloody fight erupted on October 6, 1862, following a year of struggling to control this critical border state by the North and South. Each side claimed the allegiance of the people, and each understood its strategic and economic importance.

The Kentucky state government preferred to stay neutral however, and — taking states' rights to a new extreme — passed a Neutrality Proclamation, backing it with a threat to kill anyone who violated the edict. Leave us alone! The state, in effect, told both the Union and Confederacy to go to hell. The Confederate government sent written assurance to Kentucky's governor, promising not to "disturb the neutrality of Kentucky."[1] The Jefferson Davis administration thought that it would be great to have Kentucky in the Confederacy, but having it was not absolutely necessary for the success of the Rebel government.

President Lincoln had other ideas. He understood the importance of keeping Kentucky out of the Confederacy as it provided a buffer zone between the Deep South and the Northern tier of states. It would also give the Union control of the Mississippi River south to Vicksburg and provide a launching point from which to threaten western Tennessee. For these reasons, in the early stages of the war, Lincoln applied a gentle but firm touch to that border state to keep it from seceding.

When talking and writing about Kentucky or the rebellion, Lincoln chose his words carefully. Instead of calling the seceded states the "Confederacy," he used the phrase "so-called Confederate States of America," for he refused to give any credence to the Southern experiment. He believed it was a rebellion without basis in law and with no constitutional support.

Lincoln had very little political capital at his disposal, however, for he received only 1,364 votes from Kentucky voters in the 1860 election, and just 5 votes from Lafayette County, where many of his in-laws lived.[2] Nevertheless, he made a request to the governor for troops, expecting Kentucky to provide its quota. His request was met by a sharp rebuke from Governor Beriah Magoffin, who wrote to Lincoln's secretary of war: "Kentucky will furnish no troops for the wicked purpose of subduing her sister Southern States."[3]

Subsequent events suggest Lincoln was undismayed by the rejection. Still, he was concerned that the Kentucky state militia might cast its lot with the Confederacy, so to prevent that he directed a naval officer, Lieutenant William Nelson, to discreetly assist and equip loyal elements of the militia. Working cloak-and-dagger-like, and acting on the president's orders, Nelson went to Lincoln's close and loyal friend Joshua Speed, who, although a Kentucky slave owner, was anxious to help.[4] Speed was from an old and aristocratic Kentucky family and apparently had no problem believing in both slavery and the Union. But it was his belief in Lincoln that motivated him to take great risks.

The clandestine work paid dividends, as Nelson succeeded in placing over 5,000 guns into the hands of Unionists, while the secessionists were only able to get their hands on some antique flintlocks.[5] As time went on, every indication coming from Kentucky convinced Lincoln that the majority of that state's people were opposed to secession, and that if otherwise left alone, Kentucky would eventually side with the North. For most of 1861, both armies waited at the border of the contested state, waiting for favorable signs while attempting to recruit men to their cause. It seems that Union recruiters had the edge.

The South had very strong ties to Kentucky, and despite the promises of non-intervention, the Confederacy wasn't about to concede the state. Governor Magoffin was anti-secessionist but a strong supporter of slavery, which he believed to be morally defensible, and in his heart of hearts, he was for the South. Louisville was very antebellum in its outlook, with significant business and railroad connections to other Southern cities.

The state laid claim to many old-line, aristocratic families and was the birthplace of Confederate president Jefferson Davis and General Albert Sidney Johnston, the officer who would travel from California and take control of all Rebel forces in Kentucky. It was also the home of former vice president John C. Breckinridge. He favored neutrality for Kentucky, and after the battle of Bull Run he went to his home state and pleaded with Kentuckians to be calm.

A great number of people in the region identified with Ohio rather than Dixie. Among the prominent Union families were the McCooks of Ohio and the Crittendens of Kentucky, both on track to play critical roles in the struggle for the state. As much as the Southern element wanted to pull the state into the Confederacy, the federal element desired to preserve their beloved Union, regretting the loss of any state. Toward that end, the Department of the Cumberland was organized on August 15, 1861, consisting of Tennessee and Kentucky.[6]

It was said that Lincoln so valued Kentucky that he said "he hoped to have God on his side, but he had to have Kentucky."[7] After all, he was born there and his wife's family, the aristocratic Todd's, were Kentucky folk, although not all of them were on the side of the Union. In fact, throughout the state, strong feelings on both sides of the question led to the disruption of communities and bloodshed, with neighbor shooting neighbor.

Then, on September 4, 1861, while false reports of the death of Jefferson Davis appeared in Northern newspapers, the South made the first move toward forcibly taking control of Kentucky. General Leonidas Polk, in charge of Confederate forces in western Tennessee, ordered General Gideon J. Pillow to invade and capture Columbus, a town situated near a series of high bluffs overlooking the Mississippi River. The impetuous Pillow, an eager, head-down

fighter whose judgment was often questioned, was only too happy to comply. Once there he busied himself with fortifying the bluffs, cutting down every tree in sight. He placed his guns in position and from there commanded a critical stretch of the Mississippi River, essentially blocking all traffic.

Once again the South "fired the first shot," this time in defiance of the wishes of Jefferson Davis, but playing into Lincoln's strategy. Two days after Polk's forces entered the state, a Union army under Brigadier General U. S. Grant crossed the border

Alexander M. McCook posing in his army uniform with sword and gloves. McCook was thoroughly military and enjoyed the formalities, accoutrements and routine of military life. This photograph shows him as a one-star brigadier general. He was promoted to that rank after serving with gallantry and skill at the battle of Bull Run.

under the pretense of wanting to save Kentucky from "Rebel invaders." The governor angrily ordered both armies out, but the legislature voted in favor of removing only the Rebels. Aggressive and intuitive by nature, Grant — then an unknown quantity — was only too happy to accept the "invitation" to stay, after taking Louisville and Paducah.[8]

And stay the Union did, causing the South to increase its efforts at winning the "war within the state" of Kentucky. Finally, on September 25, 1861, the Kentucky legislature ended its neutrality and took the side of the Union. The legislature passed a bill calling for 40,000 volunteers for the Union army. It passed by wide margins in both the House and the Senate.[9]

Undaunted, in November 1861, secessionists from 68 Kentucky counties came together at Russellville to create a pro–South provisional government with Bowling Green as the capital city. The delegates elected George W. Johnson, a big-hearted, secessionist planter, as the provisional governor who quickly applied for admission to the Confederacy. It was accepted, and in December, a confident Confederacy added another state to its confederation, signifying the belief that Kentucky was theirs to keep, and demonstrating their willingness to fight to keep it.[10]

But the North persisted, and for all practical purposes, Kentucky was on the Union side for good, despite Governor Magoffin's Confederate sympathies. The newly created Department of the Cumberland, under Brigadier General Robert Anderson, moved its headquarters from Cincinnati to Louisville, beginning a long Union presence in the "bluegrass" state. Anderson's gallant effort at Fort Sumter caused the public to repose special trust in his abilities. He consulted with Brigadier General Alexander M. McCook about the needs of his department and dashed off an urgent request to army headquarters. In a letter dated September 28, 1861, he asked for "all the regiments you can spare," and "the sooner the better." He also asked that McCook be ordered to come down and assist in what he perceived to be an emergency.[11]

Not long after his letter to McCook, Anderson was relieved due to a serious illness. His replacement was Brigadier General William T. Sherman, whose recent performance at Bull Run drew favorable reviews. Sherman's first task after assuming command on October 8 was to gather together all available regiments and organize them into an army. Just about everything needed to make war was in short supply, especially men, arms and ammunition. Feeling the need for help, Sherman summoned Brigadier General Alexander M. McCook to come to Louisville to assist in the work.

On October 5, 1861, McCook was assigned to the Department of the Cumberland and ordered to "repair to Louisville" and report to the department commander.[12] About a month earlier, on September 3, 1861, he received a brigadier's star.

A proud and patriotic McCook reported as ordered and was sent to the

Union camp at Nolin Creek along the Louisville and Nashville Railroad, with instructions to take command of all United States forces in the area. Sherman called on McCook to move forward as quickly and carefully as possible, but to "act on the defensive" until he was "much strengthened," closing his message with an ominous admonition: "The safety of our nation depends on you holding that ground for the present."[13]

McCook named the campground "Camp Nevin" after the owner of the land, a man said to be a "wealthy and violent secessionist."[14] It was the ground — formerly a plantation — upon which the genial Ohio general organized his division and set about getting his new soldiers acquainted with army life. The weather was wet and cold, and soon disease broke out among the men, including measles and pneumonia, causing camp to become "one vast field hospital."[15] Grave diggers were kept busy at Camp Nevin due to the high disease-related mortality rate.

Due to overcrowding and terribly unsanitary conditions, death by disease was not limited to Camp Nevin. It was destined to be a major factor in the war, as diphtheria, typhoid, dysentery, malaria and other maladies took two lives for every one lost to gunshot.

Bad conditions and death from diseases notwithstanding, McCook and his subordinates were determined to convert volunteers into soldiers, and drill and more drill was conducted until the men were in fighting trim. McCook was all army and a stickler for adherence to regulations, and though he frequently disciplined his erring soldiers, his actions could be tempered by humor. One observer recalled visiting Camp Nevin and seeing men "patrolling back and forth with rails instead of carbines." The disciplined soldiers were forced to "present arms" when McCook appeared. He was observed to show a "suspicious twitching about the corners of his mouth, which dispersed into a broad smile" when he passed by the silly-looking soldiers.[16] It was not by the book, but McCook enjoyed it nevertheless.

McCook had been cast suddenly into an important leadership role and was trying to be creative while teaching young soldiers the need for discipline in ranks. Sherman expressed great confidence in McCook whose reckless sense of self-confidence made him feel equal to the challenge. He had been tested under fire at the battle of Bull Run and earned his promotion to brigadier general because of his valorous conduct, the youngest brigadier in the army.

On October 13, 1861, McCook relieved General Lovell H. Rousseau at Camp Nevin. By early November, McCook had taken charge of four brigades under Brigadier Generals Thomas J. Wood, Richard. W. Johnson, Lovell H. Rousseau and James S. Negley, men with whom he would serve for the next couple of years. He gave his division a tentative title: the "Central Division."[17]

General McCook was quickly earning a favorable reputation. When the 1st Ohio Infantry was sent to Kentucky, it was temporarily attached to another commander, causing the infantrymen to voice their opposition to the arrangement. It was reported that "this did not suit the First — they were anxious to return to their idol — McCook." The excitement subsided when the men of the 1st Ohio volunteers learned that the assignment away from General McCook was only temporary.[18]

Anson G. McCook, now a major, wanted his newly recruited 2nd Ohio Infantry placed with General McCook, but it was instead attached to a division headed by Brigadier General William "Bull" Nelson.[19] This was the same William Nelson whom Lincoln had selected to secretly place guns in the hands of pro–Union Kentuckians. Nelson left the navy, became a general in the army and acquired a nickname that fit his hulking size and fighting disposition.

On November 10, 1861, Sherman designated McCook's division as the 1st Division, Department of the Cumberland.[20] Sherman called the gathering troops at Camp Nevin "good material, but devoid of company officers of experience." The heady Alex McCook, however, was optimistic and was looked upon by observers as capable of holding forth against the Rebel army at Bowling Green under General Simon Buckner.

A report circulated that Buckner was planning to lure McCook into a "Bull Run trap" complete with "masked batteries and curvilinear earthworks." According to the article in the *Chicago Tribune*, Buckner was plotting to dupe and destroy McCook and then move on. The reporter, however, claimed to know better and wrote: "McCook is careful, knows with whom he has to deal, and, we predict, will prove himself the man and the mettle for any of Buckner's emergencies."[21] But the McCook/Buckner battle never took place, thus depriving both men the chance to gain battle laurels. There would be no "second Manassas" in Kentucky.

McCook's attitude reflected his supreme belief in his leadership abilities. In a letter to Ohio governor William Dennison, the optimistic general bragged that he was in command of "the most important army in the field," and that he could "break the back of the rebellion in three moves."[22] He did not elaborate on the "moves" he would implement to bring the war to a quick end, nor did he mention any role that General Sherman might play in the scenario.

Actually, Sherman was troubled and did not share McCook's optimism. Because of the recent disaster at Bull Run, Sherman held a fatalistic view of the Union army. He believed it to be inept, essentially an untamed mob, without collective will and in no position to fight for the North and win. Placed in this unenviable position, he was fearful, believing that the enemy occupied much of Kentucky with greater numbers than what the Union had available for combat. He was disappointed in the number of Kentucky recruits joining the Union. Sherman believed an army of 50,000 men would be the minimum needed to make a move against the Rebels led by his former West Point friends:

Polk, Beauregard and Braxton Bragg. Still Sherman seemed determined to fight, telling his officers, "Each man must understand that he is to stand and fight down to the stubs."[23]

McCook was showing every indication that he would be one to fight and fight hard, for he was suited for the routine of military life and its many challenges. On November 4, 1861, he sent a letter to his commander explaining, "We are all well" and "ready for any emergency." He also expressed frustration with "runaway Negroes," six of whom came into his camp, complaining that their "masters have run away and joined the southern army." McCook said, "As you have the political fortunes as well as the military in hand, I would like some information on the subject."[24] It is doubtful that McCook was trying to irritate Sherman, but the letter was probably not well received.

Sherman was bearing up as best he could under the stress of command, when McCook gave him a headache in the form of another letter dated November 5, 1861, asking for instructions on how to deal with runaway slaves, or in his words, "contraband." McCook considered the question one of vital importance to the people of Kentucky and wanted to make sure he was handling the matter correctly in view of national policy and objectives.

McCook stated: "Ten [slaves] have come into my camp within as many hours, and from what they say there will be a general stampede of slaves from the other side of Green River. They have already become a source of annoyance to me, and I have great reason to believe that this annoyance will increase the longer we stay. They state the reasons of their running away their masters are rank secessionists, in some cases are in the rebel army, and that slaves of Union men are pressed into service to drive teams, etc."

McCook suggested that if the slaves were allowed to stay with the army, "our cause in Kentucky may be injured." He didn't trust the Kentuckians, doubted their loyalty and had "no great desire to protect her pet institution, slavery." Still he wanted to return the slaves to their masters, as a "matter of policy." He wrote, "I am very far from wishing these recreant [sic] masters in possession of any of their property, for I think slaves are no better than horses in that respect." He put some of the runaways to work as they were "handy with teams," but on the whole he found the matter "embarrassing" and sought Sherman's advice and judgment.[25]

It was said that McCook held the "Southern view" with regard to handling fugitive slaves. In the early stages of the war, McCook was complimented by Southern newspapers for "his courtesy in returning slaves that followed the Union army."[26]

Journalist and historian Whitelaw Reid claimed that McCook was sympathetic to slave owners who came into his camp looking for runaways. In his two-volume history of the Civil War, Reid wrote about a "well-publicized" meeting between McCook and a slave owner during the war. McCook, according to Reid, was always anxious to return slaves and "treated the slave owner with utmost courtesy."[27]

While Sherman generally opposed the expansion of slavery and believed it contributed to cultural sloth and infamy, he did not advocate the immediate abolition of approximately four million slaves. As such he was quick to criticize both the abolitionist and the slave master. And yet he failed to see the changed thinking about slavery among his fellow Northerners, including his younger brother Senator John Sherman who was an abolitionist. It was never a moral issue to General Sherman, and as time went on, his authoritarian attitude toward blacks meant he was out of step with men such as his brother, Lincoln and even Grant.

Sherman wrote back on November 8, snappily telling McCook to honor the laws of Kentucky, refuse the runaways and return them to their masters, as he had no instructions from the government to do otherwise. To deny the slaveholders of their "property" would be to send the wrong message to the people of Kentucky and throughout the South. Sherman declared that this is not a war to overthrow slavery and it would be wrong to publicize it as such. "You will send them away."[28]

The issue could have been easily settled by simply abiding by the Confiscation Act, recently passed by Congress and signed into law by Lincoln. This act authorized the seizure of all Southern property used for a military purpose, including slaves. As a result of the act, Lincoln said that officers "neither should nor would send back to bondage such as come to our armies."[29] Due to their high rank, both men should have known about this new law, and if they did, they chose to ignore it.

Nervous and irritable, angry with "meddlesome" reporters (he imprisoned one and threatened to hang another as a spy) and at odds with his position in the army, the quirky Sherman was ill prepared to deal with the sensitive slavery issue. The weight of his problems resulted in numerous examples of peculiar behavior. On one occasion he was walking with an unlit half-smoked cigar when he spotted a soldier puffing smoke. He asked the soldier for a light and in response the man offered the cigar. Sherman used it to light his half-smoked cigar and then tossed the stump, keeping the soldier's fresh cigar. Walking away, he thanked the bemused soldier who simply said, "That's cool, isn't it?"[30]

Sherman's family had a history of mental illness, and he had become so emotionally unstable that he was barely able to handle his military responsibilities. While he was a man of high intelligence and married into a rich and prominent family, he had yet to experience success commensurate with his intellect and abilities. In truth, Sherman was haunted by the specter of failure, and following the disaster at Bull Run, he internalized the rage he felt, turning it against himself. He would pace the corridor of Louisville's Galt Hotel for hours,

Newspaper vendor and cart in a Union camp. While reporters were often hated and their articles slanted or inaccurate, soldiers of all ranks eagerly bought and read newspapers. The cart in this photograph sold newspapers from New York, Philadelphia and Baltimore, three cities that contributed a large number of the newsmen who traveled with the armies and reported on the battles.

as if in a trance, smoking heavily, plagued by self-doubt while trying to sort everything out. Was it madness or troubled genius that plagued him so?

After consulting with McCook, Sherman complained to his superiors that the lack of arms and ammunition would mean that moving forward "with our present force ... would be simple madness."[31] This and other aspects of his behavior caused observers to think he was unbalanced and showing signs of insanity; reporters picked up Sherman's heated explanation, mixed in some gossip and ran with it, thus becoming insensitive germ carriers that threatened to destroy his military career.

Although his brother John, the senator from Ohio, was a Republican, General Sherman was aligned with the Democrats. But he hated politics and politicians so much that he quit voting after the election of 1856.[32] He was impolite and caustic in his relationship with the Lincoln administration, demanding more and more of everything. Major General George B. McClellan became greatly concerned and assigned a staff member to watch Sherman.

Rumors of his bizarre behavior made their way to Washington where the assistant secretary of war declared, "Sherman's gone in the head, he's looney."[33]

From there the story got worse. The *Cincinnati Commercial* from Sherman's home state announced to the reading public: "GENERAL SHERMAN INSANE." This condemnation, presented to a wide audience, was drawn from Sherman's request for 200,000 troops to keep Kentucky in the Union. He believed that the Union was greatly outnumbered when in fact the opposite was true. Although Sherman was erratic and unstable, the insanity charge was reckless and unfair, and only fueled the fires of hatred between the general and the news media.

In the early 1860s, reporters were thought of as a lowlife class — keyhole peekers, shameless liars and scandalmongers — men who would print anything to make a buck. Sherman once contended that the press had ruined many officer's careers and said that if the "press can govern the country, let them fight the battles."[34]

It was not only Sherman who hated them, but the army as a whole disliked and distrusted reporters. Although most eager to buy and read newspapers, enlisted men and low-grade officers frequently expressed disgust and disappointment over the reporting of the war. One sergeant wryly suggested that it is inadvisable to "swallow anything whole" that appeared in newsprint. Many soldiers believed that anxious reporters simply invented their stories to suit themselves or their intended audiences.[35]

General McCook was proud to say that the "abolitionist press" was free in its criticism of him, and that he could expect the negative reporting to continue.[36] At every opportunity McCook attempted to muzzle the press, and tossed out of his camp none other than Whitelaw Reid, the Cincinnati reporter who would go on to a long and distinguished career in the newspaper business.[37]

Although both McCook and Sherman were enemies of the newsmen, it was the latter that drew the sharp rebuke from reporters. A correspondent from the *Daily Times* of Cincinnati blasted Sherman for his critical remarks about Kentucky and Kentuckians, saying, "General Sherman has unfortunately made himself unpopular in Kentucky."

McCook, on the other hand, was spared any criticism. In the same article that castigated Sherman, McCook was called a "man of ability and energy, and at the same time, with manners of a gentleman." Noting that McCook "inspires both love and respect," the correspondent made it clear that he preferred General McCook to General Sherman.[38]

Both McCook and Sherman were trying hard to win a war and paid scant attention to the sensibilities and rights of reporters operating under the protection of the First Amendment of the Constitution. The generals were doing what they thought was right and grudgingly tolerated the persistence of the newsmen. While they too, in some cases, lacked an understanding of the

Constitution, the journalists were at least on the winning side of the issue. In the first year of the war, an estimated 500 reporters from the North roamed the battlefields and followed the armies.[39] They were just as devoted to reporting the war as McCook and Sherman were set on winning the war. In this clash within a clash, the reporters were destined to emerge as the winners. In the meantime, the "crazy Sherman" stories had negative consequences, for he was relieved of command.

Whether it was the pressure from the press or of his own volition, or a combination of these ingredients, at his request, Sherman was relieved by McClellan and replaced within a few days of his letter to General McCook concerning the disposition of runaway slaves. On November 11, 1861, Major General Don Carlos Buell, another Ohio native son, was appointed to command the Department of the Ohio, and Sherman was moved to the Department of the Missouri in St. Louis.

Buell was a West Point graduate of 1841, finishing 32nd in his class. He was a career military man, having served in both the Mexican War and the Seminole Indian War in Florida. He took great pride in military life and its structure and insisted that all who served with him conduct themselves with the same sense of dignity and professionalism. He was a burly man of great physical strength, and thought to be sincere, cordial and a gentleman, but he was nonetheless stern and rigid in matters of military discipline and justice. Buell was a soldier through and through, and selected as his wife the widow of a general. Since he was a "pro-slavery" Democrat married to a Southern woman, he was looked upon by some Republicans with suspicion and doubt.[40] Nevertheless the Lincoln administration hoped his strong military background would result in victories.

The new commanding officer went to work as if he would live up to Lincoln's expectations. One of Buell's first moves was to rename his army, calling it "the Army of the Ohio." Next he restructured it into six infantry divisions, all supported with artillery.

Major General George H. Thomas was placed in charge of the 1st Division consisting of five brigades, one of which — the 3rd — was commanded by Colonel Robert L. McCook, older brother to General McCook. Included in Colonel McCook's 3rd Brigade was his highly regarded 9th Ohio Volunteers, made up of German immigrants from Cincinnati and better known collectively as the "Dutchmen." The 2nd Minnesota and 35th Ohio rounded out his brigade.

The 2nd Division was placed under the command of General McCook.[41] It was essentially the 1st Division renamed, as it contained the brigades of Rousseau, Negley, Johnson and Wood. Captain Daniel McCook, Jr., served as the assistant adjutant general to his older brother, Alexander.[42]

As Buell was well known for his "slow coach," cautious and methodical tactics, it was generally believed that he would spend an inordinate amount of time organizing his army, drilling his men, and would not, therefore, launch a serious campaign until after the first of the year. It was expected that his sore-footed troops would resent him and an impatient administration in Washington, D.C., would hound him until he attacked somebody, somewhere.

Buell's first serious encounter with the Rebels was at Mill Springs on January 19, 1862. Mill Springs was then a small town near the Cumberland River in south central Kentucky, 90 miles east of Bowling Green. Confederate forces under the leadership of Brigadier General Felix K. Zollicoffer were encamped near Mill Springs. They dug trenches and built cabins on the north side of the Cumberland River, at the junction of Fishing Creek, with lines strung out along both streams.

The colorful and popular Zollicoffer, a former congressman from Tennessee and a journalist known for his fiery editorials, was hoping to lure more young Kentucky men to his ranks and drive the "Northern hordes across the Ohio River."[43] While he was not a military professional, the 50-year-old Zollicoffer shocked both Northern and Southern military men with his bold and successful forays in Tennessee and Kentucky. By comparison, the Union forces in Kentucky seemed moribund, leaving Lincoln very frustrated and impatient for some action. With Buell at the helm and the able Thomas his second in command, Lincoln was hoping that someone would "do something."

But a cautious Buell, seemingly in no hurry, was keeping an eye on Zollicoffer while paying greater attention to Brigadier General McCook's division that had moved into and was occupying the town of Munfordville, Kentucky. McCook was under orders to make certain that the railroad bridge over the Green River was not destroyed by Confederate troops. Unfortunately, it was partially destroyed, and McCook's men immediately set about repairing it. Maintenance and control of the huge bridge was vitally important, as it was needed to maintain the flow of supplies for the Union forces into middle Tennessee.

Within a short time of establishing his position at Munfordville, McCook received a dispatch from Buell of an unusual nature. McCook was ordered to deny a request from a Confederate surgeon who asked that his wife, two other ladies and the corpse of his child be allowed to pass through to Louisville. Considering it an act of impudence, Buell directed McCook to deny the request "courteously" and point them in another direction.[44] There were other priorities that needed attention.

Major General Thomas, like his commander, was also unlikely to charge into battle in hot haste. But he was anxious to move against the Zollicoffer. He sent a dispatch to Buell, advising that "the enemy [is] encamped at the mouth of Fishing Creek," and "can be captured" if a Union force intercepts at Somerset and "gets in their rear."[45] Buell simply replied: "I am letting him alone for the present."[46]

In a letter to his friend, General McClellan, on December 8, 1861, Buell stressed the pressing need to whip his army into shape, "now little better than a mob." While he was concerned with Zollicoffer, Buell didn't wish to "fritter away" his organizational effort by pursuing "these roving bugbears."[47]

When it was finally decided to move against Zollicoffer, Buell acted swiftly and hit hard. He ordered Thomas and Brigadier General Albin F. Schoepf, a native of Austria and in command of Thomas' 1st Brigade, to conduct a coordinated attack against the Rebels at their Mill Springs works. The decision was made after a reconnaissance by Schoepf revealed the location of the enemy and the extent of his armed strength and fortifications. The Union forces included two of Colonel Robert L. McCook's regiments. They were well-seasoned troops following a successful western Virginia campaign, where a big chunk of the Old Dominion was safely in Union hands.

A fierce battle was fought on the 19th, resulting in a Union victory over poorly armed and rain-soaked Rebels. Zollicoffer, the "bugbear," was killed and his small army routed. The Union forces were widely praised for their win at Mill Springs, and the happy result was a major boost for the North and for the morale of federal troops. Buell was off to a good start as commander of the Army of the Ohio. So was Robert L. McCook. Seriously wounded while leading a bayonet charge, he emerged as a heroic figure, thereby adding to the growing reputation of the "Fighting McCooks."

Following the impressive win at Mill Springs, General McCook was ordered to march his division to the mouth of the Salt River and board transports that would take his men to Fort Donelson, where he would join General U. S. Grant. Therefore on a cold and snowy February 14, McCook's division set out on what proved to be a useless assignment and a miserable trek through mud and snow. By the time the division was in position to assist Grant in his assault on Fort Donelson, the battle there was over and the fort was in Union hands.[48]

The ousting of the Confederates at Fort Henry and Fort Donelson in northwestern Tennessee by General Grant caused the South to change its plans in favor of another offensive strategy. Having met with defeat in Kentucky, there was no choice but to abandon the Bluegrass State as well as Nashville, Tennessee. The greatly diminished and scattered Rebel forces under the command of Major General Albert Sidney Johnston retreated south, intending to gather at Corinth, Mississippi.

Buell's next step was to advance his army in the direction of Nashville after the Confederate forces abandoned that city. In doing so, he ignored Lincoln's plan to establish a presence in East Tennessee, liberate the Union supporters and keep the Rebels out. But Buell consolidated his army and moved to the Tennessee capital city, while the Rebels returned to East Tennessee to punish the anti-secessionists. The angry Confederates arrested and jailed many of the Union loyalists and hanged five men whom they deemed to be the greatest offenders.[49]

The violence did not escape the scrutiny of the news media, and the *New York Times* launched an editorial plea for help, calling attention to the helpless people of East Tennessee who were the victims of "terrorism." The *Times* called it despotism most foul, with the "necks of the people all beneath its iron heel."[50]

The approximately 10,000 to 12,000 loyalists in East Tennessee, holding out bravely for rescue, added additional pain to Lincoln's already overburdened psyche. He wanted desperately to get Union troops into that mountainous area so he might be able to accomplish in East Tennessee what he did in western Virginia. Buell no doubt understood the value of assisting the beleaguered people, but —fixed thinker that he was — setting up shop in Nashville was more important that lurching his way through roadless mountains.

Nashville was about to become the first Southern capital city to be occupied by a Northern army. It was a thoroughly modern and prosperous young city of about 30,000 people, second in importance to New Orleans in the Confederate west. Located in a rich, agricultural region, it had factories, colleges, luxury hotels, a paid fire department and was well connected to other cities by five railroads. It also had a cannon foundry and was General Johnston's well-equipped military headquarters. Nashville was critically important to the South if the Confederacy was to regain control of Missouri and Kentucky.

When the people of Nashville learned of the fall of Fort Donelson, panic began to spread throughout the city, which was already lacking confidence in Johnston's ability to protect them. The bad news came just as folks were on their way to the city's churches. Suddenly, Sunday devotions were forgotten, and soon a large crowd assembled at Johnston's headquarters and anxiously asked if the general intended to fight. To their shock and dismay, they were told that Johnston intended to evacuate.

On February 16, 1862, Johnston began moving out of Nashville. At that same time it was rumored that Buell was coming to Nashville with a large army and conquest on his mind, causing people to flee the city in droves. Seven trainloads of women and children, with men clinging to the tops of the cars, left Nashville. Among others taking flight were hundreds of sick and wounded soldiers who abandoned their comfortable hospital beds and began limping and lumping out of town.

Able-bodied soldiers, too, made their departure, leaving the city at the mercy of lawless mobs who took to looting and wrecking. They were joined in the streets by poor people who saw the chance to fill their baskets with food. Many food seekers were trampled by thugs and deserters; some shopkeepers were shot during the melee. Fortunately, Confederate General John Floyd arrived in the city and took control and ended the deadly chaos. Order was finally restored by the army and a proper evacuation was under way, after two suspension bridges over the Cumberland River were destroyed. Johnston retreated with his five brigades in the direction of Murfreesboro, a small town about 35 miles southeast of Nashville.[51]

The lack of bridges did not stop Buell's army. He took possession of the city of Nashville on February 25, 1862, after a meeting with a citizens committee. The Union soldiers were not well received. Buell noted that "the people appear to look upon us as invaders." While waiting for the arrival of his other divisions, Buell advised his superiors that moving into Tennessee was a risky move, noting the strength of the enemy.[52]

General McCook's division arrived at Edgefield on the Cumberland River, opposite Nashville, on March 2, 1862, having been on the march for most of February. During the winter campaign McCook became familiar with much of Kentucky and Tennessee, and the country folk, many of whom resented the presence of Union soldiers.

On a rainy night McCook and his staff stopped at Bell's Tavern near Kentucky's Mammoth Cave, hoping to get fed. The lady of the house, being a strident secessionist, refused to serve them. Later when McCook's servant prepared some ham and coffee for the hungry men, the tavern hostess threw sand in the coffee and mud on the ham. Nevertheless, McCook and his staff salvaged enough food and drink for supper, but they turned to eating only after he tied up the angry woman.[53]

The majority of the women of Nashville were secessionists or sympathizers, including the widow of former president James K. Polk. She was living in comfort in a fine brick mansion, at the expense of the federal government, when General Grant and his staff paid a visit. A correspondent from the *New York Times* who accompanied the general noted that she was polite in a forced and cold-shouldered manner, and that she neither made any pro–Southern remarks, nor did she say anything that could have been construed as pro–Union or patriotic. Grant and his staff departed after a short visit, leaving the bitter old lady alone with her sentiments and memories. The correspondent noted that the widow of President Polk seemed content to be alone, trusting that the presence of her late husband's tomb on the property would be sufficient protection from would-be pillagers.[54]

Thomas' division arrived at Nashville at about the time that McCook's division made its appearance. The city was quiet when they entered. The Confederates were moving toward Murfreesboro, burning bridges behind them. General Richard W. Johnson of McCook's division recalled that the weather was miserable and cold and that his uniform froze to his body. His brigade set up camp within a stone-walled enclosure, with nothing to burn to keep warm. They did, however, have a couple of barrels of whiskey to provide some nighttime comfort.[55]

During the day, Union troops were busy dealing with Nashville residents who returned to the city. Each one had to take a loyalty oath in order to be granted parole. One man, a minister, was ordered by McCook to say a prayer for President Lincoln "or be hung." An angry McCook told the minister that the Union had been lenient on pro-secession folks but that officers would resort to the rope if gentle methods failed. McCook did not hang the man and instead granted him a parole.[56]

By March 6, all six Union divisions were present in Nashville, and Buell commanded an army whose total strength was about 75,000, although not all of his troops were present for duty.[57] With much of the South terribly disheartened over the failure of the Kentucky campaign, combined with the loss of Forts Henry and Donelson, it appeared as if Buell and Grant were in position to do what the Army of the Potomac had been unable to do: crush the Confederacy.

CHAPTER 6

The Battle of Shiloh: The First Day

And ere dusk had set in the firing had nearly ceased, when, night coming on, all the combatants rested from their awful work of blood.
—*New York Times*, April 10, 1862

In 1862, Shiloh Church was a humble place of worship, and services there were infrequent. Built in 1854 of rough-cut wood and a clapboard roof, and overpowered by its natural surroundings, the small, isolated Methodist Episcopal Church was not an imposing sight. The walls were cracked and the windows were without glass, causing one observer to call it the "best ventilated church you ever saw."[1] It was of no importance to anyone except the rural folk who worshiped there, and yet the high drama of events that unfolded on Sunday, April 7, 1862, drew the church out of obscurity and into permanent focus and scrutiny. It presents a luminous and lasting image, remembered for all time, for the "battle of Shiloh." It was there that the Sabbath was mugged and a churchyard was turned into a killing ground.

Shiloh Church was built in the Tennessee wilderness, where the rough monotony of the land was broken by a few 40- to 80-acre farms. Much of the area was uneven, heavily timbered, with sloughs, ridges, streams and deep ravines. It was not easy terrain for soldiers who would be required to march forward and then form and maintain a line of battle.

The word "Shiloh" is of Biblical origin, coming from the first book of Samuel. It was a reference to a religious center where Jewish people made annual pilgrimages. The word also meant "peace."[2] How strange, then, that one of the bloodiest battles of the entire Civil War was fought in the churchyard and in the surrounding countryside. For two April days in 1862, peace was bludgeoned almost beyond recognition save for sheer mockery of the word.

In March, military strategy was focused on the western theater. Both armies were planning, maneuvering and hoping to outwit and therefore outfight the other. The Union army of the west was riding high on a series of successes, the brightest of which was a stunning victory at Fort Donelson, under the leadership of Major General Ulysses S. Grant. Not only were the Confederates driven out of a strategic point on the Cumberland River, but the defeat resulted in the capture of thousands of Rebel troops. To further aggravate and injure the South, on March 13, Congress passed an article of war making it a court-martial offense for any officer to return escaped slaves to their masters.[3]

While the sound whipping at Fort Donelson stung the South and subjected its leadership to harsh criticism, it buoyed up the spirits of the North to the point of over-confidence. The Northern public was pleased; many believed the war would come to a quick conclusion followed by a restoration of the seceded states to the Union.

Grant was operating under the direction of Major General Henry W. Halleck, whom President Lincoln had placed in charge of the Department of the Mississippi on March 13, 1862. This was an uncomfortable alliance, as the two men disliked one another, so much so that Halleck removed Grant from his command for failure to file reports.

But the allegation proved to be untrue, and Halleck begrudgingly placed Grant back in command of the Army of the Tennessee. While he disliked the casual and usually disheveled Grant, Halleck understood Grant's fighting instincts and knew that he had no better choice from among the many federal generals. The goggle-eyed Halleck could be caustic and hypercritical and was never well liked or understood by the public. But he was good at organization and administration and seemed ideally suited to plan the next big move, the one that was expected to crush the life out of the Confederacy. "Old Brains," as he was called, was good at making difficult choices as long as he had sufficient time to think things through and weigh the politics of his decision.

Choosing Grant may have been a difficult decision for Halleck because of some unsavory remnants lingering in the former's past. Grant was a West Point graduate who served in the Mexican War. In the peacetime military, however, Grant seemed out of place and resigned from the army because of excessive drinking. He also floundered as a civilian but was given a new lease on life after the Civil War started, where his real skills — leading men in battle — came to the fore. Grant proved he could think and act under pressure while he commanded a division of two brigades at the battle of Belmont in southeastern Missouri, and he became an overnight sensation when he demanded an "unconditional surrender" from the Confederate commander at Fort Donelson.

After resuming command of the Army of the Tennessee, Grant made his headquarters at Savannah, Tennessee. From there he monitored the Rebel army under General Albert Sidney Johnston, situated in nearby Corinth, Mississippi.

Following their loss of Forts Henry and Donelson, along with the defeat at Mill Springs, the Confederate leadership decided to pull out of Kentucky rather than risk further defeats in that state. With Kentucky seemingly out of danger, Lincoln and his generals could focus on other key cities and towns such as Corinth, a railroad center, where the enemy was gathering and poised for an advance toward the Union position.

Grant's position was tenuous; his army was divided, with two divisions on the banks of the Tennessee River: one at Pittsburg Landing and one upriver at Crump's Landing. The remaining two divisions, his veteran units, were at Savannah. Grant saw the need to gather his forces, coordinate with Major General Don Carlos Buell and the Army of the Ohio and prepare for the enemy. On March 19, 1862, a seemingly uneasy Grant sent a message to Buell, saying he was "a little anxious to learn your whereabouts." He warned of a large Rebel force gathering at Corinth, only 20 miles down the road from Shiloh Church.[4]

The 59-year-old Albert Sidney Johnston — in charge of all the western

Confederate forces — was so determined to serve the South that he rode on horseback across the country from Los Angeles to Richmond to join the cause.[5] He was the highest-ranking field officer in the Confederate army, and much esteemed by President Davis, his former classmate at West Point.

While Johnston was brutalized by much of the pro-Rebel Tennessee press over recent losses, including Fort Donelson, Davis refused to dismiss him to appease an angry public. To Davis, Johnston was the greatest, most capable commander in Amer-

Major General U. S. Grant. The Ohio general was in command of the Union Army of the Tennessee at the battle of Shiloh. Grant was a plainspoken man whose unkempt and unmilitary appearance belied his quiet genius for leading men in battle. As a civilian, his life was one of mediocrity, but his work as a field commander in the Civil War elevated Grant to the role of general of all federal armies and eventually to the presidency.

ica.[6] After all, he had more than proved himself in both the armies of the United States and the Republic of Texas.

Johnston arrived in Corinth on March 24 and took charge of the Confederate forces that had been under the command of the neat and pompous, and always energetic, Brigadier General Pierre Gustave Toutant Beauregard. The "hero of Fort Sumter," the ego-driven, self-styled Napoleon in gray, and architect of the Confederate victory at the first battle of Bull Run, was easily the most popular general in the South. While it was rumored in the Northern press that he had died from typhoid, he was very much alive, his reputation was soaring and he was in every respect seen as a hero. But he proved to be an irritant to an equally egotistical Jefferson Davis, who sent him west to get him out of Virginia.

But Beauregard was a natural soldier and was generally liked by the troops, so he just had to be useful somewhere. Beauregard's soldierly panache was welcomed by Johnston, and the two generals immediately set out to develop a strategy to stop Grant. They were depending on the divisions of Generals William J. Hardee, Braxton Bragg, Leonidas Polk and John C. Breckinridge. These men were backed up by other capable brigade and regimental commanders with battlefield experience and West Point credentials.

Elected in 1860 to the U.S. Senate from Kentucky, Breckinridge was not a professional soldier. But he was a prominent and promising man facing a difficult decision. After waffling for a time, he escaped capture by Union troops by slinking out of Kentucky and into Virginia, where he pledged himself to the Southern cause.[7] He was appointed to the rank of brigadier general in November of 1861, and was thereafter expelled from the Senate.[8]

Breckinridge was reviled in the North and was handled roughly by the Northern press. A Cincinnati newspaper said that the former senator had taken to heavy drinking and was considered a "common drunkard" who suffered from "the delirium tremens."[9] When the battle of Shiloh erupted, Breckinridge was in command of the reserve corps.

Johnston's army numbered up to about 40,000 ragged, sickly, ill-trained and poorly armed men. Few had seen any combat. This gathering of men was more like a semi-organized, half-starved mob than an army, made worse by the antics of feuding commanders and a commanding general whose self-esteem and reputation had been weakened by a series of setbacks.

Brigadier General William T. Sherman was Grant's principal division commander, having been rehabilitated by Halleck, who understood the political strength of Sherman's family. Sherman was allowed to create his own division and take the field with Grant. He was in fighting form, having at last seemingly conquered the mental maladies that haunted him during the early stages of the war. Gone were all the twitches and other nervous habits, replaced by a calm, methodical manner and demeanor; the realist had returned. His reformed behavior inspired his troops, convincing them that he was rational and clearheaded.[10]

Sherman and Grant worked well together and respected each other, having been friends since their West Point days. Both were thoroughly devoted to the cause and put the interest of the Union above personal goals. In doing so they strengthened their friendship, and that in turn strengthened the Union army.

Sherman was directed to make camp at Pittsburg Landing and prepare space for the entire army. Pittsburg Landing was a docking station on the Tennessee River, nine miles upriver from Grant's Savannah headquarters. Sherman examined the nine-mile rolling plain that spread out from the landing and decided that there was room for 100,000 men. With their backs to the river, a creek on both of their flanks and the Confederate pickets near their front, the Union troops were camped in a large patch of land roughly shaped like a triangle. Shiloh Church stood near the center of the camp.

Next Sherman played a feint in the direction of Corinth, based on word from Union sympathizers that the Rebels were expecting an attack. This ploy was intended to mask a cavalry raid on the Memphis and Charleston Railroad toward Farmington. The ploy was aborted when the Rebels learned of the raid. The raid having failed, the Union high command shifted gears and planned a full-scale invasion in conjunction with the army of Major General Buell, then in charge of the Department of Kentucky and stationed in Nashville.[11] While Halleck gave the order to make a strike against Corinth, he wanted Grant to move cautiously and wait until he was joined by Buell before he started shooting.

Grant — always the aggressor — was anxious to get moving before Johnston got his army ready. He gathered a veritable armada of steamboats — 82 in all — from St. Louis to transport his troops.[12] Soon the campground at Pittsburg Landing was teeming with Union soldiers as boat after boat docked and men streamed ashore. Sherman's 5th Division, consisting of mostly Ohio men, camped near Shiloh Church, about a mile and a half from the landing. By the end of March, Grant had about 34,500 men at the landing with more on the way. The massive amount of tents blanketing the countryside made a very impressive sight, and the mood was good among the men who whiled away time playing poker when they weren't drilling.

Meanwhile Buell's divisions were on the move in the direction of Pittsburg Landing. His army consisted of five divisions totaling 37,000 troops. Halleck's plan was to have Buell unite with Grant no later than March 24, thus fielding two armies whose combined strength equaled about 70,000 men. While Buell was not known for moving fast, everything depended upon speed and efficiency, and a little luck.

When Buell commenced to march on March 16, 1862, his 2nd Division,

William T. Sherman was a brigadier general who worked well with Grant at the battle of Shiloh. The two men became good friends. Sherman was also well acquainted with General McCook, as they both served in the same division at Bull Run. Although Sherman went on to great success in the Civil War, his early experiences as a commander were marked by nervous irritability and internal rage that nearly ruined him.

commanded by Brigadier General Alexander M. McCook, led the way southwest from Nashville. McCook's division consisted of three infantry brigades and three artillery batteries, only one of which reached the field of battle. The 4th Brigade, consisting of six regiments, was led by Brigadier General Lovell H. Rousseau. The four regiments of the 5th Brigade were led by Colonel Edward N. Kirk, and McCook's 6th Brigade, also made up of four regiments, was commanded by Colonel William H. Gibson,[13] a substitute in place of the seriously ill Brigadier General Richard W. Johnson.

General McCook's brother, Captain Daniel McCook, serving as assistant adjutant general, was part of his staff. Their cousin, Lieutenant Colonel Edward M. McCook, commanded the 2nd Indiana Cavalry in the 4th Division led by Brigadier General William Nelson.

General McCook's division made its way steadily and confidently through the beautiful farm and plantation country of central Tennessee that flowed and fluttered in cotton and wheat fields. They watched with great curiosity as gangs of slaves worked in the fields. Everything was going well when the division was suddenly forced to halt at Columbia on the Duck River on March 19 because the bridges they intended to cross had all been burned. Engineers immediately began reconstructing the bridges.

Buell wrote to Halleck on March 25, assuring "Old Brains" that the bridges would be completed by the time he (Buell) arrived at Columbia. The crews were still working on the 26th, when Buell arrived to study the dilemma. With Halleck fuming at his St. Louis headquarters, the bridge crews finally completed their work on March 31, 1862.

On that same day, Grant, feeling a bit restless, wrote to McCook: "The two cavalrymen sent by you have arrived. I have been looking for your column anxiously for several days so as to report it to the headquarters of the department, and thinking some move may depend on your arrival."[14] Grant wasn't expecting to fight at Pittsburg Landing; rather he wanted to hit the Confederates at Corinth with his army and Buell's divisions. Time was of the essence, and time was running out.

As it turned out, one division of Buell's army didn't wait for the convenience of a high-and-dry crossing. At the urging of Brigadier General William "Bull" Nelson — who was fearful that Grant was in mortal danger — Buell allowed the 4th Division to ford the river on the 29th and get a head start. In doing so, Buell ignored protocol, as the honor of being the lead division would normally have gone to McCook who had seniority. Nelson crossed with his division without McCook's knowledge, meaning that after a ten-day delay, Buell's men were on the move again, beginning an 82-mile march on a narrow country road to Savannah.

Although the road was muddy and crossed by numerous creeks, the men were in high spirits, many of them thinking they were off to the last battle of the war. The country folk along the way proved to be mostly pro–Union, and the men were uplifted by the sight of women and girls waving small American flags. The inspired soldiers marched on, feeling the pride of their profession, and anxious to shoot some Rebels while a few remained as targets.

When it was learned that Buell was on his way to connect with Grant, Johnston decided to strike the encampment at Pittsburg Landing. Believing he had to protect Corinth at all costs, he devised a plan with the aid of his generals. It was not badly designed despite being the product of desperate thinking. He was hoping to move fast and hit hard before Grant was reinforced by Buell. Johnston was yearning to win a battle, rescue his career, turn the tide in favor of the South and restore popular support to his side of the war.

Johnston's plan was essentially to hit the entire Union front, with emphasis on the left flank, thereby severing its connection with Lick Creek on the south end of the line. Then the Rebels would proceed to roll up the Union line, pressing it into a corner formed by Owl Creek and the Tennessee River, but away from the boats at the landing. If this worked, Grant's forces would be trapped with no means of escape, thus forcing him to surrender or be wiped out.[15]

Although Johnston was "officially" in charge of the Southern army, Beauregard was "effectively" in charge. He took control and came up with a method to implement the plan that was dangerously inept, but Johnston gave it his stamp of approval. The plan was highly impractical in view of the untrained, unready troops, field officers who were uninformed and a terrain that was not conducive to effective troop movement or communication. But as it turned out, it almost worked, owing to the willingness of the Rebel troops to plunge headlong into disaster, fight like demons and die in droves. They were expected to do all this on a single biscuit a day. On April 3, with drummers drumming, the Confederate army marched away from Corinth, in good spirits, looking for a fight in Tennessee.

The success of the plan depended on the ability of the troops to move fast and surprise the enemy. Unfortunately, their progress was slow due to rain and muddy roads, further complicated by the lighthearted and undisciplined attitude of the troops. They should have been moving fast and quietly, but there was a tendency to talk and laugh out loud, and worse yet, to randomly shoot at birds and animals. At one point, an entire regiment fired a round in unison. The careless behavior gave their commanders fits.[16]

Then General William J. Hardee's division engaged in a sharp skirmish with federal troops on April 4, 1862, the day originally set for the attack. This untimely incident caused Beauregard to lose his enthusiasm for an attack. Yet despite the indecision of Beauregard and the urging of General Leonidas Polk, who wanted to call off the attack and save the starving troops for another day, Johnston ordered an assault to commence at daylight on April 6, 1862. "I would fight them if they were a million," he said, with a hint of fatalism in his voice.[17]

On the other side of the war, Grant relaxed his guard, as he did not expect an attack. He believed the impending battle would take place at or near Corinth, and he had the luxury of selecting the time and place to attack. Still he sensed that the battle would result in high casualties, writing his wife Julia about the "terrible sacrifice of life that must take place."[18]

The Union soldiers lazed away in their tent city, disdaining the safety of entrenchments. Sherman's men settled in on all sides of Shiloh Church; he ignored warnings from Rebel prisoners that a huge army was poised to strike.

When a cautious colonel warned that great numbers of the enemy might be near, Sherman sneeringly rejected the warning. He told the colonel to pack up his regiment and go back to Ohio if he was so fearful.[19]

The situation seemed scripted for disaster. A leisurely Sherman was in charge at the camp, while Grant was at Savannah, waiting for Buell, nursing an injured ankle after his horse fell and pinned him in the mud. "Bull" Nelson's division arrived at Savannah on April 4, but Grant ordered him to go into camp there rather than continue on to Pittsburg Landing. He wrote to Halleck saying that he had no concern over an imminent attack. But he was essentially hemmed in on all four sides. The Tennessee River was at his rear, and the two, roughly parallel, streams that ran into it made up the other sides. Finally, on the fourth side, Johnston's Rebel army waited, occupying a wide front.

Grant was well on his way to the first serious blunder of his illustrious Civil War career. He would forever regret his lackadaisical attitude, especially because it was expressed in writing to Halleck — his antagonist — and made a part of the permanent record of the war.

While the federal troops were alerted to the presence of a large Confederate army, the Rebels nevertheless struck first and gained the advantage. Hardee's division of 9,000 men poured into the Union lines, and over the next three hours the Confederates steadily drove them back. From 6 to 9 A.M., Hardee kept up his frontal assault, essentially destroying three enemy brigades, with bodies piling up on both sides. With his entire army of 40,000 engaged in battle, it looked as if Johnston would have his big victory over Grant's Army of the Tennessee.

Grant arrived at the Landing at 8 A.M. and was greeted by total chaos. Nonetheless he thought only in terms of winning the battle, which a lesser man would have concluded as being lost. Not Grant. He coolly took stock of the disaster in the making and ordered up more ammunition. He sent a message to General Lew Wallace to bring his division up to the front where more men were desperately needed. He also sent word to General Nelson to get his division over from Savannah.

By 11:30 the federal right wing had been crushed, and frantic Southern soldiers began ransacking the Union camps: food at last. At this point, Sherman, with the assistance of General John A. McClernand's division, made the first counter-attack, gaining back some ground and slowing the Rebel momentum. The ransacking Rebels were caught up in looting and gorging and were low on ammunition. Using this to their advantage, the Union commanders regrouped.

The battle raged into the afternoon with men dying at a frightful rate. The chaotic pattern of the long battle was such that survivors of shattered units on both sides would be sent fleeing to the rear, meeting fresh units on the way to the front. When one side got the advantage, the other would be sent reeling back, amid heavy losses. At one point the Rebels captured some federal artillery and turned the big guns against the Yankees. The guns were retaken but at the cost of many lives.

The mad pace and noise of the battle was terrific, and men on both sides were strangely transformed into demonic, half-human killing machines, motivated by the desire to kill and kill savagely. A battle-crazed Union soldier jumped on an artillery piece, "crowed two or three times and then fell badly wounded."[20] The killing was personal and close up, setting a new standard for battlefield deaths and a harbinger of the high casualties that would be tallied over the remainder of the war.

The madness seemed to infect the generals too, as General Braxton Bragg ordered eight ill-advised and nearly suicidal frontal attacks into the teeth of Yankee guns, suffering about 2,400 casualties from approximately 10,000 men — members of a volunteer army that he contemptuously called a "mob."[21] Use them up, was Bragg's policy and practice. He was always careless with the lives of his men and was therefore not well liked. And yet in obedience to his orders they charged headlong into deadly gunfire, while it was erroneously reported that Bragg, himself, had been killed.[22]

The division of General Benjamin M. Prentiss became separated from the main body of Union forces at a wooded place called the "Hornet's Nest." Prentiss and his men bravely held their ground until forced to surrender, and in doing so gave Grant time to reorganize. He sent word to Buell, noting that his desperate situation could only be saved by reinforcements. Grant later described the fury of the battle in an otherwise terse report, calling it the "most continuous firing of musketry and artillery ever heard on this continent."[23]

At least Grant lived to tell the tale. Not so for his adversary, however. The Confederates absorbed a terrible loss when Major General Johnston died, having bled to death from a wound to his right leg just below the knee. Riding on his horse, "Fire-Eater," he had exposed himself to gunfire all day and when finally shot refused medical attention. By 2:30 in the afternoon he was gone. The distinguished general died to the sound of the Rebel yell, as the battle raged on without intermission. Having died on a high note, he was spared the sting of another disastrous defeat. News of Johnston's death was kept from the men.

The *New York Times* excitedly reported that Johnston was hit by a cannon ball. This was wrong, of course, but newspapers including the *Times* had limited access to facts, and it was more important to print something than to ignore the story altogether. How Johnston died was not as important as the fact that he died. For it meant that Beauregard was entirely in control, although it was reported erroneously that he had an arm blown off.[24]

About one o'clock in the afternoon, Buell and his staff arrived at Pittsburg Landing on a small steamer. The first sign of battle he saw was in the form of

4,000 to 5,000 terrified stragglers, clamoring for cover along the riverbank. The sight defied description. Buell — accustomed order and discipline — was shocked and angered at what he had seen.

He met briefly with Grant, asking about a plan for a retreat. Grant vetoed the idea, still believing he could win what appeared to be a no-win situation. And by 4 P.M., it looked worse as the mob of panic-stricken stragglers along the bank increased. Grant pleaded in vain with the frightened men, urging them to find courage and rejoin the battle. But they had lost faith in Grant; they felt betrayed and believed he had lulled them into thinking no attack was imminent.

Sherman still commanded about 18,000 men who were not yet terror stricken. He formed a line of defense against the onrushing Rebels that extended about a mile and a half in length. This line held its position until about 5 p.m, with Sherman showing great combat mettle in his first fight as a divisional commander. But he needed help and soon got it.

The 1st Brigade of Nelson's division, under the command of Colonel Jacob Ammen, arrived at about five o'clock. He too was greeted by the grand gathering of terrified soldiers, now about 15,000 in number. It was an embarrassment for Ammen and his small brigade of about 550 troops who with fixed bayonets and colors proudly displayed were ready to fight. With a band playing, the lead brigade of Nelson's division marched forward toward the fighting. This display of discipline and pride inspired a few stragglers to find their rifles and get back into the action.[25]

When General "Bull" Nelson saw the frightened mass at the river's edge, he was enraged and began cursing them, calling them cowards — and worse. He was a nasty, foul man by reputation, and when angered, he could out-yell and out-swear most men. Nelson ordered his first company to charge into the mob with sabers. He only succeeded in causing some of the skulkers to trample others. An exasperated chaplain tried to rally the stragglers but he failed too.

Despite the chaos at the landing and the growing band of stragglers, Grant felt his chances at success were increasing, and that when all of Buell's army was in the field, he could win the battle. He downplayed the tragic events that had just transpired. And despite Buell's anger and apparent contempt for him, Grant stayed calm and kept planning.

Both sides ceased fire as nightfall came; both Grant and Beauregard felt good about their circumstances despite the great slaughter that day. Beauregard telegraphed Richmond proudly announcing that his army had won a "complete victory." An elated Jefferson Davis informed the Confederate Congress that the federal army was beaten to the point of annihilation.[26]

Grant, however, saw the results as decidedly undecided. He looked forward to launching a strong counter-attack while Beauregard expected to finish off a greatly weakened enemy. When Sherman remarked that the Union had gotten the worst of it that day, Grant said with confidence that they would whip the Rebels when the fight resumed in the morning.

That night Beauregard and his generals met in Sherman's tent on the Shiloh campground so recently occupied by Union troops. Beauregard heard a rumor that Buell had diverted his troops toward Decatur, and was wistfully happy about his prospects for finishing off an unreinforced Grant the next day. Beauregard's army of 40,000 had fought bravely but chaotically and mostly beyond his control. But they had taken about 3,000 prisoners including a general, and Beauregard believed he had accomplished a great deal.

In truth, had Beauregard continued the assault into the evening, he might have completed the rout and won a great victory. But he stopped; his men were exhausted and hungry, and there were wounded to care for and dead to bury. Beauregard also had a sad responsibility to attend to and formed a detail of officers to take General Johnston's body back to Corinth.[27]

During the night, the reveling Rebels looted the Union camps, helping themselves to food and camping amenities that seemed like luxuries. Those damn Yankees ate well. The Rebels were celebrating what they considered to be a great victory, as if there might be some minor mopping up the next day, and then they would march away in triumph. A sense of complacency set in as it was believed that the enemy had escaped across the river. So the Rebels plundered and partied by candlelight, the sounds of their antics interrupted by the groaning and moaning of thousands of wounded and dying men, lying somewhere out there in the darkness. Rain that night compounded their misery. In war there are two kinds of men: those who survive the battle and celebrate life and those who suffer alone in the dark waiting to die.

CHAPTER 7

The Battle of Shiloh: The Second Day

> It becomes my duty again to report another great battle fought
> between two great armies, one contending for the maintenance of
> the best government ever devised, the other for its destruction.
> — Major General U. S. Grant

At the end of the first day's battle, the Southern army was, in fact, a mess, terribly disorganized and ready to be driven back in defeat. And Union men were on the way, capable of doing just that. During the night, more of Brigadier General William "Bull" Nelson's men arrived followed by Brigadier General Thomas J. Crittenden's division. Crittenden's men were quickly brought ashore so the transporter could pick up Brigadier General Alexander M. McCook's division, waiting at Savannah.

General McCook had pushed his men hard in an effort to get to Savannah, and when he arrived during the night, he found that no arrangements had been made to ferry his troops to the Landing. An angry McCook roused sleeping boat captains from their beds and in short order, boats were ready.[1] While the exhausted Rebels were resting in Union tents, with a hard rain falling, the odds were shifting against them.

Captain Daniel McCook later wrote an article about the battle that was published in *Harper's New Monthly Magazine*. He recalled, in flowery, melodramatic language meant to bring out the "glory" of the thing, that the night was "an agony of rumor — rumors of defeat, of panic, of men rushing into the river, of the annihilation of the army." Dan McCook was thoroughly imbued with the martial spirit, and yet he hoped that, while passing that terrible night on the steamboat *Tigress*, the enemy would draw back and there would be no fighting in the morning.[2]

The rain let up about 3 A.M., and by five o'clock in the morning on April 7,

1862, Nelson's men were on the move. By eight in the morning, Crittenden's brigades had formed up on Nelson's right. The confident and disciplined Union line moved into the battlefield of the previous day, walking over the bodies of dead soldiers. They met sporadic fire as they advanced. Seeing the well-ordered movement of Buell's regiments, Sherman and his men were inspired.

As the steamer *Tigress* inched its way toward Pittsburg Landing, Dan McCook was convinced that a terrible fight was in the offing. He recalled hearing an infantry band perform a rousing rendition of "Il Trovatore" against a backdrop of gunfire, and the music had an inspirational effect on the men of the 2nd Division.

Disembarking at the landing with the 2nd Division, and eager to join the fray, Dan McCook was amazed at the chaos. In his *Harper's* article he described the bedlam at the riverside. He recalled seeing supplies scattered about, anxious officers "rushing around," trying to gather stragglers, and soldiers, "sutlers, camp-followers and even women adding their voices to the Babel of sound."

He was shocked at the sight of "thousands of soldiers, panic-stricken ... hiding under the bank," some of whom tried to discourage the 2nd Division troops from marching off to fight.[3]

The chaos was almost too much for Captain McCook who had already been exposed to battle at Wilson's Creek in Missouri. It was like watching the angels of death swirling in the low clouds, like a powerful storm, about to destroy everyone on the ground. And worse yet the division had to march by or over acres of dead and wounded men of both uniforms. With images of death and sounds of suffering everywhere, General McCook's division had reason to be disheartened.

Daniel McCook, Jr., was a prominent member of the family called the "Fighting McCooks." With the rank of captain, Daniel served at the battle of Shiloh as an aide to his brother, General McCook. Daniel's account of the struggle published by *Harper's New Monthly Magazine* reveals in excruciating detail the terrible suffering and high casualties of the two-day battle. Despite the carnage and loss of life, the Union victory was cause for great celebration in the North.

General McCook's businesslike report, however, makes no reference to the dead from the previous day's battle. McCook's explanation of his role in the battle lacked the high drama of brother Dan's article. The general states that he arrived at Pittsburg Landing at 5 A.M. on the 7th, when his 4th Brigade under Brigadier General Lovell H. Rousseau was disembarking. He reported to Buell and received his orders, directing him to place Rousseau on Crittenden's right, thus extending the Union line of march.[4] McCook rode out with the 4th Brigade, and when he came upon the 1st Ohio Infantry — his original regiment — he stopped to greet the men he led as a colonel at the battle of Bull Run, less than a year before. Trying to inspire his old regiment, McCook said that he would "blow his brains out" if any member of the 1st Ohio ran from the fight.[5] He expected no straggling from the veteran regiment.

After seeing to the placement of Rousseau's men, McCook ordered Colonel Edward N. Kirk's brigade to stand in reserve until needed. That need was quick in coming. General Braxton Bragg hurled four regiments and a battalion against Rousseau's brigade near the Duncan farm. When McCook saw that Rousseau had been hit by a superior force, he ordered Kirk to join in the attack. Soon a portion of Gibson's brigade arrived and McCook ordered him to "form a line in the rear of the center, to be used as circumstances might require." McCook's men advanced at a steady pace, facing a vigorous attack on his right and center, but the "steady valor of General Rousseau's brigade" repulsed the Rebels. Soon they reached the campground that General John McClernand's men were driven from the day before. It was there that a reinforced enemy made a desperate stand against McCook's men.

They were up to the challenge, however, and Rousseau's brigade of resolute, well-trained troops pushed the Rebels steadily up Corinth road, toward Shiloh Church. The advance of the 4th Brigade was a major factor in Beauregard's decision to order a retreat.[6] McCook reported with pride that Rousseau had the "pleasure of retaking McClernand's headquarters." The fighting that swirled around Shiloh Church was just as furious as it had been the day before.

With McCook directing the traffic, his regiments moved forward, firing into Confederate ranks, while others moved back to replenish their supply of ammunition from the ordinance wagon, whose timely arrival contributed to the overall success. Everything seemed to be working as McCook skillfully deployed regiments to plug gaps or to support troops under heavy fire. At one point during the fierce fight, General McCook ordered his brother Captain McCook to take a message to Colonel August Willich. And sensing that he had sent his brother on a very dangerous assignment, he said calmly, "Goodbye Dan."[7] Fortunately for the family, however, Dan McCook returned safely.

When the enemy shifted its focus from McCook's right to his left, he had a regiment ready to stem the tide, always arriving at the very moment it was needed. At one point, McCook contends that 10,000 Rebels were directed at his two brigades but they held their ground despite being very tired and facing overwhelming odds. McCook's 1st Ohio fought with skill and valor in the thick of it, losing 50 men dead and wounded.[8]

At about 3 P.M. on the second day of the battle, General Grant ordered a charge of the enemy, across an open area, to be led by Illinois troops. According to Lucius W. Barber of the 15th Illinois Infantry regiment, the troops were weary from battle, but rose to the occasion, inspired by the presence of Grant who was there to supervise the charge. The men greeted him with rousing cheers that picked up their spirits and enlivened their senses. Barber recalled in his memoirs that "the brave McCook" came riding forth with sword in hand, shouting, "Now give them a touch of Illinois! Forward! Charge!" Then with one "wild shout," the Union troops sprang forward, driving the Rebels before them.[9]

By about 3:30 P.M., the Rebel retreat began as Beauregard was convinced by his staff that any further attacks would be futile. His adjutant general compared the Confederate army to a lump of sugar about to be dissolved in water, suggesting it would be "judicious" to leave with what they had left. It was an apt metaphor. Seeing the futility of it all, Beauregard ordered a retreat, his grand plan for success a failure and his ragged but gallant army defeated and demoralized. After Beauregard organized a covering force, the defeated and weary army began a sad walk back to Corinth.[10] The shooting stopped, and an exhausted and relieved Union army surveyed the battlefield with dead bodies in every direction.

McCook noted in his report that his brigade commanders performed admirably, supplying leadership and inspiring confidence in their men. Colonel Kirk, for example, seized the flag of the 34th Illinois when its commanding officer, Major Charles H. Levanway, was killed, and rallied the fallen officer's soldiers. Kirk was severely wounded in his shoulder and yet continued to direct his troops. McCook made sure that his commanders, including Kirk, were recognized for their valor and courageous service to the Union.

He said, "The bravery and steadiness of the officers and men under my command are worthy all praise, considering the circumstances surrounding them." Then he reminded those who would read the report that the day before the battle, his men had marched 22 miles, and a "portion of them stood all night in the streets of Savannah in a driving rain, without sleep." And once they reached the landing, "the head of my column had to force its way through thousands of panic-stricken and wounded men before it could engage the enemy."

General McCook commended his personal staff including his brother, Captain Daniel McCook, and even put in a good word for his superiors for the manner in which they dispatched orders to him. He closed by stating that he suffered 93 men killed, 803 wounded and 9 missing, numbers which to McCook were small considering the desperate nature of the struggle. Lieutenant Colonel Edward M. McCook duly reported that his cavalry regiment was not involved in the action, having been ordered by General Nelson to remain on the opposite side of Pittsburg Landing.[11]

Edward's cousin, Alexander M. McCook, had been tested by fire more severely than any time previous, including the first battle of Bull Run, and he handled it very well. He was part of a team that came to the rescue of Grant's army[12] and had a hand in saving "Sam's" career, and probably that of Sherman as well. In his entire Civil War career, General McCook would never experience another battle that turned out so well from his personal standpoint. He was cited for gallantry and promoted to major general.

Other reports are generous in their praise for General Alexander M. McCook at the battle of Shiloh. Among them, Colonel W. H. Gibson said, "I must thank General McCook for the labor and energy he has shown in bringing his division to that state of discipline and skill which renders it at once an honor and an ornament to the armies of the republic."[13]

In his memoirs, Sherman also complimented McCook for coolness and skill during the heat of battle. He wrote that in order to "give personal credit where I think it is due ... that General McCook's splendid division [Rousseau's brigade] from Kentucky drove back the enemy along the Corinth road."[14]

That was for the record. Off the record, McCook was heard to say that many Iowa and Ohio regiments were "the greatest cowards in the world."[15] Was he referring to men under his command, or did he intend to denigrate those Iowans and Ohioans who were among the cowering masses, huddled and hidden along the riverbank? Whatever his motivation, the remark is unfortunate in view of the great sacrifice made by so many men that day. Even the skedaddlers contributed something before they skedaddled.

The curtain was drawn on the worst battle up to that point in the Civil War, and the surviving players were left with an unforgettable sight. With the guns silent, it was time to deal with the eerie drama of death. It was like a scene from Dante's vision of hell; the sight of broken and bloated bodies lent a ghastly, surreal, dreamlike appearance to the area, but the terrible stench made it all very real. There were tents shot full of holes, horses dead and bloating, and worst of all there was the suffering of the wounded for all to hear, as they groaned in pain and begged for attention, death or just a drink of water.

For Colonel Edward M. McCook, mere words to explain what he saw were valueless. He wrote: "I can't describe the horror of the field — no one can." The roar of artillery and musket shot stayed in his head for days following the battle.[16]

The horrors of the battle also left their mark on Captain Daniel McCook. He recalled the "stony, glaring eyes and blue lips, the glistening teeth, the shriveled and contracted hands, the wild agony of pain and passion in the attitudes of the dead." He was moved by the "mangled form of one of my best loved classmates dressed in a rebel uniform."[17] After the shooting subsided, Daniel McCook found and buried his friend, placing on the fallen Rebel's chest a miniature of a girl. He confessed that it was the saddest night of his life.[18]

Medical supplies were insufficient, doctors were in short supply and overworked and there was no place for many of the wounded to lie in comfort. The dire need for medical personnel sent doctors from the northern cities rushing to Pittsburg Landing. Among them were Dr John McCook and Dr. George McCook.[19] Ambulances circulated among the wounded and surgeons did their best to attend to

After the battle of Shiloh was over, Alexander M. McCook was promoted to the rank of major general, as shown in this photograph. McCook's division in the Army of the Ohio fought with great courage and was in part responsible for turning the tide in favor of the Union on the second day of fighting. The battle of Shiloh represents the pinnacle of McCook's Civil War success.

the suffering, but the numbers were overwhelming. While the suffering men were not unappreciated, many were neglected and left to die on Shiloh's stench-ridden, blood-polluted acreage.

Not long after the shooting stopped, civilians arrived hoping to find their loved ones, dead or alive. In one instance, a woman roamed the shabby, makeshift graveyard hoping to find her husband, a lieutenant in an Illinois regiment. Searching among the graves, she came across her husband's dog that had followed him to Shiloh. The half-starved dog was sitting by a grave that, when opened, revealed the body of the dead lieutenant. The sad widow, along with the faithful dog, took the remains of her husband back to some quiet prairie cemetery in Illinois.[20]

Many men were buried poorly in shallow graves, and in the years following the battle of Shiloh, roving hogs dug up and ate the dead. It was said that the free-ranging hogs were uneatable "on account of their living off the dead."[21] It was all too hideous to be real, and yet so many men carried the terrible memory with them until, dying at an older age, they were given a much more civilized burial.

Among those abandoned by the retreating Rebels was Kentucky's "provisional governor" George W. Johnson. Despite having a withered arm, he insisted on fighting and was serving on Breckinridge's staff when he was badly wounded during Monday's fight. Johnson was discovered by General McCook, who recognized him from a meeting of the two at the 1860 Democratic National Convention in Charleston, South Carolina. McCook made sure that Johnson saw a doctor, but he later died of his wounds.[22]

Another Rebel captured by McCook's division was a badly wounded Marshall Polk, an officer from Tennessee who attended West Point with Alex. Now enemies, during those formative and innocent days, the two men were friends.[23]

The Lincoln family felt the impact of the battle of Shiloh in a personal way. Samuel Todd, a younger brother to Mrs. Lincoln, was among the casualties. Having chosen to fight for the South, he was killed on the second day of the battle.

The Yankees were glad to see the Rebels leave, and no one, including Grant, was anxious to pursue them. McCook, in fact, pleaded with Grant, begging that no more be asked of the troops that fought so hard that day.[24] The men needed rest, he insisted. In fact both armies had fought themselves into a state of mind-numbing exhaustion, and both seemed to be drained of the desire to shoot and kill anymore that day. Duty and honor be damned if only for a short while.

Sometime after the battle, Grant wrote an article on Shiloh for *Century Magazine*. In doing so, he harshly criticized McCook for his unwillingness to press his men any more that day. Years later when Grant penned his famed *Personal Memoirs* he apologized to McCook, regretting the injustice, for McCook's division had traveled hard and long to get to Shiloh in less than desirable weather conditions, and once there, "did as good service as its position allowed." Remembering McCook's gallantry and loyalty, and that of his brothers and cousins, Grant said, "General McCook himself belongs to a family which furnished many volunteers to the army."[25]

Although the Union merely regained ground that it had lost and not an acre more, it had earned a hard-fought victory at Shiloh, which was reward enough. It is significant to note, of course, that instead of destroying the Union army or driving it out of Tennessee, the Confederates were forced to pack up their dead commanding general, fall back on Corinth, and leave Grant's army in possession of Shiloh Church and its environs. The Confederates came and fought hard, but did not conquer.

The immediate concern for the Union was to clean up the mess. Burial details were put to work on both sides as Beauregard sent a detail back under a flag of truce, in accordance with Grant's consent. The Rebel dead buried in front of McCook's division alone totaled 680, a bloody indicator of the ferocity of the fighting.[26] The combined casualties for two days of intense fighting was 17,897 dead and wounded, a statistic that horrified the public on both sides, shifting the pre-battle optimistic mood to post-battle gloom. Shiloh ranks seventh on the list of the bloodiest battles of the Civil War.[27]

Nevertheless the Northern press proclaimed it a grand victory with happy headlines. Bell-ringing celebrations erupted throughout the North as people saw in the victory at Shiloh, relief from the sting and humiliation of Bull Run. Congress took a day off, and Lincoln issued a proclamation of thanksgiving. Grant, who turned defeat into victory, suddenly found himself a hero.[28]

But after time for reflection, attention turned to what went wrong, and Grant was heavily criticized. The public groaned under the terrible weight of large numbers of dead and wounded. Grant was accused of being caught off guard and drinking too much, and many called for his removal. Lincoln was urged to sack Grant, but he refused to do so, telling critics that Grant fights and therefore he could not be spared.

As good as he was, Grant learned as he led, and after Shiloh, he "gave up all idea of saving the Union except by complete conquest."[29] Despite the terrible toll of the battle, he had the will to fight on. Yet Grant seemed ready to give in to the pressure and resign, but Sherman encouraged him to stay in the army; they had become and would remain good and trusted friends.

On the other side, Beauregard — who insisted on calling it a Confederate win — was lambasted for his failure to attack the Union lines late in the first day of battle, when he had a chance to finish off Grant and his exhausted and bloodied army.[30] Shiloh was a terrible blow to the South as stories were told of fields turned red with blood. Saddened southerners learned about a mass grave that contained over 700 dead Rebels. Forced to contemplate the horrendous loss of life and the concomitant blow to its pride, it is no wonder that the "South never smiled after Shiloh."[31]

In the North, the press made sure that Shiloh wasn't forgotten, and it became, next to Gettysburg, the most controversial and criticized battle of the entire Civil War. The two-day fight, the high casualties and the conduct of its leaders raised questions that screamed for answers. The newspapers, of course, were very anxious to provide explanations. Unfortunately, the articles the battle spawned were designed to sell papers more so than to get out the truth. As one would expect, Grant was the recipient of the harshest criticism and blame, signaling to all that a change of command was in the works.[32]

On April 11, 1862, Major General Henry W. Halleck arrived at Pittsburg Landing to take command, thus pushing Grant aside for a second time. He thanked both Grant and Buell and their men for winning the two-day battle. Then, after instilling strict disciplinary measures throughout all levels of his army, he set it marching, albeit slowly, toward Corinth. He had a field command and was determined to make the most of it, his way, and show the unmilitary Grant how things should be done.

General Grant would have to wait for the assessment of latter-day historians to receive credit for his persistence and aggression at Shiloh, both of which were largely responsible for pushing the Confederates back across the border and well into Mississippi. For despite his mistakes and lack of preparation, it was his steady leadership and coolheaded judgment that won the day. He could have adopted Buell's thinking and pulled away, allowing the South to claim victory, but he stayed and fought and with the aid of Sherman, McCook and other generals drove the enemy back, arguably softening them up for Halleck's easy conquest of Corinth.

It is the battle of Shiloh, however, not the conquest of Corinth, that is remembered in history. Shiloh changed the face of the Civil War. Glory lost its "l." Gone were any romantic notions of a light war fought in gentlemanly fashion. Gone were any thoughts of a quick victory by either side. All such thoughts were lost in the wreckage of war. The terrible carnage, the high, unprecedented number of casualties, and the acres of mangled bodies — some headless, others legless — scattered amid the debris of battle, caused the survivors to realize that in a nightmarish fight to the finish, the end was nowhere in sight. The public on both sides were not long in coming to the same conclusion. After one year of fighting with light to moderate casualties, the warring parties left military pomp and circumstance behind and plunged into the fatal darkness of all-out war.

CHAPTER 8

The Corinth Campaign:
Halleck's Slow-Coach Operation

Richmond and Corinth are now the great strategical points of the
war, and our success at these points should be insured at all hazards.
— Major General Henry W. Halleck

After the smoke, dust and death settled in at Shiloh, Major General Henry
W. Halleck, in charge of the western-based Union forces, was determined that
such a disaster never be repeated. High-casualty battles were a dreadful waste
of men and material to the man who looked at war as a chess game. It was a
match of wits, a brainy contest where battles were won by the general who
could outthink his opponent. In Halleck's thinking, a bloody mess didn't necessarily equate to a successful campaign. Halleck was a planner, a plodder, a
fixed thinker and a textbook military man. After all, he wrote one of the most
widely read books on battle tactics entitled *Elements of Military Art and Science*.

Having decided to pull his tired army back after the bloody fight at Pittsburg Landing, Confederate General Pierre G. T. Beauregard retreated to
Corinth, Mississippi, a tiny village tucked into the northeast corner of the
state. The nearest city of importance was Memphis, 90 miles to the east. While
it was not a major urban area, Corinth did have two important railroads that
ran through it. The village was Halleck's target, for where there were railroads
there had to be Rebels.

Halleck would now put all his military expertise to good use and punish
and push Beauregard and his Rebel army out of Corinth and deny the Confederates the use of the railroads. Like other cautious, methodical generals,
Halleck believed it was more important to capture and control a place than to
destroy an army. If enough key places were captured, the enemy would be
forced to surrender.

Halleck graduated from West Point in 1839, third in his class, with a brilliant academic record.[1] He was married to a granddaughter of founding father Alexander Hamilton and was living in high style in California when the Civil War started, a rich man, having enjoyed success in a law practice, along with interests in a bank, two railroads and a lucrative mercury mine. By August 1861, however, he was back in the east and in the army again, working under his mentor General Winfield Scott for a lot less money. Like so many others who answered his country's call, it was where he wanted to be. And like so many other men eager to serve, he just had to find a way to fit in where he could do the most good.

Unfortunately, Halleck was not the kind of man who made friends or influenced others. His brusque manner, his rather snooty and abstract personality, and his flabby and unkempt appearance put people off. While he was uneasy around other men, it was said that Halleck could cast a stare like a dagger into another's psyche, and his glassy, goggle-eyes gave way to rumors that he was an opium addict.[2] He did, in fact, use opium, but it was for the purpose of easing the pain of hemorrhoids.[3]

Working from his post at the Department of the Missouri, after replacing General John C. Fremont, Halleck approved and supported General U. S. Grant's taking of Fort Henry on the Tennessee River and Fort Donelson on the Cumberland River in February of 1862. Both were important waterway victories and were the cause of wild celebrating throughout the North, because Grant had created an opening into Tennessee.

Grant's reputation was on the rise. After bloody Shiloh, however, Halleck reined in his aggressive field commander and decided to put his own hands on the controls. Halleck decided that Grant, while

Major General Henry W. Halleck, nicknamed "Old Brains," came into the Civil War after an outstanding record at West Point and successful business ventures in California. The goggle-eyed Halleck was caricatured and criticized as much as or more than any other leading figure of the Civil War because of his appearance and personality. He was not impressive in his brief stint as a field commander on the Corinth campaign, but Lincoln found him to be useful, and Halleck served throughout the rest of the war at a desk in Washington, D.C.

a courageous fighter, was too reckless for command. To make matters worse, Halleck heard that Grant was drinking again.

If Grant was haunted by his past, Halleck was inspired by the present. He could do without Grant, for he had at his disposal three large armies totaling over 100,000 men and clearheaded generals to command them. He had the Army of the Tennessee, on paper, still Grant's army, the Army of the Mississippi under Major General John Pope, and Major General Don Carlos Buell's Army of the Ohio. How he would manage this huge army was an open question, for Halleck had yet to hold a field command in the Civil War.

Halleck clearly liked Buell more than Grant, and showed it by talking freely and friendly with the former while behaving far more formally to the latter. Like everyone else, Halleck knew what happened at Shiloh. It was the arrival of Buell's divisions at Pittsburg Landing that provided the winning edge for the Union. Grant had shown extraordinary toughness and resolve throughout the two-day battle, but the unprecedented number of casualties was cause to reserve judgment on his worth. It would take time for the country to appreciate Grant's battlefield savvy and his motivation to fight hard, make sacrifices and win.

General Halleck entered into his new assignment with a full measure of self-confidence. Efficiency and systemic order were the hallmarks of his military character, and both attributes would be put to the test. He was in charge of the largest army ever assembled on the continent. And with firmness and dedication, his sights were set on Corinth. To Halleck, the small, obscure Mississippi town was the "greatest strategic point of the war."[4] He sent a wire to Washington announcing the departure of his army, saying, "Our army will be before Corinth tomorrow night."[5]

On May 1st, having completed all preliminary details, the Corinth campaign was at last launched. Halleck started to move, albeit very deliberately, with Pope's army leading the way. Thinking in terms of concentration, communication and coordination, and leaving nothing to chance, the thoughtful and efficient general — his 111,000-man leviathan divided into three wings — began its conquest of Corinth. "Tomorrow night," however, was about four weeks away.

Still the army was at last leaving Pittsburg Landing, a terrible pit of death and suffering. Heavy rains that came after the fighting ended raised havoc with the burial crews, and bodies were washed out of the ground. The stench of decay lingered overhead while civilians attended to wounded relatives or searched for the graves of loved ones. The grief-stricken folks were joined by whisky peddlers, prostitutes and curiosity seekers. The surviving soldiers were only too glad to leave that dreadful place that would, however, linger on in memory.

Among those on the tedious march was Dr. John McCook, attached to the Army of the Ohio. The doctor spent a considerable amount of his time nursing and cooking for his son Edward who was too sick to ride a horse. The elder McCook believed that Ed would have died had he not been attended to for some two weeks. Yet despite his onerous responsibilities, Dr. McCook recalled that the great army on the march was a spectacular sight with "colors flying and thousands cheering."[6]

Other McCooks in Halleck's grand army included Dr. George McCook, a brother to Dr. John McCook. Captain Daniel McCook, Jr., was an officer on the staff of his older brother Alexander, the general. Also included in the Army of the Ohio was Colonel Robert L. McCook, a brigade commander. Robert was an older brother of Alexander. Robert had distinguished himself in the western Virginia campaign and in Kentucky at the battle of Mill Springs, where he was severely wounded while leading a bayonet charge. The popular and likeable Robert L. McCook was a rising star in the Union army.

The right wing of the military behemoth was formed by the Army of the Tennessee, under the direct control of General George H. Thomas. In the center was Buell's Army of the Ohio, including the division of General McCook, marching in a reserve capacity. On the left marched General John Pope's Army of the Mississippi, fresh from an impressive victory at Island No. 10 in the Mississippi River. Capturing the island in the Madrid Bend of the river meant that, except for Fort Pillow, the great waterway was Confederate free and open for federal use all the way to Memphis. Pope's star was just then on the rise.

Grant—whose victories at Forts Henry and Donelson were seemingly forgotten—tagged along, officially the second in command to Halleck. On paper he was still commander of the Army of the Tennessee, but he had little authority and Old Brains paid him no mind, except maybe to cast a hard, goggle-eyed stare at the dehorned general. Grant recalled that he once offered a strategy suggestion, and Halleck "pooh-poohed it, and gave me to understand that when he wanted my advice he would let me know."[7] Another general said that Grant's assignment as "second in command" was equivalent to being "the fifth wheel to a wagon."[8] If Halleck meant to make Grant feel useless, he succeeded.

The pace of the advance was slow and deliberate and was made even slower due to roads that were bad or washed out altogether by rainy weather. The country was a bog-filled wilderness, thus requiring numerous detours. Over the first two days Halleck's rain-soaked army logged in 12 miles, approximately halfway to Corinth.

There was some fighting to break the monotony of marching. On May 3 and 4, skirmishing broke out at Farmington, Mississippi. On the 9th the fighting was more severe as the army closed in on its target. Sporadic fighting continued as Halleck advanced, forcing the Rebels to move back toward their fortifications.

If Lincoln was waiting for news of a great battle between Halleck and Beauregard, he ended each day with disappointment. And yet the president was a man of measured patience. He had an uncanny ability to judge the military capability of his generals, and Lincoln was just then giving Halleck his big chance to lead.

Halleck was in charge and was leading, but he was in no hurry to reach his destination. If the going was really rough, the army was lucky to travel a mile and a half in a day's march, and then dig in and wait maybe a day or two. At the end of a day's march the routine was the same: dig four hours and sleep six. The next morning, tired soldiers left their entrenchments to plod along, only to stop and dig down again when the army halted. And not just ordinary ditches, but complex trenches like the ones that Halleck saw when he visited France before the war.

The extremely slow pace of the march gave bored soldiers the chance to slip away and engage in looting. Stopping at isolated plantations, hungry soldiers gathered in food and supplies, and made their way back to the rest of the army. One victim of federal foragers complained that they took everything he had except his "hope of eternal salvation."[9] Everyone, it seems, was made to feel the cruel lash of war.

Meanwhile, the waiting Confederate army had swollen to about 84,000 with the arrival of three divisions led by Major General Earl Van Dorn. In the night, trains arrived bringing more troops, while excited deserters and wild rumors emanating from Corinth boosted the Confederate strength to astronomical numbers. But if the extra-cautious Halleck was worried, he tried hard not to show it.

While the Union army was engaged in its snaillike march toward Corinth, Beauregard was making plans for a great battle. Although he was not a colorful man, he could inspire his soldiers and the Southern press. On May 2, he issued an emotional proclamation, warning his men that the "invaders" were "on our soil." He told his soldiers that they must decide if they were "freemen or vile slaves of those who are free in name only." He reminded his army of its gallant effort on the "ever memorable field of Shiloh." Pumping them up for another great battle, Beauregard told his men that someday their children would proudly proclaim, "Our fathers were at the Battle of Corinth."[10]

Beauregard was also hard at work constructing huge and elaborate walls, breastworks and other forms of fortification. As if trying to out-build Halleck — or just preparing to defend against a Yankee horde — Beauregard transformed Corinth into a fortress.

Actually, Corinth was an affliction, an open sewer of the worst kind for the occupying army, as sickness, including dysentery, typhoid and measles, coupled with seriously wounded men, added thousands to the inactive list.

Attending to the multitude of wounded kept the medical teams busy, but their patients were dying in droves. The civilian population was forced to confront the horrors of war as the bodies and amputated limbs piled up for all to see. In raw numbers the Rebel effectives were only about 51,000.[11]

The slow-moving invaders finally halted about three miles outside of Corinth, where Halleck decided to close up all three wings and make a united front. After this was accomplished, the Union forces pushed forward, and a serious entrenchment began, followed by a siege and artillery bombardment of Corinth. Two large armies were seemingly about to collide in the northern Mississippi town, but there would be no journalists to witness the event, for Halleck ordered all of them back to Pittsburg Landing.

Actually on May 13, Halleck issued an order that all "unauthorized hangers on" must sever all connections with his army and depart from every camp. Those who failed to obey would be put to work digging entrenchments. This edict was viewed with disfavor by General Pope, a self-styled glory hound who seemingly could not get enough self-serving publicity. He questioned the meaning of Halleck's order and was told that reporters were the same as "unauthorized hangers on." But with the departure of newsmen, "unofficial" reporting was continued by "uniformed correspondents," meaning that Pope and his exploits continued to be featured in the newspapers.[12] In actuality, the Corinth campaign was covered by newspapers, including the *New York Times*, as much as was any other military movement of the war.

Minus the "hangers on," Halleck and his huge army had advanced to a point where it had to fight or go somewhere else. Having never led an army into battle, he seemed uncertain as to the proper course of action. Reports and rumors of the strength of the Rebel army caused Halleck to lapse into a state of extreme caution. Whatever the consequences, he would not be flushed out by what he believed to be overwhelming odds.

Then he made a decision. Instead of preparing to attack, he ordered his troops to dig deeper and harder. They obeyed and kept up the accursed digging as best they could, the work made more difficult when the Mississippi heat replaced the Mississippi rain. There had been some skirmishing, exchange of cannon fire and sharpshooting, but no general engagement by the opposing armies. Beauregard wanted to attack a wing or two, but each time he was ready, he discovered that Halleck was too well concentrated and entrenched. Meanwhile, Union generals of a more aggressive slant grew restless, itching for action.

Finally on May 26, with all three wings of the ponderous, burrowing army moving into position, Halleck ordered Buell's center wing to attack and clear out the Rebels concentrated near the Saratt house and drive them "behind Bridge Creek." Buell chose General McCook's reserve division to handle this task. The house was on the Saratt plantation. Among its features was a hill that Buell wanted cleared of Confederate pickets so that his army could occupy it and use it as a vantage point from which to strike Corinth. Since Corinth was situated on defensible terrain, the Union needed to clear and use the hill.

The next morning early, before dawn, an enthusiastic General McCook had his division up and out of their trenches and on the move. He sent the brigades of General Lovell H. Rousseau and General Richard W. Johnson advancing up the hill, side by side. His other brigade, commanded by Colonel Frederick S. Stumbaugh, was held in reserve, positioned at Johnson's rear. Colonel Robert L. McCook's brigade was selected to support Rousseau. The plan was to take the occupying Rebel pickets by surprise with an overwhelming force.

General McCook's plan worked very well and with light casualties, unlike most of his assignments. Johnson's brigade encountered heavy skirmishing, but after a half hour of shooting, the Rebels were driven off the hill. Johnson and Rousseau found themselves the sole occupants of the hill and immediately ordered their men to dig in. Heavy artillery was brought up, and rounds were blasted toward the Rebel lines. Beauregard fired back halfheartedly, but the Union was fully and firmly in control of the high ground, giving Halleck a decided advantage. He was now free to begin his all-out bombardment.[13]

Finally, on May 28, after an incredible four weeks of snail like progress and seemingly acres of infernal trenching and tunneling, Halleck was ready to strike a mortal blow at his enemy. He had moved his entire line to within one-half to three-quarters of a mile from the Rebel front. At this point Halleck brought up the heavy siege guns.[14]

McCook's division engaged in a little hot fun with Beauregard too, as he ordered his artillery to open a "heavy fire of grape and canister on the enemy." After about 30 minutes of loud pounding, the Rebels withdrew, and McCook ceased firing. In his report, McCook states that the "rebels retreated in great confusion, leaving many of their dead and wounded behind."[15]

As the Rebels were trying to conceal their true plans, they maintained a strong front throughout the day of the 28th. Thus the artillery duel continued intermittantly all day as well as did infantry gunfire. The next morning, the big guns were unleashed again accompanied by musket fire. By nine o'clock, the musket fire ceased although some artillery continued throughout the day.[16]

Halleck didn't have to expend any more canister or grape, for unbeknownst to anyone in his army, Beauregard decided to evacuate the heavily fortified Corinth, and did so in the stealth of night on May 29 after destroying excess supplies. Beauregard was able to load his soldiers on trains and move them away and yet convince Halleck that the Rebels were there in great numbers. After emptying the town of troops, the last train came back empty, and following Beauregard's order, those few people still in Corinth let out a loud yell so as to convey the belief that a large body of men had just arrived.[17]

Beauregard's great hoax had its intended effect as Halleck expected to meet with strong resistance. It was not until the morning of May 30, that Halleck realized he was shelling an empty town. His big guns boomed and blasted while his infantry advanced toward the walls, expecting to face heavy fire. When they reached the breastworks, however, no one fired back, much to their relief and surprise. Big guns seen from a distance were just logs or "Quaker guns." The real artillery was gone with the rest of the Rebel army. Corinth was a fortress in disguise.

Realizing that the occupying army had gone, the Union troops stormed into the town finding it a burning, smoldering mess. General McCook casually reported that he "had the pleasure of entering with my division the deserted earthworks and encampments of the rebels."[18] The mayor of Corinth surrendered the town to General William Nelson.[19]

Beauregard had been very thorough, leaving little of value for the Union army to salvage; what could not be hauled away by the retreating Rebels was destroyed. In a final bit of humor, someone left a message carved in wood which read: "These premises to let. Inquire of G. T. Beauregard."

Halleck — not known for having a sense of humor — examined the burntout premises. With no Rebel army to fight, he was left in control of Corinth, the town now in ruins that he had set out to capture. To every man who participated in the slow march to the Mississippi destination, it was a wretched and shabby trophy of war. The much-ballyhooed-battle, so vigorously played up in the press of both the North and South, fizzled out ingloriously.

To follow up his hollow victory, Halleck immediately sent six divisions, including Colonel Robert L. McCook's brigade, in a feeble pursuit of the retreating Rebel army, but soon called it off. Halleck's purpose at this point was to drive Beauregard as far south as possible. His thoughts were not on catching up with Beauregard, but on Washington. For he knew he had to prepare a report to Stanton that would offset the criticism that was sure to come from unimpressed third parties.

While Halleck was satisfied with the result, there was a feeling of dissatisfaction among some of the men and officers. General Johnson was mystified that Halleck "did not let loose those dogs of war."[20] The enemy escaped just when it appeared that their defeat and capture were imminent. For this Halleck was criticized and blamed; the men thought he had been out-generaled. The Corinth campaign was another example of "many cooks under a worse than doubtful chef."[21] The "chef" was chided for capturing some "Quaker guns," a handful of Rebels and a burned-out town shielded by five miles of crude fortifications. The great but agonizingly slow Corinth campaign — a month-long snipe hunt that ended with Halleck holding an empty bag — had finally ground to a halt.

Halleck placed General McCook's division in charge of Corinth. After McCook settled in to garrison the town, his men found that it was already occupied — by lice. His itchy soldiers, who had labored so long and hard to get to Corinth, were stuck in a place almost as bad as Pittsburg Landing.[22]

Still there was considerable value in this strategic victory, for the loss of Corinth meant that the Confederates would evacuate Fort Pillow on the Mississippi River and leave Memphis undefended and ripe for capture. Naval forces took control of Memphis on June 6, 1862, and a new base of operations was established for further incursions into the heart of Tennessee. General William T. Sherman understood this when he praised his friend Halleck, calling the result a "victory as important as any in recorded history."[23]

Others were not so kind. The *Chicago Tribune* said the effort was "tantamount to defeat," and the *Cincinnati Commercial* waxed sarcastic when it reported that "Beauregard had achieved another triumph."[24] In the same vein, frustrated General John Logan angrily declared that his men would not dig "another ditch for Halleck, unless it is to bury him in."[25] On the whole, Halleck was seen as far too timid by many of the aggressive generals under his command.

Lincoln, however, was impressed with Halleck, who had experienced his first and last field command. On July 11, 1862, the president appointed "Old Brains" general-in-chief, in charge of all Union forces. Halleck accepted the promotion with some reluctance. He had no desire to become bogged down in the nasty politics of war, nor was he anxious to intervene in the quarreling among egotistical generals and politicians. So he lingered in Corinth, in the western theater of the war, where he felt comfortable and useful.[26]

Not so for the bulk of his grand army. General Alexander M. McCook's division left lice-infested Corinth on June 11, 1862, toward Florence, Alabama.[27] Other elements of Buell's Army of the Ohio moved east into Tennessee with their sights set on Chattanooga. Pope left the Army of the Mississippi and went to Washington where he was placed in command of a newly created Army of Virginia on June 27.[28] Grant reassumed command of the Army of the Tennessee and established his headquarters at Memphis. He ordered divisions of Sherman and John McClernand to engage in railroad repair in western Tennessee.[29]

Halleck finally arrived in Washington in late July. He was given an office where he would coordinate with Secretary of War Stanton, along with other desk officers and generals in the field. The *New York Times* called Halleck's promotion one that would be "regarded with high satisfaction by the country." While acknowledging that Halleck "is not known to the country as a brilliant leader of armies in the field," his West Point background showed that he was a "safe and thoroughly reliable commander, an excellent disciplinarian, and a master of the theoretic art of war." The even-tempered editorial indicates that the *Times* was willing to give Halleck a chance to succeed in his new position while inviting the public to do the same.[30]

For General McCook, the cadence of army life would quicken over the next several months, a rather dramatic change after participating in the mind-numbing, overly cautious Corinth campaign. If he was looking for something more challenging, McCook would find it in the woods and mountains, and along the rivers of Tennessee. He would find it in the fast and furious pursuit of General Braxton Bragg's army as the Confederates made an earnest bid to retake Kentucky and threaten Ohio. For the remainder of 1862, General McCook and other members of the "Fighting McCooks" would become an integral part of the changing landscape of warfare as both sides of the horrible conflict picked up the pace of the fighting and dying.

CHAPTER 9

The Race for Louisville

The greatest recorded speed for a long distance march since Caesar's march against Pompey's sons.

—*Boston Transcript*, June 13, 1903

On July 25, 1862, Major General Alexander M. McCook wrote to Colonel James B. Fry from his camp in Battle Creek, Tennessee, warning that a large force of Rebels some 40,000 strong was expected to gather in Chattanooga. They were preparing for an invasion of middle Tennessee, according to an Atlanta newspaper. In closing, he said: "I will watch them."[1] By that he meant his spies would watch them and report to him, for no doubt McCook got the newspaper from a spy. All generals utilized spies for intelligence purposes, and McCook found them very useful. He had spies working undercover in General Braxton Bragg's headquarters.[2]

Keeping vigilant and advancing the Union cause was consistent with the pride McCook felt about his martial accomplishments. In another communication, he advised Fry that he had "four men in the mountains, neither of whom knows the others are there."[3] McCook was acting in accord with the prevailing practice: do not let a spy know that you have other spies out spying.

Colonel Fry was the chief of staff of Major General Don Carlos Buell, commander of the Army of the Ohio, the pride of the Northwest. It was looked upon as one of the greatest armies ever assembled in the world, having rescued Grant while scoring a major victory against the South at Shiloh. In the American mind its reputation and promise were greater than its eastern counterpart, the Army of the Potomac. The North could not have been faulted for wanting to raise its exalted band of fighters, like a noose, above the Rebel army.

Alex McCook was undoubtedly feeling good about himself just then, having been tested at Shiloh and promoted to major general on July 17, 1862, because of valorous service at that battle. He had done his part during the Corinth campaign, although neither McCook nor any other commander was asked to do much more than march and dig entrenchments. But that was all in the past. Now in command of the 1st Army Corps of the Army of the Ohio, he was Buell's "strong arm and willing heart,"[4] and he seemed anxious to stay in his commanding officer's good graces.

Daniel McCook, Jr.— now a colonel and no longer serving on his brother's staff, was in charge of the 36th Brigade, General Philip H. Sheridan's division of Major General Charles C. Gilbert's 3rd Army Corps. Daniel's youngest brother, Lieutenant John J. McCook, served on his staff. Major Anson G. McCook was also with Buell's army along with his 2nd Ohio Infantry Regiment in Brigadier General Lovell H. Rousseau's division. Anson had previously done a short stint with General McCook's division at Battle Creek, about 20 miles from Chattanooga. It was there that "Fort McCook" was created in honor of General Alexander M. McCook.[5]

The McCook family was riding a wave of success when tragedy struck. On August 5, 1862, while very sick and riding in a carriage, Brigadier General Robert L. McCook was overtaken by mounted Rebel guerrillas. While attempting to stop the carriage, he was shot and mortally wounded, the second McCook to die in the Civil War. He was 35 years old. McCook was traveling with a light escort about three miles in advance of the main body of his brigade when he was overtaken near New Market, Alabama.

His weakened physical condition combined with the ruthless manner in which he was overtaken and killed set off a firestorm of controversy throughout the federal army. The public and the press were also outraged, calling his death a cowardly assassination rather than an act of war. Expressions of sympathy to the McCook family flowed from the officers who served with the fallen general. Members of McCook's 9th Ohio, seeking revenge for the death of their beloved commander, scoured the countryside in the vicinity of the attack, burning and destroying property and randomly killing suspicious men.

A search for Robert L. McCook's killer eventually led to the arrest of Frank Gurley, allegedly a Confederate officer. Gurley was tried, convicted of murder and sentenced to hang, but through appeals from Confederate officials, his execution was postponed and he was eventually released from custody.

A sorrowful General Alexander M. McCook sought permission from General Buell to escort his brother's body home for burial. Buell refused to grant permission, saying, "It is painful to be compelled to refuse your request, but I feel that your services at this time are most important, indeed indispensable."[6] Buell was referring to the threat posed by a large Confederate army, now gathered in Tennessee. Since a major battle was expected, McCook understood and accepted the refusal in good faith, knowing that the need for his service in the field outweighed his desire to join his family and attend Robert's funeral and burial at Spring Grove Cemetery in Cincinnati.

The Confederate army that General McCook and General Buell were watching and were ready to fight was that of General Braxton Bragg, for the North Carolinian did indeed have plans for a major campaign against the North. In June he replaced General Pierre G. T. Beauregard whose towering ego and pie-in-the-sky ideas about running an army proved unsuitable to Jefferson Davis. Beauregard had neither the will nor the desire to handle the tedious, day-to-day grind of a field commander.

Bragg, on the other hand, seemed to be just the ticket, and by early August the Union brain trust knew that he was up to something big. McCook's spies reported seeing large numbers of Rebel troops boarding train cars. It was believed that Bragg was most likely headed for Nashville. As if expecting a hard march to catch Bragg, McCook wrote to Fry, saying, "For God's sake, send me all the shoes to spare and at once."[7]

Ensconced in Washington, D.C., but seemingly within yelling distance, Major General Henry W. Halleck was excited too, telling Buell to get moving. Halleck had assumed command of all the Union armies on the 23rd of July, and he wanted action. "There is great dissatisfaction here at the slow movement of your army toward Chattanooga. It is feared that the enemy will have time to concentrate his entire army against you." At this point it was believed that Bragg could be cut off at Chattanooga, and a great battle was expected there.[8]

Halleck's annual report indicates that the Union was fearful of the Confederate strength and discipline, along with its "rigidly enforced conscription." It was feared that the South was planning to invade and reestablish a strong presence in Arkansas, Missouri, Tennessee and Kentucky. And worse yet, the Rebels were looking to set foot in Ohio, Indiana and Illinois, "while our attention was distracted by the invasion of Maryland and Pennsylvania and an extended Indian insurrection on the western frontiers."[9]

Halleck was a stiff-necked but thin-skinned man who, as a field commander of the Corinth inchworm-like campaign, moved about as slow as any general in any war. As a desk commander, however, he expected his field generals to be more aggressive, to find the enemy and fight, so his impatience was really put to the test by Buell's deliberate attitude. Finally, tired of giving direction, he said simply: "March where you please, provided you will find the enemy and fight him."[10] He might have added "and defeat him," for above all else, Halleck hated the thought of losing, especially when the loss was accompanied by great losses of men and supplies.

Buell — every inch a soldier — did get marching, but not in time for a fight at Chattanooga. Instead he left his headquarters at Huntsville, Alabama, and came up through Tennessee intending to intercept Bragg somewhere along the way. To do so Buell needed to maintain pinpoint coordination with his division commanders. While on the move through Tennessee, McCook assured Buell he was ready for the enemy, and "if my cavalry do not fight you will never hear from them. I have given my infantry orders to shoot every one of them that runs to the rear."[11]

At Murfreesboro, Buell gathered his divisions together, expecting to meet Bragg in battle at or near Nashville. While at Murfreesboro, Buell's army was strengthened by two other divisions sent from the Army of the Tennessee. The concentration of all Buell's forces in one place allowed Bragg to select either Nashville or Louisville as his destination.

Bragg chose the latter. And in a bold and deceptive move, his troops marched from Chattanooga to Glasgow, Kentucky, 110 miles south of Louisville, in 17 days, destroying miles of railroad, burning bridges and tearing down telegraph lines as he progressed. Along the way he recaptured Munfordville and received the cheers from pro–Confederate folks in Lexington and Glasgow. He headed an army of five divisions consisting of about 35,000 men.

In a showy display of conceit, Bragg claimed that he was on his way to Kentucky to "liberate" its people from Yankee tyranny. He brought a large supply of extra rifles expecting that Kentucky boys would rally to his banner and join the Southern cause.[12] His true intent was to prevent Buell from carrying out his designs on Chattanooga.

Bragg's army moved in close coordination with that of General E. Kirby Smith, who at the head of about 9,000 troops had moved into central Kentucky from northeastern Tennessee. The two Southern generals had met in Chattanooga and come up with a plan of conquest. They wanted to reclaim middle Tennessee and invade and retake Kentucky, destroying as much infrastructure and supply lines as possible to keep Buell off guard, and maybe even draw U. S. Grant out of western Tennessee.[13]

Buell learned of Bragg's movements while in Murfreesboro. He was almost as alarmed as was Halleck, and it got him going. The Army of the Ohio had penetrated deep into Tennessee and northern Alabama and was forced to turn around and head north, thus giving up so much hard-gained territory. Taking Chattanooga would have to wait for another campaign. Moving forward with all possible speed, Buell pushed through Tennessee, stopping for a short time in Nashville. General McCook requested Buell's permission to burn Nashville, calling it the most "treasonable place in the Southern Country," with the exception of Murfreesboro.[14] Buell wisely denied the request, believing it was absolutely necessary for the Union to hold and preserve Nashville.

After leaving a strong force in Nashville, the Army of the Ohio pushed on in a desperate, all-out race with the enemy while the people of the North waited breathlessly. For a time both armies marched north through Tennessee on a roughly parallel course. Buell was aided by a packet of letters that were taken off a dead Rebel officer. The letters — which first fell into McCook's hands — explained Bragg's campaign plan.[15]

Using the letters and other resources at his disposal, Buell — with a smaller but formidable army — managed to reach Louisville ahead of Bragg, thus reestablishing a strong presence there. The forced march was one of the most punishing of the entire war, leaving scores of exhausted and footsore soldiers very unhappy with their commander. They cursed Buell and openly called him a traitor, or worse, as they marched through a wasteland. From Bowling Green to Louisville, the dusty trail was marked by dead animals and wrecked railroads. It was made worse by the lack of water and daily skirmishing. Despite the hardships, the miserable soldiers maintained a strong, steady pace toward their destination.

Not to be outdone, however, Bragg's army kept pace. The Rebels turned toward Frankfort, a Kentucky city that boasted the highest percentage of slaves (52 percent of the slave population) in the state. There he established a puppet government friendly to the Confederacy.[16] While "Governor" Richard C. Hawes, a fumbling old man, made his "inauguration" speech, the sounds of federal guns could be heard in the background. He finished talking and meekly went into hiding while Bragg took to the field.

The stage was set for a showdown over the ultimate control of the state of Kentucky. The rival generals were well acquainted, having fought with distinction as junior officers in the Mexican War. Both men were successful at West Point and each showed great promise. It was commonly believed that both were destined to move up in rank, to be leaders, although Don Carlos Buell was considered the best prospect of all.[17]

Buell was deliberate and a plodder, but he never lacked self-confidence. What he did lack, however, was public support. The Northern press made sure everyone knew that the Confederates were on the move in great numbers, and Bragg seemed to have a free hand to do what he wished. For this, people blamed Buell, cursing his slowness and ineptitude. Newspapers, politicians and ordinary citizens expressed no confidence in Buell, believing that he had mismanaged the best army ever given to a general and squandered a golden opportunity to strike a deadly blow against the South. Kentucky was being ravaged again and Indiana and Ohio were threatened, and a sense of fear and gloom pervaded the North.[18]

Buell's grand army consisted of approximately 58,000 effectives, of which number 22,000 were raw troops, lacking discipline and training.[19] It was divided into three corps, under the commands of McCook, Crittenden and Gilbert, from first to third, respectively. Major General George H. Thomas was second in command.

Bragg's army was divided into two wings, commanded by Major General Leonidas "the Bishop" Polk and Major General William J. Hardee. Although many of the troops were new to the army and therefore untested, morale was high and the boys were in good spirits.

Buell's Army of the Ohio, with Crittenden's division leading the way, entered Louisville on September 27. The men had marched a remarkable 120 miles in one week. Ragged and dirty, they were cheered by the civilians of Louisville and later fed and given fresh drinking water.[20]

On September 29, the last of Buell's divisions entered Louisville. The next day Buell was ready to move out and find Bragg when an order came from Halleck relieving him from duty and placing Major General George H. Thomas in command. This didn't sit well with Thomas, who liked and respected Buell, and he strongly objected to Halleck's move. So due to Thomas' insistence, Halleck rescinded his order, allowing Buell to resume command.[21] But the threat of removal hung over Buell's head, nevertheless.

As if Buell needed another headache, a violent quarrel between two generals left one dead and the other under arrest. Major General William "Bull" Nelson — one of the heroes of Shiloh — was Buell's man in charge of the defenses of Louisville, an important supply depot. Nelson was a member of an old and prominent Kentucky family and was instrumental in keeping his state in the Union. Lincoln was well served by Nelson in the early stages of the war, when the latter smuggled guns into Kentucky to arm the Union recruits.

Nelson was recovering from a battle wound when he returned to Louisville in order to beef up the defenses of that city. He was expected

Brigadier General Jefferson Davis, in a blue uniform, was not in any way related to the Confederate president of the same name. He spelled his first name "Jef" for the sole purpose of distancing himself from the Davis of the South. While he was a solid soldier and dedicated Unionist, his hotheaded nature almost proved to be his undoing. He shot and killed fellow general William "Bull" Nelson following a quarrel in a Louisville hotel. But due to strong political connections, Davis was never charged with a crime. Instead he was attached to General McCook's corps as a division commander.

to recover fully and return to duty as he was a huge man with a strong constitution and an aggressive temperament. Anson McCook described Nelson as a man known for his "peculiarities and eccentricities."[22]

The other general in the deadly affair, Brigadier General Jefferson C. Davis, was sent to Louisville by Major General Horatio G. Wright, the commander of the Department of the Ohio. Davis was assigned to take charge of the defenses of Louisville. Since he shared a first and last name with the pres-

General William Nelson was called "Bull" due to his hulking appearance, his frequent use of profanity and his aggressive fighting temperament. Lincoln found him useful in the early stages of the war, when Nelson secretly armed Union loyalists in Kentucky. He went on to serve with gallantry at Shiloh where he was wounded. During the Perryville campaign, Nelson was shot and killed by Jefferson Davis as a result of a bitter argument between the two Union generals.

ident of the Confederacy, Unionist Davis styled himself "Jef" to distinguish himself from the leader of the rebellion.

Nelson and Davis had vastly different personalities and physiques but had been on friendly terms, having served together in the Charleston, South Carolina, harbor in the late 1850s, and more recently at Corinth. At first everything went well as Nelson assigned Davis to the task of organizing an odd mix of local men into ranks of disciplined soldiers. But Davis chafed at having to do such undignified work, since he was regular army and a division commander. He began to question Nelson's authority. At the Galt House, the finest hotel in Louisville, the two men argued over the issue, and the hotheaded Nelson ordered Davis out of the city. A fuming and insulted Davis left Louisville and went to Jeffersonville, Indiana, just across the Ohio River, but was too angry to stay.

The next morning, the 28th, Davis was back in Louisville, the same day that the main body of Buell's army tramped into town. With him was a group of supporters including Indiana governor, Oliver P. Morton. Davis and his friends went to the Galt House looking for Nelson. About 7:30 A.M., they found him in the lobby, after he had just finished eating breakfast. Davis confronted Nelson in the great hall of the hotel and demanded an explanation for having been relieved of duty. Angry words were exchanged, and Nelson dismissed Davis by saying "go away you damned puppy."

This time the insult was unbearable. Davis reacted by crushing a calling card into a ball and flipping it into Nelson's face. Nelson, a hot-tempered man of brute strength, slapped the much smaller Davis and called him a coward. Davis turned toward his friends, was handed a revolver and without hesitation shot Nelson at point-blank range in the upper chest.

Nelson unsteadily made his way up the staircase and collapsed. He requested that someone get a minister. "I want to be baptized," he said. "I have been murdered." When his friend General Crittenden came to his side, Nelson said, "Tom, I am murdered." In a short time he was dead.[23]

Davis was placed under arrest as Kentuckians expressed outrage at the death of one of their own. Army officers, hardened by battlefield deaths, were shocked at the thought that one general could shoot and kill a fellow general. A mob quickly formed in the street near the Galt House, and there were threats to take Davis out and hang him. The town — and army — found itself divided into one group that lamented the loss of Nelson and another that sympathized with Davis. This led to a fistfight between Indiana Governor Morton and General Jeremiah Boyle. Morton was getting the worst of it when Alexander McCook took off his coat and broke up the fight, threatening to "head his division and 'clean out the town.'"[24] Soon after, order was restored.

The violent interlude and the uncertainty over the fate of General Davis was not sufficient to interfere with the need to engage in serious battle planning.

In fact the shooting was easily set aside during the state of emergency that had spread fear throughout Kentucky and across the river into Ohio. Keeping with their sense of duty, Buell and his generals soon relegated the Nelson tragedy to the back burner while concentrating on the threat posed by Bragg and his Confederates. Military justice could take care of Davis while Buell's army dealt with the Rebels.

CHAPTER 10

The Battle of Perryville

We are very sure that if he [General Buell] could have ordered supports for [Major General] McCook at an earlier hour than he did order them the attack would have been repulsed with less loss to himself and greater to the enemy.

— War Department, April 13, 1872

On October 1, 1862, Major General Don Carlos Buell's army moved out to find the enemy, marching toward Bardstown, Kentucky, to the tune and beat of fife and drum, where it was expected a fight would take place. Major General Henry W. Halleck found it necessary to "urge upon the importance of prompt action," fearing an attack on Cincinnati by a portion of General Braxton Bragg's command.[1] But Bragg backpedaled to Perryville without making a stand, perhaps looking for a more favorable place to fight. Buell's army marched forward in pursuit, and by the 7th found itself close to Perryville, a small town about 60 miles southeast of Louisville.

Up to this point, the main problem was obtaining drinking water in a hot, drought-stricken part of Kentucky. As a result, Union troops, dressed in new wool uniforms, suffered from heat and thirst, and finding water became a priority. Thirsty soldiers, desperate for a drink, were forced to slurp up muddy water from stagnant streams, some of which were contaminated by dead and rotting animals. An Illinois soldier called them "hog puddles" and complained that the men had to hold their noses when they drank the filthy liquid.[2]

It was expected that abundant water would be found at nearby Doctor's Creek, a tributary of the Chaplin River, and it was imperative that the Union secure the creek. The 11th Division of General Charles C. Gilbert's 3rd Army Corps under Brigadier General Philip H. Sheridan was given the task of taking possession of Doctor's Creek. Early on the morning of the 8th, Sheridan ordered the 36th Brigade commanded by Colonel Daniel McCook, Jr., with a battery of artillery, to cross the creek and secure it. It was soon discovered that in order to claim the creek, it was necessary to take and control the range of hills that fronted the Chaplin River. For this Sheridan brought up an additional brigade of infantry and another battery of artillery.

According to Sheridan, there was little resistance from the Rebels, and soon the hills were under Union control and a much-needed water supply was at hand.[3] Colonel McCook's report, however, notes that while his "regiments were fresh from their homes they moved steadily up the hill driving the enemy, who contested warmly every step."[4] This was the beginning of the battle of Perryville.

Sheridan's men started digging in to establish a position, annoyed constantly by Rebel sharpshooters. He found it necessary to send a brigade to chase them away, and in doing so discovered a large body of Confederates formed in a battle line on the opposite side of the Chaplin River. Then, while standing on high ground, he spotted on his left the 1st Army Corps led by Major General Alexander M. McCook marching forward on the Mackville road toward the Confederate battle line, apparently totally unaware of the presence of the enemy.

Sheridan tried to get the attention of someone in McCook's corps by using his signal flags but was unsuccessful. A short time later, the leading regiment was under heavy attack as if it had been delivered up to the enemy, setting off a battle that the Army of the Ohio was not just then expecting.[5] With soldiers falling like cut grain, it didn't take long for McCook and his men to realize they were in a desperate fight.

The day was not unfolding in accordance with Buell's plan. A battle was not expected until the next day. Buell had given written instructions to McCook, telling him to march at 3 A.M., "precisely," and pull up even with Gilbert about three and a half miles from Perryville, conduct a reconnaissance of the area, find water if possible and get his troops settled in for the night, but "do not permit them to scatter." After these tasks were completed, McCook was to report in person to Buell for further instructions.[6]

Instead of a quiet evening spent in anticipation of a battle the next day, McCook and his men were caught up in a wild and desperate fight. From the measured tone of McCook's report of the battle, however, it is clear that he understood and followed Buell's instructions, even though he started about two hours late. McCook marched at five o'clock in the morning of October 8, 1862, with just two of his divisions, the other (Sill's 2nd Division) having been detached to march on Frankfort to monitor Confederate general Kirby Smith. Brigadier General Lovell H. Rousseau, whose 3rd Division contained the more experienced troops, took the lead, marching with extreme caution, "having heard previously that the enemy were in force at Harrodsburg."

When his men pulled up abreast of Gilbert's 3rd Army Corps, McCook methodically went about positioning his forces, marking out his line of battle and arranging the artillery. He ordered General Rousseau to send a line of skirmishers to examine the woods that lay to the front and left of his divisions.

McCook, following instructions, then rode off to report to Buell who was situated about two and a half miles to the rear. He arrived at about 12:30. Since Buell was not expecting an attack until the next day, he ordered McCook to conduct a reconnaissance of the Chaplin River in order to secure much-needed water. Returning to his corps, McCook "went forward in person to the high ground overlooking a portion of Chaplin River" and "advanced to within 600 yards of the river, and saw the water." It was bad water, but drinkable.

McCook then sent for two of his brigade commanders, Brigadier General James S. Jackson and Brigadier General William R. Terrell, showed them the water, and marked off their line of battle supported by an artillery battery. He ordered Terrell to advance his brigade downhill toward the water, led by a body of skirmishers. McCook recalled seeing no enemy troops while standing on the high ground, except for some cavalry on the hills on the opposite side of the river. These were scattered by a few well-placed artillery rounds. "Not being apprehensive of an attack, I left this position and moved toward the right of the line." That was about 1:30 in the afternoon.

McCook then decided to ride into the woods where he sent the skirmishers, but Jackson urged him not to go. He (Jackson) said "Providence had been kind to me and that some lurking scoundrel might shoot me." Acting on intuition, McCook changed his mind and did not enter the woods.

Within half an hour, McCook's left was under a fierce assault that began with an attack on the 33rd Ohio Infantry, the skirmishers he sent into the woods toward Doctor's Creek. Buell was wrong; Bragg had ordered an attack. McCook immediately reinforced the 33rd with two other regiments, including Major Anson G. McCook's 2nd Ohio. Terrell's brigade absorbed the worst of the initial attack. Still, according to General McCook, Terrell did "everything in the power of a man" to rally and lead his men. General Terrell was hit by a shell that blew away part of his chest, and the survivor of the battle of Shiloh died at 2 A.M. the next morning.

General Jackson, whose uncanny warning kept McCook away from the surprise attack, was killed in the first few minutes of firing. To Lieutenant Colonel John Beatty, it seemed that the sky was on fire with bullets, shells and explosions, like "all hell had broken loose."[7] The fighting was furious, characterized by desperate bayonet charges and surging masses of struggling men, grappling hand to hand amid the noise and fine madness of war.

By 2:30 P.M. McCook realized he was under attack by a force that outnumbered his troops by three to one. The ground they fought on was that chosen by the Confederates, and McCook was a stranger to it. The area was characterized by hills and deep ravines that allowed Rebel troops to hide and attack at will. It was ideally situated for an ambush. McCook believed that

Bragg himself was on hand to conduct the battle aided by the corps of Leonidas Polk and William J. Hardee.

Out-generaled and out-gunned, with everything working against him, McCook was in big trouble and he knew it. So he dispatched his aide-de-camp, First Lieutenant L. M. Hosea, to General Sheridan of Gilbert's left division for assistance on his right. At 3 P.M. he dispatched another aide, Captain Horace N. Fisher, to the "nearest commander of troops for assistance." Captain Fisher met Brigadier General Schoepf and reported the condition of McCook's pinned-down soldiers. Schoepf referred Captain Fisher to Gilbert who referred him to Buell.

McCook's report does not reveal what, if anything at all, his aides were able to accomplish. However, judging from the way in which the battle progressed and ended, the aides' efforts were ineffective and in vain. By the time contact was finally made with Buell, it was late in the afternoon and most of the damage had been done. When told about the rout of McCook's corps, Buell was perplexed, thinking the news was exaggerated. Nevertheless, he ordered Gilbert to send two brigades to assist McCook who was desperately trying to piece together a defense against Bragg's fresh, well-organized regiments.

While his aides were out looking for help, McCook remained in the "rear of my left center" until he witnessed the Union right completely routed and driven back. He then rode off to his right to discover that it was "turned by a large force of the enemy." A disaster was in the making. Men and officers were being shot up — dying quickly or slowly, but with soldierly anonymity, and still the Union forces fought gallantly and skillfully. Soon, Rousseau's "line was compelled to fall back" to prevent it from being annihilated by the enemy.[8]

Among Rousseau's regiments, Major Anson G. McCook's 2nd Ohio was in the thick of it. After his horse — a high-spirited black Morgan called "Nig" — was shot and wounded, Major McCook found a gun beside the body of a dead man. He fell in line and, shoulder to shoulder with his privates, fired upon the enemy, to the inspiration of his men. McCook shot a Rebel who was about to bayonet a wounded Yankee. In the next instant, another Rebel described as "a burly rebel, weighing over 200 pounds," took aim at McCook from close range. Just then Private William H. Surles stepped in front of his commander, fired and killed the enemy soldier, thus saving Anson G. McCook's life. Surles was later awarded the Congressional Medal of Honor for conspicuous gallantry.[9]

The day was finally saved by the timely and skillful use of the big guns, along with the fortuitous arrival of two brigades from General Robert M. Mitchell's 9th Division from Gilbert's corps. McCook ordered them in battle line and along with their artillery "repulsed the wicked attack for the first time." By this time it was nearly dark and still there was no sign of Buell or members of his staff. Mercifully, both sides ceased fire. At last it was quiet.

Believing the attack would be renewed the next morning, McCook spent much of the evening preparing for it, arranging the alignment of his exhausted and hungry troops — troops that fought all day with little or no water.

The sun set bright red against a cloudless sky, a dramatic and mocking reminder of the blood that was still leaking from bodies and soaking into the ground. The sun was replaced by moonlight so illuminating that it was possible for the shooters to pick their targets and the fighting could have recommenced. But there was to be no more fighting at Perryville, called by McCook the battle of Chaplin Hills, as the Confederates pulled out during the night, taking with them the rifles intended for recruits that never materialized. The withdrawal also meant that the South would never again seriously threaten Kentucky. That much was accomplished primarily by McCook's portion of the Army of the Ohio.

A total of five McCooks participated in the Perryville campaign: General Alexander M. McCook and his brothers Daniel and John, along with cousins Anson and Edward, whose cavalry brigade patrolled the front.[10] They were all burdened by the loss of Robert L. McCook, killed by Rebels that summer. No doubt they all felt and shared the pain of their loss, but none of them excused themselves because of it.

General McCook termed it the "bloodiest battle of modern times for the number of troops engaged on our side," approximately 14,000. His casualty list was high and he closed his report by lamenting the loss of Generals Terrell and Jackson and so many others. McCook commended many of his men and officers, especially those of Rousseau, saying, "If there are or ever were better soldiers than the old troops engaged I have neither seen nor read of them."[11] As he did at Shiloh, Rousseau came through doing all that was expected of him and more.

Colonel Daniel McCook, whose brigade spent much of the afternoon on the hills above the furious battle below, was forced to watch Rousseau's division under attack. In his testimony at the post-battle inquiry, Colonel McCook was upset that Gilbert pulled his (McCook's) brigade out of line at about 2 P.M., and ordered it back upon the hill from its position in the woods, because his troops were "raw." Once in position on the hills that it took earlier that morning, the brigade withstood two Rebel attacks. Then, with the division and two batteries lying idle, Daniel McCook said he "begged General Sheridan to at least allow us to open on them with artillery." The request was denied by Sheridan acting through Gilbert. McCook was told that this action "might concentrate the fire of the enemy's artillery upon our troops." McCook's response was that the troops could have been moved out of harm's way simply by taking them down the slope.[12] Finally, after watching Rousseau's men "pulverized" by Rebel artillery, Sheridan authorized Colonel McCook to open up on the enemy.

Colonel McCook later found out that at about 2:15 that afternoon, Rousseau had sent a dispatch stating that he was being attacked, and that the dispatch went through the signal office, meaning that Gilbert, or someone on his staff, knew of the attack. Learning this made the high-strung McCook extremely angry, resulting in a "burst of indignation of mine, coupled with a few oaths, demanding of General Sheridan why we were ordered out of those woods."[13] The larger question, of course, was why a division was lying idle when it was obvious that those fighting needed help. It was pointless to obey an order "not to bring on an engagement" when a fierce battle was well under way.

Clearly, Dan McCook wanted to help his brother, but he also wanted to get into the fight because he saw an opportunity to attack the flank and rear of the enemy. He believed that there had been an inexcusably poor exercise of leadership at the battle of Perryville. And while he didn't name names, it was certain that the main target of his criticism was General Gilbert.

Others were equally critical. A member of the 9th Ohio Infantry regiment, serving in Gilbert's corps, recalled, "Our division, ready to attack, waited in reserve, idle," while General McCook and his corps "practically fought the battle themselves." The men were eager to move forward and "reinforce McCook," but the order never came. Moreover, several brigades were idle and unable to attack, "and without orders to attack!" After waiting all day, darkness fell and it was too late.[14]

While General McCook must have felt that Gilbert and the rest of the army failed him, his report is calm and businesslike, free from rancor and with no indication of who was to blame for the calamity.[15] He gave praise and credit where both were due, and laid down some mild criticism for less-than-stellar performance of a few officers and some "green" troops from Jackson's division. He knew that someone else would assign blame for what went wrong that day. Although he was bloodied badly, he was not forced to retreat, so no one could claim he "lost" the battle.

If the Union effort suffered from mistakes and indecision, the Confederates were just as bad. Bragg lacked sufficient intelligence to launch an effective attack. Instead he repeated the futile tactics he pursued at Shiloh, hurling large groups of men *en masse* into the brunt of enemy fire. His losses were staggering. Because his men fought hard and with gallantry, the Rebels drove the surprised Yankees back and gave Bragg a chance to win.

It was not to be, however, and since the Confederates left the field of battle in despair and disarray, the Union could claim victory. Many newspapers jumped on a few details and rumors and wrote it up as a win, including the *New York Times*, which declared "VICTORY IN KENTUCKY" on October 11, 1862. The article offered very few details, stating only that Buell attacked Bragg and after a "short but terrific fight" the Rebels retreated with federal troops in pursuit. It was rumored that Bragg, himself, was killed.

All this proved to be wrong, of course, but it would take some time for the newspapers to catch up with what really happened along the Chaplin River that October day. Bragg, far from dead, summed it up succinctly, stating, "The ground was literally covered with his [McCook's] dead." In addition to the men they killed, the Rebels managed to capture some 400 prisoners and the "servants, carriage and baggage of Major-General McCook." Bragg's report comes off like a claim of victory, but he was forced to acknowledge the awful nature of the battle, calling it "the severest and most desperately contested engagement within my knowledge."[16]

Knowing that he was greatly outnumbered by the Army of the Ohio, Bragg retreated toward Harrodsburg ten miles to the north, to join the division under General Kirby Smith. Smith favored staying and fighting, because their combined forces evened the odds, but Bragg vetoed the idea. He had just fought one of Buell's three corps to a standstill and understood that a retreat was preferable to fighting the entire Union army. Furthermore, young Kentuckians failed to join his army, and he was greatly disappointed; Kentucky would have to do without Bragg's help.

On the Union side, Buell did not mount a pursuit. He lacked the ability to arm and feed his soldiers sufficiently so as to launch another battle. He was too far from his base of operations and lacked the resources to haul supplies over the great distance.

Bragg and his army departed Kentucky in a fit of anger, feeling betrayed by the people they came to "rescue." Unwilling to accept that most Kentuckians favored the Union or just wanted to be left alone, the Confederates left the state, seeking only revenge and retribution. One unit captured 12 men and hanged them, one at a time, from a convenient tree branch.[17]

Brigadier General Phil Sheridan, who had a limited role in the battle, had a negative view of the fight and the outcome. In his memoirs he states that the troops under the command of Major General George H. Thomas and Brigadier General Thomas L. Crittenden were idle that day "for want of orders," although near enough to participate. And much of Gilbert's corps also stayed on the sidelines (or, as was the case with Daniel McCook's brigade, were ordered there). While he did not fault General McCook, or anyone else, the battle of Perryville, he wrote rather vaguely, "remains in history an example of lost opportunities."[18] It is also the history of the 916 Union soldiers killed that day, nearly all of them from McCook's corps.

While the common soldier was not privy to statistics and the reports of their commanding officers, information nevertheless, made its way down to their level by way of the "grapevine telegraph." After the battle of Perryville, the foot soldiers that did the fighting learned that "Buell got mad at McCook for bringing on the battle without his orders, and he left him to fight it out without his help."[19] Anger permeated the ranks of the Army of the Ohio over the manner in which the fight was fought, much of it directed at Buell. The biographer of the 9th Ohio said Buell's "garish torpor at Perryville" matched his "glaring lassitude at Shiloh."[20]

Journalist and historian Whitelaw Reid thought McCook was the responsible culprit. In his two-volume history about Ohio and the Civil War, he states McCook "brought on the battle of Perryville, contrary to the spirit of his instructions and before the army was prepared to sustain him."[21] Reid, however, had an unfriendly run-in with McCook prior to Perryville, so it is possible he may have been influenced by that experience when he faulted his fellow Ohioan.

The blame game has been going on for a long time. The writer of an excellent history of the Army of the Ohio, after a detailed analysis of the battle, all but cleared Buell of responsibility and laid it squarely at McCook's feet for his "refusal to make timely calls for help." Instead of sending riders out to Gilbert and to the nearest commander in the area, he contends that McCook should have directed an aide to go directly to Buell. By failing to do so, McCook "put the entire army at risk."[22]

In his unpublished memoir, Anson G. McCook, who fought that day, saw it differently. He leveled harsh criticism at Buell while strongly defending his cousin Alexander, whom he openly admired. He insisted that Buell knew that General McCook had made contact with the enemy and that there was no excuse for not sending someone on a 15-minute ride from his (Buell's) headquarters to McCook's position to become fully apprised of the emergency. For further proof, Anson said Henry Villard, a correspondent with the *New York Herald*, who was present at the battle, later wrote in his memoir that Buell was "informed by signal message as early as two o'clock of the rebel attack upon McCook," and did nothing.[23]

In a time when newspaper reporters were not held in high repute, Villard was one of the exceptions, for he commanded some respect. He spent eight months with Buell on the various campaigns of the Army of the Ohio, and none other than President Lincoln met with Villard to sound him out. After his tenure with Buell ended, Villard sat down with the president and answered every question asked of him, talking about "the principal commanders under Buell," speaking with "entire frankness." The president asked him to return, for Lincoln found young reporters like Villard to be most useful. Apparently Lincoln did not hear anything about McCook that would cause him to discipline or relieve the general following Perryville.[24]

Lieutenant Colonel John Beatty, whose Ohio regiment was one of the units that bore the brunt of the Rebel attack, came away from the battle feeling less than glorious about it. He blamed "McCook's foolish haste" for the carnage that took place and censured Buell for "being slow." He openly disliked West-Pointer General Alexander M. McCook. Beatty, who styled himself as a "citizen soldier," suggested that "petty jealousies" were the cause of the slaughter of so many good men, so badly used up by poor leadership.[25]

The top brass took a similar view and ordered an inquiry into Buell's conduct and lack of action. Where was Buell, and what was he doing, while McCook's men were being shot to pieces? Why did he not send help? How could he not hear the sounds of battle only two and a half miles away? Buell, of course, had his side of the story that he later defended with great vigor.

McCook's father was "concerned about some report" that Buell, Crittenden and Rousseau were "in Louisville together and he feared they were doing something against Alexander." As such, Daniel McCook, Sr. — who always went to extraordinary means to promote his sons — assumed a protective stance. But George W. McCook called the report nonsense because it was clear that Bragg "made the attack," and besides, Crittenden would never be a party to the backstabbing of his friend.[26] Nevertheless, with questions mounting, all knew that an inquiry was at hand.

A commission was formed that included Major General Lewis "Lew" Wallace, who was under official scrutiny because of his conduct at Shiloh, Brigadier General Edward O. C. Ord, and of all people, Brigadier General Albin Schoepf, who had served under Buell on the day of the battle of Perryville. Their purpose was twofold: examine Buell's conduct at the battle and consider his failure to pursue and destroy Bragg when the opportunity was ripe. Since McCook was a major player in the battle, he became a flash point at the inquiry and testified in great detail under heavy and tedious questioning.

After he was sworn in, McCook proceeded to explain in great, mind-numbing detail — such as only a general in the army could appreciate — each and every road and route he took on his way to Perryville, being careful to mention all the bridges, creeks and hills he crossed. After an exhaustive survey of his long march, the questioning began on specifics.

McCook was permitted to range far and wide in his responses when he chose to do so, subject to objections, of course, by Buell or members of the commission. At one point he interjected that Buell was "the most uncommunicative general I have ever seen or heard of." McCook explained that he only assumed the Army of the Ohio was headed for Kentucky, because he believed that Bragg was going there; he was never told of their destination. He also complained that he was not sufficiently informed as to the location of other units.

McCook had a hard rebuke for Gilbert too. Had he secured the cooperation of Gilbert, the battle, he said, could have resulted in a "complete victory." Gilbert's forces were near enough, no more than 350 yards away. But Gilbert was nowhere to be seen when the fighting was fierce and deadly. McCook testified: "I thought it was his duty to cooperate with me on that day. It is the duty of a general to relieve a brother general, whatever his orders may be."

When asked about his post-battle meeting with Buell, McCook spoke at great length, expressing the frustration he felt at the time, having just endured a tough fight. Buell, he said, expressed surprise, saying he knew nothing of the battle until 5 P.M. that day. McCook castigated Buell for refusing the loan of even one brigade to bolster his position that night of the battle. "He told me I should not have another man. I was at that time very much vexed and provoked." McCook felt he was entitled to assistance, for his men were exhausted and hungry and because he expected to be attacked the next morning.

McCook was questioned about the lack of pursuit of the enemy following the battle. Did he know of any reason why Bragg's battered army was not run down and defeated? "No reason, whatever," he replied. "I believe they should have been vigorously pursued the next morning at daylight." While this was damning testimony, Buell made no comment, but he later had plenty to say.

McCook continued to testify, answering questions seemingly without hesitation, speaking like a confident man, like a good soldier who did his duty and was entitled to be proud about it. Although the line of questioning didn't seem to fit a pattern, and much of it seemed irrelevant and far ranging, his responses were consistent with his reports, and he was never cross-examined in a way that suggested the commission was questioning his veracity. Overall his testimony hurt Buell in some ways, but McCook was equally quick to defend his commander. Buell, he said, was expert in matters of organization and discipline, and was a tireless worker. "I believe General Buell's army was the best ever put in the field ... there was never a more untiring general than General Buell."

When asked about the influence of the newspapers on the morale of the army, McCook responded with a few testy and off-the-wall remarks about reporters who followed the army. He recalled that a certain "pest" of a correspondent called Buell an "ass," and for that, McCook sought to expel him from camp. Reporters, he said, are "the worst enemies of the army," giving away critical information to the enemy. "I had a correspondent of the *Cincinnati Gazette* arrested and put out of the army because he published things he had no business to."[27] While it was not relevant to the subject of the inquiry, McCook left no doubt about his opinion of the press and its role in the war, and relished the chance to condemn it.

The commission members took turns questioning McCook, who remained sharp throughout the proceedings. Each officer seemed to have his own area of interest whether it was in troop movements, the size of each army or more pointed matters such as dissatisfaction of the men.

When asked about a petition regarding the removal of Buell, McCook said he never saw that piece of paper. He quickly made it known that there was a general feeling of discontent among the men on the march from Nashville to Louisville. "They [the troops] complained of being marched to death and of being half fed." He also said that Buell spent too much time in his quarters and too little time circulating among the men, and felt that "had he visited his camps more, reviewed his troops more, and shown himself more to his soldiers, a different state of feeling would have existed."[28]

The general consensus among many of Buell's officers was that he lost the luster he gained at Shiloh, and over time, their respect for him diminished. Brigadier General J. B. Steedman was questioned by the commission and echoed this sentiment, and for good measure added a bit of unique testimony about McCook's attitude toward Buell. One day while engaged in conversation with a group of officers, McCook slammed his fist on Steedman's knee and blurted out, "Don Carlos won't do, he won't do. General, there is considerable feeling in the army on the subject."[29]

What did testimony such as this have to do with an analysis of the battle of Perryville and its aftermath? Well, nothing, maybe, but the commission was giving Buell a thorough examination and making an overall evaluation of his ability to command. Finally, after slogging through reams of seemingly irrelevant and repetitious testimony, much of it speculative and conflicting, the commission summed up its findings.

First of all, the commission ruled that "there can be no question about its being the duty of somebody to assist McCook." His corps was being chewed to pieces while thousands of other soldiers sat idle. It was simply a matter of then determining who was in a position to come to the rescue.

Gilbert was deemed to be the guilty party in that regard. The commission took Gilbert to task rather roughly for his failure to fully reenforce McCook when so requested. He was judged to have been close enough to McCook's men to be aware of the desperate situation. Sending a mere two brigades late in the day was insufficient relief. Since he was a West Point graduate in the class of 1846, who served with distinction at Shiloh and Wilson's Creek (in Missouri) where he was severely wounded, a better performance was expected of him.

McCook was not free from blame either, as the commission was of the "opinion that General McCook's failure to send up instant notice of the attack upon him in force was equally culpable." There was testimony from Colonel J. B. Fry, Buell's chief of staff, that McCook's aide-de-camp did not arrive with news of the battle until about 4:30 P.M.[30] There was also some question about McCook's failure to conduct proper reconnaissance that might have revealed the location and number of enemy troops.

But the sternest rebuke was for Major General Don Carlos Buell, in command and therefore the one to bear ultimate responsibility for the success or failure of the campaign. The commission found that he should have been on the field of battle, having heard the sound of artillery about 2 P.M. that October 8. Instead of checking it out, he blithely dismissed it as a waste of ammunition. His willingness to fight Bragg and his loyalty were called into question by witnesses who suggested he favored the South.

In this regard Buell was handicapped because he once owned slaves. And if that wasn't bad enough, he openly favored returning runaway slaves to their masters, so he was not liked by abolitionists and their newspaper allies. Although in March of 1862, Congress passed legislation forbidding army officers from allowing slave hunters to take runaways, Buell openly defied the order. This caused dissension in the ranks of the Army of the Ohio as a growing number of officers and enlisted men were opposed to slavery and the Buell policy.

Anson McCook was among them. He once refused to turn over a fugitive slave and ordered a slave hunter out of his camp with a stern warning to permanently stay away. Anson took the anti–Buell position that black men who voluntarily entered the lines of the regiment "were under the protection of the flag and ... free men."[31]

For an example of Buell's unsympathetic attitude toward blacks, his opponents could point to the harsh order he issued to General McCook on June 21, 1862. McCook's division was crossing the Tennessee River near Tuscumbia, when Buell ordered him to prevent fleeing slaves from getting across the river, thereby stranding large numbers of black people who were then exposed to recapture and retribution by angry slaveholders.[32]

In sum, the officers in charge of Buell's fate and future learned too much that they didn't like about him. They said: "In our judgment the opportunity slipped through General Buell's absence from the field or on account of his ignorance of the condition of the battle."[33] Buell could have excused his "absence from the field," for the day before the battle he was thrown from his horse and suffered a dangerous cut in his thigh. But he was not a complainer and, to his credit, never used his injury as a mitigating factor, and besides, there was no excuse for failing to send members of his staff to McCook's position.

It was later determined that due to an unusual natural phenomenon known as an "acoustic shadow," caused by the wind and the peculiar topography of the area, Buell did not hear the terrible sounds of battle so close by, aside from the artillery barrage early in the afternoon. Buell later wrote that he "received with astonishment" the information that severe fighting had commenced, for he had not heard so much as a musket shot. He reasoned that the lack of knowledge of the raging battle was "probably caused by the configuration of the ground, which broke the sound, and by the heavy wind which it appears blew from the right to the left during the day."[34] But all this information was not available to the commission, and that body made its decision on the testimony of its witnesses along with pertinent documentation, thereby sealing Buell's fate.

He was ruled guilty of serious omissions on the field of battle, and that, coupled with his unpopularity among the troops and some officers, sealed his fate. It was essentially an inglorious end to an otherwise meritorious military career by a proud, professional soldier who was fired because he wasn't quite good enough. There was no hard evidence that he was disloyal or sympathetic to the South despite his "soft war" approach, and he was brought down by circumstances and unpopularity more than lack of ability.

It could also be said that Buell was ousted by bad luck and low-grade intelligence. And the same could be said of Bragg. While both armies were out and about, feeling out the area for each other, a portion of each unexpectedly met, and upon contact ignited the bloody battle of Perryville. Buell was wrong for concluding that he was confronted by Bragg's entire army, and Bragg was mistaken for thinking that only a portion of his adversary's army was in place. And to top it off, it was the elemental need for water that brought both sides to the Chaplin River where so many met their deaths in the heat and dust of a Kentucky autumn. It was like some unavoidable tragedy, or as one soldier said, "enough to make angels weep."

The lack of water put an even more tragic spin on the battle of Perryville. It meant that surgeons patched up wounds and cut off limbs for two days, almost non-stop, without washing their hands. Thus the risk of gangrene was even higher than usual in that season of suffering.[35] Rushing about among the piles of blackened and mutilated dead, looking for wounded to treat, the medical personnel had to deal with buzzards and animals that were chewing on corpses. George W. McCook said that some wounded men waited for as much as a week for treatment.[36] An Indiana soldier recalled how awful it was to "witness such a smell of human beings and the hogs eating the dead bodies," proving that the sideshow of the war was more macabre than the main event.[37]

The Civil War challenged, tested, humbled and crushed many good and well-meaning men on both sides of the conflict. Compared to the many that were brought down by a combination of misfortune or bad judgment, few have been elevated to the status of heroes. Few were those who came through unscathed by the righteous harping historians. Far too many men had their Civil War record defined by a single incident.

Buell accepted his fate, believing on principle that he had chosen the best course of action as a commanding general. He chose not to turn and strike at Bragg because much of the army consisted of "raw and undisciplined" troops, and he wanted to wait until Sill's division arrived, for then he would have his entire army together. Further, he would have faced an enemy with an equal number of men, on ground that was selected for the occasion. Buell later reflected, "I am not willing to admit that I might have failed." But he wanted to leave an impression: could another man be so certain of success under the circumstances?

He wrote thoughtfully, "In my judgment the commander merits condemnation, who, from ambition or ignorance or a weak submission to the dictation of popular clamor, and without necessity or profit, has squandered the lives of his soldiers."[38] But "popular clamor" was that he lacked aggression and failed to lead, and for those reasons, he was loser in the public mind and guilty in the opinion of the commission.

Nor was Buell the only one brought down by the commission. During the inquiry Gilbert was ridiculed by General Ord who referred to him as a mere captain, a "quartermaster or assistant quartermaster, disguised ... in a major general's uniform." Another witness accused Gilbert of denying his parched men a drink of water from a supply he kept all to himself and his staff. "He had a guard over it and would not let them have a drink."[39] Thought to be petty, quarrelsome and unqualified as well as a miserable failure and a fraud, Charles C. Gilbert was relieved and was never given a field command, doing desk duty for the remainder of the war. He joined the growing ranks of trashed officers.

Alexander M. McCook survived with his rank and position intact, although his reputation was slightly wounded. But he recovered, kept his command and the way was shown for him to redeem himself in future battles. After all, he was a fighter and Lincoln needed aggressive men who would fight.

In the years that followed, men affected by the events of October 8, 1862, would rethink and refight the battle of Perryville. Arguments, recriminations, charges and counter-charges were hurled about like canister and grape. The level of anger and disappointment never seemed to diminish, and Perryville was not without its ghosts. Anson McCook was one of those who couldn't get it out of his craw. Thinking about the ill-starred battle with his cousin Alex in mind, he wrote: "Although over forty years have passed since that October day in 1862, it is difficult to write with moderation in regard to the indifference shown to the many appeals for help."

CHAPTER 11

Rosecrans Takes Command

Press them hard! Drive them out of their nests! Make them fight or run!
— Major General William S. Rosecrans

Following the bloodletting at Perryville, the Union army limped south into Tennessee, as if it had suffered a defeat. Actually, the Army of the Ohio under Major General Don Carlos Buell succeeded in driving the Confederates out of Kentucky and appeared to be in a halfhearted pursuit of the enemy. But this result was lost on the public and press, and Buell received no credit for keeping Kentucky under Union control. Instead he was blamed for allowing General Braxton Bragg and his Southern army to escape into Tennessee after the battle of Perryville. The crushing blow was not delivered, and President Lincoln relieved Buell of command on October 30, 1862, less than three weeks after the Union victory at Perryville.

Buell — who lacked rapport with the common soldier and was compromised by his pro-slavery attitude — was replaced by Major General William S. Rosecrans, a man who many thought would motivate and inspire the Army of the Ohio to great achievement. Rosecrans accepted his assignment with grace and dignity, and with kind words to the man he replaced. In a letter he praised Buell knowing that the outgoing general was too "true a soldier to permit this to produce any feelings of personal unkindness between us." Rosecrans described himself as "neither an intriguer nor a newspaper soldier," but rather a soldier who goes "where I am ordered."[1]

Rosecrans was a West Pointer, having graduated fifth out of 56 in 1842. Just the opposite of the quiet and moody Buell, Rosecrans was a colorful, fiery and flighty man of great intellectual capacity. He was learned, versatile, articulate and liked to talk. His subordinates soon learned the loquacious general was also an energetic and voracious worker who needed little sleep. He was usually the first officer on his feet in the morning and the last to get into his blankets at night.

Prior to taking charge of the Army of the Ohio, Rosecrans distinguished himself in western Virginia, where he commanded an army that kept General Robert E. Lee at bay, and at Corinth, Mississippi, where he served under Major General U. S. Grant after Halleck moved on to Washington, D.C. Rosecrans came to Tennessee fresh from an October 4 victory at Corinth, having saved the town for the Union and kept Grant's lines of communication open.[2]

Big things were expected of the mercurial and brainy Rosecrans. Because of his success in the early stages of the war, he was popular in the public mind, and some would say the popularity went to his head. He was not above playing army politics, and it galled him that other generals whom he considered inferior, such as Don

Major General William S. Rosecrans was appointed to command the Army of the Ohio following the battle of Perryville. He brought impressive credentials to the position, having been successful in the western Virginia campaign. Much was expected of the talkative, energetic and deeply religious Ohioan with a workaholic attitude toward running an army.

Carlos Buell, Thomas Crittenden and Lew Wallace, were senior in rank. While these men would pose no impediment to his climb up the Union ladder, Rosecrans' icy relationship with the iron-willed General U. S. Grant opened the door for a future collision.

Rosecrans took charge of an army in bad shape, populated by demoralized, angry, unpaid men in the mood to desert. It was believed that about 7,000 of Rosecrans' soldiers were absent without leave, about one-third of his total force.[3] But the flashy Rosecrans seemed inspired by the mess he inherited, and on November 4, 1862, he ordered his troops out of their camp. Their lethargy shaken off, the army marched along the Green River toward Nashville, with the right wing of the army under Major General Alexander M. McCook leading the way. The Confederate forces having retreated to Murfreesboro, about 35 miles to the southeast, the Union army took charge of Nashville, where Rosecrans established his headquarters.

According to a reporter for the *New York Times* who accompanied the army, the city of Nashville bore a sad and desolate appearance that only war can cause, having been reinvaded and reoccupied by the Union army. The listless streets and their neglected structures were in bad shape; scores of trees were cut down for firewood. Most of the "prominent" families had vacated the city, and males in general were in short supply, leaving a largely female population that heaped verbal abuse on the hated Yankees. Like a blue tide, General Rosecrans' "grand army" poured into the conquered city in waves, turning the erstwhile distinctive Southern city, once again, into an armed camp. Its churches, schools, asylums, colleges, hotels and mansions were quickly occupied by the troops, and its warehouses were raided for food and supplies.

The state capitol building — its landscaping unfinished — that once rang out with Southern anger and defiance was now under the quiet control of the military governor Andrew Johnson, who was working "day and night to restore the civil laws of his State."[4] Elsewhere in the building, the *Times* reporter was impressed by the sight of scores of sick soldiers in dirty, tattered uniforms who sought some form of comfort, lounging amid their rusty weapons, knapsacks and blankets. The Union army settled in as best it could in the city that General Alexander M. McCook wanted to burn during the first occupation.

Rosecrans' entire army consisted of about 35,000 men. Despite the *Times* reporter's uplifting description, it was far from "grand." Sensing this, Rosecrans immediately set out to whip his sick and tired army into shape, asking his generals to instill a sense of discipline, order and pride. A strict routine was adopted including regular drilling. He set an example; he challenged his soldiers and officers. He cared about the men and staffed his army with plenty of doctors and chaplains. The troops responded having found a commander they liked and respected. They nicknamed their talkative and amiable general "Rosy."

Rosecrans' army was reorganized and divided into three "wings," each under a commander of major general rank. The left wing was commanded by Major General Thomas L. Crittenden, the center by Major General George H. Thomas, and the right by Major General Alexander M. McCook. Despite having been hit hard at Perryville, McCook was not demoted or relieved of duty but granted more onerous responsibilities. His ability to handle large bodies of troops was suspect, but his courage and loyalty were never questioned, and since he was always anxious to fight, he was still very valuable. After the Army of the Ohio was reinforced, McCook's corps consisted of 15,832 men, made up of three divisions of infantry and nine batteries of artillery. Each division had its cavalry escort of one or more companies.

General McCook's brother Colonel Daniel McCook, Jr., also occupied a position of importance, serving under General Thomas as a brigade commander in charge of four regiments of Illinois infantry and the 52nd Ohio Infantry. Their youngest brother, Lieutenant John J. McCook, was assigned to the staff of General Crittenden. Their cousin Major Anson G. McCook was the commanding officer of the 2nd Ohio Infantry Regiment in Thomas' corps.

Of Rosecrans' three commanders, Thomas showed the most promise. He was from Virginia, but unlike fellow Virginian Robert E. Lee, Thomas was a firm supporter of the Union, and was known for his careful, methodical and mature thinking. Some of his pro–Confederate relatives could not accept his loyalty to the Union, and for that he was written out of the family permanently. But he had made the choice that he could live with and was satisfied.

Thomas was a heavy man

Major General Thomas Crittenden came from a prominent Kentucky family. His father was a U.S. senator who opposed secession while his alcoholic brother George chose the Confederate side of the war. Thomas Crittenden commanded a division in Rosecrans' grand Army of the Ohio. A proud man fond of showy displays of bravado, Crittenden found good company in the friendship of Alexander M. McCook.

whose dour countenance mirrored a serious attitude toward life. But he could smile and had the common touch, and "Pap" or "Old Slow Trot," as he was called, was very popular with the rank and file. He had a close relationship with Buell, was actually senior to Rosecrans and became upset when he was passed over in favor of Rosy. Still he understood a soldier's duty and was determined to apply his considerable leadership skills to the Union cause.

Crittenden came from an old and well-established Kentucky family of divided loyalties. Older brother George was an alcoholic Confederate major general, just then serving on another front after suffering a resounding defeat at Mill Springs, Kentucky, in January. Their father, former Kentucky governor John Crittenden, was a powerful political figure, having served as the U.S. attorney general and in the U.S. Senate. Thomas L. Crittenden was a lawyer by profession. He was showy, free with his use of booze and profanity and unafraid to raise his family's status and position when he needed the clout.

The Lincoln administration seemed pleased that Rosecrans was making progress in getting his army into shape for a campaign against the South, but as time went on, appreciation turned into impatience. Would the vaunted Rosecrans turn out to be another linger-in-camp, spit-and-polish general à la George B. McClellan? The administration urged Rosecrans to strike a blow against the Rebels, but the lively general kept deflecting the barbs, saying he needed more supplies or that the timing was not right. As November gave way to December, it appeared as if Rosecrans was going to let the rest of the year slip by without a fight.

He did, however, engage in a brief war of words with his counterpart. When Bragg sent a crippled Confederate soldier into Rosecrans' lines with a letter asking for safe passage, Rosy became infuriated and showed a bit his hot temper. Rosecrans "respectfully" demanded an explanation for this highly irregular request. How, he asked, in a dispatch to Bragg, would anyone know that the man is not a spy? And how can Bragg expect Rosecrans to care for wounded Rebels?[5] But the matter faded away without incident with the approach of the holiday season, as a lighter and happier mood prevailed at the Union camp.

The Rebel army seemed to be inclined to enjoy the holidays, too, with music, parties, balls and conjugal visits. Major General McCook, encamped on Mill Creek, five miles south of Nashville, came in contact with two Southern women who gave him a copy of the Murfreesboro *Rebel Banner*. From that newspaper he learned that Confederate president Jefferson Davis visited Murfreesboro and delivered a high-spirited talk to the troops in mid-December.

In a message from his headquarters to Rosecrans on December 14, General McCook sounded confident, noting the significance of a visit to enemy troops by their commander-in-chief, but he was "ready to whip any given amount of men who will honor me with an attack."[6] Davis, on the other hand, departed Bragg's camp at Murfreesboro believing that a winter fight would not be necessary, thinking that Rosecrans had taken up a defensive position only.

But Rosecrans had other ideas, and after considerable prodding from Washington, he placed all commanders on alert on December 15. He warned them that reliable sources indicated a possible attack by the Rebels near Stewart's Creek. All his generals in blue were advised to be battle ready, "to ride your lines frequently, and above all, ... see that officers, non-commissioned officers and men are thoroughly instructed in, and that they practice, the rules and directions laid down for the performance of outpost and patrol duty."[7] After several weeks of preparation, Rosecrans was ready for a major offensive against the South to take place over the holiday season. Christmas was destined to be wet, cold, bloody and anything but merry.

The holiday season was under-celebrated in Ohio as well, as civilians were burdened with thoughts about soldiers far from home. Mary McCook, a cousin to Alex McCook, and others were busy "sewing constantly," making "flannel shirts" for Union soldiers, believing that "charity begins at home."[8] Her mother Catherine seemed to dread the passing of time: "We seldom indulge in any merriment as I feel all the time anxious and uneasy about our dear boys for they are constantly exposed to every danger."[9] Her health weakening, she could only sit and wait for letters, hoping for good news, all the while knowing that more fighting and dying would soon occur.

When at last the Union army was reinforced, well equipped and ready to move, Rosecrans called his commanding generals together for a consultation and inspirational lecture. The generals seemed up to the challenge that lay ahead. McCook — his round face beaming — was especially buoyant in his outlook, noting his experience at Shiloh and Perryville, while boasting about the fighting ability of his corps. Crittenden was equally cheery, although he knew from experience that Bragg, for all his faults, could be a shrewd and effective leader, a man difficult to outthink. After the astute and levelheaded Thomas entered the room, Rosecrans revealed his strategy before a blazing fire. Later the group toasted to their success with hot toddies, and Rosecrans closed dramatically, saying, "Press them hard! Drive them out of their nests! Make them fight or run!"[10] They expected to meet Braxton Bragg's Army of Tennessee at Stewart's Creek within a short time.

If Lincoln could have heard Rosecrans' inspiring and emotional appeal, he would have been pleased. For the Union needed action; moreover it needed a victory very badly in view of a recent disastrous defeat at Fredericksburg, Virginia, and the lack of progress on other fronts. Eighteen sixty-two was a bleak year for the Union. Public support for the war was weakening and would certainly diminish even further unless there was a win somewhere in the South, and Lincoln had his hopes tied to Rosecrans and the Army of the Ohio.

Throughout much of 1862, Lincoln contemplated slavery and what to do about it until his mind ached. He was pestered constantly by anti-slavery senators, congressmen, and by well-meaning abolitionist groups, and their newspaper allies, including Horace Greeley's *New York Tribune*. Lincoln opposed slavery on moral grounds, but he had to move carefully in view of his overriding goal to preserve the Union.

Lincoln, however, was a man who used all the tools at his disposal, including the press. He would not hesitate to clamp down on a newspaper for publishing a story that endangered the Union war effort, but he generally steered a middle course between those who supported an unfettered press and those like Secretary Stanton and General W. T. Sherman who would have destroyed it. Lincoln once said that he wanted Greeley "firmly behind me," for it would be "as helpful to me as an army of one hundred thousand men."[11]

In a letter to Greeley dated August 22, 1862, Lincoln staked out his position with firmness and clarity. "I would save the Union," he wrote. "If I could save the Union without freeing any slave, I would do it; and if I could save it by freeing all the slaves, I would do it; and if I could save it by freeing some and leaving others alone, I would also do that." The abolitionist Greeley no doubt was dismayed that Lincoln proclaimed his primary purpose was to save the Union, and that destroying slavery was a secondary purpose that just might be accomplished in the process of saving the Union.[12]

Lincoln had to consider the border states and the possible negative reaction to emancipation in Maryland, Kentucky and Missouri. He grappled with thoughts of the Founding Fathers and their compromise on slavery, dealing with it in such a way that it would eventually be rejected by the people. The word "slavery" is not mentioned in the Constitution but it pervaded the sacred document like a ghost or an evil spirit that would someday have to be exorcised.

To the Founders, slavery was a bad idea, and after having been sufficiently tested, it would be outlawed. This made good sense to Lincoln, but compromises had failed or, as was the fate of the Missouri Compromise, been declared unconstitutional by the U.S. Supreme Court in the famous "Dred Scott Decision." Now America was engaged in a terrible Civil War with slavery at the heart of the matter.

Each day Lincoln came face to face with the burning issue and knew that he had to make a decision — and soon. He told two Unitarian ministers, "When the hour comes for dealing with slavery, I trust I will be willing to do my duty though it costs my life. And gentlemen, lives will be lost."[13] By degrees, Lincoln had abandoned his original, "soft on the South" approach to winning the war. He became convinced that the South would not surrender unless it was thoroughly beaten and its "peculiar institution" swept into the trash heap of history.

Congress, cleansed of Southerners, was in the mood to cooperate. In the summer of 1862, it passed a confiscation act that permitted the president to "employ as many persons of African descent as he may deem necessary and proper for the suppression of this rebellion." Congress also repealed a law dating back to 1792 that prohibited black men from serving in the army.[14] As sure as time marches on and leaves progress in its wake, the tide was turning against slavery.

Following the Union victory at the battle of Antietam near Sharpsburg,

Maryland, on September 17, Lincoln announced his preliminary Emancipation Proclamation to the nation, with an effective date of January 1, 1863. In doing so, Lincoln was offering the South the chance to lay down its arms. The choice was theirs; the South could either give up their fight or give up their slaves. The South had until January 1, 1863, to decide.[15]

Lincoln and others on his cabinet felt that in freeing the slaves in those states that were in open rebellion, the South would be further weakened. Abolitionists had long insisted that by freeing a slave, the South would be denied a worker and the Union would gain one. Lincoln came to understand this, and yet he was concerned about feeding and caring for thousands of ex-slaves who would flock to the Union lines, and equally concerned about the possible negative impact emancipation might have on his army, especially the soldiers from the border states of Kentucky, Missouri, Maryland and Delaware where the proclamation did not apply. And if by chance he gained another major victory at or near the time of the effective date of the Emancipation Proclamation, so much the better. But where would it come from?

On December 24, 1862, Rosecrans gave the order to move out. McCook was to lead the way, marching toward the town of Triune by way of the Nolensville pike with two divisions in front and one in reserve. Triune was 28 miles from Nashville. Thomas was ordered to march down the Edmonson pike and take up a position at Nolensville, 13 miles from Triune, and Crittenden was ordered to advance to La Vergne by way of the Murfreesboro pike.[16] La Vergne was a village located about 11 miles from Nashville. The actual departure from camp came two days later.

McCook's immediate task was to attack the town of Triune where he was expected to face Confederate lieutenant general William J. Hardee, a former friend from Georgia. Called "Old Reliable," Hardee was a West Point man who enhanced his military standing by contributing to the publication of a textbook entitled *Rifle and Light Infantry Tactics*, published in 1861, just in time to be useful to both sides of the war.[17]

Before the war and while McCook was teaching at West Point, he made a special trip to New York to visit then–Colonel Hardee and his family. In a letter to a mutual friend in New York, dated November 29, 1858, McCook said, "I have concluded to hasten my visit to New York," to "be in the city with the Colonel."[18] One senses that the two men enjoyed a warm friendship four years before they were about to face off at Stones River. If he defeated Hardee, forcing the Rebel general to retreat toward Shelbyville, McCook was to pursue with two divisions while the third was to push on toward Murfreesboro.[19]

Among McCook's division commanders was Brigadier General Jefferson C. Davis, who had been indicted for manslaughter after shooting and killing General Nelson in Louisville. But Davis had powerful friends in high places, most importantly Indiana governor Oliver P. Morton, and was never brought to trial by courts-martial or civil authority. Within a month after the shooting he was ordered to duty again and soon thereafter was part of Rosecrans' new Army of the Ohio, serving under McCook. Brigadier General Richard W. Johnson and Brigadier General Philip H. Sheridan were also each in charge of a division in McCook's corps.

Events of the 26th seemed to go in favor of the Union plan. McCook broke camp and proceeded down the Nolensville pike, steadily, over rough and rolling terrain, skirmishing as he went along in a cold, hard rain. He met with considerable resistance from cavalry and artillery and ended the day with a "brisk fight." But the darkness found him in control of Nolensville and the hills that fronted the town, with a loss of about 75 dead and wounded.[20] All in all, McCook's encounter with Hardee was successful.

The next day McCook, brimming with confidence, continued his pursuit of Hardee on the road to Triune. Unfortunately the weather was uncooperative and Hardee escaped in the fog. By the time McCook's corps arrived in Triune, it was deserted except for some cavalry, the main body of enemy having fallen back to Murfreesboro. He learned that just the night before, the town of Triune honored Hardee with a dance. Union skirmishers — in no mood for a party — pushed the Rebel cavalry back, and McCook's men had the now cheerless town to themselves. As the windy and rainy weather was miserable, no further pursuit was made that day. Despite the hardships of pursuit, McCook's men were "in glorious spirits, and only want a chance."[21]

And it was looking more and more like they would get the chance. In the afternoon of the 28th, McCook sent a dispatch to Rosecrans saying that he had questioned some prisoners and runaway slaves who entered his lines. He learned that "Hardee's entire corps had been drawn up in the line of battle the evening before, the nature of the ground being entirely in the enemy's favor, they knowing it perfectly well." For the first time, McCook was showing signs of concern, noting the unfamiliar and rough terrain and the persistence of bad weather.

Rosecrans' chief of staff, Lieutenant Colonel J. P. Garesche, fired back a dispatch from the commander. Get ready. "Everything indicates a determination to fight us." Thomas and Crittenden were moving into place. "Push on to Murfreesborough [sic] with all your force."[22]

At 10:45 P.M., McCook sent his last dispatch of the day, indicating he would be ready to move the next morning. He wrote, "I will take all my wagon train with me over into the valley of Stewart's Creek" and cross it. "My column threatens the enemy's communications, and I expect to be strongly resisted tomorrow. Will do everything mortal man can do to gain my position."[23]

On December 29, McCook's forces advanced to within five miles of Murfreesboro and took up a line of battle at Wilkinson's crossroads. At one o'clock in the morning on the 30th, McCook received orders to report to Rosecrans' headquarters for another late-night session. The sleepless, hands-on Rosecrans was well known for his late-night meetings and long, moonlight rides, and his subordinates generally looked upon these activities with displeasure. (Doesn't the man ever sleep?) On this night it was McCook's turn to be chastised for slowness in carrying out orders.

McCook arrived at 3:30 A.M. and received further orders from his impatient commanding officer. He was to prepare for battle without further delay. The left of McCook's line, commanded by Brigadier General Sheridan, was to close up against the right of Brigadier General James S. Negley of Thomas' corps. To the right of Sheridan, the division of Davis was stretched out, all three brigades in line with no reserve. Then McCook's right extended his line "forward until it became parallel, or nearly so, with Stone's River, the extreme right to rest on or near the Franklin road."[24] The extension was completed with two brigades of Johnson's division placed on the right of Davis, with one brigade in reserve.[25] This is important because of what happened the next day.

His forces in place as ordered, McCook advanced along Wilkinson pike in the mid-morning, taking fire from stubborn enemy sharpshooters and skirmishers, firing away from heavy cover offered by a cedar thicket. Still the right wing moved forward, gaining ground a few feet at a time. The troops pushed on throughout the day, guarding the right flank from a possible surprise attack.

On the afternoon of the 30th, a civilian who lived along the Franklin road was sent to General McCook by General David S. Stanley, the chief of cavalry. The man claimed to have been within the Confederate lines and willingly revealed to McCook that Hardee's troops were extended far beyond the Franklin road, meaning he overlapped the Union forces. A concerned McCook sent the man under guard to Rosecrans so he could repeat his story. McCook expected to receive orders to realign his troops to avert a possible surprise. But he received no such instructions and by his own volition placed the two brigades in position to reinforce his right.[26]

Then at 6 P.M., McCook received new orders from Rosecrans. He was to start "large and extended camp-fires" on his right, "to deceive the enemy, making them believe we were massing troops there." The order was carried out, and soon the desired number of fires were burning for a distance of almost one mile from the right of McCook's line.

McCook surveyed his line of battle and declared it to be sound and solid. "My line was a strong one," he wrote in an official report, "open ground in front for a short distance." Rosecrans sent further instructions for the next day when a major fight was expected, ordering McCook to fall back slowly if the enemy attacked, "refusing your right, contesting the ground inch by inch."[27]

That evening McCook and other officers again reported to Rosecrans' headquarters for a discussion of the battle plan. Rosecrans stressed the need for McCook to hold firm for at least three hours while Thomas and Crittenden advanced. Crittenden was to lead the attack against the rebels with support from Thomas, the goal being to crush the Confederate right.

Rosecrans said to McCook, "You know the ground; you have fought over it, you know its difficulties. Can you hold your position for three hours?" McCook replied, "Yes, I think I can."[28] Rosecrans was placing a great deal of confidence in McCook, and the overall success depended upon the Ohioan's ability to hold firm while the main attack against the Confederates would be made by Crittenden on the far left of the Union line.

McCook later insisted that he did not attend the meeting with Rosecrans and the other corps commanders on the evening of December 30. Rather he reported to Rosecrans of his own volition, "through a sense of duty." He was accompanied by General David S. Stanley, and explained to Rosecrans — in Stanley's presence — the position of his divisions. It was then that Rosecrans asked if McCook could hold his lines, and McCook said, "Yes, I think I can." McCook's response was meant to convey his confidence that he could hold off the same contingent of Rebels that he had fought earlier that day. This conflict in the record is important in light of what happened the next day.[29]

At any rate, that fateful night of December 30, 1862, the right wing of Rosecrans' army was dangerously close to the left wing of the enemy. In fact the opposing lines were so close in places that the enemies could hear one another's music. Bands from the North played rousing versions of *Yankee Doodle* and *Hail Columbia*, while their Southern musicians countered with *Dixie* and *The Bonnie Blue Flag*. All musical competition was ended, however, when one of the bands began playing *There's No Place Like Home*. At once soldiers on both sides began singing, and soon a massive chorus of homesick voices filled the cold night air with a heartfelt song.[30]

The Union army was about to test the mettle and skill of a Confederate army under the direction of Major General Braxton Bragg, a crafty, acerbic man of poor health, but with the ability to develop sound military strategy. A West Pointer, who finished fifth in his class in 1837, Bragg was known for his inability to get along with his subordinates — many of whom hated him and wanted him removed from command. Still, he was favored by President Davis, who trusted his judgment. Bragg could be efficient and smart, but also indecisive and reckless with his men. Which Braxton Bragg would show up at the next battle?

Bragg's Army of Tennessee consisted of 37,702 men, divided into two wings, one led by Lieutenant General William J. Hardee, and the other by Lieutenant General Leonidas Polk. Both generals were experienced and capable. Polk was the Episcopal Bishop for Louisiana and is frequently referred to in the literature as the "Fighting Bishop." Both generals aligned their men on the west side of Stones River while the division of Major General John C. Breckinridge manned the right flank on the east side in order to offer some protection to Murfreesboro. Bragg's men had dug an extensive line of rifle pits on both sides of the river, making his position all the easier to defend, but he wasn't thinking defensively.

Bragg's cavalry was in the hands of General Joseph Wheeler, a capable man who, over time, earned a reputation as one of the great horse soldier commanders on the Confederate side. Always aggressive, "Fightin' Joe" Wheeler took his regiments out and around the flank and rear of the Union army on the 30th of December. He struck McCook's large wagon train near Lavergne, burning and destroying 300 wagonloads of valuable army supplies, estimated to have been worth a million dollars.[31]

McCook didn't know it but his luck had taken a turn for the worse. He returned to his camp near the Gresham house feeling that there would be little pressure on him because the Confederates would be drawn toward Crittenden's assault. He settled in for the night, expecting a relatively easy day the next day since Rosecrans had decided to attack the Confederate right with the left wing of his army. McCook had his orders: hold the Union right.

Then, during the night, Sergeant Lewis Day of Colonel William P. Carlin's 2nd Brigade of Davis' division heard noise that resembled a troop movement. He reported this to his superiors, but nothing was done. Later, Brigadier General Joshua W. Sill, a brigade commander in Johnson's division, also heard suspicious noises and went to Sheridan with his concerns. According to Sill, the Rebel troops were so close he could actually hear the slight ring of metal against metal from swinging canteens and rifles. Both men proceeded to McCook's headquarters where they found the general asleep on a bale of straw. They roused him from his slumber and reported their suspicions. McCook dismissed their concerns out of hand, saying only that Crittenden's attack would ward off any threat to the right wing.[32] McCook believed that Johnson's division, as presently staffed, was strong enough to take it to the enemy in front of it.

What the celebrated Ohioan didn't suspect was that Bragg was planning a sneak attack of his own — against McCook's position. Like Rosecrans, Bragg also planned to attack his opponent's right. The troop movement that night was no doubt Bragg's response to the extra campfires. So as it turned out, Rosecrans' plan to fool Bragg was about to backfire. Bragg was "tricked" into thinking he was facing a larger force, and in so thinking, he beefed up his strength until it was far superior to that of McCook — and very close to Union lines.

Sheridan had a terrible gut feeling about it all. Unlike McCook, he and Sill were unable to sleep, so Sheridan reformed his alignment and sent two reserve regiments forward to reinforce Sill. Then he went about setting up his artillery for an attack he felt was certain to happen.[33] He would get little sleep that night.

CHAPTER 12

The Battle of Stones River

> We have fought one of the greatest battles of the war, and we are victorious.
>
> — Major General William S. Rosecrans

The morning of December 31, 1862, was deceptively quiet for the Union army camped near Murfreesboro, Tennessee. At about 6:30 A.M., Major General Alexander M. McCook enjoyed a leisurely shave, and other officers talked calmly with each other. The 6,200 soldiers from Brigadier General Richard W. Johnson's division were casually drinking coffee and eating a meager breakfast. Then Bragg's attack began.

Johnson's pickets saw the Rebel mass first. A sudden wall of "butternuts" — so-named because of their peculiar, homespun uniforms — came rushing forward out of the trees, 4,400 strong under General John McCown. Most were veteran Texans and Arkansas men, all battle worn and determined. They got up earlier than their enemy, disdained breakfast in favor of a belt or two of whiskey and were therefore fired up and formidable.

The Rebels' first targets were the brigades of Brigadier General Edward Kirk and Brigadier General August Willich on the Union extreme right. The element of surprise was so successful that before long, a rout was in the making. McCook later reported that "they [Johnson's division] were attacked by such an overwhelming force that they were compelled to fall back."[1] This understatement looked good on paper but failed to describe what really happened as the Union troops, taken utterly by surprise, dropped everything, broke and ran in panic through the cedars, many of them falling to Rebel minié balls. As they ran from the Rebel onslaught, many could be heard yelling, "Sold again! We are sold again!" Kirk was wounded in the first hail of gunfire. Sill was killed trying to gather his troops and offer resistance. He was wearing General Philip H. Sheridan's uniform jacket when he was picked off by a sniper.

It was a terrible, unforgettable sight, this massive explosion of violence.

Those regiments that tried to resist were overrun by both Rebels and a stampede of insensible and bleeding bluecoats. The retreat — if one can dignify it as such — was completely disorganized because horrified men simply forgot they were soldiers and desperately wanted a place to hide. One of the desperate men in recalling the incident said: "I felt as though I would like to be all legs, with no other purpose in life but to run."[2]

The mass flight, although instinctive, was contagious, gathering strength as it went on its way. The fleeing mob overran the field hospital that was soon behind enemy lines, the doctors, too, facing bullets and bayonets. More than 1,000 Union soldiers were captured along with many artillery pieces.

While the debacle on the right was happening, the rest of Rosecrans' plan of attack was right on schedule, going exactly as planned. The left under Crittenden crossed Stones River and was driving the enemy before it. Then about 7:30, a message came from McCook saying he was "heavily pressed and needed assistance." Not knowing of the rout in progress, Rosecrans' return message was that McCook "make a stubborn fight." Soon another message came from McCook, saying that Johnson's division had been shattered and troops were on the run. Hearing this bad news, Rosecrans had to abandon his attack on the Confederate right and go to the aid of McCook.[3] The battle plan changed from offensive to defensive.

The shattered Union right was saved from complete disaster by a gutsy and fierce counter-attack by Sheridan's forces. Always a man of action and a natural fighter, Sheridan didn't wait for Rosecrans to arrive. He stood his ground, and his division stood with him. His artillery poured shells and death into the Rebel ranks that had turned and charged toward Davis' flank, having finished off Johnson. The Rebels fell back in the face of Sheridan's murderous guns, and the fighting general known as "Little Phil" used the time in an attempt to rally some of the fleeing Union soldiers. Unfortunately the divisions of both Johnson and Davis crumbled in disarray and death. Davis' division, however, must be credited with some staunch resistance to the Confederate tide before it collapsed, for his men were up early and under arms and therefore not caught unaware.

The fighting on both sides became intense with thousands of guns pouring deadly fire into uniformed ranks. Wounded and dying men fell upon a carpet of bodies, making a thick layer of dead and disabled soldiers. Artillery blasts shattered trees that fell upon the dead and living alike, creating additional casualties.

Among the Union casualties that day was one of the three women in uniform who fought beside the men. A young woman disguised and hiding under the alias of Frank Martin was wounded in the shoulder. Another woman, Frances Louisa Clayton, was fighting beside her husband who was killed. She had no time to collapse in grief, and with a fixed bayonet, she stepped over his body and charged the enemy along with her comrades. The third woman was a sergeant who was five months pregnant at the time of the battle.[4] Proving that the strangeness of war is immeasurable, the female sergeant was serving and fighting while bearing a burden that no man can be forced to bear.

Major Anson G. McCook and the 2nd Ohio were in the heavy fighting. The regiment was under the command of Lieutenant Colonel John Kell. The maddening pace of the fight began to wear Kell down, and he paused and turned to McCook and said, "Major if I am killed I want you to promise to send my body home." McCook understood the gravity of the request as the regiment marched across the field to face the enemy. Yet his reply was laced with unexpected humor. "Colonel," he said, "this regiment is like the Democratic party, where none resign and few die, and I don't know but my chances to be killed are as close as yours." Nevertheless, Anson McCook promised to comply with Kell's wishes. Within a short time, he was approached by Kell's own son, a private in the regiment, who was carrying his father's dead body.[5]

Soldiers on both sides fought with purpose and madness, throwing themselves into the teeth of battle like meat into a grinder, at times completely out of control, until the act of dying seemed to inspire more death, until death itself resembled a living organism, surging like a raging river. Throw yourselves into it, boys (and girls), for cause and comrades. There's no better way to die than to perish in battle for your country.

At some point during the mad episode of official business, General McCook's official papers fell into the hands of the enemy.[6]

By 9:00 A.M., the Union right — or what was left of it — had been under attack for three hours, with Sheridan providing the most courageous and competent leadership. General McCook has been accused of failing to take charge of the situation. It has been said that neither he nor Johnson could be found for the first hour of battle. One writer states: "He [McCook] was as invisible as Sheridan was ubiquitous," and that rather than assisting his most able division commander, McCook "drifted aimlessly" in the rear.[7]

Finally, Sheridan too was forced to retreat, but did so with military order. After four hours of deadly fighting, Sheridan and his division — minus 1,600 casualties, including three brigade commanders — drew back and assumed a defensive position. He came across Rosecrans and calmly reported, "Here we are; all that's left of us."[8] It was indeed a terrible day for the Union at Stones River, and it was still morning.

That afternoon, the Confederates hoped to duplicate their success by attacking Rosecrans' center. By this time the Union forces were not in line, but rather strung back in the shape of a V. In the middle of this formation Rosecrans placed 50 big guns that threw deadly fire into the onrushing Confederates. On and on they came, only to be driven back with great losses. The tide had turned.

A reporter for the *New York Times* who witnessed the fierce fight said the "scene at this point was magnificently terrible," fought with splendid determination by both sides. He was especially impressed with the Union batteries "vomiting smoke and iron missiles" upon the gray-clad Rebels "with awful fury." "Shell and shot fell around like hail."[9]

Between 5 and 6 P.M., the battle that raged for approximately 11 hours was over for the day. Both sides had fought themselves into delirious exhaustion. The South had done its very best, but just as at Perryville, was unable to deal the North a deathblow. The cost in lives lost and men wounded added up to about 7,000 on each side. Casualties and rumors of casualties piled up with great rapidity; it was even reported from Louisville to the *New York Times* that Bragg was killed.[10] It was, of course, not true; he was just as much alive after Stones River as he was after Perryville when he was also rumored to have been killed.

Hardee was able to brag that with 12,000 men, the Confederate troops "utterly routed McCook's corps, ascertained by his captured returns to have been 18,000 strong." He also claimed to have taken 4,000 prisoners and "twenty-three pieces of cannon."[11] Truly, their West Point friendship was dead, dead, dead.

Nightfall came on cold and bitter, and both sides withdrew to rest and recover from the day's deadly work, contemplate their harvest of death and think about tomorrow. There was nothing to eat, many of the Union soldiers had lost their blankets and to make matters worse, no fires were permitted. The best the battle-worn troops could do was to lie down someplace and think of the warmth of home and family against the backdrop of the terrible nightmare they had just experienced.

The battlefield, now strangely silent, except for the moans and cries of the wounded, was awash with dead and injured bodies, blue and gray, men and horses piled one on top of another. The wounded men who didn't die fell asleep. It was so cold that many injured and disabled soldiers were stuck to the ground, frozen in their own blood. The acrid smell of gunpowder lingered above the bodies, rising in the air, mingling with other natural elements, the combination of which formed the nauseous perfume of death that only a combat soldier knows.

It was an unhappy New Year's Eve that wore a mask of death, a hideous sight to behold, which once seen would never be forgotten. One veteran officer could not describe it except to say, "I never saw a greater number of men and horses killed than there was upon a few acres of ground covered by the Rebel advance, on the north side of Stone [*sic*] River."[12] Abraham Lincoln had a dream about gunfire, seeing dead bodies and crowds of the curious reading the casualty list posted at Washington's Willard Hotel.[13] And there would be more carnage in the following days.

That night Rosecrans gathered his generals for another strategy session. Although personally shaken by the terrible events of the day, Rosecrans was far from finished. In fact it could be said he was more determined than ever to defeat Bragg. Earlier in the day Rosecrans witnessed the horrible decapitation of his chief of staff, Lieutenant Colonel J. P Garesche by cannon fire. Although he was splattered with the blood and pieces of brain of his fellow officer, Rosecrans shook it off, and his military instincts took control.

According to Rosecrans' recollection, McCook advised retreat while Thomas and Crittenden were willing to defer to their commanding officer's decision. Fight or flee, it was up to Rosecrans. And he resolutely decided to stay and fight, "eat corn for a week" if necessary, but fight and win the battle — or die in the attempt.[14]

Although the Union right had been routed and driven back two or three miles, Bragg was not in control of the road leading back to Nashville. This was a plus for Rosecrans. There would be no retreat.

Later, Rosecrans and McCook surveyed the rear of the army near Overall Creek. Some years later, McCook told Crittenden that Rosecrans was checking the area, seeking out an avenue of escape, just in case it was necessary to retreat. As they rode over the area, they saw something that convinced them that they had no choice but to stay and fight. Firelights in the background indicated that the Confederates had managed to move around to the Union rear, thereby cutting off any possible retreat. McCook then agreed with Rosecrans: fight and die if need be, but fight. What they didn't know, however, was that the lights were not from Rebel soldiers but from federal cavalrymen who were burning wood to provide some warmth and comfort for the wounded.[15] Once again, torchlight illusion played an important role in the scheme of things.

Meanwhile, back in Bragg's headquarters, the Confederate commander was feeling good about the day's battle. While his losses in dead and wounded were heavy, he did succeed in driving back the Union right and center. He felt that Rosecrans had no choice but to withdraw.

Rosecrans, however, was made of sterner stuff. He hatched new plans and, thinking that Bragg would go after his left, deployed Crittenden on high ground, above McFadden's Ford, on the east side of Stones River. But as it turned out, there was comparatively little action on New Year's Day.

The big news on the first day of 1863 was the announcement by Abraham Lincoln of his Emancipation Proclamation, freeing slaves in the seceded states. While anti-slavery Americans throughout the North waited anxiously for the expected news, Lincoln acted, keeping his promise. It was after the battle of Antietam that Lincoln told his cabinet, "I made a solemn vow before God that, if General Lee should be driven back from Pennsylvania, I would crown

This unusual photograph provides a look inside of a slave pen in Alexandria, Virginia. It shows the doors to the cells where slaves were kept prior to being sold. It is a sad and solemn reminder of a time when an entire race was denied its humanity and was treated no better than livestock.

the result by the declaration of freedom to the slaves."[16] Although the fight at Stones River had yet to be decided, the president was ready to carry out his promise.

Early in the day the president shook hands with long lines of well-wishers at the New Year's reception until his right hand was painfully swollen. Later in his office, at 2 P.M. that day, in the presence of Secretary Seward, Lincoln dipped his pen in ink, paused to allow his hand to stop trembling, and then signed the historic document, saying, "I never, in my life, felt more certain that I was doing right, than I do in signing this paper. If my name ever goes into history it will be for this act, and my whole soul is in it."[17] It was the act of a great man so often laid low by sadness and melancholy, suddenly experi-

encing a rare moment of happiness. Knowing he was doing
the right thing, Lincoln was
fully caught up in the excitement of the moment.

If anyone was looking for
something to turn the tide in
favor of the Union, this was it.
This daring, revolutionary act
changed everything. In the
years leading up to the election
of Lincoln and the ascendancy
of the Republican Party, there
was a growing sense in the
North that the salvation of the
Union depended upon the
destruction of slavery.

For too long churches in
the North avoided the issue,
preferring not to make waves,
while Southern churches used
the Bible to justify enslaving
"inferior beings" for their own
good. Southern church leaders
had, in effect, placed an asterisk
in the Bible next to the Golden
Rule. Lincoln read the Bible
too and wanted Southerners to
see the "good book" as an
instrument of God's grace to all
mankind, and to understand
that freedom does not spring
from the enslavement of others.

A dark, haunting ugliness
had settled over the land, creep-

President Abraham Lincoln's genius as president
and commander-in-chief was evident in many
ways, but it truly stands out in his signing of the
Emancipation Proclamation, freeing slaves in all
states in open rebellion against the federal government. His whole soul was in the act, and if
he was to be remembered for anything he accomplished during his presidency, he could wish for
nothing better than credit for his role in ending
slavery in America.

ing into the collective conscience of a growing number of people. The "peculiar
institution" had become incompatible with civilized conduct, and so long as
the specter of the slave master and plantation culture loomed on the horizon,
America would be denied its place among the advanced civilizations of the
world. The prevailing and often unspoken sentiment was that slavery should
die the death, and with Lincoln's pen, the dagger was applied. There would
be no turning back.

With the signing of the great Proclamation, the slaves in most Southern states were free at last — at least on paper. But more importantly for the immediate present, the numbers turned sharply in favor of the Union, as blacks were to be used in the cause. Instead of sending fugitive "contraband" back to their masters, they would be enlisted, and paid, to do assorted grunt work for the Union army. But there was more. In time thousands of ex-slaves were formed into regiments and fought, with valor, for the Union cause — their cause. The Proclamation was a powerful incentive.

Lincoln understood full well the moral aspect of ending slavery. It was something that he felt good about doing in a personal way. He knew that he could not wipe away the awful stain of slavery; it would remain a part of America's history. But by ending slavery and pointing the country in the right direction, he was doing what was right and long overdue. And he did so with a personal satisfaction that was for him, alone, to feel.

The president knew there would be others who would criticize his Proclamation, and to them he would argue political necessity. Freeing the slaves was almost a desperate deed, done to win the war and save the Union. After all, from the outset, Lincoln insisted that the war was fought to preserve the Union. It was simple logic: slavery had to die so that the country could live.

In the early stages of the war, Lincoln was willing to let the Union reunite, unchanged and with minimum casualties. Now, more than two and a half years into the war, and thousands of casualties later, Lincoln and his administration came to the conclusion that a more radical strategy was in order. And by denying the South the use of slave labor, it was believed that their economic and military underpinnings would be fatally damaged. If it played into Lincoln's personal desire to end slavery, so much the better.

He was satisfied that he had acted wisely and prudently, under the war powers granted to the president by the Constitution. To the Congress and the country, Lincoln said, "In giving freedom to the *slave*, we *assure* freedom to the *free*.... We shall nobly save, or meanly lose, the last best hope of earth."[18] To the Confederacy, which violated the Constitution by making war on a constitutionally-ordained government, and to the North as well, Lincoln wrote, "I invoke the considerate judgment of mankind and the gracious favor of Almighty God."[19]

On January 2, 1863, it was apparent to Bragg that Rosecrans would not pull out and that another attack would be necessary. He had successfully hammered the Union right and center, so it seemed the time was right to hit the left. For this task, Bragg chose the division of Major General John C. Breckinridge of Kentucky.

Breckinridge was more than just another general in gray. He was known throughout America, having served as vice president of the United States under

James Buchanan. The hard-drinking Breckinridge was also known, and apparently was once well liked, by the McCook family, now his enemy. At the 1856 Democratic National Convention in Cincinnati, his name was placed in nomination for vice president by George W. McCook.[20]

Breckinridge was a staunch pro-slavery candidate for president in 1860 and made a very creditable showing at the polls, winning most of the South. While he lost the presidency, he was elected to the U.S. Senate by the Kentucky legislature. Despite having been defeated in the presidency contest, Breckinridge was on good terms with Lincoln, and was a distant relative of the president's wife. When the new president and Mary arrived in Washington, Breckinridge paid them a courtesy call.[21] Lincoln liked his fellow Kentuckian and once said, "I was fond of John and regret that he sided with the South."[22]

Following the battle of Bull Run, but before he joined the Rebellion, Breckinridge was seen talking to Confederate prisoners at Fairfax and Centreville. The *New York Times* reported rather pointedly that he "does not, in his interviews with them, conceal his sympathy with them and their cause."[23] The *New York Tribune* was even more critical, calling Breckinridge a traitor and a spy who should relinquish his Senate seat and join the secessionists.[24]

The newspapers were right to be concerned, for Breckinridge, known for his moderate views, spoke in the Senate during an extra session and made an impassioned appeal to his colleagues to bring an end to the war. Fending off accusations of treason, he ex-

Confederate General John C. Breckinridge had served as vice president under James Buchanan and was well acquainted with Lincoln. Unlike other prominent Kentuckians, he sided with the South, making him one of the most hated and reviled leaders of the Confederacy and a conspicuous traitor. He commanded a division at the battle of Stones River and was routed by Union forces.

pressed faint hope that the Union would be kept whole. But he wanted "a peaceful separation of these states," if disunion was inevitable.[25]

In the summer of 1861, Breckinridge's 16-year-old son Cabell ran off and joined the Rebel army. The ex–vice president, too, followed his heart and joined the generals who went south, hoping to encourage his fellow Kentuckians to do likewise. On October 8, 1861, at Bowling Green, Kentucky, Breckinridge issued an address to the people of his state, condemning Lincoln as a dictator. He said he was glad to give up six years in the Senate "for the musket of a soldier."[26]

Because he had served in high positions of public trust, he was thought of by the Union as a traitor — not just another Rebel — and if captured on the field of battle, he might have been hung. But the Union command knew he was a brave and able officer who possessed the loyalty of his Kentucky troops, dubbed the "Orphans" brigade because they knew that with their native state on the side of the Union, there would be no going back home. ·

Breckinridge objected vigorously to the attack, as ordered by Bragg, because his reconnaissance revealed a strongly entrenched Union force just waiting to annihilate his beloved "Orphans." But Bragg was adamant, and since he didn't like or trust Kentuckians the sentiment was that he would simply use them up and if he got lucky, so much the better. So the attack was made on the Union position above McFadden's Ford, and after an initial success, the Rebels were hit hard by Yankee batteries and driven back amid great slaughter. The Rebels retreated in disorder, and hundreds surrendered. A Union private recalled that many Southern soldiers "fell to their knees and begged mercy," insisting that they were conscripted to fight for the South.[27] Nearly one-third of Breckinridge's "Orphans" were lost, and for all practical purposes, the battle, too, was finally finished. It was one of the bloodiest and hardest-fought battles of the entire Civil War.

The next day, in a cold rain, a disconsolate Bragg withdrew his tired survivors with the advice and consent of his generals Hardee and Polk. According to Bragg's report, it was McCook's personal papers, describing the size of the Union army, that convinced the Confederate commander to retreat. He learned he was outnumbered, and a retreat was the prudent course of action.[28]

With the Rebels gone, the task of burying the dead — hundreds and hundreds of bodies — was left to the Union. As some men had lain on the ground for five days, the burial detail was faced with a task almost as awful as the battle itself. The Union lost one man to death, injury or capture for every three who fought.[29] When the dead, wounded and missing were all accounted for, the loss for both sides combined was 32 percent, a Civil War record.[30]

While the burial details were at work, McCook, Crittenden and Major General Lovell H. Rousseau got rip-roaring drunk, an undignified example that was not lost on the more sober and serious officers. But it was their way of relaxing and unwinding in the aftermath of the awful battle. No one could be faulted for wanting some form of escape.

That they could drink meant they had survived the battle and would be able to fight another day. In fact, none of the three McCooks who saw action during the Stones River campaign were injured, although General McCook had a horse shot out from under him. A witness said the horse was "blown to atoms by a shell, and although severely bruised," McCook "soon remounted and rode to the front of his gallant division."[31]

Major Anson G. McCook was commended by General Rousseau for his gallantry on the field and recommended for promotion to colonel. In the thick of the fighting on the right-center, he stepped forward to take command of the 2nd Ohio Volunteer Regiment when its commanding officer, Lieutenant Colonel John Kell, was killed.[32] Another "Fighting McCook" was added to the roster of heroes.

Colonel Daniel McCook's moment of danger came while he was away from the field of battle, escorting a train of 95 ammunition and hospital wagons to the Union lines. As the train progressed to within seven miles of Nashville, it was attacked by Confederate cavalry under General Wheeler. Colonel McCook led a counter-attack that dispersed the enemy horse soldiers. In his report McCook said he "was completely surrounded by rebels — wounding at least one with my pistol."[33] Colonel McCook and his men were greeted warmly by war-weary troops when his train arrived at the Stones River battle site.

On January 5, 1863, Rosecrans wrote to Major General H. W. Halleck in Washington from Murfreesboro, "God has crowned our arms with victory. The enemy are badly beaten and in full retreat."[34] Not satisfied with one message, Rosecrans penned another to Secretary of War Edwin S. Stanton, saying, "We have fought one of the greatest battles of the war, and are victorious. Our entire success on the 31st was prevented by a surprise of the right flank; but nevertheless, [we have] beaten the enemy after three days' battle."[35]

While the Union could claim a win because Bragg left the battlefield, it was hardly a definitive victory; it was a non-defeat. Nevertheless the news was received in Washington with great rejoicing. Lincoln sent his best wishes to his conquering general: "Your dispatch announcing the retreat of enemy has just reached here. God bless you, and all with you! Please tender to all, and accept for yourself, the nation's gratitude for your and their skill, endurance, and dauntless courage."[36] It was not one of Lincoln's most eloquent writings, but it was effective in conveying his happiness for a win, at long last. Eighteen sixty-two had been a hard year for Lincoln.

Secretary of War Stanton, normally a sourpuss and not known for acts of gratitude, was also swept away by the euphoria, writing to Rosecrans: "There is nothing you can ask within my power to grant to yourself or your heroic command that will not be cheerfully given."[37]

The news media played it to the hilt as well, causing pro-war sentiment to soar and celebrate while Copperhead hopes dampened. Just when the anti-war Democrats were gaining popularity and power, and people were becoming war weary, headlines throughout the North described a big victory at Stones River. Having received dispatches from Rosecrans, the *New York Times* on January 6, 1863, shouted VICTORY! The *Chicago Tribune* called it a Union rout, won largely by troops from the Northwest. Much of the North erupted in joy while pro-war meetings and demonstrations heaped praise on Rosecrans and his brave soldiers, thus quieting the anti-war element. The general assemblies of Ohio and Indiana passed resolutions thanking the heroic Rosecrans for his "great victory."[38]

After the cheering subsided and the official reports were turned in, the administration, the press and public got another look at the battle of Stones River. The reports made it clear that serious mistakes were made. With so many casualties inflicted on the Union right, the victory was tainted. Why wasn't the Union right reinforced or better prepared when it was known at the highest levels that Confederate troops were massing there? The finger-pointing started, and attention was turned to what went wrong and who was to blame. And much of the focus was on General Alexander M. McCook. Should McCook have taken action to strengthen his position despite orders to the contrary? His paper-thin line was stretched out from Wilkinson pike to the Franklin road, with Hardee in a position to flank him.

McCook had his detractors in the Army of the Ohio. He never seemed to win the affection of his men, and certain officers thought of him in uncomplimentary terms. He was full of confidence and often too anxious to get his men in a fight, thus placing them unnecessarily at risk. Colonel John Beatty, who served under Thomas, called McCook a "chucklehead," a snide reference to a perceived lack of intelligence, maturity or good judgment.

Beatty acknowledged that after the battle, McCook complimented him for having fought well. Beatty went on to write in his memoir: "He [McCook] should know, for he sat behind it [Beatty's command] at the commencement of the second assault ... but soon thereafter disappeared."[39]

In his *Army of the Cumberland*, published in 1882, historian Henry M. Cist castigated both McCook and Johnson for ignoring the apparent danger and not reinforcing the Union right. But he placed an equal measure of blame, and ultimate responsibility, on Rosecrans for trusting McCook's "ability to withstand the attack on his faulty line." Rosecrans should have known better than to entrust the "safety of his whole army to McCook alone."[40]

Before going into combat, good planning is necessary, based on reliable intelligence, but it is equally important to react quickly and correctly to sudden, intervening factors. In other words, a military leader has to be able to "think on his feet." Some of his colleagues and many historians have concluded that Alexander M. McCook lacked this ability. Because of this, he failed at critical times, to the detriment of his men and his place in Civil War history. After his divisions were hammered at both the battles of Perryville and Stones River, it was clear to many that he was unable to manage troops on a large scale.

McCook's official battle report of January 8, 1863, indicates otherwise. In it he sets forth his role in the bloody events in a calm, evenhanded manner, explaining step by step the actions he took on December 31, 1862, while Bragg's left was hammering his right. "I was in the rear of the center of my line when this attack commenced; therefore I did not see all the column that attacked and turned my right; but it can be safely estimated that the rebel force outnumbered ours three to one." He did not criticize his troops for running in chaos, because "over such ground [thick brush and heavily wooded] it was almost impossible for troops to retire in good order," especially when under attack by superior numbers.

McCook left the impression that he was in control throughout the long morning. He explained that "General Sheridan's division was ably maneuvered by him, under my watchful eye." He met with General Rousseau and posted his division so as to "repel the attack." He went on to say that he took charge of the panic-stricken soldiers of Johnson's division and reformed them in the rear of Rousseau's division. Nowhere does one read about an inept commander, struck by fear and confusion.

McCook wrote: "In strict compliance with my orders, and the knowledge I possessed of the position of the enemy, which was communicated to my superior, also to the generals under my command, I could not have made a better disposition of my troops." He reported 542 killed and 2,334 wounded. He closed his report with high praise for his officers and men, expressing great sadness over the loss of so many able and brave soldiers. In short, he concluded that everyone in his corps, including himself, did the best that could be done under the circumstances.[41]

Rosecrans' official report of February 12, 1863, covered the Stones River campaign in greater detail than did McCook and with no small amount of praise for his men for their boldness, bravery and sacrifice under fire. He began with commendations for his three wing commanders, lauding both Major General George H. Thomas and Major General Thomas L. Crittenden for their skill as leaders, and to "Major-General McCook, tried, faithful, and loyal soldier, who bravely breasted the battle at Shiloh and at Perryville, and as bravely on the bloody field of Stone's River."[42] High praise such as this can hardly be construed as placing blame for failure to perform. According to Rosecrans, McCook had performed valiantly, a hero among heroes.

On the same day, however, Rosecrans sent a letter to Halleck with a different slant on the battle of Stones River and one of its key participants, General McCook. Rosecrans suggested that had "not the direction and extension of our right wing been so faulty, there would have been one day to the battle of Stone's River, and no organized rebel army left after it." He confessed to Halleck that he "trusted General McCook's ability as to position, as much as he knew I could his courage and loyalty. It was a mistake."[43] While this letter does not condemn McCook or recommend an inquiry, it does deflect some of the blame for the disaster of December 31 away from Rosecrans and onto his right-wing commander.

A report from Cincinnati that was printed in the *New York Times*, from a correspondent who was at the scene of the battle, pointed an accusing finger. "I suppose I shall raise a storm about my head for saying so, but I can't from all that I have heard, come to any other conclusion than that the right wing of our army was completely surprised." He suggested that either Johnson or McCook (or both) were to blame, that "the sentiment of the entire army is extremely hostile to both," and that an investigation would follow.[44] McCook's conduct, however, was never the subject of an investigation, and he retained his command of the right wing of the Army of the Ohio.

Years later an officer who served with Brigadier General Horatio P. Van Cleve's division of Crittenden's wing during the battle of Stones River came forth to defend McCook's role in the holiday-season bloodletting. In 1892, at Los Angeles, Lieutenant Colonel James H. Woodard presented a paper to the California Commandery of the Military Order of the Loyal Legion of the United States. The paper describes and re-fights the terrible battle, including details about strategy that are not revealed in official reports.

According to Woodard, when McCook made his visit to Rosecrans' headquarters on the eve of the battle, he expressed his concern about "having to fight the whole Rebel army." Rosecrans simply restated his orders as if uninterested in McCook's assertion. Then at 3 A.M. on the 31st, McCook sent a dispatch to Rosecrans that said enemy troops were massing "far beyond his right."[45] Once again, there was no reaction from Rosecrans. (Unfortunately for the record, McCook's report makes no mention of this dispatch.)

Woodard was ordered to ride around to the Union right that night, and having done so, he witnessed the Rebel troop movements. He rode with Sill and Sheridan to see McCook. His recollection of what McCook said is far different from what Sheridan remembered. When told about the troop movements on the right, McCook replied: "I have reported to Gen. Rosecrans all of the facts which you give me. I have been advised by Johnson and Davis of the situation, but my orders from Gen. Rosecrans are very definite ... the plan of the battle is for the attack to be made by our left wing. In fact, Crittenden and Thomas are expected to do most of the fighting."[46]

McCook restated his orders. His job was to hold the Union right. Rosecrans, McCook explained, was fully aware of the enemy buildup, but he was also of the belief that the expected attack by Crittenden would draw the Rebels back toward the action on the Union left. Go back to your camps and get some rest.

Later the next morning, with the battle raging and troops running wild and out of control, Woodard recalled that McCook was fully in charge, "trying to re-form Johnson's broken line." McCook was also seen ordering Davis and Sheridan to charge the enemy and later directing the division of Rousseau. Woodard concluded that it was "apparent that the whole battle was being fought by McCook, as was the case at Perryville."

Was McCook over-anxious to fight? Nonsense, wrote Woodard. McCook did not attack but was instead attacked by a superior force that, using the element of surprise, gained the upper hand. McCook, like any good soldier, was simply following his orders and improvising in accordance with the dictates of the action at his front. He stood his ground and rallied his troops, and under the circumstances, according to Woodard, Thomas or Grant could have done no better.[47]

Cist disagreed but conceded that McCook showed great courage under fire, and did "all he could do to aid in repairing the great disaster of that day … to the best of his ability."[48] And a reporter who witnessed the furious fighting, and wrote about it in a breathless article for the *Times*, supports Woodard's view of McCook. He recalled that McCook was "brave to a fault, and self-possessed. He narrowly escaped death many times."[49]

John Fitch, who served under Rosecrans and authored a history of the Army of the Cumberland that featured the battle of Stones River, also said that McCook was in the thick of it, risking his life to rally his men, and for a time was reported as killed. According to Fitch, McCook "rode to and fro through the fiery storm, losing his horse, struck dead under him."[50]

General Richard W. Johnson had a similar view of his comrade and commanding officer. In his memoir, Johnson said that the night before the battle, McCook gathered his division commanders together and explained what was expected of them. Later that night, when Johnson learned of the Rebel troop movement, he went to McCook, who in turn went to Rosecrans. But Rosecrans thought it was inadvisable to make changes in the alignment of the Union right. (Again, McCook's official report of January 8 makes no mention of this.)

The next morning, Johnson was having a cup of coffee with Willich when a shot was fired, setting in motion the terrible battle. He witnessed the onrushing Rebels and recalled that the "color of their uniforms blending with the gray of the morning rendered their movements discernible only by the terrible fire of artillery and musketry." Johnson said, "McCook was everywhere urging the men to deeds of noble daring, and proved himself a hero worthy of the honored name he wore."[51]

Despite Johnson's insistence that he was in a position to witness the Rebel attack, at least one other Civil War historian has disagreed. That writer stated: "At time of attack, Johnson was not on the front line in person, but was at division headquarters, where he was too far in the rear to give direct orders."[52] This is yet another example of inconsistency in the record as reflected by differing and diverging contentions and conclusions.

It is clear that Johnson's explanation of the battle was committed to print in an effort to "set the record straight" and to correct many errors and misperceptions. He was especially adamant in stating that his camp was situated about a half mile from his brigades. Johnson wrote, "I mention this distance because it has been asserted by some camp followers that my headquarters were a mile and a half in the rear of my line." While his book is not a tirade of anger and indignation, Johnson felt he and the rest of McCook's wing did the best they could, having been attacked and overrun by an enemy in superior numbers.[53]

Johnson seemed especially perturbed by the persistent belief that the Union right was taken by surprise on the morning of January 31. "Time has not corrected this error," he wrote. When his book was published in 1886, there were "thousands who believe our right was attacked while still in bed." Preposterous! This could not happen to an army commanded by the "ever vigilant McCook," a man "who belongs to a race of soldiers," whose "courage has been tested by contests as fierce as ever shook the earth or crimsoned the battle-field." Johnson no doubt felt better for having told his side of the story, but he had to resign himself to the realization that differences of opinion would long outlive all who fought in the battle of Stones River.[54]

Another writer — a soldier turned historian — William Dodge Sumner came out strongly in defense of McCook. Dodge wrote that Rosecrans' order to start a series of fires on the Union right on the night of December 30 backfired. Seeing the fires, Bragg immediately, and logically, massed troops on McCook's front. Thus the Union was vulnerable and overrun the next morning due to Rosecrans' miscalculation, not due to McCook's inaction or poor judgment.

Alex's family, of course, defended him. Cousin Anson — whose conduct at the battle earned him promotion to colonel — said, "He who has earned the sobriquet of 'Fighting Alex' made a desperate but apparently unavailing resistance." Although Alex "did not win many laurels in the fight," Anson believed it was due to bad luck, not bad judgment.[55]

Despite lapses in judgment that might have prevented or mitigated the disaster of December 31, the overall public perception — with the exception of some journalists — was that McCook, along with every other man and officer, fought a hard fight, giving all they had to give for the Union. With all the blood shed on the field of battle, there was no need to bleed anyone further by way of an inquiry or investigation. The war had lasted long enough for knowledgeable people to understand that in pursuit of ultimate victory, good men must die and some battles would not unfold and end according to plan.

That may have been the conclusion of Lincoln, Halleck and Stanton, for they had access to all the reports, correspondence and newspaper articles and took no adverse action against McCook or any other officer who fought at Stones River. Lincoln was especially pleased with the result, thanking Rosecrans for a "hard-won victory, which, had there been a defeat instead, the nation could scarcely have lived over."[56]

It appears that the entire Washington military establishment was pleased with the effort and result, as was the general public. After all, the retreat of Bragg meant that the Union was firmly in control of much of Tennessee, including Nashville. Everyone moved on, leaving it for latter-day historians to engage in second-guessing the strength and weakness of men long dead, meaning the verdict of history remains scolding and accusatory.

Sensing that so much had been accomplished, the Army of the Ohio was elevated and renamed. On January 9, 1863, by General Order No. 9, the War Department, by direction of the president, created the Army of the Cumberland. It was divided into three army corps, "to be known as the Fourteenth, Twentieth, and Twenty-first."[57] Major General A. M. McCook was placed in command of the 20th Corps, a move that can only be interpreted as an expression of confidence in him as well as a promotion.

Amid a swirl of bad post-battle publicity, Alexander M. McCook took leave and got married in Dayton, Ohio, on January 29, 1963. His bride was the lovely and talented Kate Phillips, a member of a prominent and wealthy Dayton family. The Phillips family enjoyed a long and proud pedigree that reached back to the days of William the Conqueror and 11th-century England. Alex met Kate in 1861 when he was in Dayton drilling new recruits. He was smitten. He sang to her, he courted her, he made her laugh, and they fell in love.[58] Alex won the heart of the belle of Dayton, and Kate, in her glory, was carried off by her gallant young general.

Their wedding was a lavish, expensive and splashy affair — the great social event of the season. Among the guests were Robert Todd Lincoln, son of the president, the governors of Ohio and Indiana, several generals, the parents of the groom and his brother Colonel Edwin S. McCook and wife. The long list of dignitaries attests to the political strength of the McCook family. The wedding ceremony was said to be the "most brilliant hymenial [sic] demonstration ever made here."[59]

Following the ceremony and reception, the newlyweds and the wedding party took a train to Cincinnati to be honored at another big event. Alex and Kate went to Louisville on the steamer *General Buell* and had their pictures taken at the Galt House. It was then that the golden carriage turned into a pumpkin, for the fun was over for the happy couple. Alex had to get back to his corps. An article in the *Cincinnati Daily Times* said McCook will no doubt, "fight all the harder now that he has two unions to defend."[60]

For General Alexander M. McCook and the rest of the proud Army of the Cumberland, serious challenges lay ahead — challenges that would call into play all the talent and character of the entire officer corps. And after the next major battle, everything would be sorted out for General McCook.

For some months after the battle of Stones River, Union troops remained in the area. Among them, Joseph A. Hamilton of the 15th Indiana Infantry Regiment participated in an unlikely event along that river: he got married. His bride was Francillia L. Bean of Chicago, who was drawn to the field of battle because of her desire to "minister to the wounded, sick and dying." The May wedding was well attended by men and officers of the Army of the Cumberland, including three major generals and many ladies. While it lacked the extravagance of the McCook-Phillips ceremony, many of those present called it one of the most romantic weddings they ever attended.[61] A battlefield was a strange place for a happy, young couple seeking perpetual union. It was far from a reunion of the warring elements, but it was as if some ethereal form of decency had been restored to a place so recently ravaged by gunfire and death.

CHAPTER 13

The Tullahoma Campaign and the Advance to Chattanooga

Chattanooga is ours without a struggle and East Tennessee is free.
— Major General William S. Rosecrans

Not long after the shock and carnage from the battle of Stones River was folded into the public mind, the War Department divided the Army of the Cumberland into three corps. The top brass discarded the old wing designations. The reconstituted army set in for the rest of the winter, healing and regrouping while enduring cold, wet weather made worse by an abundance of mud and a scarcity of food.

The inaction during those trying times was the subject of some grumbling in the press and by others more comfortably situated. Although impatience was evident throughout the North, people were willing to wait for winter to pass. When the weather improved, however, all excuses were rejected as the nation waited for Rosecrans and his army to do something spectacular.

Come spring 1863, the Army of the Cumberland was an army in search of a strategy for staging another major battle. Commander Major General William S. Rosecrans' agile mind was working, the wheels were turning, but not fast enough to please the Lincoln administration. Throughout the Civil War, the men in charge of directing the war effort at the national headquarters believed the country was on the edge of a hellish abyss, and they acted accordingly. Much as they had hounded Buell, Halleck and Stanton prodded Rosecrans to get moving and resume killing the enemy. But the prickly commander was in no hurry.

The thin-skinned Rosecrans could dish out the sarcasm and return invective as well as anyone in the army, and he seemed to have just the biting retort needed for the occasion. He would move when he was ready, and not a minute sooner. Rosecrans was convinced that Halleck and Stanton kept turning down his request for supplies because they wanted to force him into making a move before he was ready, thereby causing him to fail. He even threatened to resign rather than give in to haste.

Rosecrans knew he would not be forced to resign, nor would the administration replace him. Lincoln liked him, and he was seen by many as the Union's top general, a savior — the one military man whose record of accomplishment pointed toward greater things, the soldier who had the ability and will to defeat the South. He was a celebrity general and could afford to be obstinate and act only when the time was right.

Despite his anger at Halleck and Stanton, Rosecrans was always respectful to Lincoln and addressed him kindly in letters, preferring to go directly to the president. Lincoln returned the kindness, even when he gave Rosecrans a bit of a push to get him moving. After Vicksburg fell to the Union on July 4, 1863, he reminded Rosecrans that there would be no Southern army creeping up from behind so might it not be a good time to move toward East Tennessee? "Be assured," Lincoln wrote, "I think of you in all kindness and confidence; and I am not watching you with an evil-eye."[1]

When some Republicans, hostile to Lincoln, asked Rosecrans if he would be interested in running for president in 1864, the general reminded them that the current president was just what the country needed.[2] Truly, Rosecrans wanted to make a move to please Lincoln and show the country that he was the genuine article, but he stuck to his guns. While he was not another McClellan, he refused to move precipitously.

Besides, the winter weather was a factor. During the three months following the battle of Stones River, continuous rain made muddy roads impassable. In the meantime, the inactive army spent months healing, drilling and fortifying itself in Murfreesboro, while Rosecrans and his generals worked to resupply their men in preparation for an inevitable march deeper into the South. Death and suffering aplenty was in the offing.

There were diversions, including an unexpected visit from none other than C. L. Vallandigham, the erstwhile friend and political ally of the McCook family. He was escorted into Rosecrans' lines at Murfreesboro after having been arrested and convicted under General Order 38, enacted by General Ambrose Burnside, then in command of the Army of the Ohio at Cincinnati. Burnside was upset over Copperheads in general and Vallandigham in particular, and when the latter publicly accused the Lincoln administration of lying to the people about the goals of the war, he was taken into custody by 150 soldiers who, in the dark of night, broke down the door to his house and dragged him away to prison.[3]

Burnside had acted without consulting Lincoln or members of the cabinet. This left Lincoln in a dilemma, for he didn't want to undercut General Burnside, nor did he want to deal with criticism from conservatives, as well as some

Republicans, who insisted that the former Ohio congressman was merely exercising his First Amendment rights. Lincoln cleverly took a third alternative
and banished Vallandigham to the Confederacy for the duration of the war.
When the "traitor" was presented to Rosecrans, the angry commanding general
upbraided the famous Copperhead and warned Vallandigham to never again
show up at the Army of the Cumberland headquarters, saying, "If you do …
I'll be God damned if I don't hang you."[4]

Vallandigham — who considered himself a loyal American — was turned

over to the Confederates who
were none too happy to see
him, even though they loved his
anti–Lincoln stance. Eventually
he ended up in Canada where
he was free to harangue against
Lincoln and his pro-war administration.

Southern sympathizers
such as Vallandigham were
examples of Northern support
the South was counting on to
maintain its offensive. In the
summer of 1863, after more
than two years of fighting with
heavy casualties on both sides,
the South remained confident
and defiant. The *Richmond
Examiner* spoke for Southern
resistance in an editorial supporting slavery and the rebellion. The *Examiner* proudly
declared that the South had
rejected liberty, equality and
fraternity, and in its place "sub-
stituted Slavery, Subordination
and Government." This was

Clement L. Vallandigham of Ohio was a thorn in the side of President Lincoln, having
emerged as an outspoken opponent of the war. As time went on, the erstwhile friend
and political ally of the McCook family became known as one of the most powerful
Copperheads in America. After Vallandigham was arrested, Lincoln had him banished
to the Confederacy. The South was none too happy to have him, however, and Vallandigham found his way to Canada where he was free to rail away against the Union
war effort.

necessary because, while "among equals equality is right, among those who are naturally unequal [the black race] equality is chaos," for the "slave races" are "born to serve" and the "master races born to govern." Harkening back to the "fundamental principles" of ancient times, the *Examiner* lectured the North and proclaimed that for all time to come, "our Confederacy is a God-sen [*sic*] missionary to the nations with great truths to preach."[5] The hard-hitting editorial was a rallying cry for the South and a sign to the North of hard fighting yet to come.

After the somewhat comic Vallandigham interlude, Rosecrans' army returned to mundane tasks until the sameness of army routine was softened in early June by a double hanging. It took place on June 9, and the victims were two Confederate officers who arrived at Fort Granger, near Franklin, Tennessee, posing as Union officers. They were in uniform and presented documents, bearing Rosecrans' forged signature, to show that they were inspectors for the U.S. Army, sent to inspect fortifications of the Cumberland department. "Colonel Auton" and "Major Dunlap" were in reality acting on orders from General Bragg.[6]

Federal officers were suspicious from the outset and Rosecrans was wired for his insight. He knew nothing about the men or their supposed mission and ordered them arrested and tried by court-martial. If convicted, they were to be hung immediately. The two men, whose real names were Colonel Lawrence Williams Orton and Lieutenant Walter Gibson Peter, confessed to being spies when confronted with proof of their deception. The two men were sentenced to be hanged by a drumhead court-martial. They were allowed to sleep on it and were hung the next morning. Orton was the cousin of the wife of Confederate general Robert E. Lee, and was also thought to have served as Bragg's chief of artillery. Witnesses said they died "like brave soldiers."[7]

It was rough justice, but all spies knew they could expect nothing less than a stout rope and a short drop should they be apprehended. In the final analysis they were just more casualties of war, their personal significance and sacrifice lost in the whirlwind of the larger tragic episode. Events of death during the Civil War were far too common to elicit anything more than a fleeting sense of gloom and even less of pity. Bury the bodies. A spy was usually forgotten minutes after the last shovel of dirt was tossed on his grave.

Major General Alexander M. McCook — who did not attend the hangings — seemed to be in good spirits and enjoying camp life. About a month following the battle of Stones River, he took leave and married his sweetheart, the pretty Kate Phillips of Dayton, Ohio, on January 27, 1863. Kate came south to visit her new husband in Tennessee in the early spring. A contemporary noted that her "beauty and gentleness" were a rare treat for the men of the

Army of the Cumberland.[8] W. T. Sherman knew her well and said, "A more lovable creature never existed on earth."[9]

The weather was nice during Kate's visit, and she and Alexander rode together proudly in the presence of the soldiers, as the general was fond of military showmanship. He undoubtedly enjoyed showing off his pretty wife too. McCook believed he was a winner, so he acted like one.

In April, McCook and Brigadier General Jefferson C. Davis journeyed back to the Stones River battle site with some laborers to gather some small cedar trees. Mrs. McCook planned to take them to Louisville for planting. In a letter describing the incident, Davis, a sarcastic fellow, couldn't resist suggesting that guerrillas might capture her before she reached Louisville.[10]

Of course Davis wouldn't wish for that, for he and McCook were good friends. They both were made for soldiering and life on the march, courting danger. But not everyone was impressed with McCook's habitual grin and spit-shined posturing. Brigadier General John Beatty, who commanded a brigade under Major General George H. Thomas, described McCook as "young and fleshy," taller than Rosecrans, with a weak nose "that would do no credit to a baby." McCook, he said, has a "grin which excites the suspicion he is still very green or deficient in the upper story."[11]

Since Beatty blamed McCook for the disaster at Stones River, he could not fail to find something negative about the brash young general. There was jealousy in the ranks throughout the army that often resulted in pettiness, character attacks and backstabbing. A great deal of jealousy was leveled at the youthful McCook who went from a colonel to a major general in a very short period of time. Many other observers leveled their opinions at McCook, and most were negative or insulting. For example, he was called "a good fighting man, but coarse and without dignity." But the same soldier said, "We have confidence in him in battle."[12] The wife of another general called McCook an "imposter as a general." And yet, if he was aware of the sharp criticism, McCook did not show it. On the other hand, the dashing general with "twinkling bright, china blue eyes" never seemed to be troubled by self-doubt.[13] He was the commander of an entire corps, a proud soldier doing his duty for his country. The military was his home and career.

Besides, not all senior officers in the Army of the Cumberland found him objectionable. Colonel Hans Christian Heg, a Norwegian-born commander of the 3rd Brigade in Davis' division of McCook's corps, often mentioned the general in letters to his wife. For the most part the letters were cordial and indicate that Heg respected McCook and looked forward to his contacts with McCook. When Mrs. McCook arrived, Heg said, "Mrs. Gen Mc.Cook is here. Yesterday I had an introduction to her by the Gen. She is a very pretty little woman."[14] Had Heg disliked McCook, what better opportunity would he have had to vent his disapproval than in letters to his wife?

Another fellow officer of importance liked General McCook. General William T. Sherman, who practiced law with Daniel McCook, Jr., before the war, was openly friendly to Alexander M. McCook. Although he was once quoted as saying McCook was a "juvenile," Sherman admired his energy, willingness and dedication to the army.[15] Their friendship dated back to Bull Run where they served with competence and courage in Tyler's division. They remained friends for life.

Much was expected of McCook because he was one of the "Fighting McCooks," a member of a renowned military family. He had been an instructor at the West Point military academy, and the Lincoln administration kept waiting for that experience and ability to show itself on the field of battle. He would have that opportunity in the coming months, as Alexander M. McCook would be tested as he had never been tested before. No one doubted his personal courage, but there were many who believed he lacked the ability to command anything more than a division. He had bravado and love for the army, but did he have greatness in him? He had proved that he was not afraid to fight and risk death. But could he lead when all seemed lost?

In the summer of 1863, Rosecrans' Army of the Cumberland was organized into three corps. The 14th Army Corps was under the command of Major General George H. Thomas. It consisted of four infantry divisions, each one backed by three batteries of artillery. Major General Thomas L. Crittenden commanded the 21st Army Corps, consisting of three divisions with an artillery regiment for each. Alexander M. McCook commanded the 20th Army Corps, a unit similar in size to that of Crittenden. His 1st Division was commanded by Brigadier General Jefferson C. Davis, the 2nd Division by Brigadier General Richard W. Johnson, and the 3rd Division by Major General Philip H. Sheridan. All three commanders were experienced and capable, and all served under McCook at Stones River. On June 30, 1863, McCook had a total of 16,047 men and 54 big guns present and ready for action.

A Reserve Corps under Major General Gordon Granger included an infantry brigade headed by Colonel Daniel McCook, Jr. Daniel's cousin, Colonel Edward M. McCook, was in charge of a brigade in the cavalry corps commanded by Major General David S. Stanley. Captain John J. McCook, Daniel's youngest brother, was Crittenden's aide-de-camp. The Army of the Cumberland was well stocked with McCooks

The army looked grand both on and off paper and consisted of 97,142 "aggregate present" officers and men at arms.[16] Among them was Brigadier General James A. Garfield, Rosecrans' chief of staff, the man always at his commander's elbow, writing and dispatching detailed orders with clarity and often with great rapidity. Garfield was ambitious and talented, and was as anxious to pursue his personal goals as he was in being a loyal, team player. He was instrumental in shaping up the Army of the Cumberland during its long encampment at Murfreesboro. Rosecrans trusted Garfield implicitly, as he trusted Thomas, McCook and Crittenden.

Overall, the army and its leadership suited Rosecrans. Garfield, however, believed it could be improved. He "begged" Rosecrans to oust McCook and Crittenden in favor of Generals Don Carlos Buell and Irvin McDowell. Garfield doubted McCook's abilities because he (McCook) ordered a fugitive slave out of Garfield's camp during the Corinth campaign. Garfield did not dispute McCook's personal bravery, but he believed "misfortune [in battle] followed him like a specter."[17]

When the Army of the Cumberland was finally set in motion, it did so without one of its own. A soldier named David Blaser was shot for desertion. Not only had he deserted, but he joined the Confederate army. He was court-martialed and executed by a firing squad on June 20, 1863.[18]

Although the actual number of troops that marched out of Murfreesboro on June 24, 1863, was about 70,000, at long last, Rosecrans' army was ready to contest the Confederate Army of Tennessee still under the command of gloomy, acerbic and perpetually unpopular, but always dangerous, Major General Braxton Bragg. The coming clash of arms would add many thousands to the roll of the dead, wounded and missing.

Rosecrans' initial move was a gem, a sterling example of tactical genius. He directed his huge army on an 11-day, 80-mile sweep of middle Tennessee, during which time he completely outmaneuvered Bragg, also a capable strategist. Union losses were about 600 killed and wounded, making it an almost bloodless campaign by Civil War standards.

This was the Tullahoma campaign, an outstanding military feat that was never highly publicized. And yet its strategic importance cannot be denied, for Rosecrans prevented Bragg from dispatching troops to relieve the siege of Vicksburg where General U. S. Grant was putting the squeeze on the occupying Confederates. Despite this almost bloodless success, Rosecrans failed to impress Washington, as no major battle was fought and the Confederate Army of Tennessee was still intact, although now driven all the way to Chattanooga.

General McCook was very impressed with the progress of the great army during the Tullahoma campaign. His upbeat report sparkles with compliments to his division commanders, his personal staff and his entire corps. He wrote, it "affords me the greatest pleasure to report to the general commanding the gallant Army of the Cumberland that I have not heard a word of murmur or complaint in this corps from the highest officer down to the youthful drummer. Officers and soldiers vied with each other in the performance of their duties, and I have yet to hear of a single straggler."[19]

While Rosecrans no doubt took great pleasure in McCook's report, his

Tullahoma success had the misfortune of being overshadowed by dramatic, Fourth of July Union victories at Gettysburg and Vicksburg. Every Civil War buff and historian can cite the importance of driving Robert E. Lee and his army back to Virginia, badly beaten, but Tullahoma was quickly forgotten. And yet thanks to Rosecrans and his corps commanders, Thomas, Crittenden and McCook, Bragg and the Confederates possessed but a small corner of Tennessee: the town of Chattanooga

Chattanooga had long been the focal point of the Lincoln administration war planners. By taking it, the Union could block any attempt by the South to invade Kentucky or middle Tennessee. And capturing Chattanooga would, at long last, allow the North to rescue the eastern Tennessee loyalists, one of Lincoln's most cherished goals.

A city of about 2,500 people, Chattanooga was an important railroad and supply center, with connections to other points in the South including Memphis and western Virginia. It was looked upon as an ideal place from which to launch an invasion into Georgia and strike at the heart of the Deep South, which up to this point had been largely untouched. Divide the South and end the war. For these reasons, the Union wanted to take Chattanooga, and the Confederates were just as determined to hold it.

The recent fortunes of war favored the Union. Victories by Meade at Gettysburg and Grant at Vicksburg were cause for rejoicing in the North while a mood of gloom and doom settled in throughout the South. All summer long, deserting Rebels showed up in Union lines with depressing tales to tell. Colonel Edward M. McCook, commanding a division of Union cavalry, reported to Garfield that a deserter from the 5th Arkansas insisted that both men and officers would refuse to follow Bragg, believing his case to be "hopeless."[20]

With each bit of favorable information, Rosecrans' mind swelled with confidence, believing the South was ready to cave in. Everything pointed to dissension in the Southern army, including a false report that John C. Breckinridge killed Bragg as a result of a long series of difficulties between the two generals.[21] All the news — true or false — that flowed into the Union lines was good, and Rosecrans had cause to look forward to the decisive and destructive defeat of the Rebel army he was pursuing. Then he would march through Georgia to the Atlantic Ocean. It was his chance to prove he was America's great general, the savior of the Union.

Before he could take another hit at Bragg, Rosecrans had to repair the railroad back to Nashville and bring up supplies needed for a major campaign. In the meantime, his men rested again, McCook's divisions settling in at Winchester. While the men enjoyed the fishing and hunting, McCook's generals engaged in partying. Jef Davis, who was fond of music and liquor, took advantage of the respite to indulge in both, along with his comrades.

One story that has survived tells of McCook and his division commanders sitting on a porch, engaged in storytelling and jokes. An observer noted that they "acted more like a lot of boys, and when you come to think that the oldest of them had not yet reached forty, they weren't *very old* men." All were making merry when the usually impulsive Sheridan decided he wanted a drink. He asked Davis abruptly, "Haven't you got anything to drink around this camp?" Davis, of course, always seemed to have a generous supply of booze and he hauled it out, and soon McCook and his generals were enjoying whisky and cigars.

That summer, Alexander M. McCook was forced to accept the loss of another family member to the sad fortunes of war. On July 21, his father, Major Daniel McCook, died of wounds received at the battle of Buffington's Island on the Ohio River. Major McCook had been stationed in Cincinnati, serving as paymaster for the federal army, when he volunteered to join the Union forces marshaled to find and defeat Rebel raider John Hunt Morgan. General Morgan and his cavalry had invaded Indiana and, while cutting a path of destruction, crossed into Ohio.

Although he was 63 years of age, Daniel McCook, Sr., was especially eager to find and fight the invaders. He was convinced that Frank Gurley, the man the Union deemed responsible for killing his son General Robert L. McCook, was riding with Morgan. Major McCook was obsessed with killing Gurley, and while in line with other infantrymen skirmishing with the Rebels, he was shot and killed, becoming the third "Fighting McCook" to die from battle wounds.

Alexander had little time to mourn the loss of his father, for by mid–August, the Army of the Cumberland was on the move again, undertaking one of the biggest and most dangerous operations of the entire war. It was in pursuit of a Confederate army of unknown size. In order to find it and fight it, Rosecrans' troops had to traverse a series of mountainous, heavily wooded, unknown terrain, through the dust and heat of a very dry summer. Rosecrans knew Bragg was out there someplace, expecting an attack. To find him meant traversing many ridges broken by gaps, creeks and valleys. The Union supply train was immense, consisting of about 400 wagons that sometimes impeded the flow of troop movements.

Although Bragg was ill and almost incapacitated, he knew that the Cumberland Mountains would slow down the federal troops. The Cumberland range consisted of a long plateau that started at the bank of the Tennessee River southwest of Chattanooga and then sloped off abruptly into the narrow river valley northwest of that city. Lookout Mountain, a principal obstacle, was a one-hundred-mile natural landmark that stretched out below Chattanooga, shaped much like a hand with one finger pointing west and another thumblike appendage to the east. It was about 2,400 feet above sea level — high, rocky, rugged, well timbered and difficult to cross except on the roads built in the narrow gaps. Then there was Missionary Ridge, a well-forested, rocky hill about 500 or 600 feet in elevation that could be crossed relatively easily at any point. These natural obstacles presented the Union army and its commander with a challenge, but Rosecrans felt up to it.

While the Army of the Cumberland was winding, climbing and gapping its way to the south and east, the Army of Tennessee was whiling away its time in Chattanooga. Idle troops were bored and hungry, as food was scarce. Bragg was sick and confused, and in this state of mind, unable to move against Rosecrans, or even make plans for action. And as usual, Bragg had been quarreling with generals. Following the loss at Stones River, Breckinridge was so angry at Bragg that he threatened to resign and challenge his commander to a duel.[22] Bragg's two wing commanders Lieutenant Generals Leonidas Polk and D. H. Hill didn't like him either, and seemed to delight in acts of disobedience or stall tactics. Thus Rosecrans was able to make his painstaking journey at his leisure, although experiencing some skirmishing along the way.

Rosecrans reasoned that Bragg's Army of Tennessee was slowly retreating into the interior of Georgia, so his initial plan was to spread his army out and cut off the Rebels. At this point he had the numerical edge and the psychological advantage as well.

Bragg's army was in a state of low morale and was little more than a disheartened and hungry mob. A soldier from Breckinridge's "Orphans Brigade" who kept a journal complained of poor rations consisting of corn meal, with "a good deal of the cob" ground up in the meal, and "the poorest kind of blue beef."[23] Lousy and little food, ragged uniforms, inferior weapons and shaky leadership: the outlook wasn't very good, but there was one bright spot in Bragg's bleak picture. The Confederate cavalry was still superior to that of the Union, although about equal in the number of men and horses.

McCook's corps was on the Union right with Sheridan's division at the end of the line at Stevenson, Alabama, which at the time served as Rosecrans' headquarters. As the army prepared to cross the Tennessee River, McCook ordered all sutlers to close shop. One of the sutlers, a Jewish fellow, had been doing a brisk business and wanted to stay open four hours longer. With this in mind, he pulled up in front of McCook's headquarters with four baskets of champagne in his cart. Seeing this, McCook said, "Well, we can't send the champagne back so we will send for all the good fellows to come and drink it up and as soon as it is finished, the Jew must close." The champagne was consumed, and the happy merchant departed, leaving behind a group of even happier soldiers.[24]

Pursuant to orders, McCook moved the divisions of Johnson and Davis across the Tennessee River and reported that things were going "swimmingly." Crittenden's corps made a showy move toward Chattanooga, trying to attract

Bragg's attention. Meanwhile, Thomas, the center, moved in utmost secret, albeit very slowly. All three corps were at this point invisible to the Rebels as Bragg had no pickets or spies to pick up their movements. Even so, the Union army, moving in three pieces, was hampered by communication problems. For days at a time, there was little or no contact between Rosecrans and one or more of his distant corps.

Rosecrans wanted all elements of his army in place by September 3, ready for a coordinated attack on Chattanooga. So far his plan was working. Although he was late in reaching his destination, Crittenden's noisy diversion finally did attract Bragg's attention. Part of the plan was to trick Bragg into thinking that Crittenden's corps was Rosecrans' entire army, while the other two corps under McCook and Thomas crossed the Tennessee River near Bridgeport, Alabama, downriver from Chattanooga.

The plan was working. Now fully aroused, Bragg believed that the main Union striking force was about to hit Chattanooga. On September 2, after a council of war, he ordered his troops to pull out of Chattanooga and regroup in LaFayette, Georgia. This done, Crittenden moved into Chattanooga and occupied it. Once again, it appeared as if Rosecrans' brilliance won the day; it was another relatively bloodless coup. On September 9, 1863, an elated Rosecrans telegraphed Halleck the good news: "Chattanooga is ours without a struggle, and East Tennessee is free."[25]

Brimming with confidence, Rosecrans was even more certain that the Rebels were on the run, and ripe for the picking, if only he could catch them. The hunt was on in earnest. He ordered Crittenden to leave one brigade at Chattanooga and send the rest of his corps further east, across Missionary Ridge, hoping to cut off the Rebel retreat. McCook and Thomas were to move through the gaps in Lookout Mountain and cut off any attempt by Bragg to retreat to the west. In doing so, Rosecrans continued to spread out his forces.

What the Union brain trust didn't know is that Bragg had finally come up with a plan of his own. He only appeared to be retreating, while in actuality he was plotting a strike at the Union left. The sullen deserters tramping into Union lines with depressing stories were deliberately sent out by Bragg to convince the Union generals that the Army of Tennessee was on the brink of collapse. But in fact Bragg was being reinforced: first by Major General Joseph Johnston and then by Major General Breckinridge's division from Mississippi. He wanted President Davis and General Robert E. Lee to send Lieutenant General James Longstreet's troops from the Army of Northern Virginia. Lee, however, was lukewarm on the idea, for Longstreet had over the course of many battles proved to be an excellent field commander. For that reason, Lee was not willing to be without him.

Although still very ill, Bragg snapped out of his lethargy and went to work. He also received an unexpected bit of good luck. On September 5, 1863,

Bragg got his hands on a copy of the *Chicago Times* that revealed the federal plan in detail. He learned about Crittenden's move toward Chattanooga and Thomas and McCook's movements over the mountains. Bragg laid out a plan by which his army would move out toward Rome, Georgia, in four columns and strike the enemy while its forces were divided and spread apart.

Bragg had a good chance at succeeding just then, had he been healthy and decisive enough to follow through. The federal forces were just too far apart and vulnerable to being chewed up in three big bites. For example, on September 11, McCook was completely out of touch. He had been encamped at Alpine, Georgia, for three days, not knowing what to do, while wondering when orders would come from headquarters. McCook discovered the presence of the Rebels at Pigeon Mountain, only a few miles away from Alpine. He had strayed too far south of the Rebel position. He became greatly concerned and nervous over the isolation of his corps, fearing an attack. But sometimes fortune favors the foolish, for Bragg was not aware that McCook was ripe for the picking. Having escaped a potential disaster, McCook finally received orders from Rosecrans and had his men on the move toward the rest of the army.[26]

From his desk in Washington, General Halleck sensed Rosecrans' army was in trouble. Believing that the Confederates were planning an attack to turn the Union right (meaning McCook), he ordered Major General Ambrose Burnside to hold East Tennessee to protect Kentucky, and move his infantry toward Chattanooga, "as rapidly as possible," to "connect with Rosecrans." Burnside was told to be prepared to take control of Chattanooga, should Rosecrans be attacked. Halleck wrote to Rosecrans, saying he could count on Burnside's support in case of an attack and also alerted Grant and Sherman.[27]

It was then that Rosecrans saw the flaws in his plan. It dawned on him that the Confederates were not retreating but were preparing to fight. Furthermore, Davis and Lee changed their minds. Longstreet and two divisions were on the way by rail from Virginia. Rosecrans knew about the "secret" Southern plan, however, because the story was published in the *New York Herald*.[28] Once again a newspaper provided valuable intelligence.

Rosecrans had to change his strategy fast and move his corps closer together, for his dispatches were not reaching his commanders. In his official report, Rosecrans acknowledged that Bragg had been reinforced, and therefore it was "a matter of life and death to effect the concentration of the army."[29]

He needed help from Washington and requested that General Ambrose Burnside be ordered to come down from Knoxville for support. Washington did dispatch someone: Assistant Secretary of War Charles A. Dana arrived in Rosecrans' camp on September 11, with a letter of introduction from Secretary of War Edwin Stanton. While he was supposedly there to assist any way he could, most of the men, including Rosecrans, took a skeptical position, believing Dana was a spy for Stanton, a bird of "evil omen," up to no good.[30]

Soldiers of all ranks looked for the time when Dana would be picking someone's carcass.

Dana was an experienced journalist who broke into his chosen profession as the managing editor for Horace Greeley's *New York Tribune*. As a young man, he tended to favor idealistic and utopian societal schemes and organizations, looking toward some benevolent socialistic society as the remedy for social ills. He favored abolition. As years passed, idealism was replaced with the outlook of a cynic, and finally it was said that a hardened Dana believed in nothing—not man or God—except putting out a good newspaper.[31]

Prior to his assignment with Rosecrans, Dana spent some months with Grant and Sherman on the Vicksburg campaign and learned to admire and respect both men very much. While he was loyal to the Union cause, and wanted to help it succeed, he tended to panic when under pressure and was prone to send messages that were incomplete or over-exaggerated. Although not impartial, he was a good observer, and when not unduly pressed, he was a reliable messenger, just what Stanton wanted. Lincoln called Dana the eyes and ears of the government at the front. Men at the front called him a "loathsome pimp."[32]

Rosecrans was puzzled and suspicious at first, but due to his convivial nature, he soon warmed up to Dana and went on his way, planning for a major battle. He wanted to attack Bragg at LaFayette on the 13th, but only if McCook could close up soon enough. It seems Rosecrans was overly optimistic as usual. Crittenden was just then at Lee and Gordon's mill on Chickamauga Creek, fully ten miles away from Thomas' left flank at Cooper's gap. Thomas was separated from McCook by 30 miles of "uncertain mountain trails."

Granger had finally gotten his reserve corps up to Rossville. He was a regular army officer, small in size but harsh and imposing in appearance. He was a strict disciplinarian, a martinet, who had low tolerance for any unmilitary behavior, including foraging. If there were no government rations for the troops, they were expected to go hungry and wait for the supply wagons.

While undergoing the forced march to reach Rossville, the advance troops made camp, and despite Granger's "no foraging" order, they set out to find something to eat. When soldiers ate from the supply wagons, the meager meal usually consisted of some meat—bacon or beef—and a breadlike concoction called "hard tack." It got its name from the fact that it was so hard that "it might be tacked upon a roof of a house instead of shingles."[33]

Although he understood Granger's cruel and unyielding attitude, Colonel Daniel McCook was sympathetic and told his men, "Get to the woods boys and keep out of sight." Unfortunately, many were caught red-handed when Granger arrived in camp. When he saw the stolen chickens and other delights, Granger lost all self-restraint. The irate and diminutive commander then sent out a mounted patrol to round up all foragers; he decided to make an example of all those who disobeyed his order. Soon men from every regiment were hung by their thumbs from trees near Granger's tent.

Outraged officers and soldiers demanded that Granger relent, and a war of words almost erupted into bloodletting. Granger, whose wrath was out of control, ordered artillery fire into the protesting soldiers, but the gunners refused to fire. At this point Colonel McCook and Brigadier General James B. Steedman intervened and negotiated a "truce" between Granger and his angry officers. The men were cut down, and the anger soon subsided. But the damage had been done, and Granger was thereafter hated by most of his corps.[34]

While this nasty episode was playing itself out, Rosecrans continued to arrange his army so as best to stave off an attack. At this point, he was no longer the hunter and had assumed a defensive attitude. There would be no swift-paced march into Georgia, no overrunning and defeating Bragg. Still, at this point, the devoutly religious Rosecrans may have felt some divine intervention on his behalf, for Bragg fell back to vacillating again.

Truly, the Rebel army had missed its opportunity to strike and defeat a portion of Rosecrans' widely scattered forces. The dour and cadaverous Bragg hesitated, and when he did give orders, his generals were either too slow or simply refused to move at all. They seemed to be especially pleased to be able to frustrate their enfeebled leader. Hard as he tried, nothing seemed to go right for Bragg who "wore failure like a habit."[35] The inaction and infighting by his subordinates bought time for the Union army as Rosecrans struggled to bring his troops together.

Getting McCook to close in on Thomas was especially challenging. Upon receiving orders, McCook set out from Alpine on the 13th intending to march toward Thomas on a direct route toward Dougherty's Gap. At 11:30 that morning, McCook sent a message back to Garfield confirming that he was on his way. He also mentioned that a captured Rebel lieutenant warned of a huge Southern army gathering at LaFayette. The prisoner also stated "that he is morally certain that re-enforcements are coming from Virginia by way of Atlanta,"[36] an obvious reference to General Longstreet.

Then that afternoon McCook received another order telling him to join Thomas at Steven's Gap. McCook misunderstood the order, thinking that he now had to abandon the direct route. He didn't realize that Garfield meant that he should continue toward Dougherty's Gap, but simply take a different route to get there.

A very confused General McCook sent a message to Thomas stating he would have to re-cross Lookout Mountain and march north through Lookout Valley to get to Steven's Gap. The change in plans brought about by Garfield's vague order meant an additional 25 miles of hard marching. Vowing to do all that "mortal men can do," McCook pushed his troops through the brutal heat, all day on the 14th, with many of his men falling out exhausted along the way. Finally, he was forced to halt at sunset. Just then he received another dispatch from Garfield, telling him to discontinue his current route, turn around and resume the direct route.

McCook was angry. He fired back a message which in essence was a refusal to turn back. He said, "I will be pained to take my troops over that route again; they certainly will feel as if I were trifling with them. I will suspend the movement until I hear from you."[37] His men were dead tired, and he was frustrated because of conflicting orders.

When Rosecrans read McCook's testy message, he relented and sent back an order telling McCook to continue his current route but leave two brigades to guard Dougherty's Gap. Satisfied that he now knew what he had to do, McCook pushed his men harder than they had ever been pushed before. On the 16th, they covered an estimated 26 miles over very rugged country, and finally, late that evening, the tired 20th Corps lumbered into Steven's Gap.[38]

McCook's message to Thomas indicates he was still in good spirits, despite the forced march, much of it without water. He mentioned that he didn't know the whereabouts of Colonel Edward M. McCook's cavalry division. But he noted that his cousin took "his crowbars and implements for destroying railroads, and I think he is up to some devilment." As for himself, McCook declined to meet with Thomas that evening, due to the long ride and little sleep for the past two nights.[39] Indeed, due to the confusion caused by the orders, a relatively short 12-hour march became a torturous trek of 108 hours.[40]

Rosecrans finally had his three corps close enough to one another so that a coordinated attack — or defense — was possible. On the 17th, his army was stretched out on or near the west bank of Chickamauga Creek, a meandering stream that meant "River of Death" in the Cherokee language. With Bragg facing him on the opposite side of the creek, hidden by the dense woods, Rosecrans began to concentrate his strength on the left of the Union line, with McCook at Crawfish Springs on the right. To the rear loomed Missionary Ridge. The Cherokee people were gone, having been displaced by an alien culture, but Chickamauga Creek was flowing full strength, presenting challenges for both the North and the South.

The Union army was ready for a fight, but there was to be no battle on the 17th. Rumors floated about that Longstreet's Virginians had arrived to assist Bragg. Colonel Robert H. G. Minty, a cavalry brigade commander, picked up the talk and went to Crittenden with the news. Crittenden merely laughed and insisted that Longstreet was in Virginia. He was unconvinced and unworried. Dana was in accord. He sent a dispatch to Stanton on the 17th, saying, "We are still without information of Longstreet's arrival."[41]

On September 18, the first shot of the battle was fired. A soldier from the

7th Pennsylvania Cavalry fired on a group of officers in gray. He missed, but it was a start.

Meanwhile, on the Union right, at Crawfish Springs, General McCook was relaxed and ready for a fight too. Most of the Union cavalry was under McCook's control. He reported that his guns had been silent all day on the 18th, but that his men had their rations and ammunition. General McCook closed his dispatch to Garfield saying, "My men are confident. Let us in."[42] Late in the afternoon, McCook received a terse message from Rosecrans: "Move up."[43] Soon no one would be relaxing or laughing.

CHAPTER 14

The Battle of Chickamauga

> My report to-day is of deplorable importance. Chickamauga is as
> fatal a name in our history as Bull Run.
>
> — Charles A. Dana

The terrible battle of Chickamauga erupted full blast on Rosecrans' left on September 19, 1864. While it was believed that just one enemy brigade had crossed Chickamauga Creek, in actuality General Braxton Bragg's Rebel columns crossed the creek in force during the early hours of the morning, preparing to wheel to the left and hit the Union left flank. What Bragg didn't know, however, was that during the night Major General George H. Thomas moved his corps from the right to the left flank, thus reinforcing it. The Union plan was to line up along the west side of LaFayette Road, hold it and stand firm between Bragg and Chattanooga.

The woods were dense and tangled, and both sides were unaware of the presence of the other while feeling their way forward. Soon the fight was on as Rebels and Yankees met in a sudden, head-on collision, amid heavy musket fire. Once again two great western armies from the North and South were locked in a furious struggle to the death with both sides charged with desperate, animal determination.

Thomas was in charge of the Union left that was heavily assaulted by the Rebels. He shuffled brigades in and out of battle, trying to anticipate where the Rebels would come from next. Still he maintained the edge and blunted Bragg's flanking movement. Bragg, on the other hand, found himself backed up against the Chickamauga Creek, with just a few places to cross or ford, should he have to retreat.

It may have been fortuitous or it may have been good judgment, but lucky for the beleaguered Major General W. S. Rosecrans, he had his best general (Thomas) at the helm when the fight started. Attempting to direct the thrust and parry of his army, Rosecrans dispatched orders from Widow Glenn's small cabin, located on a hill to the rear of Major General Thomas J. Crittenden's position.

First one side would have the advantage and would drive the other back amid heavy casualties; then the tide of battle would turn the other way when reinforcements threw volleys of lead into their rivals. At times regiments fought on their own, without direction, as if caught up in an instinctive drive to inflict injury and death. Once the fighting became intense, it remained intense so that all day long, as the battle raged, the deadly contest gave out one, long continuous roar, with dense clouds of smoke fouling the air. Because of the smoke and the thickness of the entangled vegetation, it was difficult for a soldier to see much beyond the end of his rifle. This battle, like so many others in the war, was fought as much by ear as it was by eye.

On the Union side, Crittenden was performing with both skill and valor. He rode up and down LaFayette Road, dubbed "the Bloody Lane," rallying and directing troops. Rosecrans recognized this and placed him in charge of the Union center. This meant that Major General Alexander M. McCook was protecting the right at Lee and Gordon's Mill on the southern end of the Union line where it was still relatively quiet.

At ten o'clock that morning, McCook received his first dispatch of the day from Headquarters Department. In it, Garfield told McCook to hold the right where he was, close to water, and make "dispositions to relieve [division commander under Thomas] General Negley."[1] Fifteen minutes later McCook was ordered to send a division to Widow Glenn's with orders to support Thomas.[2] He sent Brigadier General Richard W. Johnson's division. Soon thereafter he sent Davis and his division. At this point two-thirds of his corps was out of his control.

Then at one o'clock in the afternoon, he received the following from Major General James A. Garfield: "General Thomas is heavily engaged, and Palmer and Johnson have been ordered up to support him. All goes well thus far. A considerable cavalry force of the enemy has got in behind us, and are threatening our trains. The general commanding directs you to hurry [Colonel John G.] Mitchell's cavalry in upon our right, and send a detachment to look out for our rear."[3]

The pace of fighting was quickening, and Rosecrans — who ate and slept very little but smoked constantly — was showing signs of cracking under the strain of battle. Once again, as at Stones River, Bragg had by surprise gained the advantage. Yet Rosecrans desperately tried to maintain self-control despite his weariness. Late in the afternoon, Rosecrans decided to get McCook more involved in the fight. McCook was needed at Viniard Farm where the fighting was heaviest and casualties were piling up at an alarming rate. Garfield sent McCook another dispatch: "The tide of battle sweeps to the right. The commanding general thinks you can now move the two brigades of Sheridan's up to this place. Leave one brigade posted at Gordon's Mill ... if the right is secure come forward and direct your forces now fighting."[4]

In response, McCook sent General Philip H. Sheridan with two brigades, those of Lieutenant Colonel Luther Bradley and Lieutenant Colonel Bernard Laiboldt. McCook's report indicates he personally arrived at the scene of the battle "at the close of the engagement on the 19th" to supervise the efforts of his generals. His report praises the fighting of both Johnson's and Davis' divisions. Johnson fought on the extreme left of the line of battle, "driving the enemy more than a mile, capturing seven of the enemy's guns and a large number of prisoners." He lauded Davis' division that fought "against vastly superior numbers."[5]

The noise of the battle was positively deafening, as if all the demons of every war in man's past had risen up and out of the bloody ground to join in the mad orgy of gunfire and death. Men who had fought at Antietam and Bull Run were later to say that by comparison, the battle of Chickamauga was by far the loudest. And in the midst of it all, soldiers on both sides were falling fast as regiments and brigades disintegrated in the withering fire. Call it courage or call it madness, but the mind-set on both sides was fight to the death. It was what soldiers called "battle rage," a bizarre state of mind where "things of the body are forgotten," amid the "roar and din of musketry."[6] Through it all, telegraph service was surprisingly effective and Charles Dana managed to send seven messages to Stanton relating the progress of the battle.[7]

When daylight finally and mercifully gave way to darkness, and the sound and fury of the fight fell silent, every Union unit except two brigades had thrown themselves into the epic struggle. As a result, the Union troops still controlled the main roads leading north, thus securing their line of retreat. Rosecrans had lost a lot of men but surrendered no ground.

It was estimated that the first day of fighting resulted in about 6,000 to 9,000 Confederate casualties and about 7,000 Union losses, killed, wounded and missing. And for all the sacrifice and suffering, the outcome was still in doubt. It was a stalemate. To the exhausted soldier, too tired to do anything but find a place to collapse, the coming of the morning was sure to mean the resumption of fighting.

The night brought its own form of torment. Though the guns were silent, the wind came down from the north, blowing cold through the woods. Men on both sides shivered in the unseasonable cold, especially the Rebels whose clothing was inferior to that of the Yankees. Neither side was permitted to light fires. So to keep warm, men "spooned" in groups on the bare ground, trying to sleep, on what for many would be their last night among the living.

The minor luxury of a dreamless sleep gave way to the moans and wails of the wounded, lying alone and helpless by the thousands. Disabled, cold and bleeding, begging for water, a friend, a mother or death, their piteous cries

Major General Alexander M. McCook always took pride in his military bearing and appearance. In this photograph he looks very regal and proud on his horse. Unfortunately, at the battle of Chickamauga, McCook's army career met with disaster as the Army of the Cumberland sustained a resounding defeat. McCook, Rosecrans and Crittenden were relieved of duty and subjected to official inquiries into their conduct at that terrible battle. While McCook's bravery was never questioned, his judgment was deemed suspect.

grew to a haunting crescendo, an overpowering, terrible sound that took on a character more disturbing and far more unforgettable than the booming of artillery and musket fire.

Meanwhile commands on both sides had plans for the next phase. Rosecrans—all thoughts of conquest gone—called his generals together to patch together some type of defense. He was now convinced that Rebel General James Longstreet was either on the scene or close to it. Rosecrans was outnumbered and out-generaled; staggered, but far from beaten, he ordered logs to be cut for defensive breastworks.

At Widow Glenn's cabin, Rosecrans, Thomas, McCook, Crittenden and other generals conferred. Thomas slept through most of the session, waking up long enough to say, "I would strengthen the left." Rosecrans was anything but his usual loquacious self; his jovial side had given way to gloom and fatigue. Still he managed to think clearly enough to devise a battle plan.

At 11:45 P.M., Rosecrans handed a message to Thomas that sounded deceptively simple but not entirely optimistic: "The line of battle for to-morrow is your present line, and a line which General McCook will form from your right to this place [Widow Glenn's]. General Crittenden will be held in reserve on the eastern slope of Missionary Ridge, in the rear of your right. You will defend your position with utmost stubbornness. In case our army should be overwhelmed it will retire on Rossville and Chattanooga."[8]

The Union would defend LaFayette Road on its front and the Dry Valley Road (that led back to Chattanooga) on its rear. McCook was ordered to place the divisions of Davis and Sheridan on Thomas' right. He was to "refuse his own right in order to protect both Widow Glenn and the Dry Valley Road." He had a mere five brigades to hold a line about a mile long, a far cry from the corps he commanded when he crossed the Tennessee River. The repositioning of his troops meant McCook would get very little sleep that night.

About midnight the planning and ordering were concluded. And though he was very tired, Rosecrans could not break his custom of doing a bit of post-meeting socializing. He ordered some food and coffee for his generals and asked Alexander M. McCook to sing "The Hebrew Maiden's Lament," a ballad that had been popular for about 15 years. McCook, who was a good singer, sang to the generals about shedding bitter tears, and when he was finished, the meeting broke up.[9]

Meanwhile Bragg conducted his own strategy session with his generals. Longstreet, who was fully expected to arrive that night, would take charge of the left wing, and Lieutenant General Leonidas "Bishop" Polk would command the Rebel right. Bragg would attack with both wings and resume the pounding of the Union troops. Polk left the meeting upset because he wanted more support for his unit. But then a petulant attitude by Polk toward Bragg was the norm, as the two strong-willed men disliked one another intensely.

James "Pete" Longstreet arrived at the Rebel camp about eleven o'clock that night and found Bragg asleep. While there was a measure of distrust between the two men, they sat down and methodically discussed the coming fight and studied maps of the area.

When Longstreet left Virginia, Robert E. Lee simply said, "General, you must beat those people."[10] Lee called Longstreet his old warhorse, and Pete's presence gave Bragg an advantage over Rosecrans. But Bragg was so sensitive to possible interference from other generals that he probably didn't fully appreciate the importance of having Longstreet, one of the ablest of the Confederate commanders, at his disposal.

Overall the Confederate plan was vague and uncertain. A firm strategy was lost because of exhaustion and indifference on the part of Bragg and his generals, whose lack of confidence and dislike of their commander was an excuse to drift back to their camps, fall asleep and leave the next day to the whims of fate.

Sunday, September 20, 1863, dawned dim, with smoke and fog obscuring the vision needed to see and shoot at the enemy. Thus no attack at dawn was practicable. Even so Polk was slow to prepare for the day's fighting that he had been ordered to start. An angry Bragg set out to apply a verbal lash or two on his recalcitrant generals. Why wasn't Breckinridge up and shooting?

Rosecrans was quick to take advantage of the fog and Rebel complacency, and set about rearranging his right, stationing Sheridan near Widow Glenn's house. While he was clearly suffering from the lack of sleep, Rosecrans heard pre-dawn Mass and then dutifully inspected his line. In doing so, he found that McCook was not yet in position. Rosecrans angrily confronted McCook and rebuked him for his slowness and because his line was so strung out that it was a "mere thread." McCook was told to close up at once; Rosecrans wanted no repeat of the kind of rout that occurred at Stones River.[11]

Rosecrans wasn't finished yelling. After leaving a chastened McCook, "Old Rosy" engaged in a shouting match with Brigadier General Thomas J. Wood, whose skin was far thinner than that of McCook. Under the terrible pressure of command, Rosecrans was experiencing a mood swing, showing his angry side, and his generals got an all-too-familiar dose of his wrath.

It wasn't until about nine o'clock that firing started on the Union left, when Breckinridge hit Beatty's brigade hard at Kelly field. Once again Thomas was being challenged, most likely thinking about his advice to Rosecrans at the council of war the evening before when he insisted that the left be strengthened. Rosecrans didn't have to be reminded, and he immediately sent an order to McCook instructing him to be prepared to send reinforcements to Thomas.

Fighting on the left was furious but the Union lines held, due in large part to the log breastworks. True to form, Bragg attempted to weaken Thomas' position by massing men against the defenses. As at the battle of Stones River, Breckinridge's men were badly hammered. And once again the former vice president of the United States came close to routing his opponent, but ended up losing about a third of his division, including two brigade commanders. Among the Confederate casualties was Brigadier General Benjamin Hardin Helm, a much-respected brother-in-law to President Lincoln.

Polk wasn't finished, however, and he sent General Pat Cleburne's division at the Union left, slamming into Richard W. Johnson's division. For about an hour the Rebels attacked the well-camouflaged Union troops. For all their valor the Rebels died in droves as the slaughter was immense and the sound of musketry deafening. The savage bloodletting of the day before returned with renewed fury.

Strangely, a bewildered white dove was seen flying over the battle ground, in and out of the smoke and dust until it landed on an artillery piece. It was caught by an artillery man whose dirty hands smudged its white feathers with black powder. The soldier, content merely to touch the symbol of peace for a moment, let the bird go, and it disappeared in a cloud of smoke.[12]

The ethereal intervention had no effect on the pace of the battle. And finally, after about three hours, the morning fighting on the Union left subsided, and the Southerners fell back to regroup; their losses were staggering. Rosecrans' plan was sound and was working.

All morning long, Rosecrans kept troops in motion, moving from right to left to reinforce Thomas. In doing so, Rosecrans was so busy giving orders that the usually reliable Garfield couldn't keep up. To help out, Rosecrans ordered Major Frank Bond, his senior aide-de-camp, to write orders. Bond, who lacked Garfield's cool, facile mind and knowledge of his commander's style, couldn't write with the same speed and clarity.

For example, at 3 P.M., Bond sent a message to McCook directing him to send a brigade from Sheridan "to support Davis, who is hardly pressed." Minutes later, he corrected the message, noting correctly that Davis was "hard pressed."[13] This lack of clarity interfered with Rosecrans' ability to relay orders to his generals.

And he still had Longstreet to contend with. While Union troops were fighting desperately to repel the Rebel attack on the left, the diminished right was struck a mortal blow at the hands of Longstreet's corps. This shocking development resulted in large part from one of Rosecrans' hastily written orders.

While he was being assailed on both fronts, Rosecrans frantically tried to fashion a strategy to thwart defeat. He turned to Garfield to dictate yet another order, when he noticed that his chief of staff was preoccupied. Turning to Bond, he dictated the following order to General Thomas J. Wood: "The general commanding directs that you close up on Reynolds as fast as possible and support him." Major General John J. Reynolds was the commander of the 4th Division of Thomas' corps. The order was marked "gallop," meaning it had to be delivered as speedily as possible.

The order was given in response to yet another request by Thomas for assistance on the left. Thomas wanted General John M. Brannan's division, which was supporting Reynolds, and Rosecrans wanted him to have it. And when Brannan pulled out, Wood was to fill the vacant space.

Rosecrans didn't read the order as written by Bond and it was indeed taken away at a gallop by Lieutenant Colonel Lyne Starling. As Starling started on his way, Rosecrans shouted that Wood was to align himself on the left of Reynolds, not behind him. This correction was repeated by Garfield as Starling rode off to deliver the order.

When the courier reached Wood, his division was in line, ready to face the approaching enemy onslaught. His troops were already skirmishing.

Alexander M. McCook and Wood were standing next to a tree when the message was delivered at about 11:00 A.M. Wood read the order. And despite the attempt by the courier to explain its true intent, Wood, still smarting from Rosecrans' sharp, insulting rebuke earlier that day, decided to interpret it according to the written words. So strong was his anger that he was willing to let his personal feelings take precedence over his duties as a division commander during the boiling point of a desperate fight.

Wood supposedly said, "Gentlemen, I hold the fatal order of the day in my hand and would not part with it for five thousand dollars."

He immediately began withdrawing his troops from the battle line, while his brigade commanders shook their heads in disapproval. Wood later insisted that he asked McCook to fill the gap and McCook agreed to do so. McCook just as strongly insisted that he made no such promise because he had insufficient troops available.[14]

McCook's official report indicates that at about 11:00 A.M., he was carrying out an order from Rosecrans to send two brigades of Sheridan's division at the double-quick over to support Thomas. It was then that, to his great surprise, Wood was pulling out of line.

Wood's petulant response to a poorly worded order proved costly in more ways than one. This act, more than any other by either side during two days of fighting, precipitated a Southern victory. Wood's impulsive action became the subject of controversy and argument for decades. General David S. Stanley, in his memoirs, said Wood's action was "in the highest degree criminal." He blamed the Chickamauga defeat squarely on Wood.[15]

In Wood's official report, he repeated, verbatim, the order he received from Major Bond. And then he stated, "When I moved my command to go to the support of General Reynolds, the gap made in our lines was not closed by troops on my right, and the enemy poured through it very soon in great force." While he doesn't place any blame on anyone, Wood makes it clear that he expected McCook to fill the gap.[16]

Rosecrans' dispassionate post-battle report is not finger-pointing either. He simply states that "General Wood, overlooking the direction to 'close up' on General Reynolds, supposed he was to support him, by withdrawing from the line and passing to the rear of General Brannan." Calling it an "unfortunate mistake," Rosecrans said the gap in the line of battle invited the enemy to take "instant advantage" of an error of tragic proportions.[17]

The uncanny timing of events could not have been worse for the Union. Seeing the inviting gap of several hundred yards between the Union center and right, Longstreet's troops poured through it in great strength, eight brigades in five columns, crushing the weakened federal line. The Union right was cut off and subjected to a fearful attack by overwhelming firepower. The Union center was turned and shattered. Demoralized troops were on the run on the

Dry Valley Road toward Rossville. The Union headquarters at Widow Glenn's was overrun and the staff scattered.

Dana was taking a nap at the Widow Glenn cabin when the shooting and shouting woke him up. He panicked when he saw troops running away from the gray onslaught. He noticed that Rosecrans crossed himself and realized they were really in trouble. Soon thereafter Rosecrans composed himself and attempted to rally his troops, but the panic among them was contagious. The rout was on. Once again the Union right, such as it was at the time, was being crushed and scattered. Rather than watch any more of the madness, Dana mounted up and galloped, non-stop, for Chattanooga. The assistant secretary of war was not about to become a casualty or a prisoner.

At some point during the disaster, the Widow Glenn log cabin was hit by a Rebel blast and went up in flames. Fortunately, no one was in the cabin at the time, for Rosecrans and his staff officers were on their horses, desperately trying to restore some order to the chaos and stem the tide of runaway troops.

McCook tried to resist the Rebel assault with two brigades of Davis' division and one brigade of Sheridan's division consisting of about 1,200 men, but it was hopeless. Confederate General John B. Gordon recalled in his battle memoir that McCook and Sheridan rode at the head of their troops leading them in a gallant and fearless charge against the Southern front. And Dana, who had no love for McCook, reported back to Stanton that "McCook, with the right of his corps and [Colonel John T.] Wilder's mounted infantry, attempted to recover the day, but it was useless."[18]

In his weighty book, *Annals of the Army of the Cumberland*, John Fitch described the efforts of McCook and Crittenden as heroic. Fitch, who served as provost judge of the Army of the Cumberland, was quick to note that both generals did their best with depleted commands, most of their men having been shifted to the left to support Thomas. And yet in the chaos and confusion, they "labored with all possible zeal and ardor to repair the disaster of the hour." Both generals rode about like men possessed, trying desperately to gather their men together and continue the fight. While he was careful not to mention General Wood by name, Fitch said the gap left in the Union line, caused by an "error in the movement of a division," allowed the Rebels to annihilate the federal right and center. McCook and Crittenden were not to blame.[19]

McCook's report states that five brigades of his corps were cut off from the rest of the Army of the Cumberland, and yet they put up a strong resistance. He was further hampered by the lack of cavalry, as mounted troops ordered to report to him failed to do so.[20] McCook concluded that "no troops fought with more heroism or suffered greater losses than these five small brigades, their loss being over 40 per cent of the number engaged in killed and wounded."[21]

Sheridan was nearly overcome by despair. Two of his brigades — those of

Bradley and Laiboldt — were decimated, the latter as a result of an order by McCook. A man who liked a good fight, Sheridan would not remember this battle with any fondness. He had suffered through two days of seeing his division badly used up.

He, McCook, Rosecrans and Crittenden were faced with the smoke-plumed wreckage of two corps of a great army. Lifeless and suffering bodies were everywhere; riderless horses meant that dead and wounded colonels and generals were lying or limping amidst the carnage. Dispirited and exhausted soldiers wandered about in a daze; the army was transformed into a zombie-like band of men lost in a cloud of smoke, chaos and defeat. Each soldier acted as if he were grappling with a near-death experience, each one sleepwalking with a desire to wake up in a place of safety and sanity.

The surviving commanders were battling private thoughts that no one can ever know, and facing misgivings over bad strategy and questionable decision making. Each had to face his role in the disaster and the need to make decisions for himself and for the fleeing troops. For military men in positions of leadership, it is times such as this that decisions are made that make or break careers.

Overwhelmed by the terrible turn of events, and reduced to a silent caricature of his former self, a crestfallen Rosecrans decided to leave the field of battle, and in the company of Garfield and a few others, he started up Dry Valley Road, in the direction of Thomas' position. Meanwhile Sheridan led his tired, thinned ranks toward Missionary Ridge, having come to the conclusion that all was lost; he would let his men go on their way and save themselves. They had suffered so much in two days of fighting that he could ask no more of them.

McCook and his staff came upon part of Rosecrans' cavalry escort. After stopping to assess the situation, McCook spoke with an old man whom Rosecrans impressed into service as a guide. According to witnesses, McCook drew his revolver, placed the barrel at the old man's head and said: "If you guide us into rebel lines I will blow your head off." McCook, well-known for his cursing, used other vivid language during his admonition of the reluctant guide.[22]

The guide led the group away from the fighting to a point beyond Dry Valley Road. Possibly feeling somewhat safer and perhaps a bit ashamed over leaving the field of battle, McCook spoke about hooking up with Thomas. About that time he came across a wounded officer from the army engineers who advised McCook to forget about joining Thomas, for he too was beaten and in retreat. McCook and his entourage continued on their way to Chattanooga.

Crittenden had become separated from Rosecrans and McCook, and tried to rally some stragglers. But he, too, believed that all further resistance would be futile, and speculating that McCook and Rosecrans were captured or dead, he pressed on to Chattanooga.

Meanwhile Rosecrans, after consultation with Garfield, decided that someone should go find Thomas. Rosecrans sent Garfield, who was only too glad to go. He returned to the action, and in doing so, turned away from a mistake that, had he made it, would have ruined the political career he had in mind. Rosecrans continued on to Chattanooga where he would take up the task of reorganizing his scattered and dispirited army, while future president James A. Garfield made his way back to Thomas and into history as a hero. It was a calculated move. He was willing to risk death not only for his country and comrades, but for the sake of his political ambition.

Thomas had gained some advantageous high ground on which to make a stand. He was joined by Granger who decided that despite orders to the contrary, he would see what he could do to help out. Granger ordered Daniel McCook to stay behind and cover the Ringgold Road on the Union left. His last words to Colonel McCook: "Hold the road to the last extremity." McCook replied, "When my brigade retreats he [Granger] can report Dan McCook among the killed."[23] Granger later ordered McCook to forget about guarding the road and instead take a position on an open ridge, northwest of the McDonald farm. Dan McCook and his brigade were soon in the thick of the fighting.

Granger found Thomas where the latter had rallied the troops on a place called Horseshoe Ridge, high ground that the triumphant Rebels felt they could and must take to make their victory complete. Thomas stubbornly and courageously directed the battle, holding off the Rebels. He was fighting with the divisions of Baird, Brannan, Johnson, Palmer, Wood and Reynolds. Sheridan had returned and joined the fight with about 1,500 of his division.

But Thomas, too, felt that his men had done all they could and ordered a retreat after nightfall. At about ten o'clock on the night of the 20th, Daniel McCook's brigade trudged away from Horseshoe Ridge onto McFarland's Gap Road, the last Union unit to leave the battlefield. He reported the loss of just two men.[24]

The savage, two-day battle was over, and the Confederacy was in possession of the field of battle. Bragg sent a telegram to Richmond, thanking Almighty God for bestowing the South with a win. But much to the anger of his commanders, Bragg did not pursue the broken Union army and finish the job. At this point he had no idea as to the extent of his victory; his army was exhausted and had suffered an immense number of casualties. One writer estimated the South lost 2,673 killed, 16,174 wounded and 2,003 missing, for a staggering total of 20,950 men. The Union losses were smaller but no less significant: 1,656 killed, 9,749 wounded and 3,774 missing, for a total of 16,179 casualties out of 57,840 men who were on hand for the battle.[25]

Having stayed and fought while his fellow generals left the field of battle, George H. Thomas earned the title the "Rock of Chickamauga." The newspapers picked up the story and Thomas' sudden fame was blazing across the North. Meanwhile, the reputations of Generals Rosecrans, McCook and Crittenden were for all practical purposes ruined. Their decision to depart from the fighting was upsetting to both men and officers, and public opinion turned against McCook and Crittenden. Although they may have believed they made the right decision, a general leaving a field of battle always looks bad. Dana, who disliked all three, did his best to undermine any chances they had at maintaining their commands, proving to be a "spy" after all. He reported that several generals, including Sheridan, Wood and Johnson, refused to serve under the disgraced generals who witnesses said ran from the battle like scared rabbits.

Interestingly, Dana apparently forgot that he too mounted up and ran like a scared rabbit.

Some newspapers added to the chorus of condemnation. The *Cincinnati Weekly Gazette* said McCook's decision to "take the road lying through the valley, thus losing two days," was "one link in the chain of blunders which the disasters of Chickamauga may be ascribed."[26] This is a reference to McCook's long march over a circuitous route during the week before the battle. That same newspaper said McCook

Major General George H. Thomas, friend and colleague of McCook, not only survived the battle of Chickamauga, but emerged as its hero. His corps stood its ground while those of McCook and Crittenden were routed, and Thomas became known as the "Rock of Chickamauga." He was chosen to replace Rosecrans as commander of the reorganized Army of the Cumberland. When the war ended, Thomas was considered one of the Union's greatest generals.

deserved the criticism that was leveled at him because of an "unbroken succession of disasters he has brought upon his commanders." The *Gazette* concluded that McCook had at last fallen out of favor after having been granted the "forbearance of General Rosecrans," as well as the press and public.[27]

While the *Gazette* was quick to jump to the defense of Rosecrans, it showed no mercy or respect for the highest-ranking member of the "Fighting McCooks." Although the *Gazette* was informed of Wood's withdrawal of troops and the subsequent rout of the overwhelmed Union right by onrushing Rebels, it nevertheless speedily denounced McCook. For "McCook disappeared from the general history of the battle ... extricating himself from his demoralized and routed corps."[28] McCook and Crittenden were "in disgrace" and would face charges for their misconduct.[29]

A general in Davis' division added to the condemnation. Years later while penning his memoirs, Brigadier General William P. Carlin concluded that McCook was at least indirectly responsible for the Union defeat at Chickamauga. Because McCook's march over Lookout Mountain to reach Thomas at Steven's Gap took three and a half days, the delay in uniting the army resulted in the stunning loss.[30]

The *New York Times* printed an anonymous letter from a soldier or an officer who said that "McCook and staff came riding by going from the field." When asked about the status of the battle, McCook reportedly said, "This is the worst whipped army you ever saw." The man said he "felt like cursing the man that would leave the field, as McCook had done."[31]

The happy Confederate post-battle report praised its left wing that went crashing into the Union right, causing McCook and Crittenden to flee "before the heroes of Manassas and Murfreesborough [*sic*]."[32] It may be true that the South "never smiled after Shiloh," but one would not stretch poetic license too much to suggest that the Confederacy broke into a cheery grin after Chickamauga.

Of course had McCook caught a bullet and died in the midst of the disaster, he would have been a hero, and the public and press would have sung a different tune, celebrating the "gallant general" who was killed while trying to rally his troops. This is probably what the gruff and blunt General Stanley — who was hospitalized with dysentery and fever at the time of the battle — had in mind, when in his war memoirs, he said that "McCook might have saved his reputation by joining either Davis's or Sheridan's Division of his own Corps."[33]

While public opinion and negative press coverage were damaging, Dana delivered the death blow. He sent a poison pen dispatch to Stanton on the 20th, saying it was the "blunder of McCook in marching back from his previous advanced position" that "cost us four days of precious time." Had McCook not blundered, the "disaster might perhaps have been avoided."[34]

Stanton convened a meeting with Lincoln. There Stanton presented his case for removing the three generals he didn't like, especially Rosecrans. Lincoln's secretary, John Hay, was present at the War Department meeting and heard Stanton say: "No, they need not shuffle it off on McCook. He is not much of a soldier. I never was in favor of him for a Major-General. But he is not accountable for this business. He and Crittenden both made pretty good time away from the fight to Chattanooga, but Rosecrans beat them both."[35]

Navy Secretary Gideon Welles wrote in his diary that McCook and Crittenden "wilted" when they were needed the most and instead of staying on the field galloped off to Chattanooga and "went to sleep."[36] All in all the facts, as known in Washington, painted a grim and unflattering picture of the generals known for their unselfish service and gallantry. Based on Dana's letter, the facts as the president knew them, and Stanton's urging, Lincoln signed orders relieving McCook and Crittenden.

Stanton, of course, was a friend of the McCook family, a friendship that dated back to the 1840s. During the Civil War, the hardworking Stanton was known as a "bull-head" because he was opinionated and extremely stubborn.[37] Although he was noted for his curt responses, cutting, hurtful remarks and dagger stares, he once showed a softer side. In 1847 Stanton penned a tender letter to Margaret McCook, the wife of his friend George W. McCook, saying, "The disposition and capacity to excite love, belongs to all women; in various degrees

Edwin M. Stanton, secretary of war in the Lincoln administration, was a mystery man of many faces who, while running the war department with skill and efficiency, built a power base that exceeded that of any other member of the cabinet. Before the war, Stanton was a law partner of George W. McCook, a brother of Alexander, but the good relationship formed from the law practice only went so far. Stanton convinced Lincoln that General McCook should be removed from command because of the rout of the Union right at Chickamauga.

to be sure, and with power according to the endowments with which they may have been blessed."[38]

Stanton, whom Lincoln affectionately called "Mars," was endowed with a fierce dedication to his work and would let nothing, including friendship, cloud his vision and his determination. He was obsessed with just one thing: winning the war.

Owing to the secretary's character and devotion to duty, the McCook family connection with Stanton, gained through George W. McCook's law partnership, was insufficient to save General McCook's reputation. But then the disdain that Stanton felt toward Alex McCook was met by an equal measure of contempt, for the fallen general once called the secretary "a natural born fool."[39] Furthermore, two years after the war ended, McCook took another swipe at the secretary of war, joining a group of other generals who signed a "round-robin" asking that President Andrew Johnson fire Stanton.[40]

Firing McCook and Crittenden was relatively easy, but the decision to sack Rosecrans was more difficult to make. As the sensitive president was partial to Rosecrans and had recently sent the general an encouraging message, Lincoln stopped short of firing him, despite pressure from Stanton. Lincoln had to take into account the politics of the matter, knowing that Rosecrans was very popular in Ohio where people were about to elect a governor. Lincoln wanted that office to go to a Republican.

Upon placing General U. S. Grant in charge of all the forces in the West, Lincoln found a way to relieve Rosecrans, whom he believed had become unnerved after Chickamauga and was therefore unable to act decisively. False but deadly rumors were circulating, saying Rosecrans was drinking heavily, and "his opium eating, his liability to epileptic fits" along with religious delusions had rendered him incompetent.[41] In his folksy yet blunt style, Lincoln said that Rosecrans was acting "confused and stunned like a duck hit on the head."[42] He gave Grant the option of keeping him or replacing him. Grant chose the latter. General Thomas would take Rosecrans' place.

Dana had urged Stanton to impress upon Lincoln the dire need to sack all three troubled generals, saying that there was "grave unrest" among other officers that threatened the *esprit de corps* of the Army of the Cumberland. Dana claimed to have overheard an officer saying that if McCook retained his command, "the right will be licked again." So the bloodless deed was done although there was opinion floating about that McCook and Crittenden were sacrificed for Rosecrans' shortcomings at Chickamauga.[43]

A letter from Major Anson McCook — who was absent on detached duty, thereby missing the fight — to his cousin George W. McCook expressed this concern. Writing from Chattanooga on October 8, 1863, Anson informed George of the "successful attempt to slaughter Alex," assuming that his cousin may have heard the bad news from "other sources." Anson named Dana as the responsible party. He expressed great surprise that Crittenden was brought down with Alex, saying, "I thought they would not have the courage to take off the head of so prominent a Kentuckian." Anson wrote, "I have made diligent inquiries as to Alex's conduct and can gather nothing that can possibly affect his military reputation or his character as a soldier." Furthermore, he added, Rosecrans had "assured both that it was not done at his request."

Anson explained, correctly, that Alex's corps had been greatly reduced by sending division after division to protect the Union left. He said that Alex had received an order to report to Rosecrans and finding that the commanding general had gone to Chattanooga, went there along with Crittenden in obedience of orders. Defending his kinsmen, Anson wrote: "It is unfortunate, perhaps, that they left the field at all but those who know them, know very well that they most certainly do not lack courage."

Anson was concerned over his family's reputation as well as the political nature of the demotion and wanted to caution his brash cousin — known to make rash comments — against making "unguarded expressions," or "he is a goner." Anson's anger and disgust are apparent when he says, "The whole thing is a most infamous outrage and Alex is determined to have the matter thoroughly ventilated." He closed the matter telling George, "I scarcely know what to do. My regiment is torn to pieces and that, in addition to the attempt to disgrace Alex makes me feel like resigning."[44]

A disconsolate Anson McCook conducted his own inquiry into the matter, and from what he could gather, his cousin should not have been relieved of command, nor should he have been accused of wrongdoing. He insisted that Alex and Crittenden were made scapegoats by those who wanted to cover up their own incompetence. Truly, this was a low point in the otherwise successful military service of an entire family of fighting men.

However, it wasn't all bad news and foreboding for the McCook family. General Thomas cited Colonel Daniel McCook for "gallant and meritorious conduct at the battle of Chickamauga, September 19 and 20, when he commanded a brigade of the Reserve Corps, and being posted in an important position on the afternoon of September 20, 'kept a large force of the enemy's cavalry at bay.'"[45] While he was not heavily involved in the action, Colonel McCook held his ground and was inching closer to that brigadier's star.

By order of the president, the Army of the Cumberland was reorganized, and the tattered remnants of the 20th and 21st corps were combined into the new 4th Army Corps, with Major General Gordon Granger in command — the same martinet who wanted to kill his hungry troops for trying to find food. But Granger stayed on the field of battle until Thomas ordered a retreat, so his unpopularity with his men was overlooked. He moved up while others moved down.

Generals McCook and Crittenden received their termination notices and were ordered to "repair to Indianapolis" and report their arrival by letter to the adjutant general, for an official inquiry into their conduct at the battle of Chickamauga.[46] Crittenden was upset and angry at the news and threatened to resign; McCook took it all in stride and was said to have merely accepted his fate. One of his last official acts as an officer in the Army of the Cumberland was to send a dispatch to Braxton Bragg, asking for permission to remove "bodies of certain officers" from the battlefield. It was granted.[47]

Before he left, McCook sent Rosecrans a letter in response to a claim in some newspapers that he (McCook) disobeyed an order from his commander. Would Rosecrans please be so kind as to explain what order it was he failed to obey? Rosecrans immediately replied: "I take pleasure in saying to you that no official, or other dispatches of mine, have warranted a charge of disobedience of orders by you, on either days of the battle of Chickamauga."[48]

The letter was considered just another example of Rosecrans' misplaced magnanimous attitude toward McCook. Dana couldn't resist taunting McCook, calling it a "white-washing" letter.[49] Dana was no doubt upset when Rosecrans' report of the battle of Chickamauga commended General McCook "for the care of his command, prompt and willing execution of orders, to the best of his ability."[50]

Interestingly, Rosecrans' commendations did not include General Wood, but he had high praise for George H. Thomas, America's new hero and star general. Thomas, whose sense of humility would not allow him to revel in his new status, replaced his good friend William S. Rosecrans, albeit reluctantly. As each man looked to the other with the highest respect, there was a smooth transition of command.

While reorganization was taking place, the government tried to keep a lid on the Chickamauga debacle, exercising its censorship powers. That didn't stop Henry Villard, a reporter for the *New York Tribune*, who traveled to Chattanooga to gather information. He found many men eager to talk, including McCook and Crittenden, both of whom wanted to get their version of the story out.[51] While McCook distrusted journalists, he was willing to use them in emergencies such as the one he was facing, sensing a chance to defend himself.

McCook was not without support from other officers. One of the first to rise to McCook's defense was William Dodge Sumner, who had served in the 2nd Division, Army of the Ohio. In a book that came out in 1864, Sumner blamed the press for working up negative public opinion about McCook. Sumner flayed McCook's "maligners" from the press who had been waiting like vultures for the chance to destroy him. After the defeat at Chickamauga, the press let loose with "its denunciations" and "vile slanders," poisoning public opinion.

Reminding his readers that a man is innocent until proven guilty, he slammed all those who condemned McCook before any charges were filed or evidence considered. Shame on the newspapers and shame on their gullible readers, for they were not satisfied with the bloodshed on the field of battle, and instead wanted more victims. In Sumner's eyes, General McCook was a hero who "so frequently defended the honor of his country's flag ... baring his own bosom to ... their [the Rebels] missiles of death." Such a man should be praised and honored, not condemned nor called a coward.[52]

Rosecrans, McCook and Crittenden learned what other deposed generals understood; sometimes your best is not good enough in an unforgiving world that demanded miracles from mere mortals. If generals and those around them failed, the critics forgot that these men risked their lives and served their country. One bad decision in the midst of chaos and wholesale destruction had the unholy power to stay with an officer for life. Instead of gratitude, the three men, who dearly loved the military and their country, were handed their official heads, subjected to the indignities of an official investigation, and then, like condemned felons, were left with bitter memories to wear like weighted chains.

"McCook ... seemed to be possessed by a strange fatality," wrote General William B. Hazen, a survivor of the battle of Chickamauga. Looking back on Perryville and Stones River, Hazen recalled that McCook "assumed a kind of boastful over-confidence that in war always presages failure" because it usually results in the lack of thoughtful planning needed for success. Call it too much bluff and bluster. Hazen believed this was McCook's chief character flaw, and it led to his undoing.[53]

Another general who served with McCook throughout the Tullahoma and Chickamauga campaigns, namely James A. Garfield, scarcely mentions him in his book of Civil War letters, except to say that his brother officer had a good singing voice.[54]

On October 6, 1863, Alexander McDowell McCook wrote a good-bye letter to his corps, telling the men matter-of-factly that he had been relieved of command and ordered to appear before a court of inquiry. While he regretted having to bid good-bye to the corps, he expressed a willingness to appear before the board and testify as to his actions on the 19th and 20th of September. He welcomed a "thorough investigation of my conduct during the two memorable days of Chickamauga, for I do not fear the issue."

Rather than give in to bitterness and blame, McCook tendered his thanks for the loyalty extended to him, and asked his men and officers to obey and follow their new commanders. He urged them to serve with "discipline, zeal and patriotism in our great cause and never lay down your arms until this unholy rebellion is crushed and the Union is permanently restored."

As he was proud to serve, he refused to slam the military. Instead McCook saved his invective for the newspaper community. He couldn't resist taking a shot at war reporters, saying to his men: "You have been slandered and maligned by news scribblers, who unfortunately, in our country, mold the public mind." But he had faith that the official record would "do you justice before the world."

General McCook closed with a wish that his men would "prosper as a corps and as individuals" and be blessed with ultimate victory for the "nation and glorious flag."[55] Then he and his staff departed Chattanooga for Indianapolis, as ordered, trusting that the official record would vindicate him so that he would be returned to command. He was just 32 years old and wasn't ready to retire or take a desk job. He was thoroughly military, devoted to the Union, and would welcome any new assignment where he could serve.

CHAPTER 15

The McCook Inquiry

I think, from what I saw, that he [General McCook] did everything
a general officer could do. I do not think he was responsible for the
repulse of our troops on the right.
— Brigadier General J. C. Davis

By direction of the president of the United States, the official army inquiry
into the conduct of Major General Alexander M. McCook, during the battle
of Chickamauga, convened on January 29, 1864, in Nashville, at the Saint
Cloud Hotel. Generals Crittenden and Negley were subjected to separate proceedings. McCook faced three army judges, namely Major General David
Hunter, Major General George Cadwalader, and Brigadier General J. S.
Wadsworth.[1]

McCook was familiar with Hunter, both men having served at the battle
of Bull Run at the outset of the war. Hunter—who was wounded at Bull
Run—was from Virginia. He graduated from West Point in 1822, and was
said to be an ugly man. Although he was courageous, he was not one of the
great warrior generals of the Union. But he was a strong supporter of Lincoln,
and as a result, Hunter was made the fourth-ranking volunteer general when
the war began. An ardent and angry abolitionist and prone to bouts of violent,
irrational behavior, he made waves in April 1862 when he ordered slavery abolished in Florida, Georgia and South Carolina, a move quickly voided by Lincoln, who was not yet ready for emancipation.

In the later stages of the war, Hunter—dubbed "Black Dave" by Southerners—was thought of as a vandal or worse, because of his wanton and widespread acts of destruction.[2] Jefferson Davis once issued orders that Hunter was
to be considered a felon, and if captured, he was to be executed. Southerners
would have gladly hung Hunter, had he been taken prisoner.

Hunter always seemed to turn up in a prominent role. In 1860, he warned
Lincoln the candidate of a plot to assassinate him should he be elected.[3] In

February 1861 Major Hunter escorted President-elect Lincoln from Springfield, Illinois, as far as Buffalo, New York, where he was forced to leave the bodyguard entourage following an injury caused by a large crowd of people struggling to see the president on his way to his inauguration in Washington.[4] After the assassination of the president, Hunter accompanied Lincoln's body back to Springfield, and he was one of the presiding judges at the military trial of the Lincoln conspirators. Through his zealous efforts, the court found all alleged conspirators guilty of murdering the president, and four of them were rushed off to the gallows.[5] Understandably, he was widely hated in the South.

General Cadwalader was a lawyer from a distinguished Philadelphia family. He had served with distinction in the Mexican War. He was engaged in a successful law practice when the Civil War broke out. He was never assigned to a battlefield position, but he was in command at Fort McHenry in April 1861, when Lincoln suspended habeas corpus and arrested and jailed the strident Maryland secessionist, John Merryman. Chief Justice of the Supreme Court Roger Taney, a Southern sympathizer, issued a writ of habeas corpus while presiding over a circuit court and cited Cadwalader for contempt of court when the general refused to release Merryman. Nothing came of it, however, as Lincoln ignored Taney's writ. Cadwalader spent most of the war on garrison duty, serving on boards of inquiry and military commissions, and as an advisor to the president and secretary of war.[6]

General Wadsworth's life was much more eventful and shorter. He was from Geneseo, New York, and studied law at Harvard which led him to politics, first as a Democrat, and in 1856 as a Republican. While he had no formal military experience, he was staunchly pro–Union and volunteered when the Civil War broke out. He served at the first battle of Bull Run as an aide to General Irwin McDowell, who was instrumental in getting Wadsworth promoted to brigadier general. He became the military governor of the District of Columbia in 1862, and ran for governor of New York on the Republican ticket and lost. He returned to the military and served honorably and bravely in the Army of the Potomac, and some months after the McCook inquiry, General Wadsworth was mortally wounded at the battle of the Wilderness.[7]

The proceedings that Wadsworth and his fellow generals presided over were essentially held in secret, and the results were not made public until after adjournment. The atmosphere was somewhat informal and disinterested, and at no time did any of the judges on the court of inquiry show any hostility to McCook. If the judges conducted any depth of preparation, it did not show up in the proceedings. McCook, himself, was better prepared and at times dominated the inquiry. The judges, by comparison, were rather passive.

McCook was allowed to question all witnesses, subject to objections as to relevancy. He was permitted to bring in his own witnesses. McCook spoke freely and confidently when it was his turn to speak, asking questions with poise and purpose, as if he wanted everything laid out on the table. He presented himself as a soldier who performed his duty as best he could under the circumstances and with no excuses or apologies. Throughout the proceedings, all persons, including McCook were referred to in the third party.

While the war of the rebellion was being pressed on all fronts by both sides, the military formalities began. The looming question, of course, was whether McCook and the other generals subject to inquiry were wrong to leave the field of battle at Chickamauga while other troops were still fighting. The court seemed to be in no hurry to get to the heart of the matter, and the first day's session yielded little of substance.

The first witness was Captain Thomas C. Williams, aide-de-camp to Brigadier General Lovell H. Rousseau. Williams had very little to say except that he did not see McCook on September 19th and 20th, the two days of fighting at Chickamauga. He only recalled seeing Johnson's division of McCook's corps, and testified that they "behaved both days with the utmost gallantry." McCook saw an opening and asked: "Who organized the division that behaved with the utmost gallantry from raw levies?"[8] Before Williams could give McCook credit, the question was ruled irrelevant, and shortly thereafter the first day's session came to an end.

The Court reconvened at Louisville on February 1, 1864. Major Caleb Bates, McCook's aide-de-camp, opened the session, explaining in some detail the posting of the 20th Army Corps on the two days of battle. He painted a favorable picture of his general, noting that McCook was in the saddle and was active and energetic in carrying out his orders, positioning troops in anticipation of an attack. The court quickly moved to events of the 20th, when Brigadier General Thomas J. Wood carried out the fateful order that left a gap in the Union lines. Clearly this would be the focal point of the inquiry.

Bates was asked, "At what time were you attacked on Sunday morning?" His response: "I think it was in the neighborhood of 11 o'clock." Bates said that when he arrived on the scene, the "line was broken and falling back fast." When asked where and what McCook was doing when the disaster was unfolding, Bates testified that the fallen general was to "the rear of the line endeavoring to reform the stragglers and get them into some order. I think the first I saw him he had a flag in his hand trying to get the men together and rally them around him."[9]

When asked if the troops were under fire at that critical time, Bates answered in the affirmative. Then the court got to the heart of the matter: "When did General McCook leave the field?"

Bates answered: "After being driven from this position, the general fell back with the others until out of fire, and there stopped and appeared to be listening to the sound of musketry and artillery." He further explained that McCook and party came across some members of Rosecrans' staff on an "eminence." The group included General Morton and the civilian guide who was to direct them safely away from the firing. They remained on the eminence for about 15 minutes, and then left for Chattanooga.[10]

Still probing, a member of the court asked, "Do you know why he [McCook] did not go to General Thomas?" Bates stated that based on available information, and stragglers who came by, it seemed unlikely that they could reach Thomas' position. Bates said that upon reaching Chattanooga, McCook went directly to Rosecrans' headquarters for orders. The court appeared to be satisfied with Bates' explanation of the tragic happenings and turned the questioning over to General McCook.

McCook sensed things were going favorably and asked Bates: "Did or did not General McCook do all in his power to rally the portion of his command that had broken?" Under oath Bates said calmly, "I think he did all that a man could do." McCook liked what he was hearing and asked: "After the line was broken by the enemy, did General McCook leave the field by his own inclination, or was he driven off the field of battle by the enemy?" Answer: "I think he was driven from the field by the enemy, unless he wished to be killed."[11]

The court interrupted McCook's line of questioning, asked a couple more questions of a general nature, and the proceedings were adjourned. McCook had more than survived the testimony of the first critical witness. A fellow officer testified that he had performed courageously and reasonably under the circumstances.

On the third day of testimony, two more of McCook's aides testified. Captain Beverly D. Williams was present with McCook at mid-day on July 20th, when disaster struck. He recalled that McCook was alert and busy, directing troops under pressure from attacking Rebels. The court members had heard all of this before and began a series of rambling, somewhat disconnected questions about what McCook did once he arrived at Chattanooga.

McCook's questions were geared to explaining his attempts to rally his troops and to show he did not simply panic and flee once the rout was on. Williams testified that "General McCook remained in the rear of the line and endeavored to rally the troops, for an hour to an hour an a half after the line was broken, before he left the field."[12] He went on to say that Rebel firing prevented McCook from going to the aid of General Thomas. He confirmed that at the time of the assault, McCook's command consisted of about 1,300 to 1,400 men from Davis' division.

McCook skillfully elicited testimony to show that at the time of the assault, Johnson's division and one brigade of Davis' division were attached to Thomas, and that Sheridan's division was marching in that direction when the Union right broke. This was very important testimony as it showed the court that McCook was severely undermanned and was facing an overwhelming enemy force.

With just the two brigades of General Davis left to resist and a gap on his left because Wood marched his men out of the line of battle, the Rebel horde rushed in. McCook then asked: "Had not General Davis but one of three things to do: submit to capture, utter annihilation, or take to flight to save his command?" Answer: "No doubt of that, in my opinion."[13] And once again on a McCook high note, the court adjourned.

On February 4, 1864, the fifth day of proceedings, Major General William S. Rosecrans was sworn as a witness. Rosecrans — who had recently been assigned to command the Department of the Missouri — was asked to explain the position of his army, and orders to his commanders on September 20, "so far as it would affect Major General McCook." Rosecrans answered in some detail, recalling that he and McCook disagreed over the positioning of the Union right. There was nothing, however, in Rosecrans' testimony to the effect the he engaged in a shouting match with the Ohio general, or that he rebuked McCook. His testimony conveyed the impression that he had every confidence in McCook's ability to handle his responsibilities on the Union right.

However, when asked, "Did the conduct of General McCook, in leaving his command at such a distance, meet with your approval?" Rosecrans said, "It did not strike me favorably." He added, "I thought it might have been possible to have done something toward gathering the rallied troops, but having no sufficient data, did not tell General McCook that I thought so."[14]

Then it was McCook's turn, and he got right to the heart of the matter, asking, "Was General McCook responsible for the breaking of Davis' line of battle; was it not mainly caused by the moving of troops to his left?" Rosecrans said, "I think the immediate cause was the removal of Wood's division from its place in line, which was done under an order to close instead of opening the line, while the enemy was advancing in force on his front." He said that the speed with which Wood withdrew his men was such that McCook had no time to fill the gap.[15]

In a bold stroke, McCook essentially established the reason for the disaster on the right and cleared himself from wrongdoing. The court heard testimony pointing the finger of responsibility toward General Wood, who was not charged or relieved from command.

McCook stayed the course, asking questions that the court avoided. He asked Rosecrans if "the disaster on the 20th" was the result of his (McCook's) disobedience of orders or "failure to perform his whole duty with the means at his disposal." Rosecrans was somewhat equivocal in his answer. He said there was a "want of vigor and close supervision" on the part of McCook with regard to the positioning of his troops, but "I do not think General McCook disobeyed or failed to obey orders on that day...."[16]

Since McCook's retreat to Chattanooga was an important part of the inquiry, he asked Rosecrans: "When you had learned the reasons for General McCook's presence in Chattanooga, did you censure his conduct?" Rosecrans said there was no censure because he was not fully apprised of the situation on the front, adding, "I regretted that he had not remained at Rossville, but do not remember that I have ever, until now, expressed that regret." It was a mild criticism at best, certainly not what the court would expect to hear from a disappointed commanding officer.

At this point in the proceedings, McCook was essentially in charge, the court allowing his effective questioning to continue. He asked Rosecrans if the withdrawal of his troops to the aid of Thomas left him enough forces to resist the Confederate attack. Again Rosecrans placed no blame on McCook, noting the superior odds that were largely responsible for wrecking the Union battle plan of the 20th.

Overall, the questions and answers went well for McCook and the court adjourned at 10:00 A.M. On paper it looked as if the press and the public had it all wrong and were unduly influenced by Dana and Stanton. Rosecrans went easy on McCook, but then he was talking in front of fellow generals — men who understood that even a well-planned battle could end in disaster. Still, to the enemies of both men, it undoubtedly appeared that their friendship and personal loyalty were showing up in the questions and answers. It was a performance that failed to please everyone.

The next day the court reopened, and the first witness to appear was none other than Brigadier General Thomas J. Wood, whose questionable interpretation of Rosecrans' mid-day order of the 20th became a huge bone of contention. A member of the court asked Wood to state "any material facts bearing upon the conduct of General McCook" on September 19 and 20, during the battle of Chickamauga.

Wood said he only had incidental contact with McCook on the 19th, but the 20th was another matter. Critical to relevant events, Wood noted that he was dismounted and conferring with McCook about the battle, when while conversing he received "an order directly from General Rosecrans to close upon General Reynolds as fast as possible and support him." Wood went on to say, "I remarked to General McCook I should move my division at once to the support of General Reynolds, and that this movement would necessarily vacate the position I was then in." Wood testified that McCook said he would move Davis' division into the position that would be vacated, and then McCook mounted up and rode off toward the right.

It seems that the interval between the battle and the inquiry caused hot blood to cool. Wood made no mention of his anger toward Rosecrans, or that his personal feelings may have tainted his decision to vacate his position without questioning the order given under the heat of battle. McCook undoubtedly felt that the confrontation should have been examined by the court. But he did not pursue that line, asking instead if Wood had any knowledge that he (McCook) failed to use everything within his means to manage his troops effectively. Wood said, "I certainly observed no want of activity or energy on his part."[17]

McCook asked one more question about the positioning of his troops and had no further questions, nor did the court. It would seem that Wood was let off easy. There was no attempt to make him the scapegoat. On the other hand, McCook was well on his way to establishing that his conduct on the 20th was not unreasonable under the circumstances. The court probably believed that prior testimony was such that there was no need for an in-depth grilling of Wood about his hasty decision to obey Rosecrans' pullout order without first questioning it. While Wood's pull out, gap-creating move would be the question for the ages, it was not deemed worthy of the court's interest. Members had heard Rosecrans testify that the gap in the line created by Wood's troop movement was largely responsible for the successful Rebel charge.

If analytical minds were at work, they might have concluded that it would have been easy for Wood to make the five-minute ride back to Widow Glenn's cabin and question Rosecrans about the order. In retrospect, it would seem to have been the logical and thoughtful thing to do. Wood had always performed with distinction; he graduated fifth in his class at West Point, served admirably in the Mexican War and performed with skill and gallantry at Stones River.

He had been royally chewed out by Rosecrans earlier that day. But to allow his anger at Rosecrans to cloud his better judgment was not the conduct that would be expected out of a general officer and professional soldier of Wood's caliber. And yet it seems likely that personal anger played a major role in the Union defeat. So the court was presented with the dilemma created by Rosecrans' hastily composed order and Wood's reaction to it — with McCook and his future as an army officer caught up in the middle of the resulting frenzy.

The remaining testimony on that day, and on the next several days as well, went favorably for McCook. Lyne Starling, assistant adjutant general of volunteers — who delivered the fatal order to Wood — said that he saw "General McCook doing everything in his power to rally the broken troops on a range of hills, just in the rear of the line of battle."[18] Colonel J. T. Wilder of the 17th Indiana Infantry agreed that McCook displayed "zeal, energy and ability" in posting his troops.[19] Captain J. St. C. Morton, U.S. Corps of Engineers, said: "General McCook appeared to be perfectly composed and appeared to be deeply sensible of the reverse of the army sustained. His disposition of the troops under his command was, in my opinion, eminently judicious."[20]

Was this an incompetent and unpopular general that the army should put on a shelf? Where were those generals and others who wanted McCook removed from command? Where were those officers who said they would no longer serve under McCook? Where was his principal accuser, Charles A. Dana? He was present when the disaster occurred but not among those who testified.

An important player in the debacle who did testify, on the 14th day of the hearing, was Brigadier General Jefferson C. Davis, a general with a checkered past, whose diminished division was routed when attacked on the Union right.

Davis, a native of Indiana, began his military career at age 18, when he enlisted in the army and served in the Mexican War. He was involved in the Civil War from the beginning, having the distinction of being at Fort Sumter when it was bombarded by Rebel cannon. Through his friendship with powerful Indiana governor Oliver P. Morton, Davis was appointed colonel of an Indiana regiment and shortly thereafter was made brigadier general. On September 29, 1862, Davis became embroiled in a quarrel with General William "Bull" Nelson. Insults led to violence, and Davis shot and killed Nelson in the lobby of the Galt Hotel in Louisville, in what some witnesses said was a cold-blooded murder. Once again Davis' friendship with the powerful Morton caused him to escape punishment and he was assigned to the Army of the Cumberland.[21] He reported for duty on November 5, 1862, at Bowling Green, Kentucky, and was ordered to command the 9th Division under General McCook.[22]

McCook must have called Davis to testify, for no one on the court asked any questions of him. Answering McCook's questions, Davis said that on the morning of the 20th, his command was positioned by "Major General McCook, commanding the corps." He said that on several occasions Rosecrans rode by his troops and made no comment as to their positioning. Later, Davis moved his troops from their reserve position to the left to close on Crittenden's right, acting upon Rosecrans' order.

McCook was using this testimony to show that his position on the right was weakened by moving Davis' troops. Davis buttressed this by testifying that he firmly believed that had he stayed in his original position, he could have staved off any rebel attack, because of the natural defenses and the fighting spirit of his men. Although his division had suffered about 1,000 casualties on the 19th, he still commanded about 1,300 or 1,400 men. He pointed the finger of responsibility away from McCook, saying, "The effect of the removal of General Wood's division left a large space unoccupied, through which the enemy advanced in large numbers."

Davis recalled that after the line was broken, he saw McCook "surrounded by his staff, engaged in rallying the troops. His demeanor was that of a general officer trying to rally his troops under desperate circumstances, under the enemy's fire." When asked by McCook, Davis said, "I do not think he was responsible for the repulse of our troops on the right."[23] Thus Davis provided powerful evidence to clear McCook's name. While his losses in the battle were heavy, and he had every opportunity at the inquiry to blame McCook's leadership, or lack of it, for the deaths of so many men, he instead upheld his erstwhile commander.

Thereafter the inquiry continued, with officers essentially providing repetitious testimony, all of which upheld McCook. If there were any witnesses in the Army of the Cumberland whose testimony might have harmed McCook, they did not appear at the inquiry. Although all witnesses were favorable to McCook, at no time did any member of the court challenge any one of them based on bias or friendship. In fact, the court was so passive, and witnesses so friendly, that at no time during the inquiry was McCook in trouble or in danger of falling under the shadow of guilty conduct. He had shown himself not only competent, but brave under fire, unwilling to retreat until there seemed to be nothing left to do. Seeking out Rosecrans for further orders was the only option left to him.

The court wasted no time in making its decision, stating, "The evidence shows that General McCook did his whole duty faithfully on that day, with activity and intelligence." The three general judges called Wood's troop pullout a "precipitate and inopportune withdrawal," without saying he should shoulder any blame for the Union defeat, but it is clear the court saw it as a critical factor. While the court did not assign a cause for the defeat, it is clear that they understood that the Wood maneuver, coupled with the small force of men available for McCook against "greatly superior numbers," was believed to be at the heart of the matter. It was simply another example of the fortunes of war. In closing, the court said, "In leaving the field to go to Chattanooga, General McCook committed a mistake, but his gallant conduct in the engagement forbids the idea that he was influenced by considerations of personal safety."[24]

The results of the inquiry were sent to the president, who declared that no further action was required and that the matter was closed. The inquiry resulted in a rout of McCook's opponents, leaving a mass of mean-spirited accusations and speculation in the carnage. A McCook supporter called the judges' decision a "triumphant vindication of his [McCook's] military character, as displayed upon the field of Chickamauga."[25] His cousin Roderick S. McCook was in accord, saying happily in a letter that Alex came through the inquiry "with flying colors."[26] Indeed it was just that. Major General Alexander M. McCook walked away with his honor intact, along with a reputation for gallantry and courage under fire that he would take to his grave.

An officer who served in the Army of the Cumberland and later became its historian took an angry poke at Stanton for ordering the inquiry. John Fitch believed that the inquiry was a vicious insult to McCook and was "an imputation on the bravery of hundreds of officers and thousands of men" that fought at Chickamauga. Fitch was personally offended by what he believed was an unjust accusation and unnecessary official proceeding which he deemed "too monstrous to be entertained."[27] It must have been particularly galling to Stanton and Dana when Fitch published his book, *Annals of the Army of the Cumberland*, with General McCook's picture on the cover next to Rosecrans and Thomas.

Generals Thomas L. Crittenden and James S. Negley were also cleared of any wrongdoing in separate proceedings. Unlike McCook who had little outside support, the General Assembly of the Commonwealth of Kentucky passed a resolution praising the patriotism and honorable service of General Crittenden, a favorite son. The members had "no doubt that the result of a fair investigation will not only exonerate him from all censure but brighten his fame."[28]

Despite this support, Crittenden's military life as a fighting general was over. He resigned his volunteer commission in December 1864, but was persuaded by President Andrew Johnson to accept a commission in the regular army as a colonel. He served until 1881.[29] Negley, too, was ignored by the high command. He resigned from the army in January 1865 and went on to enjoy a successful political career. He returned to his native Pennsylvania, and in 1868 he was elected to the House of Representatives on the Republican ticket, where he served four terms.[30]

The public and military interest in the controversy, however, had a life of its own, owing to the magnitude of the defeat suffered by the Union at Chickamauga. As a result, McCook and Crittenden were never again assigned a battlefield command. While their names were cleared, the Lincoln administration no longer had any faith in their abilities to lead an army corps — or for that matter, a division — in battle.

For McCook the disastrous Chickamauga affair was, from time to time, thrown up in his face. In 1868, Whitelaw Reid — a McCook nemesis — published a book that called the inquiry a whitewash.[31] In 1875, when Grant was president and one of the many scandals of his administration was under investigation, James Forsyth, military secretary to General Sheridan, had occasion to berate some Civil War generals who were to appear as witnesses. Among them, he called McCook a "damn fool who thinks too little and talks too much, and has just recovered his mind which he lost when he ran away from Braxton Bragg and his own army corps at Chickamauga more than a dozen years ago."[32] Sometimes the most painful and enduring wounds a soldier feels don't come from bullets and bayonets.

But McCook was responsible for some wounds. He was known to shoot his mouth off on occasion, ignoring military protocol and igniting the ire of his superiors. Not long after the battle of Shiloh, he happened to meet with a Rebel lieutenant under a flag of truce who was bearing dispatches from General Beauregard to General Buell, seeking to facilitate an exchange of wounded men. McCook was the ranking officer present and he received the dispatches. Not content with that, McCook engaged the officer in conversation, asking about the body of General Albert S. Johnston. He was anxious to know if Johnston's body had been recovered.

Then he changed the subject and inquired about the status of Brigadier General Benjamin M. Prentiss, who along with many of his men had been taken prisoner at Shiloh. Ignoring the fact that Prentiss and his men fought bravely, McCook told the astonished Confederate officer that the South should keep Prentiss and his brigade, along with "many generals of the same kind." Not satisfied with that outburst, McCook heaped compliments on the conduct of Southern troops who fought at Shiloh, and pounded Union troops from the Ohio and Iowa regiments, calling them "the greatest cowards in the world."[33]

Later that year as the Army of the Ohio prepared to move against Bragg's army at Stones River, McCook again acted with careless disregard for military custom. This time he improperly used a "flag of truce" to convey a dispatch to Bragg's headquarters. This was a "violation of military courtesy." Bragg so stated in his terse and angry letter to Rosecrans, insisting that the "use of the flag requires that it should come from the commanding general." Bragg said he was "surprised" to receive a communication from "one of your subordinates, Major General McCook."[34]

It wasn't that McCook was an iconoclast or that he disrespected military custom and protocol. In fact he loved the military and all its rituals and rites. He just seemed prone to blundering and occasional displays of bad judgment. Alexander McDowell McCook was a true "Fighting McCook," proud to serve. He was bold and daring, a man of great personal courage, but lacking in tact, maturity and common sense. In that regard he was like another reckless young Union general: George Armstrong Custer. What he did not possess, however, was Custer's luck. While Custer finished strong and was still in the saddle when the war ended, McCook was sidelined because the unfortunate events at the battle of Chickamauga, taken together with his overall record, were proof enough to the administration that he lacked the right stuff to be a good leader.

Unfortunately for the aggressive Alexander M. McCook, the men who ran the war were unrelenting, meaning he could expect to be sidelined for a prolonged period of time. Being staked out to a desk job at some relatively insignificant post far away from the hot war was unpleasant and humiliating to the man who was a soldier through and through. Still McCook had to accept the situation while he maintained his belief that he was still useful and that at some point in time, before the war ended, he would be given a field command again.

While General McCook waited, others in his family continued to serve and fight. His brother Dan was intimately involved with the Army of the Cumberland, under the leadership of General George H. Thomas, while it was

trapped in Chattanooga. In addition to Thomas, the Union army was augmented by the corps of Generals W. T. Sherman and Joseph Hooker. U. S.
Grant also made his way to Chattanooga to assist in the breakaway plan. Under
Grant's leadership, the Army of the Cumberland scored two impressive victories
over Bragg, with Colonel Anson G. McCook's brigade playing a key role. The
battles of Lookout Mountain and Missionary Ridge drove the Rebels from in
front of Chattanooga and provided the opportunity for Sherman to begin a
long and relentless campaign that took him from Tennessee to the shores of
the Atlantic Ocean at Savannah, Georgia.

General McCook could only sit and read about the great battles and victories, knowing that because of the disaster at Chickamauga, he was denied a
share of the honors and glory. Perhaps the despair he undoubtedly felt while
being left out was mitigated by the knowledge that the Union was winning the
war and that he had, early on, made important contributions. The army brass
could deny him the ability to further participate, but no one could take from
him the record of his service and accomplishments.

CHAPTER 16

Another Rebel Army
Marches North

It is almost absurd to suppose that the rebels expect to take Washington, or take any place of importance with even double the number of men which rumor assigns to them.

—*New York Times*, July 7, 1864

It was three years into the war and Confederate general Robert E. Lee was near desperate. He was confronted by the menacing army of General U. S. Grant, a man a lot like himself and a foe unlike any he had faced before. Grant had a simple plan for winning the war: find the enemy, fight fiercely and win the battle and then as soon as possible, move on to the next one. By the spring of 1864, the Army of the Potomac that floundered under the overly cautious, egotistical George B. McClellan, and others that followed him, was in fine step, full of pride and fight. In the bloody battle of the Wilderness, Grant "the Hammerer" slammed Lee like he had never been slammed before, seemingly heedless of the thousands of casualties from among the Union troops.

While a war-weary Union cringed at the heavy losses, in June Grant fell upon Lee again, like a raging plague, at the battle of Cold Harbor. Grant's dogged, head-on attacks racked up thousands of casualties on both sides, but in the war of attrition, Lee had the most to lose. Unlike other generals who chose to retreat and regroup, Grant pledged to Lincoln that he would not rest. He would fight on. The sacrifice of thousands of young lives on the altar of war caused Lincoln great grief. But he supported Grant completely, knowing that the only way to defeat the South and reunite the country was to keep the onslaught going until the Confederacy was forced to surrender.

Further to the south, Sherman's army was marching its way through Georgia, headed in the direction of Atlanta. Grant and Sherman were good friends and treated each other with the utmost respect. This blending of military talent embodied in two vastly different personalities gave Lincoln the long-sought combination he believed would bring victory. His faith in the abilities of both men was implicit and he wisely let them have their way. While he could not relax and wait for the war to end, Lincoln could reflect on the past three years and take satisfaction in the progress of events. Lincoln's hard work, dedication and humanity endeared him to the North, earning popularity and respect. To quote one admirer, the president's "Proclamation of Emancipation is riding the storm of revolution like a chariot of fire," and woe to the South.[1]

After three years of fighting, Lincoln and knowledgeable men on both sides knew that the Confederacy was in danger of losing the war. So long as Lincoln and his administration could entice and hold public opinion, the cause of the South was weakened. Time, money, arms and resolve were all on the Union side. Lee understood that it was time for launching an audacious and risky run at the North. He decided on a maneuver that he hoped would catch Grant and Lincoln off guard: an attack on Washington, D.C.

Lee was laboring under the sober realization that he was badly out-manned, and Southern boys weren't growing up fast enough to make new soldiers. His Army of Northern Virginia contained about 49,000 men. General John C. Breckinridge commanded about 9,000 and General P.G.T. Beauregard had another 7,900. Aside from that there were other small, isolated units, raiding parties and the 7,400 men assigned to guard Richmond.

Lee's military philosophy was simple and quite like that of Grant: find the enemy and fight. He also believed that the weaker side of the equation had to take greater risks. Lee was in a precarious position, and while Grant could bide his time, sit on a log, whittle and scheme out his next attack, his opponent was on a high wire in the wind with the life of the Confederacy hanging in the balance. But Lee was a man of action who would not tarry long, and in order to draw away at least some of Grant's 130,000 troops away from Richmond, he decided to send a sizeable force northward to attack Washington, or at least seriously threaten it, while raiding the rich Maryland countryside along the way.

Lee knew that attacking civilian populations and the destruction of Northern cities — especially Washington — would meet with approval and be the cause of great celebrations throughout the South. From the outset of the war, the sacking and burning of Washington was on the wish list of many Southerners. Believing this would lead to independence, a Southern woman wrote to her mother, insisting that "Washington in ruins would give peace to both sections of the country."[2]

To lead this bold diversion, Lee chose Major General Jubal Early, a West Point man who immediately quit the army after graduating in 1837. He studied law and served in the Virginia legislature. He had a family that included four children, all born out of wedlock.[3] The war brought out his fighting instincts and turned him into a gritty, hard-nosed, tobacco-chewing, Yankee-hating soldier with good leadership skills, a lover of off-color jokes and a good fight. These ingredients, combined with a rotten personality, made Early an unpopular man. His men hated him as much as the enemy, for he could unleash a harsh form of discipline that bordered on cruelty.

The cantankerous old war horse had been against secession and openly expressed sadness when he heard Sumter had been fired upon. Early cared not for old Southern ways and values, but he favored states' rights and detested all Northerners, and in the end, these factors were enough for him to throw in with the rebellion. He was anything but a fence-sitter. The desire to agitate and brawl carried him through the war years; he was doing the things he enjoyed. He served the Confederacy faithfully and competently throughout many campaigns including the first Bull Run, Antietam and Gettysburg.

In the summer of 1864, Early at 47 years old was as sharp, sarcastic and full of fighting energy as any Southern general. He also had a reputation for ignoring good advice and acting instead on his gut, taking unnecessary risks; as a result he was not well liked by his subordinate officers whom he would often criticize harshly. Nevertheless Lee needed a man with fight in his personality, and other key generals were sick or injured. He believed that if any of his generals had the qualities to pull it off, Jubal "Jube" Early was the man.[4] Lee's plan was supported by Jefferson Davis and General Braxton Bragg, who was serving as military advisor to the Confederate president.

On June 12, 1864, Lee summoned Early to his headquarters near Cold Harbor to discuss the plan he had formulated in his head. Early was instructed to take his army — the 2nd Corps, formerly under the command of Stonewall Jackson — from Richmond and move north through the Shenandoah Valley, according to his best military judgment. He would have the advantage of being familiar with the terrain.

On his way Early was to find and defeat General David Hunter whose army had been raiding northern Virginia at will. On June 11, at Lexington, Hunter burned the Virginia Military Institute and the governor's house after giving its occupants ten minutes to remove their valuables. He ordered a statue of George Washington removed and shipped off to Wheeling in Union-friendly West Virginia. All of this was the cause of outrage throughout Virginia.[5]

Stopping "Black Dave" Hunter — or better yet killing the wanton destroyer — was Early's immediate priority, and after that, anything else he could steal or destroy in federal territory was a bonus. Despite the obvious risks, Early accepted the assignment with enthusiasm, fully understanding the importance of the mission and the great opportunity for himself and the Southern cause.

Early's corps consisted of approximately 8,000 men and 24 pieces of artillery. Though small in size, it was divided into three divisions of battle-tested veterans, some of the best in Lee's army. The three divisions were commanded by Major General Robert Rodes, Major General John B. Gordon, and Major General Dodson Ramseur, the latter a mere 27 years old, in charge of cavalry. At three o'clock in the morning of June 13, 1864, they set out on their perilous mission, thin, ragged, but with good spirits and high hopes. Many of the troops were walking shoeless, as the expected shipment of footwear did not reach them in time.

Six days later, Early joined with Breckinridge, and the combined armies found and routed Hunter near Lynchburg. Early wired Lee with the good news that the hated Hunter was on the run. The enemy had not been destroyed, nor was Hunter killed or taken prisoner as Lee wished; nevertheless the mission was off to a good start. Hunter had been driven from the Shenandoah Valley, and for a time he was out of the war.[6] With Hunter retreating toward the Blue Ridge Mountains and therefore of no use to Grant, the path to Washington was temptingly left unobstructed. The timing was good, too, for Lee, Davis and Bragg had gathered intelligence indicating that the city was underdefended.

The ragtag band of Rebels, dubbed the Army of the Valley, turned north and moved out, ever watchful for the enemy, and with an ear toward Lee who might send a dispatch at any time. They would depend on the kindness of Confederate loyalists for information on the Union forces. Early could also rely on the raiding party of Lieutenant Colonel John Mosby, who was off on his own mission of plunder and destruction. Mosby volunteered to help Early.

They marched through Lexington on June 23, 1864, and in awed silence passed the grave of the revered Stonewall Jackson. On July 2, the Army of the Valley reached Winchester where its soldiers were received as heroes in a town steadfastly loyal to the South. It was here that Early learned that a federal force under Major General Franz Sigel was encamped about 40 miles to the north. Early immediately made plans to strike Sigel and brush him aside, and then, if all worked well, take Harper's Ferry.

Lee sent a dispatch asking Early to destroy railroads to prevent Union troops from reinforcing those at Washington. Keeping on the move, Early was able, through skillful use of a limited number of men, to run Sigel across the Potomac and out of the way. After that, he and his hungry men helped themselves to a rich stock of food left behind by Sigel in his haste to escape serious punishment.

The defeat of Sigel was met by an "I told you so" attitude in the media because the German immigrant's record as a field commander was dismal, after a promising start in Missouri. Southerners called him the "Flying Dutchman" because of his habit of running rather than taking a stand to face danger.[7] And yet he could lay claim to a small slice of celebrity, for the Civil War song, "I'm

Going to Fight Mit Sigel," was one of the most popular tunes of the time. It was one of a number of songs for sale in New York in *Beadle's Dime Song Book, No. 12.*[8]

Sigel's effort was not a total loss; it was a signal to the North that a serious Rebel invasion was afoot. An article in the *New York Times* reported the news of "an offensive operation which many people have for some time anticipated." Secretary of War Edwin Stanton provided information to the *Times* about the raiders after they appeared on July 3, at Martinsburgh, in the Shenandoah Valley, about 20 miles from the Potomac River. The *Times* had received numerous and alarming telegrams, with reports of a force of invaders anywhere from 10,000 to 20,000 whose intention was to invade Pennsylvania and Maryland to arouse "as much consternation as possible."

The *Times* refused to take a serious attitude toward the invaders, casually stating that it was "probable that this newly-appearing rebel force is a portion of the body sent out from LEE'S army some weeks ago, under [General Richard S.] Ewell," whose purpose was to check the advance of Hunter into the Shenandoah Valley. "There is no likelihood of anything more than this coming out of it." But the *Times* reporter was apparently unaware of Hunter's defeat, for he concluded that "General Hunter is in a position ... whence it can in two days be brought forward to operate effectively upon these rebels."[9]

Having already thwarted the Hunter threat, the invaders moved onward, toward the Potomac River, probing for the enemy. Early turned toward Harper's Ferry, but turned away when he determined it was too well defended. The tattered veterans crossed into Maryland and were struck by a flood of memories, flashbacks to the early days of the war, especially the terrible battle of Antietam that set a record for the most casualties in a single day. They were now in federal territory, among a war-weary population unwilling to sing so much as a chorus of "Maryland, My Maryland." If Early was expecting a warm welcome, he was sorely disappointed.

On July 5, the North received its first reliable information about the invasion, and it came from an unlikely source: two Confederate soldiers. The men were deserters who walked into the camp of General George Meade outside of Richmond. They confirmed that Early and Breckinridge had invaded Maryland with a "defenseless" Washington as their ultimate target. Meade took the intelligence seriously and sent a telegram to Grant.[10]

On July 6, Early set up his "north of the border" headquarters. It was reported in the *New York Times* that General Early — not General Ewell — was in charge of the Rebel invaders. Still the *Times* was loathe to assign any seriousness to the invasion, saying only that "this force is certainly too slight to be capable of anything more than a mere raid ... and the good sense of the people and the vigilance and energy of the Government" will be enough to crush it.[11] A day later, a dispatch from Washington read: "There is no authentic information here of a Rebel force in Maryland. It is thought to be a horse stealing expedition."[12]

The other side saw it differently. So far, Early's gutsy move had been successful, with his men maintaining proper discipline and more than holding their own in skirmishes with federal troops. The audacious Early was in fine tune, trusting in the old Rebel magic, hoping it would once again, as in days past, rise up and shine on him. Since Early hated the North, he most certainly loathed the *New York Times*.

Early was tempted to strike the Point Lookout Prison south of Baltimore and free 17,000 Rebels imprisoned there. Doing so successfully would more than double his small army, and give the *Times* more to write about. He didn't make the move, however, and instead trudged onward, through familiar mountains passes, always mindful that Hunter might recover and strike his rear. The long overdue shipment of shoes caught up with him on July 7.[13]

How long and how far could his army travel in the intense July heat (with or without shoes) before he encountered major resistance during his Maryland ramble? It seemed unlikely that the over-cautious General Hunter would catch up with him, but Early had to be concerned that enemy scouts or perhaps civilians would see his columns and send out an alert. He had to be vigilant should Hunter sneak up on his rear. The *New York Times* once again predicted that Hunter would "confront the rebels."[14]

No doubt recalling Lee's invasion and subsequent three-day battle at Gettysburg, the governor of Pennsylvania sounded the alarm. Governor A. G. Curtin issued a proclamation asking for a sufficient number of able-bodied men to "come forward when your homes and firesides are to be defended against a profligate horde of plunderers." General Order Number 50, dated July 5, 1864, called for all "good and loyal men" to come to the aid of their state.[15]

Early was not assigned to invade Pennsylvania, however, and he found he had his hands full in Maryland, encountering unexpected resistance. In the quiet and prosperous little town of Frederick, his men skirmished with some Union infantry stationed there. Folks coming in on the train got a scare when a group of "gray"-clothed cavalry galloped into town. They were just as quickly relieved when it was discovered that the horse soldiers were merely dust-covered Union boys.[16] Nevertheless, "great alarm and excitement prevailed" in Frederick as townspeople either left town or concealed themselves in preparation for the arrival of the Rebels.[17]

Meanwhile Mosby and his raiders were spreading panic elsewhere in Maryland. His big guns unleashed a volley of fire on a slow-moving mail train near Point of Rocks. The cannon fire set off an explosion of another sort, as wild-eyed and badly frightened passengers, many of them women, jumped out of the car windows and hid in the woods. The fireman was the only casualty, and the engineer was able to get the train moving out of harms way, leaving the frightened passengers behind.[18]

While the storm clouds gathered, the *New York Times* editorialized calmly, maintaining its skeptical attitude toward the minor "invasion" which it believed could easily be turned back. The *Times* reasoned correctly that Lee had sent Early into Maryland, hoping that Grant would be forced to send a division or two in pursuit. But this was nothing to be overly concerned about, and in fact was something to be desired. Said the *Times*, "It must not be forgotten that the more rebels enter Maryland, the less there are in front of Richmond, and it is there that the heart of the rebellion lies."

In a "bring it on" editorial on July 7, the *Times* scoffed at the notion that Early's force — or one twice the size — could "take Washington" or any other place of importance. The Maryland militias alone were capable of chasing the Rebels out or at least holding them off until Hunter arrived. The editor surmised that the best Early could do was to strike fear into the hearts of people and draw off some of Grant's men. "We want them on the Potomac; we owe it to the army at Petersburgh [*sic*] to keep them there until it has done its work."[19] Brave words indeed from the *Times*, but one wonders if its readers were emboldened or placated.

It would be interesting to know if Early read the editorial, for proud fighter that he was, he would certainly have been offended if not insulted. At any rate he was not ready to sulk, fold his tents and trek southbound, back to Virginia. He led his small army further into Maryland with Washington as his objective and in a fighting mood, driving stolen cattle and horses as he progressed.

On July 7, President Lincoln issued a "Proclamation for a Day of Humiliation and Prayer," which was scheduled for the first Thursday of August. The proclamation made no mention of a threat against Washington, but it requested that people pray for an end to the rebellion.[20] All in all, Lincoln possessed the coolest head of anyone in Washington.

Then on July 8, the *Times* also put on a more serious face and revealed much more ominous news. "There can no longer be any doubt that Gen. Lee has sent a considerable portion of his army in this direction." Rebel prisoners added to the fear factor, telling their captors that General Lee himself was leading the invasion and that the object was more than mere plundering. The invasion was for the purpose of entering Pennsylvania and other states, "and that the capture of Baltimore and the destruction of the National Capital are also aimed at."[21] Reports from troops who fought at Frederick confirmed that Maryland and the nation's capital were facing more than a raiding party. Accordingly, the *Times* increased its coverage of the unfolding events.

Word of a larger-than-expected enemy invasion reached Baltimore, where Union general Lewis "Lew" Wallace was stationed, occupied with administrative duty. While the Union still found him useful, Wallace hurt his military status by showing up late for the battle of Shiloh more than two years before the current crisis. Wallace was just then under strict scrutiny by General Henry W. Halleck, Lincoln's top staff officer, who seemed to be looking for a reason to charge the wayward general with some offense.

Wallace had a touch of the romantic about him and longed for action on the field of battle. He sensed that here was an opportunity to bounce out of his chair and dash back into the game of hot war. Reasoning correctly that Washington was at risk, he sprang into action, let Halleck do what he would. Wallace quickly rounded up all the troops, stragglers and militia he could find to defend Baltimore and its warehouses filled with supplies. He then rode out to Monocacy Junction with a force of about 2,300 men in the direction of the enemy then located east of the town of Frederick. Wallace picked his battle-ground site well, for despite his tendency to be melancholy and "blue," the Indiana native was a man of intelligence and good sense.[22]

The *Times* reported that Wallace received reinforcements, but would not state from whom or how many new men were included, saying only that "we leave the enemy to find out for themselves." The enemy was not long in finding out. On July 9, Wallace met the enemy at Frederick and was successful, although greatly outnumbered, at holding off the Rebels. Excited over his success and because he was back in action again, he wired General Halleck in Washington with news of his "victory."[23] He was, however, far from seeing the last of Early, but for the time being, Wallace and his men were blocking the path to Washington.

Early was beginning to feel a bit uneasy. He had to find a way around — or through — Wallace's well-positioned troops that now numbered about 3,350. He was unfamiliar with the lay of the surrounding land and a bit confused on where he would strike at Wallace. He thought about burning down the town of Frederick and demanded a ransom of $200,000 from the city fathers. They said they needed some time to think about it.

Knowing that time was not on his side, Early decided that he could not deliberate any longer, lest more reinforcements sent by Grant should arrive to fight. His presence in federal territory and the vast amount of exaggerated news and outright rumors had created an atmosphere of fear and panic throughout Maryland and into Pennsylvania. Yet he knew that he could not long depend on the power of fear and rumor to suppress action against him.

On July 9, Wallace and his makeshift army of soldiers and assorted, untrained and short-term volunteers were positioned near the Monocacy River, southeast of Frederick. He had been reinforced by a division from the 6th Corps headed by Major General James B. Ricketts, an advance unit sent by Grant. Ricketts' division was posted on Wallace's left, and it was there that Early decided to make his strike. General John McCausland's cavalry made a dash in that direction, crossing the Monocacy River. Early sent Breckinridge's division forth to support the attack on the Union left.

On the other side Wallace and his men understood that they needed to make an all-out attempt to stop — or at least slow down — the Early invasion. They had to protect both Baltimore and Washington, and there were no other troops within calling distance to help out. They fought hard and took heavy casualties to the tune of about 2,000 killed and wounded. Yet despite the determined resistance, the screaming Rebels, in superior numbers, overran the Union lines. Wallace was forced to retreat toward Baltimore in disorder. By four o'clock in the afternoon, the battle of Monocacy was over, and the last obstacle in the path to Washington was removed. The best Wallace could claim is that his men fought hard and made certain that Early would not have an easy time pushing the Union troops aside.[24]

Wallace could take satisfaction in that the desperate fighting delayed the Rebel advance by a day and inflicted significant damage on Early's army. He lost an estimated 800 men killed and wounded. The exhaustion following the battle, coupled with extremely hot temperatures, further slowed Early's pace.

Despite the timely and desperate effort to impede the progress of the Rebels, Wallace was not cited or rewarded by Washington. Instead — while trying to get some sleep "lying in a fence corner" — he received a midnight telegram from the dreaded Halleck. Reading it by match light, Wallace learned that he was relieved from duty.[25]

Although his work as a warrior may have gone under-appreciated, after the war Lew Wallace found his real talent: that of a writer. He gave the world the famous novel *Ben Hur*, published in 1880.

While artistic fame was in his future, Wallace's immediate concern was the status of the invasion. The shocking news of Wallace's defeat spread new and high-pitched panic in Baltimore. The Confederate strength was believed to be about 25,000, although Early's total strength was about 18,000. It was reported that General Erastus Tyler and a wounded Colonel William H. Seward, Jr., son of Secretary of State William H. Seward, were among those captured. Rebel's taken prisoner insisted that General Lee himself was directing the attack. The governor of Maryland and the mayor of Baltimore issued a joint proclamation, pleading for all citizens to man the fortifications and brace themselves for the worst. "Come in your Leagues or come in your militia companies — but come in crowds, and come quickly."[26] For the governor, help didn't materialize soon enough. His mansion outside of Baltimore was torched and burned to the ground. Fearing the worst, the citizens of Baltimore immediately began throwing up makeshift barriers to protect themselves from the Rebel horde.

Meanwhile in the South, happy emotions were at a fever pitch as news of Wallace's defeat was made known. But somehow the reporters got it wrong and people believed that the Union troops put up little or no fight at Monocacy. Rumor built upon rumor, and soon both Baltimore and Washington were conquered cities cluttered by the bodies of thousands of slaughtered Unionists.[27]

On July 11, the *New York Times* devoted its entire first page to news of the "REBEL RAID," including an update on the atmosphere in Washington. That city was jolted from all forms of complacency and had for some days been a beehive of activity, with refugees arriving around the clock. At all hours the streets were filled with "moving troops, wagons, ambulances, and as much of the pride, pomp and circumstances of war, as American's generally exhibit." In addition to the regular troops, volunteers from among the civilian population, invalid soldiers as well as those convalescing in the hospitals, were gathered for the defense of the city. Wondering what to expect next, folks were relieved to learn that Colonel Seward, wounded when his horse was shot down, had not been captured; he found a mule and escaped. According to Wallace, "he behaved with rare gallantry."[28]

Ambulances filled with wounded men arrived in Baltimore, bringing with them tales of valor from the soldiers — both veterans and recruits — who fought with desperate determination against the invaders. It was a Union loss but not one to be ashamed of, and it was with great pride that Wallace declared: "These men died to save the National Capitol, and they did save it."[29]

The Southern press found cause to crow in Wallace's defeat but dismissed the reported capture of General Tyler as the insignificant taking of a "small potato." The report was false, as Tyler evaded capture and made his way back to Baltimore. Early did, however, take prisoners, and they joined his trek toward Washington.

As news of Early's progress came in, the *Richmond Whig* bellowed, "Our people had a right to be excited. For where does the war furnish anything that approximates" the success of a surprise invasion of the North? Suddenly the South learned that a large body of its troops stole its way into Maryland, looting and destroying freely, until it found itself in a position to strike Baltimore or Washington — or both. The invasion relieved the pressure on Petersburg and was, therefore, reason for reveling.[30]

Washington was a walled city that looked nothing like the "Federal City" created in 1790 by George Washington. While it was advancing in stature and population, it was a long time in casting off its primitive aspect, and in 1861 when Lincoln assumed the presidency, the city was anything but a model of sophistication. Despite many examples of fine architecture, statutes and monuments, observers were more likely to be unfavorably impressed by its filth and bad odor, for livestock wandered freely in the city, treading among the carcasses of dead animals, "much to the disgust of our nasal organs."[31] Pollution from fires and smokestacks and canals of raw sewage made visitors and residents wish they had no sense of smell. One disgusted wiseacre said Washington air featured "70 separate and distinct stinks."[32]

Washington's population was about 61,000 people at the onset of the Civil War. Following the defeat at Bull Run, it was clear that the city had to be protected, and after more than three years of war, engineers and builders had completely surrounded Washington with fortifications. The capital was wrapped in 37 miles of "heavy earthworks buttressed with palisades, forts and heavy cannon."[33] The "state of the art" fortifications were designed to withstand a heavy attack, having been fashioned after those built by the Duke of Wellington in Portugal. An engineering team led by John G. Barnard constructed the formidable defenses.[34] Only a madman would assault the walls of Washington with infantry.

Inside the walled city people went about their business and grew accustomed to the situation. The threat from without the walls did not stand in the way of the scheduled hanging of Cornelius Tuell, a waiter turned wife murderer. *The Evening Star* covered the execution and was satisfied that it was conducted "in good order," but under heavy guard.[35] The Union generals inside the city would soon be looking for volunteers of any sort, but the condemned man was destined to escape military duty.

After learning of the invasion, Lincoln — accompanied by his cavalry escort of bodyguards — inspected the "fortifications on the exposed side of the city." He went away satisfied.[36] Washington had not seen an attack since the War of 1812, when the British stormed and burned the little city, driving its occupants, including First Lady Dolly Madison, out of town.

Major General Christopher Columbus Augur was the officer in charge of the capital defenses. He was a West Pointer and career military man who was given the wartime rank of Brigadier General in November 1861. Earlier in the war, Augur served with Generals McClellan and Nathaniel P. Banks, and neither stint of duty enhanced his military resume. In October 1863, he was assigned to the Department of Washington where he would stay until the end of the war.[37]

Among the other generals available for duty in Washington was Major General Alexander M. McCook who arrived on July 10. He was in Cincinnati when on July 7 he received orders to report to Washington, "without delay."[38] This "Fighting McCook" had done no fighting since Chickamauga, and after that ill-fated battle he had been doing desk duty while waiting for a field assignment.

He was not completely out of military step, however, and on March 13, 1864 — while in Washington waiting for orders — McCook was one of several generals invited to the "Executive Mansion" for a dinner with the president. Among the guests were Generals Halleck, George Meade and Dan Sickles, and

Secretary of War Stanton. General Grant was unable to attend, having been called away.[39]

When the Rebel raid crisis arose, McCook was put in charge of a "reserve camp on Piney Branch Creek," about halfway between Fort Stevens and the city. He was burdened by concern for his younger brother Colonel Daniel McCook, severely wounded at the battle of Kennesaw Mountain, but the emergency demanded that he put aside personal considerations. He could have asked to be excused from the assignment so that he could stay with his brother, but he reported for duty, like the soldier he was. After a brief meeting with Halleck, General McCook immediately set about inspecting the northern defenses around Fort Stevens, having never before seen them.[40]

What McCook saw was cause for concern. The northern "defenses" were feeble at best, as Fort Stevens, located about five miles from the center of the city, was manned with only 209 troops, largely inexperienced, and some

were quite literally "walking wounded."[41] The artillery was provided by the 13th Michigan Battery. For an officer who once commanded an army corps, the sight of his new "command" must have been distressing. Perhaps at no time in the history of warfare was one commander so greatly outnumbered by the enemy approaching his front.

At various times Grant and Sherman wanted to get McCook back into the hot war, but there never seemed to be a suitable opening. On April 9, 1864, in response to a request from Sherman for more generals, Grant replied: "I do not think any more generals will be sent to you unless you want Milroy, McCook or Crittenden."[42] Two

Major General Christopher Columbus Augur was the man in charge of the Washington, D.C., defenses at the time of the Early raid. In fact, there were so many generals in the capital city that Henry W. Halleck complained about the lack of privates as opposed to the abundance of brass. Among those generals who had to merge their talents and come up with a plan of defense was General McCook, who worked with Augur and was placed in command of Fort Stevens.

months later Halleck wrote to Major General Canby at Vicksburg, offering him his choice of shelved generals including McCook, Gordon Granger and Stephen A. Hurlburt.[43]

Threatened with an attack that appeared imminent, Halleck and Stanton were not about to offer up any generals. They needed all the skilled help they could get. With rumor building upon rumor as each day passed, the number of enemy troops believed to be on their way increased to an astounding 45,000, with General James "Pete" Longstreet on the way with even more men.[44]

One group that Halleck and Stanton probably counted on was the Invalid Corps. Created in April of 1863, the Invalid Corps consisted of soldiers who had suffered from injuries to the extent that their physical condition would not permit them to return to the front. By the summer of 1864, Washington was essentially a vast military hospital where thousands of sick and wounded men were being treated. The Invalid Corps was created from this steady supply of damaged soldiers.

The men of the Invalid Corps were given special blue uniforms and duties that included assisting hospital administrators. Among this category of veteran soldiers were those who still had some fight in them, and due to the expected attack, those who could shoot would shoulder a gun in defense of the city.[45]

Washington was cut off from telegraph contact with Harper's Ferry, causing the war brain trust to become more excited than usual. The goggle-eyed, nervous Halleck and gruff and bluff Stanton seemed at odds when it came to organizing their forces to meet the emergency. Halleck sent a dispatch to Grant asking for help against what he believed to be an invasion by 30,000 Rebel troops. After that both he and Stanton struggled to decide which of their generals could best take the lead.

Lincoln had high hopes for Halleck when he was given the position of general in chief. But as time went on, Halleck, more the bureaucrat than an army officer, grew less decisive and more muddled. His orders to generals in the field were often confusing and vague and therefore ignored. He was never able to take control and direct the war effort. Lincoln was finally forced to confess that Halleck was "little more than a first rate clerk."[46]

And in this latest crisis, Halleck clearly wasn't up to being Lincoln's top general. His much heralded brain was in park when it should have been in overdrive. Among his many critics was General Lew Wallace, who years later told a reporter that Halleck hated Grant so much that he (Halleck) was willing to let Washington fall to the Rebels. Wallace, of course, hated Halleck so his assertion was not given much credence, and yet all the high-level spite and malice only added to the problem of defending the city.[47]

Augur was really in charge of the whole show, but that didn't seem to register with the brain trust. Halleck was hoping for an emergent savior, and Stanton merely opted for Alexander M. McCook, the man he convinced Lincoln to fire after the Chickamauga debacle. Meanwhile, Lincoln, calm as always, reminded his secretary of war that Grant was still in charge of the army and that Grant would see to it that the nation's capital was protected.[48]

Throughout the Civil War, Lincoln was plagued by the terrible events of war, and handled each crisis with almost mystical wisdom and grace. The threat represented by Early's tattered invaders did not trouble the president as it did his nervous advisors. The president trusted his resolve, and with his eye on the goal he established at the outset of the war, he would do what he had done since taking office: lead. Knowing it was his war to win or lose, he would protect the capital city.

CHAPTER 17

The Rebel Raid on Washington, D.C.

All indications thus far strengthen the conviction that the forces of
the enemy do not exceed six or eight thousand men, and that it is
simply a plundering expedition, and nothing more.
    —*New York Times*, July 7, 1864

Secretary of the Navy Gideon Welles was trying to stay calm. Lincoln's
"Old Neptune" and diligent — and often indignant — diarist, was casting about
for accurate information on the Rebel invaders. One of the more prolific critics
during the war years, he called the invasion "very annoying" but not as serious
as those of the past. Welles was harshly critical of the war department, saying,
"Stanton seems stupid, Halleck always does." He even criticized his son, Tom
G., for joining the staff of Major General Alexander M. McCook, regretting
"his passion for service and his recklessness and youth."[1]

Charles A. Dana, still the assistant secretary of war, was especially anxious
and noisy, sounding journalistic alarms. Apparently not satisfied with Augur,
and probably still openly hostile to McCook — remembering Chickamauga —
Dana wired General U. S. Grant like a man screaming for help. He wrote:
"Unless you direct positively and explicitly what is to be done, everything will
go on in the deplorable and fatal way in which it has gone for the past week."
This was Dana's way of saying that General Henry W. Halleck, the unpopular,
confused and oft-picked-on grouch, was not up to the challenge. As for
McCook, Dana mentioned that the Ohio battle-tested general had "a lot of
brigadiers under him," but he was not authorized to leave the city.[2]

While Grant was not thrilled with the idea of sending any troops away
from Petersburg to defend the District of Columbia, he had no choice but to
send help. On July 6, he sent General James B. Rickett's division of the 6th
Corps, about 8000 men all veteran fighters. What worried him was news of

Wallace's defeat at Monocacy. Had all of the 6th Corps been available at Monocacy, the result might have been different.

Understanding that the capital was truly in danger, Grant felt better about sending help. Wallace's defeat troubled Grant and it inspired both panic and resourcefulness from among the people in walled Washington. For by 10 o'clock in the morning of July 10th, a mass of approximately 10,000 "troops" offered up their services, expecting to get direction and leadership.

But who would do the directing? In addition to Major Generals Christopher C. Augur and McCook, there was Halleck — who had some combat experience — and Generals Quincy A. Gillmore, Abner Doubleday, Montgomery Meigs and Edward O. C. Ord, the latter Grant's choice to lead. Gillmore was an engineer and Meigs a quartermaster who was busy organizing a "division" of his employees, all of whom were eager but lacked military training or experience and barely knew the barrel from the butt of a rifle. The sharp-tongued Halleck groused about the lack of qualified privates and having "five times as many generals here as we want."[3]

True, there was no shortage of brass but there was no strong chain of command and no one seemed to be able to take charge. And since there was no cavalry for reconnaissance, there was no way to determine the enemy's size or location. Furthermore, there were serious gaps in security, and bridges were not well manned. Everywhere Halleck looked, he saw decay, demoralization and weak defenses. The shaky uncertainty was strong enough to cause an earthquake. The generals seemed lost in confusion because they had no way to ascertain the strength of the enemy. Figures ranged from 20,000 to the outlandish estimate of 100,000, according to an excited picket who was certain that Lee was the head of the gigantic army.

While the city teetered on the edge of succumbing to the terror looming somewhere outside the fortifications, President Lincoln advised: "Let us be vigilant, but keep cool."[4] But just to be on the safe side, he had a ship waiting on the Potomac River, near the White House, prepared to take him out of the city to a safe place.[5]

The president may have been in more danger than he knew. Stanton was fearful and concerned that the man who had become his trusted friend was vulnerable to being killed or kidnapped. The secretary of war insisted that Lincoln take extra precautions and go nowhere without his armed guards. Stanton understood that if there was one indispensable man in America at that moment, that man was Abraham Lincoln.

As always Lincoln wanted to set a good example. So with a stern but nervous Stanton in tow, he went out among the public. He wanted the people to see that he was involved and taking action. While a sense of unease and fear pervaded the city, the two men rode through the streets in an open carriage as if making an effort to instill their feelings of confidence in others.

Lincoln held regular cabinet meetings during the crisis, and at no time during the entire ordeal did he seem the least bit fearful or concerned that the Rebels would be successful. After more than three years of fortitude, patience and suffering over the terrible losses caused by battle after battle, he was not about to lose his mind over this latest challenge. Although he understood that the toppling of the capital city would mean humiliation if not total defeat, he never believed for a minute that it would come to pass. Instead he was looking forward to the end of the war and reconstruction. His focus was on a final and complete victory over the Confederacy, with the Union preserved and slavery forever abolished. Lincoln may have been plagued by melancholy, as some writers have suggested, but he was nevertheless ruled by optimism.

Lincoln's immediate goal was to come up with a way to "bag or destroy this force in our front."[6] And by July 10, it was clear that the Rebels were advancing along the Rockville Road, for the purpose of approaching the fortifications from the north. While they were bone weary, the Rebels were excited at the prospect of attacking the Union's capital city.

Along the way the advance units of General Jubal Early's army came upon and burned the lavish Falkland Mansion of Montgomery "Monty" Blair at Silver Spring. Blair was Lincoln's postmaster general and a key cabinet member, and although a conservative, he was a staunch supporter of the president.

Later they made themselves at home at the estate of Monty's father, Francis P. Blair, fast friend of Lincoln and one of the most influential, wealthy and powerful political figures of his time. The Blairs were from Kentucky and once owned slaves, and yet when the war broke out, they were solidly pro–Union. Monty's brother, Frank Jr., was a prominent Union general, who in 1860 campaigned vigorously for Lincoln. He was a friend of both Grant and W. T. Sherman.

Since the Blairs were Southerners, others in the South believed they had turned against their own kind by throwing in with the North. Montgomery Blair had the added liability of having served as the attorney for Dred Scott, the slave whose historic bid for freedom went all the way to the U.S. Supreme Court in 1857. The well-publicized "Dred Scott decision" sent the audacious plaintiff back to bondage. The Blairs had done too much that infuriated the South, and when it was discovered that the raiders had come across the house of Monty Blair, the officer in charge said, "This house must go up."[7] They scattered books and papers and took items they considered to have value and set the house on fire.

The house of the elder Blair seemed destined for the same fate. He and his family were away at the time, on vacation further north. In a destructive mood, the Rebel soldiers began to ransack their house, tossing books and papers about, helping themselves to the contents of Blair's expensive wine cellar. The wine flowed freely, and some men dressed themselves in the clothes of the Blair women and engaged in mock dancing.

When Early and John C. Breckinridge caught up with the marauding men, the ex–vice president was furious and demanded that Early put a stop to the vulgar partying and plundering. Although Breckinridge was a thorough and unrepentant Confederate, he had once been good friends with Francis P. Blair and recalled with a hint of nostalgia that during his days as the vice president in the James Buchanan administration, he spent many peaceful visits at the mansion under much more pleasant circumstances, sipping wine and enjoying the renowned Blair hospitality. It was at the Blair house that Breckinridge made the decision to join the Confederacy.[8]

Because of Breckinridge's intervention, the great house and its invaluable contents — including an extensive library and letters to and from such notables as Henry Clay and Andrew Jackson — were spared.[9] It was a small act of decency that, however brief, upstaged the monstrous indecency of war.

Breckinridge's sympathy toward the Blairs drew fire from the Southern newspapers. The *Richmond Examiner* said the burning of Monty Blair's mansion was proper retribution for the destruction of Southern houses. "The magnanimity that spared the residence of F. P. Blair was entirely thrown away upon a creature as deeply dyed with the blood of this war as any other of his fellow scoundrels."[10] Apparently there was nothing worse than a prominent Southerner who would not severe all ties with the Union.

Following the damage at Silver Spring, a courier from the 8th Illinois Cavalry rode hard and fast toward Washington. Stopping at McCook's camp on Piney Branch Creek, he informed the general of the approaching army. McCook, his fighting spirit intact, and anxious to meet the emergency, immediately set out with his small force of men to Fort Stevens, assigning some to the rifle pits. He ordered other men into the woods to cut down trees, thereby creating obstacles to slow down the Rebels.[11]

McCook had been augmented by 1,500 civilian employees recruited by Meigs. Although still woefully undermanned, McCook ordered the Ohio militia out in a skirmish line.[12] Once again, Alexander M. McCook, the professional soldier, was feeling the excitement of impending battle.

McCook had led thousands of men in some of the fiercest and bloodiest battles of the Civil War, and after nearly a year's absence from action, he found himself in the thick of excitement again. But instead of being a part of a great army on the move and prepared to meet another great army head on, he was in an unfamiliar defensive posture at the head of an odd collection of volunteers, greatly outnumbered and totally out of context with his experience as a field commander. Nevertheless, he was placed in command of all troops "defending the Capitol on the north."[13]

In the early morning hours of July 11, Early approached Fort Stevens, marching on the 7th Street pike, a major thoroughfare leading into the city. As time passed, the merciless heat bore down on the Rebels, and along with

Soldiers pose at Fort Stevens, one of the many forts that together protected the walled city of Washington, D.C. General McCook was given the task of cobbling together a defense at Fort Stevens, at the northernmost post, five miles from the center of the city. He had at his disposal an inexperienced collection of troops including members of an Ohio militia and some civilian volunteers. It was a far cry from the heady days when McCook was a corps commander leading thousands of troops.

clouds of dust, caused many of his men to fall away in exhaustion. Still they trudged on toward Fort Stevens, the northernmost point, also the weakest link in the chain of defenses. Early was no doubt informed of this fact by the Confederate spy network, so his choosing Fort Stevens as the place to launch an attack was not by accident.[14]

Early approached Washington with only about 10,000 men available for action, and of course neither Lee nor Longstreet was present. Although not the strongest, Fort Stevens was one of the major fortifications designed to protect the key road leading into the city. Fort Stevens was named for General Isaac Ingalls Stevens who was killed in 1862 at the battle of Chantilly. It was built mainly with stone and concrete and was large and imposing in its appearance.[15]

The Rebels were met by heavy fire from Union artillery, but due to inexperienced gunners, the shells fell far beyond their intended targets. A Confederate remembered that the Rebel marchers laughed as the shells sailed over their heads, concluding that the frightened, untrained Union volunteers were aiming at the "moon and the stars."[16]

Looking toward the ramparts of Fort Stevens, Early came to the happy conclusion that it was under-manned and ripe for the picking. He was convinced that he had beaten Grant and was in a position to take the greatest prize of all, thereby elevating him above all other Confederate generals.

The decision he was about to make was of great moment, for here was the potential to upstage all the other major battles of the war. If he could capture the capital city of the United States of America, the image of a strong Union would be diminished and humiliated in the eyes of the world. A nation that could not protect its capital city would not be worthy of recognition. Other nations would then be more likely to recognize the Confederacy as a separate nation and render it assistance in money, men and supplies. But could he pull it off with a small, tired, parched and hungry army struggling against the merciless heat of summer?

About noon, as Early surveyed the city facing his army, with thoughts of grandeur and eternal fame, he noticed a dusty mist rising above the skyline. Bluecoats were on the march, marching like real soldiers, not like untrained militia. Grant's reinforcements *had* arrived. His dreams of glory dimming, Early took stock of his forces, many of whom barely straggled to the front, while others collapsed along the way. He had hoped that large numbers of Southern sympathizers would flock to his standards, but none had come except for some young Washington men who were among the "secesh" element. He and his small army were alone with two choices: attack or retreat. Early was not just yet ready to retreat. To slip away without a fight of some kind was not in his character. At the very least, Jube wanted to leave Washingtonians something to remember him by.

He sent out skirmishers that drove back McCook's pickets. Then as his troops drew nearer to the fortifications, big guns opened up, and the makeshift Yankees held their ground like veterans. The firm taste of resistance imposed upon Early a concern that blunted his normal fighting spirit. Still he had come so far and he knew that Lee was counting on him to succeed. The entire South was waiting.

Lincoln was out and about in his carriage conducting his inspection of the lines of defense, heedless of the danger. His generals were milling about; Halleck and Stanton were quarreling over who should take charge. McCook understood that he had authority over the forts on the northern perimeter, including Fort Stevens, but he was not the top dog. The confusion was apparent to the troops who would do the fighting, and the lack of leadership was anything but inspiring. Meanwhile bankers were packing up their money, ready to evacuate should the Union troops be unable to hold back the invaders. Stanton apparently had serious misgivings as well, for he removed his stash of gold from his house and hid it in the home of a clerk.[17]

Maryland refugees arrived in large flocks with their packed possessions and livestock. They were like frightened chickens, milling about while a farmer walked among them with a leg hook and hatchet. Herds of cattle running in front of the Rebels drifted into town. It was finders, keepers and the keepers were selling beef on the hoof. Freed slaves were everywhere in the city, happy to be free but laboring under the same anxiety as the whites. But even short-lived freedom was better than perpetual slavery. The sound of streetcars mingled eerily with the booming of cannons. The traffic, the wagons, the noise, the marching of soldiers, all reminded people of the first battle of Bull Run.

While a gloomy Secretary Welles complained about "dunderheads" in the War Department, the pro–South folks were in good spirits, quietly hopeful that Early would succeed. They spread rumors about the hopelessness of the defenders and that the president had been wounded in an attack. Some "secesh" were secretly making Confederate flags to wave when Early marched in triumph through the city streets.[18]

Newsboys, making more money than usual, were having a field day as the city's newspapers put out "extras," although there was a scarcity of hard and accurate information to report.[19] And yet people bought newspapers and devoured every tidbit of news, true or untrue. While the excitement of the moment stirred the blood, the people who lived in Washington were accustomed to reports of invasions and went about their daily affairs to the extent that they were able to do so.

At about noon on the 11th, all persons in attendance let out a loud cheer as men from the 6th Corps under General Horatio G. Wright marched toward Fort Stevens. They were all confident veterans who took their training in the Washington forts, so they were familiar with the guns and were able to take over for those who were about to get on-the-job training. Wright took note of the thin line of the Rebels in front of Fort Stevens and wanted to hurl his men forward to crush it. But McCook was not in a position of authority to give the order, so he deferred to Augur.

While the generals conversed, shots were heard on the left, leading them to believe that Early had at last launched his full attack. Still Augur would not give the order for Wright to march out and meet it. Wright was angered over Augur's over-cautious attitude. He was even angrier when Halleck ordered him to wait in reserve. It made no sense; the 6th Corps was sent to fight and protect the city, not to stand around and watch while amateurs were on duty.

Finally, after McCook's Ohio militia in combination with assorted clerks and other volunteers gave way, Wright was given permission to move his veterans forward. Troops from the 1st Brigade of the 2nd Division soon took back the original skirmish line. McCook reported that this was "handsomely done about 1:30 P.M." with the Union line "established at 1,100 yards in front of the works.... Affairs remained in this condition until evening."[20]

All day long, Fort Stevens was awash with curious and anxious folk who came to watch the fighting. Many, including Secretary of the Navy Gideon Welles, had the best seats in the house for the performance. He consulted with Wright and McCook and later noted in his diary that the generals assured him that an adequate plan for the defense of the city was in place.

Lincoln, too, came out to Fort Stevens to view the action. When Wright saw the six-foot, four-inch president — conspicuous in his trademark stovepipe hat — standing out front with a group of spectators like a tempting target, he was horrified but said nothing to the president. Rebel sharpshooters taking aim could see men "on the works in linen dusters and silk hats," indicating that many civilians were among their potential targets.[21]

Sharpshooters continued firing, and yet the president refused to withdraw to a place of safety. Then a man next to him was hit and dragged away. At that point a young captain yelled at the president the oft-quoted warning: "Get down, you fool." Lincoln was an astute man who always appreciated timely and sound advice so he did as ordered. The young captain was Oliver Wendell Holmes, Jr., from one of Wright's divisions. Captain Holmes was the son of the popular poet, Dr. Oliver Wendell Holmes, Sr., and was destined to be a chief justice of the U.S. Supreme Court.[22]

A chastened President Lincoln returned to the White House for the rest of the evening, but not before saying, "Good-bye, Mr. Holmes. I'm glad you know how to talk to a civilian." That night the president's secretary, John Hay, noted in his diary that "a soldier roughly ordered him [Lincoln] to get down or he would get his head knocked off." Despite the excitement of the day, Hay wrote: "The President is in very good feather this evening."[23]

At sunset those who had yet to depart from Fort Stevens looked out at burning houses, set afire by the Union artillery. Darkness settled in, the shooting stopped and the show was over.[24] The day ended with a rumor that Lincoln was among the wounded.[25]

During the night, Early received intelligence that two corps of Union troops had arrived, the 6th and 19th Corps, the later consisting of 6,000 men sent up from Fort Monroe. Still Early did not waiver. He gathered his commanders together, sipped some more of Blair's wine, and discussed strategy.[26] Despite objections raised by his subordinates, the decision was made to stay and fight. They would attack at dawn unless something occurred during the night that would cause Early to change his mind.

Early in the morning of July 12, the crowds began their return to the parapets of Fort Stevens for act 2 of the real-life drama. Everyone felt confident in the outcome due to the presence of veteran fighters. Among those expecting high entertainment were members of the cabinet and Congress and other officials and a number of well-dressed ladies. Lincoln and his wife arrived late in the afternoon to the sounds of gunfire. Others gathered on a hillside next to the fort where they viewed the proceedings, all the while seemingly unmindful of the occasional bullet that went zipping in their direction.

General Early was up and in the saddle at dawn surveying the situation, considering his next move. The morning passed without an all-out attack by either side, however, as both armies were content to wait until the other made a move. The Union was now well represented, with boys in blue in a line from Fort Stevens west to Fort De Russy and east to Fort Slocum.

While Early deliberated, possibly waiting for Union troops to come rushing out so he could pour lead into them, Wright and McCook decided to liven up the afternoon and give the crowd something to cheer about. Their focus was two houses on a hill across a ravine where Confederate sharpshooters had taken positions and were firing at their leisure, hitting Union troops. They decided the houses had to be destroyed. A reporter for *The Evening Star* watched as the 6th Maine Artillery fired a round from Fort Stevens into the cupola of a house known as the Carberry House. He gleefully reported seeing "rebels skedaddling from its shelter like so many rats."[27]

Wright and McCook pressed the issue. They organized a battle line, and at about 6 P.M. skirmishers moved out ahead of the main force. Suddenly the brigade of Union troops, led by Colonel D. D. Bidwell, charged toward the enemy and was unexpectedly confronted by the Rebel's full line of battle, and a short but hot fight erupted. In the end it was the Rebels who gave way, to the elation of the spectators who signaled their approval with cheers, shouts and applause. The *New York Times* said the sharpshooters were "becoming annoying" and approved Wright and McCook's decision to take the offensive.[28]

A cool afternoon rain provided some relief on that hot 12th of July. Later, when darkness fell, the members of the audience, like satisfied theatergoers, took to their carriages.[29] Soldiers cheered when the carriage of the president and first lady passed by the defenses.[30] Having just watched a memorable, one-of-a-kind show, those gathered doubtless felt that their time was well spent. And yet much of the city did not sleep well, fearing that the Rebels might launch a nighttime attack.

McCook and Wright could claim a measure of satisfaction. They accomplished their objective for the day: the Rebels were held at bay. The defenders' artillery blasted and burned out the houses outside of Fort Stevens and scattered or killed the sharpshooters, but at the cost of about 250 Union dead and wounded.

The show of force was apparently enough to convince Early that he would be on the losing end of a full-scale battle. While he had about 10,000 men left, his actual fighting strength was about 3,000 soldiers.[31] He began making plans to retreat. Instructing Major Kyd Douglas to bring up the rear, Early quipped, "Major, we haven't taken Washington but we've scared Abe Lincoln like hell." Then, with a disconsolate Breckinridge — denied his chance to walk his Rebel boots into the White House, for a sentimental look—leading the way, the Army of the Valley departed, leaving their dead and seriously wounded men behind. The long mission had cost Early about 2,000 men from his corps.[32]

In his autobiography, published after his death, Early admitted that he lacked the resources needed to take the city. In a mere six-and-a-half-page chapter entitled "In Front of Washington," Early said he was convinced that to attack or even stay longer would cost him his entire army. He said that having to deal with Hunter, Sigel and Wallace took up valuable time and energy and caused significant loss of life. In short, his army was played out, and so was the mission. And yet he proudly proclaimed that his march" for length and rapidity" was "without parallel in this or any other modern war."[33]

The mad ball was over, and while the outcome was worthy of praise, the vanquished host was given the "thumbs down." Breckinridge—who had grown gray and heavy—was scorned and hated all the more. It was bad enough that the former vice president chose the South, but to come back to America's capital city prepared to destroy it was enough to boil the blood of Union men. There were traitors and then there was Breckinridge, the ex–vice president and pro–slavery candidate for president in 1860 turned Rebel general—and he escaped unhung. Yet there was some closure in the victory, for every form of fright was lifted, and the walled city of Washington was restored to its former dignity.

While Early's lack of success was greeted with angry disappointment in the Southern press, Northern newspapers were lighthearted in their reporting. The *Dubuque Daily Times,* recognizing a farce when it saw one, crowed: "The Raid about 'Played Out,' Rebels Whipped, and Taking the Back Track."[34] The *New York Times* coyly suggested that the "siege of Washington" may have seemed interminable, but it was "not quite as long in duration as the siege of Troy." The reporter admitted that it "is too early for us yet to make up our minds whether we ought to laugh over the *denouement* of an affair more farcical than tragical," or be thankful that it ended with just a little humiliation in its wake. He gave the Rebels credit for brashness and guts and for making the city of Washington seem to be in far more danger than it actually was.[35]

And yet like all battles, big and small, soldiers were killed, and no amount of satire could ease the suffering and sorrow. In the aftermath there were the usual amputations, embalming of bodies, burials, carving of gravestones and grieving over lost lives, as sure as tears always flow following the effusion of blood.

A correspondent for the *Washington Chronicle* went out to inspect the field of battle and take stock of the damage done by the angry Rebels. Gazing out at the two houses destroyed by Union cannon fire, he noted "evidence of hard fighting." Disfigured trees, gutted and burned buildings and lifeless bodies scattered about were grim testimony to the intensity of the struggle. Then on

General Alexander M. McCook and his staff posing in full military regalia at his head-quarters in Washington, D.C., during the brief siege by the Confederate army under General Jubal Early. Since McCook had been relegated to desk jobs following the debacle at Chickamauga, he could not be faulted for at least trying to look important while recalling the days when he was a field general with serious combat responsibilities.

a grave near the Blair residence, the correspondent found a book taken from someone's library by a Rebel. It was volume 8 of Byron's works. Inside someone had written a cryptic note to President Lincoln, dated July 12. "Now Uncle Abe, you had better be quiet the balance of your Administration; we only came near your town this time, just to show you what we could do; but if you go on in your mad career, we will come soon again, and then you had better stand from under." It was signed: "Yours respectfully, THE WORST REBEL YOU EVER SAW."[36] Even the losers saw some humor in the event.

Early and his motley band of soldiers turned toward Virginia with no hot or serious pursuit by the Union. McCook sent two companies in the direction of the retreating Rebels, and they returned with a handful of prisoners, a clutch of ragged, wounded men.[37] Early's army would not be bagged as Lincoln had wished. Halleck, Stanton and everyone else were just glad to see them go away. At no time did the entire force of invaders get involved in the fight.

Most were waiting at the Silver Spring encampment for attack orders that never came.

While it was a serious setback for the South, Early at least made the effort, and in that there may have been some consolation. Having sized up Washington for the kill and then turned away without firing a few experimental shots would have doubtlessly left Early plagued by thoughts of "what if?" Still, it was unrealistic to think that such a small number of men, exhausted from their long march and without any means to mount or break down the walls, could have had any success against the fortified defenders. The scattered and disconnected arrangement of Early's army also prevented him from making a concentrated assault. Southern pride was not enough; he was too weak, and he knew it.

While marching away from the Union capital, Early told a Rockville citizen that he felt he could have taken Washington but would have lost 1,500 men in the process. He also said that had he succeeded in entering and capturing the city, his men would have looted the liquor stores, and in a state of intoxication, would have been beyond his control.[38] While this has the ring of a feeble excuse, all things considered, it was better to withdraw and save his men for fighting on home turf where so much Southern blood had already been shed.

To Early's credit, however, he was able to tie the Union high command in knots for about two weeks, make Halleck a nervous wreck and take a shot at President Lincoln. During the raid he wrecked railroads, looted houses, cut off telegraph communication to the outside, destroyed crops and burned down the town of Chambersburg, Pennsylvania. After it was over, he crossed the Potomac River driving a large herd of stolen cattle while carting off wagonloads of booty. He would have something tangible to present to General Lee. It would be up to Lee to decide if the mission was worthwhile.

Lee's opponent, General Grant, was extremely disappointed because Halleck had not ordered an all-out pursuit of Early. It was an opportunity lost. Nor was Grant the only critic. As could be expected, Dana ripped generals right and left in his post-siege report, venting hot wrath on Halleck, Augur and McCook. In anger and indignation, Dana lamented "the want of intelligence, energy and purpose." Dana castigated McCook in a manner that may have reminded people of the fallout from Chickamauga. Ignoring the fact that McCook was thrust into the emergency and had so little to work with, Dana complained that the Ohioan conducted no reconnaissance and had no skirmishers. Instead, Dana said, McCook "allowed the rebel sharpshooters to ... pick off men at the embrasures of the fort."[39]

If McCook had wanted to respond to the charges made by his old tormentor, he could have said that he did no reconnaissance because he had no force to use for that purpose. Since he arrived in town at the height of the crisis, he didn't have time. He could have corrected Dana on the matter of skirmishers, for he did send out a skirmish line consisting of the Ohio militia, which held up until Wright arrived with his corps. Finally, Dana was dead wrong to say that McCook allowed sharpshooters to "pick off" the defenders, for McCook and Wright used artillery to rout them out of the houses in front of Fort Stevens.

Facing a daunting challenge when he received his orders from Halleck, McCook truly did all that he could with the time and resources at his disposal. While there was much confusion and floundering during the crisis, in the end it was the combined efforts of a number of men, McCook included, that saved the day for the capital city of the United States. In doing so, the honor and dignity of the nation was upheld, and in the eyes of the world, this accomplishment cannot be understated.

The final outcome of the Civil War was not the result of a single, dramatic event, but rather a chipping away, a gradual wearing down of Southern resistance, a long series of events that, in total, concluded with the defeat of the Confederacy. The turning back of Early's raid was one such incremental step, and thousands of people, Alexander McCook included, can rightfully claim a share.

General McCook was doing his duty while bearing a personal burden that does not emerge from the records of the defense of Washington. His younger brother, Colonel Daniel McCook, had been seriously wounded in the battle of Kennesaw Mountain in Georgia on June 27. He was brought home to Ohio where he died on July 17. But before he died, W. T. Sherman promoted him to brigadier general. Daniel McCook, Jr., was but one of thousands of casualties of the disastrous battle under the leadership of General Sherman, who ordered an uphill, frontal assault on well-defended Rebel positions. Daniel's death was the fourth suffered by the McCook family in the Civil War.

After Washington quieted down, Northerners were left wondering: was Early's campaign a serious attempt to capture the Union capital city? Or was its main purpose to range freely and raid the countryside and come close enough to Washington to leave an impression? Or was the clever General Lee planning on trading a captured Washington for a threatened Richmond? A *New York Times* correspondent who lived in a house on the 7th Street pike about five miles from the city claimed to have found a document on his property that indicated that the real purpose of the raid was for plunder and to "compel Grant to release his grasp upon the very throat of the rebellion" and send a significant portion of his army to defend Washington.[40]

There was an opinion among the second-guessers that had the Rebels not spent so much time gathering loot, and instead made an immediate and direct attack on the capital before Grant's veterans arrived, the result might have been quite different and very damaging. Secretary Welles opined that because of the confusion and ineptitude on the part of the Union brain trust, "the Rebels have lost a remarkable opportunity" to capture Washington.[41] Others believed that Washington and Baltimore were adequately protected, but nothing was done to protect people in the rural areas. It was disgraceful to allow Early and his men to raid and plunder at will.

There was other residual anger as well. Monty Blair was seething mad over the loss of his house, and charged Stanton and Halleck with "incompetence and cowardice." A rumor floated out of the city that Stanton actually resigned "as a result of quarrels which grew out of the attack." This was false, of course, but consistent with the bizarre and sardonic — yet strangely entertaining — events that occurred in the nation's capital during July of 1864.[42]

On the whole, a cynical and war-weary people, loathe to assign any credibility to the Southern effort, downplayed the raid. The Rebels were mockingly reminded that they had three chances to take Washington — after the first battle of Bull Run, following General John Pope's defeat and Early's raid — and the result was the same: failure. The third time was anything but a charm, and now Northerners were saying, "On to Richmond" and let's get this thing over with.

Having turned back the third threat, Halleck and Stanton began reassigning excess generals. Among them, Major General Alexander McCook was relieved of duty in the department of Washington. He was ordered to report to the adjutant general for instructions.[43] While the defense of Washington wasn't much of a fight compared to Shiloh, Stones River and Chickamauga, there was a "Fighting McCook" in it, thereby creating another chapter in the saga of an illustrious and patriotic family.

For the audacious General Jubal Early, retribution came in the form of Major General Philip Sheridan. In August, Grant passed over Hunter and ordered Sheridan and about 30,000 men, mostly cavalry, to pursue and attack Early's ragtag but hard-fighting corps. After a series of minor battles in which the audacious Early held his own against greater odds, the decisive battle of Cedar Creek in the Shenandoah Valley was fought on October 19, 1864. Early actually had Sheridan's men retreating in chaos when the general called "Little Phil" rallied his men and gave the Army of the Valley a thrashing from which it never recovered.[44]

Sheridan was once a division commander in McCook's corps. Little Phil's success meant that McCook saw credit for victory go to a former subordinate. As the war was entering its final phases, there would be more laurels to pass out to victorious Union commanders, but none for Alexander M. McCook. He would remain sidelined for the rest of the Civil War.

CHAPTER 18

Last Years of
Service in the Army

*Alexander McDowell McCook was the member of the family who
attained the greatest military distinction.*
— *Daily Evening Telegraph*, June 12, 1903

When the Civil War was in its final stages, Major General Alexander M.
McCook was in command at the Eastern Division of Arkansas, at Helena, a
position he assumed on March 9, 1865. He would have welcomed a combat
assignment, but because of the disaster at Chickamauga he was relegated to
non-combat duty, except for the brief stint in Washington, D.C., when General
Jubal Early's ragtag band of Rebels threatened the Union capital city.

General McCook had been in the thick of some of the most significant
battles of the Civil War, including Shiloh, Stones River and Chickamauga.
Three horses were shot out from under him. His father and three brothers,
Charles, Robert and Daniel Jr., had been killed in action. Brothers John,
Latimer and Edwin suffered painful, debilitating injuries in battle, but Alexander escaped without so much as a minor wound. Now the war was almost over,
and he would never again lead an army against the South. Nor would he participate in a victory parade.

The Union army didn't seem to know what to do with General McCook,
and while he was on good terms with some of the top brass, others in high
command didn't like or respect him. Among the latter was Major General
Philip H. Sheridan, who served in McCook's corps in the western theater. In
Sheridan's mind, McCook was at least partially responsible for the loss at
Chickamauga, and "Little Phil" was not in the mood to forgive or forget.

In January of 1865, when Major General Lew Wallace was preparing to
engage in "certain secret service" for the War Department, he asked that
McCook take his place in the Middle Department at Baltimore. But Sheridan
wrote to Major General Henry W. Halleck, saying, "I am not entirely satisfied

239

to leave McCook in charge" at Baltimore. Without saying why, he asked Halleck to send someone else. Halleck then assigned Brigadier General W. W. Morris to the Middle Department and told Sheridan to relieve McCook, who outranked Morris.[1]

Wallace pressed Sheridan on the matter, again asking that McCook be placed in charge of the Middle Department at Baltimore. The record, however, doesn't indicate the nature of the communication, if any, between Sheridan and McCook. Sheridan merely replied to Halleck saying he had an excess of generals — including McCook — available for work, asking for orders.[2]

On April 7, McCook was still at Helena, Arkansas, when Major General John Pope, in command of the Military Division of the Missouri, at St. Louis, wrote to Secretary of War Edwin Stanton, asking that McCook be assigned to accompany a congressional committee formed to "examine into Indian matters" in New Mexico and Utah. Pope intimated that McCook wasn't doing anything of importance in Helena and that he wanted the Ohio general to go on the fact-finding mission because he "served long in Indian country and knows all about these matters."[3]

Receiving no reply to his first message, Pope wrote to Stanton again, this time stressing the fact that McCook requested the assignment. Pope acknowledged that McCook's brother (probably George) objected to the appointment, but urged that it be granted because "he [General McCook] is the best officer I know for this service." On the same day, Stanton grudgingly consented, saying: "Send General McCook if he desires to go."[4]

Tension between the Plains Indians and white settlers was great when McCook went west, due in part to a pair of tragic events that occurred during the Civil War. In 1862, the Santee Sioux of Minnesota — worn down by near starvation and frustration — carried out a widespread attack on the settlements in the southern and west-central part of the state, killing hundreds of settlers. The government retaliated and the Santee Sioux were pursued into Dakota Territory, where a series of battles and skirmishes were fought against the Santee and other Sioux tribes well into 1865.

The other disaster occurred in Colorado in 1864 where a Major John Chivington led an unprovoked and punitive raid on a peaceful village of Cheyenne people, massacring men, women and children. The "Chivington Massacre" shocked the conscience of the nation and angered Indians who, once again, were deceived by the army of their "Great Father" in Washington.

These bloody events were unable to dissuade McCook from taking to the frontier. Happy with the assignment that would take him to the far west again, McCook turned his Arkansas duties over to another officer and left Helena on April 27. He then started west from St. Louis, having been ordered to proceed to Fort Leavenworth, Kansas, to meet the congressional delegation and accompany it on visits to the Indian tribes. He was instructed to "escort the congressional committee — headed by Wisconsin Republican Senator James R. Doolittle — to whatever section of the country they desire to visit" in the course of their investigation.

The committeemen were looking into "errors, mistakes, frauds and wrongs of the present system of Indian policy." Fraud, graft and theft among Indian agents were rampant at the time. While Plains Indians were a disfavored class of people, the questionable and outright illegal conduct of the Indian agents was so pervasive and shocking that Congress was forced to take action. After all, public money was at stake, and a lot of it was filtering into the pockets of the agents and traders. The matter was to be fully investigated and reported to Congress so that appropriate corrective action could be taken.[5]

McCook joined the congressional party on May 16. From Leavenworth, McCook and the party went to New Mexico by way of the Raton Mountains and Fort Union. On May 31, at Fort Larned, Kansas, McCook issued his first report to General Pope.

McCook's report reveals that the army units in the field — fresh from the killing grounds of the Civil War — were planning attacks on the Indians of the Central Plains, including the Comanche, Kiowa, Cheyenne and Arapaho. The tribes were to be punished for numerous depredations, thefts and murders. Based on his personal observations, McCook concluded that a punitive campaign was wrong and not in the best interests of the army and federal government. As such he ordered Colonel J. H. Ford, who was preparing for war, to "suspend the contemplated campaign." McCook favored talks with tribal leaders with a view to moving them onto reservations where their contact with whites could be eliminated or at least kept to a minimum.

McCook explained to Pope that the congressional committee and Indian agent Colonel Jesse H. Leavenworth believed that "a peace can be secured with them and they be kept south of the Arkansas River, thus leaving the great Santa Fe Trail free from Indians," with the exception of some roaming bands of Sioux and Cheyenne. McCook — who in his younger years favored a war of extermination — insisted that the planned attack would "require 6000 men and cost millions of money," and would expose the Santa Fe Trail to danger. Furthermore, he reminded Pope that the Comanche tribes had not "committed any known acts of hostility," so "war with them is not desirable."[6]

Major General Grenville M. Dodge, also on the western frontier, intercepted McCook's dispatch to Ford and forwarded it on to Pope, with a note explaining the theft of "fifteen head of stock" near Fort Larned. Dodge viewed McCook's peacemaking attitude with disdain and was clearly trying to prove to Pope that the Indians were up to no good and were in need of punishment. Pope was in accord and told Dodge: "You must do as you think best about Ford, General McCook has no authority from me to interfere in any manner with your troops."[7]

If he was miffed at McCook, Pope didn't remove him. After all, the congressional committee also wanted no warlike tactics, and it was he (Pope) who sought out McCook's expertise. Pope may not have liked what he heard from McCook and the committee, but he had to accept that they were working toward pacifying the Indians. And besides, he had no right to recall a congressional committee, invested with the power and authority to act independent of the army.

Meanwhile, Colonel Ford continued to make his case for war, saying the "Indians are as hostile as ever," but he added that they had done little harm. McCook — along with the congressional committee — spoiled his plans. But Ford's command was at the same time diminished when much of his cavalry was ordered to be discharged from active duty.

Dodge, too, was upset with McCook and the congressional committee. He was not the kind of general accustomed to peacemaking. A man of action, Dodge acquired a reputation as an efficient and hardworking officer during the Civil War, with a record of success in battle. He was also an engineer who had worked in the high echelons of the Union spy system and was without peer in his ability to construct new railroads and repair those that were destroyed. Now that he would no longer be leading attacks on Rebels, he was anxious to turn his attention to the Plains Indians.

Dodge's tenure as Indian fighter and pacifier began on January 30, 1865, when he was assigned to the Department of the Missouri with headquarters at Fort Leavenworth, where he would report to General Pope. Dodge commenced a winter campaign against the tribes who were damaging or destroying the overland telegraph lines. Although it was with great difficulty that he got his reluctant regiments to leave their comfortable winter quarters and travel during the cold weather, he got them moving and was successful in reconnecting telegraph lines from the Missouri River to California.[8]

In the spring Dodge took to the field again after hearing "persistent rumors of another Indian uprising." He was assigned to take charge of all army units in Kansas, Nebraska, Colorado and Utah. While the officials from the Union Pacific Railroad Company wanted his services as chief engineer, Dodge postponed accepting that position in order to subdue the Indian threat to overland routes, including the proposed route of what was to be America's first transcontinental railroad.

It was during this second campaign that Dodge's aggressive stance came into conflict with the congressional committee and McCook. On June 6, Dodge infused his angry concern into a lengthy report to Pope. McCook, Dodge insisted, had it all wrong. Just ask any officer or trader on the Plains; he will tell you that the Indians were guilty of theft, murder and other "outrages" committed on many occasions.

Pope and Dodge didn't always agree, but they were both out of sync with the plans of the congressional committee. They rejected the treaty concept and believed that the army should pursue and punish the Plains Indians, force them to "respect our power and sue for peace." The army would make "informal treaties" with the Indians with no distribution of presents, goods, food or money. The conquered Indians would simply be forced to stay on reservations without the supervision of agents or traders, whom Pope and Dodge believed to be universally corrupt.[9]

Dodge, however, was a good soldier and would follow orders. He would also have his forces in position, ready to attack, should the peace efforts of the committee fail.[10] In his next correspondence with Pope, Dodge was more conciliatory. He agreed that McCook was only acting in accordance with the wishes of the committee, and if the senators wanted to treat with the Indians, Dodge would respect that effort. Should they fail — and it is clear he expected they would — he was ready to lead an offensive.[11] Apparently four years of fighting the South had no tiring effect on his aggressive psyche, and the thought of shedding more blood was not the least unappealing.

It was McCook's order, approved by a reluctant General Pope, that set in motion a peace process favored by Colonel Leavenworth, U.S. Indian agent. Leavenworth wanted peace talks and worked earnestly with the officers with troops patrolling the frontier, imploring them to comply with McCook's order. Toward this end Leavenworth wrote to Major General John B. Sanborn on August 1 with news that the president and the secretary of war had arranged for a peace commission to treat with the Indians. Should Sanborn — a Dodge subordinate — take his command south of the Arkansas River, "an Angel from heaven could not convince them [the Indians] but what another Chivington massacre was intended."[12]

With warlike army commanders chafing at the bit, but willing to stand aside, the peace process assumed center stage. Unfortunately it turned out to be a feeble effort and was crushed out by subsequent events as outlined in yet another Dodge report. On November 1, 1865, after months on the frontier Dodge was able to reassert that McCook was dead wrong. For "immediately after the issuance of this order by General McCook, the Indians made a general attack upon the entire line from Cow Creek to Fort Dodge." He was able to say, with a sense of vindication, that "all their peace talk was a ruse, a dishonest scheme."[13]

Dodge wanted to keep the warring tribes far away from the overland routes, and in order to do this, he decided that a crushing blow should be struck against the Plains Indians. Toward this end he telegraphed General Grant, "demanding his authority for starting another war against the Indians." But Grant was not supportive, nor was the administration of President Andrew Johnson. As such Dodge was not allowed to take action against the tribes, and he later insisted that the interference with his plans had laid the groundwork for the Indian wars of the 1870s. According to Dodge, the massacre of Custer's command at Little Bighorn in the summer of 1876 could have been prevented had the Indians been soundly defeated during the campaigns of 1865–66.[14]

There are no McCook reports in the official record that reflect his thoughts and efforts toward resolving the "Indian question" peacefully. But the rest of the century was marked by incidents of violence and a growing barrier of ill will between the races. What to do with the Indians and how to exploit the great American West — looked upon by many as inhospitable and uninhabitable — were destined to be the two great issues debated in the decades to come.

The scene was dominated by men like Dodge who urged the government to assign army officers to selected parts of the West to rule over the tribes with an iron hand. He believed that the federal government should not make treaties with the Indians, nor treat them as sovereign nations. Instead, officials should treat them as conquered people and "adopt all necessary measures for their government, protection, support, and future welfare as subjects or wards."[15] While Dodge's proposal did not anticipate that Indians would become American citizens, it was clearly a middle ground between those who wanted them exterminated and those who wanted them left alone to live as they had lived for centuries.

Through it all, Pope generally agreed with Dodge, and yet he once sent a report to Sherman in which he laid blame for the crisis on the attitudes of white men, who had dispossessed the Indians and destroyed their means of subsistence. "The Indian in truth," said Pope, "has no longer a country."[16]

For General McCook the frontier foray in 1865 — called by frontiersmen the "bloody year on the Plains" — was just a taste of the service he would perform in the coming years. Doubtless he felt more like a true military man while serving in the West, because the last two years of the Civil War found him on the sidelines, a restless warrior who possessed as much fighting spirit as did Generals Dodge and Sanborn.

After the war ended, McCook remained in the army and was given the rank of lieutenant colonel. The transition from volunteer to regular army meant that many brevet generals had to give up their stars for the insignia of colonel or lieutenant colonel. It was not considered a demotion, and the army would find ex–Civil War generals most useful, for during the next approximately 35 years, the primary role of the U.S. Army would be on the frontier, stationed at outposts, patrolling and occasionally fighting skirmishes and pitched battles with the Plains tribes.

For many other Civil War veterans, the end of the war meant changing from military to civilian careers. While Alexander McCook stayed in the army, his brother former brigadier general Edwin S. McCook accepted an appointment by President Grant, in 1872, to serve as secretary of the Dakota Territory, with headquarters in Yankton. Sadly, however, Edwin became entangled in the dangerous web of politics. Following a quarrel with a political enemy, he was shot and killed in Yankton. His funeral at Cincinnati was attended by his family, including his older brother, Alexander. The McCook family had suffered yet another tragic death. But as always, the family moved on bravely.

After General U. S. Grant was elected president in 1868, his trusted wartime companion W. T. Sherman took over as the top general in the army. In 1875 Alexander McCook was appointed aide-de-camp to his friend and comrade General Sherman. The friendship that took root early in the Civil War had grown warmer over the years as both men aged. Existing letters point to a relationship based on mutual respect and common interests. Unlike other generals whose relationships were poisoned by bitter, unshakeable memories and post-war recriminations, Sherman and McCook had a sincere friendship that was uplifting to both of them.

In 1880 McCook was assigned to Fort Douglas in Salt Lake City, Utah, where he served as the commanding officer. Upon joining him at the new post, his wife Kate fell ill and died at a hotel. Although devastated by the loss, McCook refused the assistance of the "foremost ladies of the city" and instead dressed and prepared his wife for burial all by himself.[17] Kate was only 44 years old and the mother of three young daughters.

Following the death of Kate, Alexander became enamored with Annie Colt from Wisconsin, a lady also admired by W. T. Sherman. The loquacious general — famous throughout the world — was reputed to be a ladies' man who enjoyed the company of pretty girls, and while not a womanizer, he was not always faithful to Ellen, his dutiful and ultra-religious wife.

When he learned that his friend Alexander McCook had found love again, Sherman wrote to Annie on August 23, 1884, extending his best wishes to the couple. Caught up in the romance of it all, Sherman admitted that he was jealous, but was equally forceful in his praise for Annie's husband-to-be whom he described as "hearty, jovial and cheery," and a man of a large, well-earned reputation. Sherman's written toast included a wish that Annie "will make his [McCook's] home what he always wants it to be — a hospitable and gracious place for his children and his host of family." He closed the letter saying that he was "hoping to see you in person at the time of your marriage."[18]

McCook was ordered to Fort Leavenworth, Kansas, where on May 13, 1886, he would assume command. Established in 1827, Fort Leavenworth was one of the military showplaces of the west, featuring modern brick buildings, stylishly built and well arranged on the grounds of the fort. Over the years it protected freight and travelers on the transcontinental trails, and served as a staging point for launching attacks on Plains Indians. The post was also the home of the School of Application for Infantry and Cavalry, created by Sherman in 1881. McCook would be in charge of the school and its instructors, among them Colonel George B. Sanford who supervised the Department of Cavalry.

McCook brought with him his belief in strict discipline. Sanford called McCook "a borderline martinet" who "lived by the book and for the book." Among his orders were bans on fireworks, gambling and a prohibition against children roaming around the parade grounds. He maintained a demanding, "no-nonsense program" of work for both officers and students and ordered that classes be held six days a week.

On the somewhat lighter side, spit-and-polish McCook was very fond of military pomp and ceremony and conducted numerous parades on the post grounds. He was also "socially inclined," and "clubs, libraries, billiard halls, canteens, schools, churches, stores and theatres" flourished.[19]

While he was stationed at Fort Leavenworth, General McCook went to Mexico City where he met with the "American Colony." He also toured a military school and visited the presidential palace. There he was warmly greeted by a Mexican officer and given a grand tour of the city in the company of a young lieutenant. McCook wrote to his wife on November 22, 1887, saying he was "not impressed" with Mexico City nor with the "Halls of Montezuma." Although he was happy to admit that he was in the presence of good people, he observed and opined — with no small measure of ethnocentrism — that the Mexican "civilization was 100 years behind ours," and would never catch up.[20]

Still he enjoyed his stay in the Hotel Iturbide and was grateful for the royal treatment he received at the hands of the Mexican government. He was introduced to the president of Mexico and gave a speech at a reception and banquet, hosted by the "American Colony." He called the reception a "great success."

The Mexican president regularly sent his carriage and coachman to McCook's hotel for trips around the city, the effect of which was to make the American army officer feel like a prince. In his eagerness to convey the joy of it all to his wife, he closed his letter saying the carriage had just arrived, "ready to carry me to the palace."[21] In the romantic heart of old Mexico, Alexander McCook, survivor of the unforgettable American Civil War, was making memories of a different sort. If only Charles A. Dana, his old tormentor from the war days, could see the redeemed and respected General McCook, basking in the glory of his high station.

According to his niece, Alexander McCook enjoyed his golden years, elevated by the respect of so many people, including other army officers. Young officers, who saw him as a Civil War icon, drank toasts to him and broke their glasses on the floor in the tradition of the military. McCook had considerable social skills and used them to entertain and make people laugh. He was a storyteller and an "after-dinner raconteur," a "hail fellow-well met," and the "life of any party." The handsome McCook with his goatee, "twinkling, china blue eyes" and "florid complexion," kept himself in good physical condition by an exercise regimen and good diet, but he was "fond of good food and wines."[22] Indeed the years following the end of the Civil War were good years for the former "Fighting McCook."

McCook returned to Fort Leavenworth after the Mexican experience and was visited by his friend and commanding officer, General W. T. Sherman. Some time after the visit, in a letter dated July 19, 1889, Sherman informed McCook that he was leaving St. Louis for New York, having just "transferred the caskets of Willie and Charles [his deceased sons] to the "side of their mother" in an adjoining lot. Then quickly changing the subject, Sherman asked a favor. It seems that when he left Fort Leavenworth, he did so without fully paying for laundry service. He said he gave the man who brought the clean clothes 50 cents. He also enclosed a dollar, asking McCook to please give it to the washerwoman who did the actual work. Sherman concluded by saying, "Let him [the husband of the washerwoman] keep the 50 cents for himself."[23] The letter was vintage Sherman prose, intensely honest and direct. Like anyone who has survived the cruel vagaries and demands of war, Sherman could switch from the grave to the whimsical in a heartbeat.

McCook remained in command at Fort Leavenworth until July 14, 1890, when he was promoted to brigadier general in the regular army and transferred to the Department of Arizona with headquarters at Los Angeles.[24] Now an old soldier nearing retirement, McCook's new assignment took him to the West Coast where he spent time in both Los Angeles and San Diego. Letters to his beloved Annie reveal an especially happy and boyish Alex McCook, as he toured Southern California and reveled in its scenery, climate and dazzling cities that reflected a charming old Spanish architecture. He was awed by the size, opulence and splendor of the new, state-of-the-art Coronado Hotel on an island off the coast of San Diego.

McCook had a cushy assignment — light-years away from the hard life of the war — and he wanted his wife and family to come to California so that they, too, could relax in the splendor of the seashore. "Since I came to this beautiful climate, I regret I did not bring you with me." Elsewhere in the letter from Los Angeles, he said, with great passion, "I do not want to grow poetical, but I wish *to God*, you were here." He insisted that he would "make the fight to remain here" and send for Annie so he could show her all "the lovely places." He had train passes for her and the children.[25]

In McCook's eyes and mind, Southern California was a vast resort, shining, timeless and magnificent — where a perfect climate was wedded to beautiful scenery, producing a forever magical world of sublime pleasure. Writing in 1890, McCook was experiencing a booming and lively California in its raw but pure state, long before it attracted the millions and the problems that came with explosive population growth. Long before smog, overcrowding, and mas-sive traffic gridlock. Long before mega-swarms of humans in constant motion, like motor-driven ants, superseded the California lifestyle that McCook knew and loved.

McCook was still in Los Angeles when he received an affectionate letter from W. T. Sherman in New York dated January 11, 1891. Sherman thanked McCook for sending a New Year's letter and then went on to discuss current affairs including the matter of a pension for Mrs. Jessie Fremont, widow of deceased General John C. Fremont.

It appears as if McCook had asked Sherman to come to California, for the legendary general struggled to explain his limited financial means, saying, "The truth is I cannot afford to visit California even if I wanted." Sherman admitted, longingly, that he missed the scenery and climate of California, from "Mendocino to San Diego — having traveled it on mule back long, long ago — 1847–9." The New York City winter was harsh, but he jokingly said, "For a 71 year old Colt I manage to get a good deal of fun."[26]

The letter to McCook was probably the last one Sherman sent to his friend and comrade, for the world-famous general died on February 13, 1891, after an illness of eight days. America lost a celebrity and a war hero while Alexander McCook lost the comfort and companionship of a steadfast friend, a man he had known, respected, served under and trusted since the first battle of Bull Run.

By the 1890s, veterans on both sides of the Civil War were dying off at a fast pace, and Alexander McDowell McCook, now reaching the "old soldier" status, was feeling the weight of years. He retired from the army in 1895 with the rank of major general, and the man Anson McCook said "had no other ambition than to serve his country" returned to Dayton, Ohio.[27]

Retirement, however, did not equate to inactivity. For later, while trav-eling abroad, McCook attended the coronation of the czar of Russia in Moscow as a representative of the United States at the request of the president. It was one of the last official acts he performed on behalf of his country.

CHAPTER 19

The Death of General Alexander M. McCook

> Perryville, Stones River and Chickamauga cannot be written without the name of McCook and the gallant men who fought under his command.
>
> —*Ashland* (Ohio) *Times*, Unknown Date

When the Civil War ended, the McCook war dead were all accounted for — Charles, Robert, Daniel Jr., and Daniel Sr., lying side by side beneath a stylish if not regal tombstone in Cincinnati's Spring Grove Cemetery. The memories of the McCook men killed in battle left the surviving family members with a legacy of pride and honor. Nowhere is this summed up better than in the writings of Anson G. McCook. In his memoirs, Anson declared that the war to put down the rebellion was a challenge to manhood that summoned courage and fortitude in every right-thinking man. He wrote: "Unless the Constitution of the United States was indeed a rope of sand and the preamble to it a jumble of meaningless words, it was the right and duty of the Government to protect it self from destruction."[1]

The cost of that protection was high and the bill was partially paid with the McCook family's best blood, but it was a cause they believed in and it was this belief that provided a measure of comfort for the survivors. When called upon to defend the nation's honor, the proud McCooks — brave and loyal to the core — rallied to the cause. Since the survivors could rejoice in a hard-earned victory, they did not question, or they were willing to accept, the depth of the sacrifice that was their lot in life. There was a grim nobility in it all, for the battle-related death's of the four men elevated the entire family in the eyes of Ohioans and the rest of the country.

And yet their losses continued. In 1869 Dr. Latimer A. McCook died. He had toiled throughout the war in anonymity as a contract surgeon with the

41st Illinois Infantry Regiment, without once taking leave. How hard he worked, how many limbs he amputated and how many lives he saved will never been known. There are no statistics to measure that kind of effort. He served at Vicksburg with General U. S. Grant and later with General W. T. Sherman on the famous march through Georgia and the Carolinas, the only McCook to do so.

Although a non-combatant, Latimer was wounded twice and left the war in poor health. Of all their boys who served in the Civil War, he is probably the least-known son of Daniel and Martha McCook. He was described as a blue-eyed handsome man with a serious outlook, and as a good doctor who always had a dog or two at his side. He never married again after his wife mysteriously deserted him, and he never fathered any children, but he liked them. As obscure as his more flamboyant younger brothers were popular, Latimer McCook's death was largely passed over. One newspaper column merely said that "he died in the West some time ago."[2]

Brother Edwin S. McCook also survived the war but died in the line of duty on September 11, 1873. He had been appointed to the office of secretary of the Dakota Territory by President U. S. Grant. While attending a railroad meeting at Yankton, the capital city, Edwin was shot and killed by a banker, Peter P. Wintermute, from a rival political group.

With the death of George W. McCook on December 28, 1877, friends of the fallen colonel were given another opportunity to eulogize both the deceased and his patriotic and noble family. George died in New York following a Christmas-day stroke, while visiting his cousin Anson G. McCook. His body was taken to Steubenville and buried in the Union Cemetery.

George was remembered as an astute man with considerable political skills, a man who forged useful connections for himself and his family, including the likes of Edwin M. Stanton and Stephen A. Douglas. He was survived by two children who inherited "a handsome fortune of this world's goods."[3]

George was commended for his reputation as a lawyer and politician, more so than that of a military man. And yet he was active during the war, as much as his health would permit, raising and training regiments in Ohio. At his funeral, his family's illustrious martial past was reprised, and mourners were told that out of the eleven McCook children born to Daniel Sr. and Martha, only four remained alive. Of the honored dead, "the father, Gen. Daniel, Gen. Robert and Private Charley were killed in the late war."[4]

When the aged and long-suffering mother of the large brood at last succumbed to death in 1879, in Lisbon, Ohio, she was almost deified, for she was "Mother McCook," the mother of many of the "fighting McCooks." Legions of women waited patiently at home while their husbands and sons fought in the war, but few, if any, were called upon to accept so much sacrifice and loss as Martha McCook.

Her obituary declared: "This woman deserves more than passing notice. As the mother of so many patriotic sons, whose deeds have shed deserved honor on the family name, she would have been held in immortal honor in Greece or Rome." She had long graced Ohio with her presence, where with the Bible and her firm yet kind discipline, she raised nine boys and three girls, and by noble example was remembered as an esteemed lady, as brave as any soldier. The Civil War brought great sorrow to her door, but with each message of injury and death, she was somehow able to withstand the impact of terrible news that would have crushed most other women.[5]

She was spared the necessity of burying her son Alexander McDowell McCook. He lived into the 20th century, dying on June 12, 1903, in Dayton, Ohio, at the home of his daughter, Kathleen Craighead. His wife Annie was by his side. He was 72 years old. A newspaper obituary called him the "Greatest of the Fighting Family," the "Fighting McCooks," who "attained the greatest military distinction." Along with the accolade, the article dredged up the disasters of Perryville and Chickamauga, two Civil War battles that reflected badly on McCook, essentially following him to the grave. While giving General McCook his due as a fighter, the article said he "lacked the experience required for the high commands that were thrust upon him."[6]

It was definitely not a heroic send-off for this McCook who went through the war without a scratch. Compared to his brothers Dan and Robert — whom he loved dearly — Alex was buried after an almost second-rate memorial that gave him good marks for loyalty and patriotism, but was woefully lacking in the type of praise heaped upon his brothers who suffered and died from battle wounds.

The last surviving member of his staff, Horace N. Fisher, wrote a memorial that may be described as an attempt to answer the critics, to shore up the general's image, honor his memory and send him into history bearing the mantle of a redeemed and enlightened warrior. Fisher had the utmost respect for General McCook, and in the sketch of his military career, he wrote about a popular and magnanimous officer who was loved and admired by his troops. It was McCook's "genial spirit" along with strict, but fairly applied discipline that made him "an ideal commander of our intelligent volunteer army." With no hint of the official criticism and malevolent newspaper treatment that dogged McCook after the battle of Chickamauga, Fisher laid out the "facts" in an effort to do justice to his "beloved commander, who has just passed away."[7]

Alexander M. McCook outlived many Northern generals as well as other men who were stubbornly critical of his war record. What it all meant to him, we can never know, but with each death he was compelled to remember either kindness or criticism. Perhaps his jovial personality, his zest for life and the high value he placed on relationships, including friendships, caused him to remember the good in men, for at no time in his later years did he become

The impressive and regal monument at the Spring Grove Cemetery was created to honor the "Fighting McCooks," the sons of Daniel and Martha McCook. Alexander M. McCook and his brothers George, Edwin, Daniel Jr., Robert and Charles are all buried at the base of the monument. Others interred there include their parents and Kate and Annie, the two wives of Alexander.

mired down in anger and bitterness. If he was deeply troubled by the thorny past, he never made a public display of his anger.

Unlike other disgruntled generals who had held high command, McCook was willing to let old wounds heal as he had no desire to pick the scab off the sores of the past. He had no stomach for refighting old battles, for there was no one he wished to bring down. Rather, he was willing to let friends and enemies alike sink into the past and allow history to deal with controversy, trusting that truth and accuracy would emerge. There is no McCook ax-grinding, finger-pointing memoir on library bookshelves, although it is certain that he was urged to write about his wartime experiences.

McCook chose not to write, however, and in some respects the record of the Civil War is diminished, for each general, good, bad or indifferent, had important experiences to share. But the war and post-war record he left behind indicates that he was satisfied that his official reports and the writings of others would tell his story with fairness and balance.

McCook's love for the army and his devotion to the cause of the Union were evidently all he needed to relax and enjoy old age with his family. After all, he was on the winning side and had played an important role in the victory over the Confederacy — a victory that forever ended slavery as well as the belief that a state could lawfully secede from the Union. He had devoted his entire adult life to the U.S. Army and was proud to have served.

Although leaving the field of battle at Chickamauga was a decision that dogged him to the end of his days, McCook would never be faulted for lacking in personal courage. He never surrendered his army, and he never forgot the sacrifices made by his soldiers, for like every other general, he had made decisions that resulted in the death of many others. Through it all, he had more than proven his bravery in combat, and he expected no less from his men.

In 1861, Alexander M. McCook and his family took a stand. In a time of great crisis, the McCook family embraced an unwavering devotion to the preservation of the Union. At a time when men were faced with standing on the sidelines or going to war, the McCooks chose the danger. Like his father, his brothers and his cousins, Alexander M. McCook had done his part. In 1903, as an old man, General McCook could surrender to death knowing that the Union was safe from the evils of slavery and secession, and had set its course toward a future that would see a strong, united America take its place among the great nations of the world.

Notes

Chapter 1

1. Bruce Chadwick, *1858: Abraham Lincoln, Jefferson Davis, Robert E. Lee, Ulysses S. Grant, and The War They Failed to See* (Naperville, IL: Sourcebooks, 2008), p. 100.
2. James F. Simon, *Lincoln and Chief Justice Taney: Slavery, Secession, and the President's War Powers* (New York: Simon & Schuster, 2006), p. 84.
3. Frank van der Linden, *Lincoln: The Road to War* (Golden, CO: Fulcrum Publishing, 1998), p. 106.
4. Leonard L. Richards, *The California Gold Rush and the Coming of the Civil War* (New York: Knopf, 2007), pp. 95–96.
5. Daniel J. Crooks Jr., *Charleston Is Burning! Two Centuries of Fire and Flames* (Charleston, SC: The History Press, 2009), p. 90.
6. Richards, p. 224.
7. Chadwick, p. 26.
8. James M. McPherson, *Abraham Lincoln and the Second American Revolution* (New York: Oxford University Press, 1990), p. 51.
9. Richard Wheeler, *A Rising Thunder, From Lincoln's Election to the Battle of Bull Run: An Eyewitness History* (New York: HarperCollins, 1994), p. 5.
10. William B. Hesseltine, ed., *Three against Lincoln: Murat Halstead Reports of the Caucuses of 1860* (Baton Rouge: Louisiana State University Press, 1960), p. 45.
11. Ibid., p. 47.
12. Chadwick, p. 49.
13. Simon, p. 11.
14. Ibid., pp. 135–136.
15. Thomas L. Krannawitter, *Vindicating Lincoln: Defending the Politics of Our Greatest President* (Lanham, MD: Rowman & Littlefield, 2008), p. 124.

16. Hesseltine, ed., pp. 88–89.
17. Ibid., p. 110.
18. van der Linden, p. 54.
19. Hesseltine, ed., p. 119.
20. William C. Davis, *Breckinridge, Statesman, Soldier, Symbol* (Baton Rouge: Louisiana State University Press, 1974), p. 250.
21. Hesseltine, ed., p. 159.
22. Ibid., pp. 156–157.
23. Davis, *Breckinridge*, p. 247.
24. Anson McCook, *Memoirs*, Unpublished (Columbus: Ohio Historical Society), p. 92.
25. Simon, p. 171.
26. Carolyn L. Harrell, *When the Bells Tolled for Lincoln: Southern Reaction to the Assassination* (Macon, GA: Mercer University Press, 1997), p. 10.
27. van der Linden, pp. 84, 88.
28. Susan B. Martinez, *The Psychic Life of Abraham Lincoln* (Franklin Lakes, NJ: New Page Books, 2009), p. 27.
29. Jay Winik, *April 1865: The Month That Saved America* (New York: HarperCollins, 2001), p. 239.
30. Library of Congress, Manuscript Reading Room (Hereafter cited as LOC), McCook Family Papers, letter Anson G. McCook to George W. McCook, October 28, 1860.
31. William Sumner Dodge, *History of the Old Second Division, Army of the Cumberland* (Chicago: Church & Goodman, 1864), p. 16.
32. Krannawitter, p. 244.
33. Michael J. Kline, *The Baltimore Plot: The First Conspiracy to Assassinate Abraham Lincoln* (Yardley, PA: Westholme, 2008), p. 20.
34. Kline, p. 27.
35. van der Linden, p. 121.
36. LOC, McCook Family Papers, letter George W. McCook to Green, Undated.
37. Simon, p. 175.

38. LOC, McCook Family Papers, letter Daniel McCook Sr. to R. H. Phelps, April 15, 1861.

39. Ibid., letter Daniel McCook Sr. to R. H. Phelps, May 4, 1861.

40. Krannawitter, p. 149.

41. *Press and Dakotaian* (Yankton, DT), December 25, 1873.

42. Dodge, p. 28.

Chapter 2

1. John G. Nicolay, *The Outbreak of Rebellion*, 1881 (New York: Da Capo Press, 1995), p. 50.

2. Connecticut Landmarks, Hartford (Hereafter cited as CL), letter Dr. John McCook to Mary Sheldon, April 24, 1861.

3. Ibid., letter Edward M. McCook to Mary Sheldon, April 1861.

4. Henry Howe, *Historical Collections of Ohio, An Encyclopedia of the State* (State of Ohio, 1900), p. 371.

5. CL, letter Edward M. McCook to Mary Sheldon, April 1861.

6. Michael Burlingame, ed., *With Lincoln in the White House* (Carbondale: Southern Illinois University Press, 2000), p. 43.

7. Teresa J. Oden, "The Fighting McCooks," *Kenyon College Alumni Bulletin*, Summer/Fall 1997.

8. William Sumner Dodge, *History of the Old Second Division, Army of the Cumberland* (Chicago: Church & Goodman, 1864), p. 239.

9. *American National Biography*, vol. 14 (New York: Oxford University Press, 1999), p. 897.

10. Dodge, p. 240.

11. Library of Congress, Manuscript Reading Room (Hereafter cited as LOC), McCook Family Papers, letter Alexander M. McCook to Daniel McCook Sr., January 3, 1855.

12. Arlene Reynolds, ed., *The Civil War Memories of Elizabeth Bacon Custer* (Austin: University of Texas Press, 1994), p. 20.

13. Catherine C. Crary, ed., *Dear Belle: Letters from a Cadet & Officer to His Sweetheart, 1858–1865* (Middleton, CT: Wesleyan University Press, 1965), p. 88.

14. Albert Kern, ed., *History of the First Regiment Ohio Volunteer Infantry, in the Civil War, 1861–1865* (Dayton, OH: A. Kern, 1918), p. 5.

15. Anson McCook, *Memoirs*, Unpublished (Columbus: Ohio Historical Society), p. 100.

16. Ibid., p. 101.

17. David Detzer, *Dissonance: The Turbulent Days between Fort Sumter and Bull Run* (New York: Harcourt, 2006), p. 92.

18. McCook, pp. 102–104.

19. Richard Wheeler, *A Rising Thunder: From Lincoln's Election to the Battle of Bull Run: An Eyewitness History* (New York: HarperCollins, 1994), p. 255.

20. James M. McPherson, *Tried by War: Abraham Lincoln as Commander in Chief* (New York: Penguin, 2009), p. 23.

21. *Cincinnati Weekly Gazette*, May 8, 1861.

22. McPherson, p. 35.

23. Detzer, p. 204.

24. LOC, McCook Family Papers, letter Daniel McCook to Robert L. McCook, July 26, 1861.

25. R. M. Johnston, *Bull Run: Its Strategy and Tactics, 1913* (Carlisle, PA: John Kallmann, 1999), p. 25.

26. T. Harry Williams, *Lincoln and His Generals* (New York: Knopf, 1952), p. 17.

27. *New York Tribune*, June 9, 1861.

28. *Cincinnati Weekly Gazette*, August 12, 1863.

29. Geoffrey Perret, *Lincoln's War: The Untold Story of America's Greatest President as Commander in Chief* (New York: Random House, 2004), p. 51.

30. *New York Times*, July 23, 1861.

31. David Detzer, *Donnybrook: The Battle of Bull Run, 1861* (New York: Harcourt, 2004), p. 236.

32. William C. Davis, *Battle of Bull Run: A History of the First Major Campaign of the Civil War* (Garden City, NY: Doubleday, 1977), p. 40.

33. Nicolay, p. 173.

34. *The Daily Times* (Cincinnati), June 5, 1861.

35. *New York Tribune*, June 19, 1861.

36. Detzer, *Dissonance*, p. 218.

Chapter 3

1. *The Daily Times* (Cincinnati), April 14, 1861.

2. *Cincinnati Weekly Gazette*, May 8, 1861.

3. *New York Tribune*, June 20, 1861.

4. David Detzer, *Donnybrook: The Battle of Bull Run, 1861* (New York: Harcourt, 2004), pp. 20–21.

5. *The Daily Times* (Cincinnati), April 24, 1861.

6. Louis M. Starr, *Bohemian Brigade: Civil War Newsmen in Action, 1954* (Madison: University of Wisconsin Press, 1987), p. 9.

7. *New York Tribune*, May 6, 1861.

8. Ibid., May 8, 1861.

9. Charles P. Roland, *The Confederacy* (Chicago: University of Chicago Press, 1960), p. 65.

10. *Cincinnati Weekly Gazette*, May 8, 1861.

11. *New York Tribune*, May 4, 1861.

12. *The Daily Times* (Cincinnati), April 24, 1861.

13. William C. Davis, *Battle of Bull Run: A History of the First Major Campaign of the Civil War* (Garden City, NY: Doubleday, 1977), p. 112.

14. Mark W. Johnson, *That Body of Brave Men: The U.S. Regular Infantry and the Civil War in the West* (New York: Da Capo Press, 2003), p. 142.

15. *New York Tribune*, June 21, 1861.

16. Davis, *Battle of Bull Run*, pp. 70–72.

17. *New York Tribune*, June 19, 1861.

18. *Washington Star*, in the *New York Times*, June 20, 1861.

19. *New York Times*, June 20, 1861.

20. Ibid., June 21, 1861.

21. Roy P. Basler, ed., *The Collected Works of A. Lincoln*, vol. 4, 1860–1861 (New Brunswick: Rutgers University Press, 1955), p. 449.

22. *New York Tribune*, June 19, 1861.

23. *The War of the Rebellion*, Official Records (Hereafter cited as OR), Series II, Vol. I, p. 757.

24. Ibid., pp. 755–756.

25. Ibid., pp. 758–759.

26. Ibid., p. 759.

27. Connecticut Landmarks, Hartford, letter Anson G. McCook to Mary Sheldon, July 10, 1861.

28. Anson McCook, *Memoirs*, Unpublished (Columbus: Ohio Historical Society), p. 110.

29. *The Daily Times* (Cincinnati), July 13, 1861.

30. Frank L. Klement, *The Limits of Dissent: Clement L. Vallandigham & the Civil War* (Lexington: University of Kentucky Press, 1970), p. 75.

31. Davis, *Battle of Bull Run*, p. 75.

32. Johnston, *Bull Run: Its Strategy and Tactics*, 1913 (Carlisle, PA: John Kallmann, 1996), p. 59.

33. *New York Tribune*, July 20, 1861.

34. *New York Times*, July 20, 1861.

35. Davis, *Battle of Bull Run*, p. 115.

36. *New York Times*, July 20, 1861.

37. Ibid., July 21, 1861.

38. Ibid., July 21, 1861.

39. Webb Garrison, *Strange Battles of the Civil War* (Nashville: Cumberland House, 2001), p. 131.

40. Webb Garrison, *Amazing Women of the Civil War: Fascinating True Stories of Women Who Made a Difference* (Nashville: Rutledge Hill Press, 1999), p. 156.

41. William Gilmore Beymer, *Scouts and Spies of the Civil War, 1912* (Lincoln: University of Nebraska Press, 2003), p. 143.

42. William E. Doster, *Lincoln and Episodes of the Civil War* (New York: G. P. Putnam's Sons, 1915), pp. 82–83.

Chapter 4

1. Margaret Leech, *Reveille in Washington, 1860–1865* (New York: Harper & Brothers, 1941), p. 99.

2. Library of Congress, Manuscript Reading Room (Hereafter cited as LOC), McCook Family Papers, letter Daniel McCook Sr. to Robert L. McCook, July 26, 1861.

3. Anson McCook, *Memoirs*, Unpublished (Columbus: Ohio Historical Society), p. 115.

4. DeAnne Blanton and Lauren M. Cook, *They Fought Like Demons: Women Soldiers in the Civil War* (New York: Vintage, 2002), pp. 8–9.

5. *The War of the Rebellion*, Official Records (Hereafter cited as OR), Series I, Vol. II, pp. 357–360.

6. McCook, p. 115.

7. David Detzer, *Donnybrook: The Battle of Bull Run, 1861* (New York: Harcourt, 2004), p. 328.

8. *New York Tribune*, July 30, 1861.

9. OR, Series I, Vol. II, pp. 357–360.

10. McCook, p. 119.

11. Louis M. Starr, *Bohemian Brigade: Civil War Newsmen in Action, 1954* (Madison: University of Wisconsin Press, 1987), p. 46.

12. William C. Davis, *Battle of Bull Run: A History of the First Major Campaign of the Civil War* (Garden City, NY: Doubleday, 1977), p. 188.

13. *New York Tribune*, July 26, 1861.

14. McCook, p. 115.

15. *New York Tribune*, July 26, 1861.

16. *Cleveland Herald*, in the *New York Tribune*, July 29, 1861.

17. LOC, McCook Family Papers, letter Daniel McCook Sr. to Owen Steen, October 10, 1861.

18. Connecticut Landmarks, Hartford, letter Dr. John McCook to John J. McCook, July 23, 1861.

19. *New York Times*, July 22, 1861.

20. Davis, *Battle of Bull Run*, p. 234.

21. *New York Tribune*, August 1, 1861.

22. Horace White, *The Life of Lyman*

Trumbull (Boston: Houghton Mifflin, 1913), p. 166.

23. Henry Steele Commager, ed., *The Civil War Archive: A History of the Civil War in Documents* (New York: Black Dog & Leventhal, 2000), p. 110.

24. B. A. Botkin, ed., *A Civil War Treasury of Tales, Legends and Folklore* (New York: Random House, 1960), p. 29.

25. R. M. Johnston, *Bull Run: Its Strategy and Tactics,* 1913 (Carlisle, PA: John Kallmann, 1999), p. 234.

26. *The Philadelphia Inquirer,* in the *New York Tribune,* July 24, 1861.

27. *New York Tribune,* August 11, 1861.

28. OR, Series I, Vol. II, p. 360.

29. *New York Tribune,* August 19, 1861.

30. McCook, pp. 119–120.

31. Ibid., pp. 122–123.

32. *New York Tribune,* August 1, 1861.

33. LOC, McCook Family Papers, letter Daniel McCook Sr. to George W. McCook, August 2, 1861.

34. *New York Tribune,* July 26, 1861.

35. Henry Howe, *Historical Collections of Ohio, An Encyclopedia of the State* (State of Ohio, 1900), p. 369.

36. *New York Tribune,* July 28, 1861.

37. *Cleveland Herald,* in the *New York Tribune,* July 29, 1861.

38. Henry Howe, *A Brief Historical Sketch of the Fighting McCooks* (From the Proceedings of the Scotch-Irish Society of America), p. 18.

39. Michael Burlingame, ed., *With Lincoln in the White House* (Carbondale: Southern Illinois University Press, 2000), p. 53.

40. LOC, McCook Family Papers, letter Daniel McCook Sr. to Robert L. McCook, July 26, 1861.

41. John Gilmary Shea, ed., *The Fallen Brave: A Biographical Sketch of the American Officers Who Have Given Their Lives for the Preservation of the Union* (New York: Charles B. Richardson, 1861), pp. 139–140.

42. Leech, p. 104.

43. LOC, McCook Family Papers, Newspaper Article, Name and Date Unknown.

44. Detzer, pp. 474–475.

45. *Cincinnati Inquirer,* March 19, 1920.

46. Johnston, pp. 254–255.

47. Ibid., p. 260.

48. Drew Gilpin Faust, *This Republic of Suffering: Death and the American Civil War* (New York: Knopf, 2008), p. 71.

49. *Cincinnati Daily Commercial,* November 14, 1861.

50. James M. McPherson, *Tried by War:* *Abraham Lincoln as Commander in Chief* (New York: Penguin, 2009), p. 41.

51. Harry J. Maihafer, *War of Words: Abraham Lincoln & the Civil War Press* (Washington, DC: Brassey's, 2001), pp. 46–47.

52. *Cincinnati Daily Commercial,* November 14, 1861.

53. Johnston, p. 236.

54. JoAnna M. McDonald, *We Shall Meet Again: The First Battle of Manassas (Bull Run)* (New York: Oxford University Press, 2000), p. 292.

55. Frank L. Klement, *The Limits of Dissent: Clement L. Vallandigham & the Civil War* (Lexington: University of Kentucky Press, 1970), p. 80.

56. Stewart Sifakis, *Who Was Who in the Civil War* (New York: Facts on File, 1988), p. 409.

Chapter 5

1. Arthur L. Conger, *The Rise of U. S. Grant,* 1931 (New York: Da Capo Press, 1996), p. 53.

2. Lowell H. Harrison, *The Civil War in Kentucky* (Lexington: University Press of Kentucky, 1975), p. 5.

3. William Sumner Dodge, *History of the Old Second Division, Army of the Cumberland* (Chicago: Church & Goodman, 1864), p. 31.

4. C. A. Tripp, *The Intimate World of Abraham Lincoln* (New York: Thunder's Mouth Press, 2005), pp. 147–148.

5. Geoffrey Perret, *Lincoln's War: The Untold Story of America's Greatest President as Commander in Chief* (New York: Random House, 2004), p. 85.

6. Frank J. Welcher, *The Union Army 1861–1865: The Western Theater* (Bloomington: Indiana University Press, 1993), p. 18.

7. Roger Tate, "The Campaign and Battle of Mill Springs," *Blue & Gray Magazine,* February 1993, p. 13.

8. William W. Freehling, *The South vs. the South: How Anti-Confederate Southerners Shaped the Course of the Civil War* (New York: Oxford University Press, 2001), p. 53.

9. Dodge, p. 62.

10. Benson Bobrick, *Testament: A Soldier's Story of the Civil War* (New York: Simon & Schuster, 2003), p. 82.

11. *The War of the Rebellion,* Official Records (Hereafter cited as OR), Series I, Vol. IV, p. 280.

12. OR, Series I, Vol. LII, Part I, p. 192.

13. OR, Series I, Vol. IV, pp. 307–308.

14. Dodge, p. 69. Camp Nevin is spelled "Neven" in other sources.
15. R. W. Johnson, *A Soldier's Reminiscences in Peace and War* (Philadelphia: J. B. Lippincott, 1886), p. 280.
16. Library of Congress, Manuscript Reading Room (Hereafter cited as LOC), McCook Family Papers, unidentified and undated newspaper article.
17. Welcher, p. 158.
18. *Cincinnati Daily Commercial,* November 19, 1861.
19. Anson McCook, *Memoirs,* Unpublished (Columbus: Ohio Historical Society), p. 130.
20. Welcher, p. 158.
21. *Chicago Tribune,* November 21, 1861.
22. Dan Lee, *Kentuckian in Blue: A Biography of Major General Lovell Harrison Rousseau* (Jefferson, NC: McFarland, 2010), p. 49.
23. Stanley P. Hirshson, *The White Tecumseh: A Biography of General William T. Sherman* (New York: Wiley, 1997), p. 97.
24. LOC, McCook Family Papers, letter Alexander M. McCook to W. T. Sherman, November 4, 1861.
25. OR, Series I, Vol. IV, p. 337.
26. LOC, McCook Family Papers, *Daily Evening Telegraph,* June 12, 1903.
27. Whitelaw Reid, *Ohio in the War, Her Statesmen, Her Generals and Soldiers,* vol. 1 (New York: Moore Wilstatch & Baldwin, 1868), p. 808.
28. OR, Series I, Vol. IV, p. 347.
29. James M. McPherson, *Tried by War: Abraham Lincoln as Commander in Chief* (New York: Penguin, 2009), p. 59.
30. Johnson, pp. 270–271.
31. Lloyd Lewis, *Sherman: Fighting Prophet* (New York: Harcourt Brace, 1932), p. 195.
32. Charles Royster, *The Destructive War: William Tecumseh Sherman, Stonewall Jackson, and the Americans* (New York: Vintage, 1993), p. 375.
33. Charles Bracelen Flood, *Grant and Sherman: The Friendship That Won the Civil War* (New York: Harper Perennial, 2005), p. 68.
34. Earl Schenck Miers, *The General Who Marched to Hell: Sherman and the Southern Campaign* (New York: Knopf, 1951), p. 28.
35. Louis M. Starr, *Bohemian Brigade: Civil War Newsmen in Action,* 1954 (Madison: University of Wisconsin Press, 1987), p. 245.
36. Gerald J. Prokopowicz, *All for the Regiment: The Army of the Ohio, 1861–1862* (Chapel Hill: University of North Carolina Press, 2001), p. 123.
37. Charles Whalen and Barbara Whalen,

The Fighting McCooks: America's Famous Fighting Family (Bethesda, MD: Westmoreland Press, 2006), p. 80.
38. *The Daily Times* (Cincinnati), November 8, 1861.
39. Starr, p. 61.
40. Larry J. Daniel, *Shiloh: The Battle That Changed the Civil War* (New York: Simon & Schuster, 1997), p. 56.
41. OR, Series I, Vol. VII, p. 467.
42. Dodge, p. 83.
43. Thomas B. Van Horne, *History of the Army of the Cumberland,* vol. 1 (Cincinnati: Robert Clarke, 1875), pp. 53–54.
44. OR, Series I, Vol. VII, p. 483.
45. Ibid., p. 500.
46. Ibid., p. 501.
47. Ibid., p. 483.
48. Lee, pp. 55–56.
49. McPherson, p. 61.
50. *New York Times,* June 18, 1861.
51. Daniel, pp. 40–43.
52. OR, Series I, Vol. VII, p. 425.
53. *New York Times,* March 28, 1862.
54. *The Daily Times* (Cincinnati), March 10, 1862.
55. Johnson, p. 186.
56. Lee, p. 58.
57. Henry M. Cist, *The Army of the Cumberland* (New York: Charles Scribner's Sons, 1882), pp. 26–27.

Chapter 6

1. Charles Carleton Coffin, *My Days and Nights on the Battlefield* (Chicago: M. A. Donahue, 1887), p. 159.
2. Larry J. Daniel, *Shiloh: The Battle That Changed the Civil War* (New York: Simon & Schuster, 1997), p. 131.
3. James M. McPherson, *Tried by War: Abraham Lincoln as Commander in Chief* (New York: Penguin, 2009), p. 85.
4. *The War of the Rebellion,* Official Records (Hereafter cited as OR), Series I, Vol. X, Part II, p. 47.
5. Steven E. Woodworth, *Jefferson Davis and His Generals: The Failure of Confederate Command in the West* (Lawrence: University Press of Kansas, 1990), p. 45.
6. James M. McPherson, *Battle Cry of Freedom: The Civil War Era* (New York: Oxford University Press, 1988), p. 394.
7. Lowell H. Harrison, *The Civil War in Kentucky* (Lexington: University Press of Kentucky, 1975), p. 16.
8. Charles Bracelen Flood, *1864: Lincoln*

at the Gates of History (New York: Simon & Schuster, 2009), p. 104.

9. *Cincinnati Daily Times*, March 10, 1862.

10. Shelby Foote, *The Civil War: A Narrative, Fort Sumter to Perryville*, vol. 1 (New York: Vintage, 1986), p. 322.

11. Daniel, p. 104.

12. Joseph Mills Hanson, *The Conquest of the Missouri, Being the Story of the Life and Exploits of Captain Grant Marsh* (Chicago: A. C. McClurg, 1916), p. 36.

13. OR, Series I, Vol. X, Part I, pp. 105–106.

14. Kenneth P. Williams, *Lincoln Finds a General: A Military Study of the Civil War*, vol. 3 (New York: Macmillan, 1952), p. 337.

15. Woodworth, p. 98.

16. Stephen Berry, *House of Abraham: Lincoln & the Todds, a Family Divided by War* (Boston: Houghton Mifflin, 2007), p. 109.

17. McPherson, p. 407.

18. Charles Bracelen Flood, *Grant and Sherman: The Friendship That Won the Civil War* (New York: Harper Perennial, 2005), p. 100.

19. McPherson, p. 408.

20. Connecticut Landmarks, Hartford, letter Edward M. McCook to Mary Sheldon, April 13, 1862.

21. Foote, p. 324.

22. *The Daily Ohio Statesman*, April 11, 1861.

23. OR, Series I, Vol. X, Part I, p. 109.

24. *New York Times*, April 10, 1862.

25. Robin Neillands, *Grant: The Man Who Won the Civil War* (London: Weidenfeld and Nicholson, 2004), pp. 60–61.

26. Harry T. Williams, *P. G. T. Beauregard: Napoleon in Gray* (Baton Rouge: Louisiana State University Press, 1955), p. 143.

27. Wiley Sword, *Shiloh: Bloody April* (New York: William Morrow, 1974), p. 377.

Chapter 7

1. Wiley Sword, *Shiloh: Bloody April* (New York: William Morrow, 1974), p. 385.

2. Daniel McCook, "The Second Division at Shiloh," *Harper's New Monthly Magazine* 28 (December 1863 to May 1864): p. 829.

3. Ibid., p. 830.

4. *The War of the Rebellion*, Official Records (Hereafter cited as OR), Series I, Vol. X, Part I, p. 303.

5. Larry J. Daniel, *Shiloh: The Battle That Changed the Civil War* (New York: Simon & Schuster, 1997), p. 268.

6. B. H. Liddell Hart, *Sherman: Soldier, Realist, American*, 1929 (New York: Da Capo Press, 1993), 1929, p. 130.

7. Charles Whalen and Barbara Whalen, *The Fighting McCooks: America's Famous Fighting Family* (Bethesda, MD: Westmoreland Press, 2006), pp. 129–130.

8. Albert Kern, ed., *History of the First Regiment Ohio Volunteer Infantry in the Civil War, 1861–1865* (Dayton, OH: A. Kern, 1918), p. 9.

9. *Army Memoirs of Lucius W. Barber, Company "D" 15th Illinois Volunteer Infantry* (Chicago: J. M. W. Jones Stationery and Printing, 1894), p. 58.

10. Sword, p. 413.

11. OR, Series I, Vol. X, Part I, p. 354.

12. Ibid., pp. 304–307.

13. Ibid., p. 317.

14. William T. Sherman, *Memoirs of General W. T. Sherman* (New York: Library of America, 1990), p. 260.

15. Daniel, p. 303.

16. Connecticut Landmarks, Hartford, letter Edward M. McCook to Mary Sheldon dated April 13, 1862.

17. *Harper's New Monthly Magazine*, pp. 830–831.

18. Ibid., p. 832.

19. Whalen and Whalen, p. 132.

20. Charles Carleton Coffin, *My Days and Nights on the Battlefield* (Chicago: M. A. Donahue, 1887), pp. 227–228.

21. Drew Gilpin Faust, *This Republic of Suffering: Death and the American Civil War* (New York: Knopf, 2008), p. 225.

22. Lowell H. Harrison, *The Civil War in Kentucky* (Lexington: University Press of Kentucky, 1975), p. 34.

23. Anson, McCook, *Memoirs*, Unpublished (Columbus: Ohio Historical Society), p. 33.

24. Daniel, p. 293.

25. U. S. Grant, *Personal Memoirs of U. S. Grant*, vol. 1 (New York: Charles L. Webster, 1885), pp. 354–355.

26. Kern, ed., p. 9.

27. *The Civil War Books of Lists* (Compiled by the Editors of Combined Books, 1993), p. 89.

28. Charles Bracelen Flood, *1864: Lincoln at the Gates of History* (New York: Simon & Schuster, 2009), p. 120.

29. James M. McPherson, *Abraham Lincoln and the Second American Revolution* (New York: Oxford University Press, 1990), p. 78.

30. James M. McPherson, *Battle Cry of*

Freedom: The Civil War Era (New York: Oxford University Press, 1988), p. 414.

31. Flood, *1864*, p. 120.

32. Arthur L. Conger, *The Rise of U. S. Grant*, 1931 (New York: Da Capo Press, 1996), p. 262.

Chapter 8

1. Stephen E. Ambrose, *Halleck: Lincoln's Chief of Staff* (Baton Rouge: Louisiana State Press, 1990), p. 5.

2. Geoffrey Perret, *Lincoln's War: The Untold Story of America's Greatest President as Commander in Chief* (New York: Random House, 2004), p. 185.

3. James M. McPherson, *Tried by War: Abraham Lincoln as Commander in Chief* (New York: Penguin, 2009), p. 119.

4. Peter Cozzens, *General John Pope: A Life for the Nation* (Urbana: University of Illinois Press, 2000), p. 66.

5. Shelby Foote, *The Civil War: A Narrative Fort Sumter to Perryville*, vol. 1 (New York: Vintage, 1986), p. 374.

6. Connecticut Landmarks, Hartford, letter Dr. John McCook to Johnny McCook, Mary, and Eliza Sheldon, June 21, 1862.

7. William M. Thayer, *From Tannery to The White House: The Life of Ulysses S. Grant, His Boyhood, Youth, Manhood, Public and Private Life and Services* (Boston: James H. Earle, 1885), p. 199.

8. R. W. Johnson, *A Soldier's Reminiscences in Peace and War* (Philadelphia: J. B. Lippincott, 1886), p. 189.

9. Dan Lee, *Kentuckian in Blue: A Biography of Major General Lovell Harrison Rousseau* (Jefferson, NC: McFarland, 2010), pp. 63–64.

10. W. J. Tenney, *The Military and Naval History of the Rebellion in the United States*, 1866 (Mechanicsburg, PA: Stackpole, 2002), pp. 179–180.

11. Foote, p. 381.

12. Cozzens, *General John Pope*, p. 68.

13. Mark W. Johnson, *That Body of Brave Men: The U.S. Regular Infantry and the Civil War in the West* (Da Capo Press, 2003), pp. 177–178.

14. Tenney, p. 182.

15. *The War of the Rebellion*, Official Records (Hereafter cited as OR), Series I, Vol. X, Part I, p. 679.

16. Tenney, p. 182.

17. Charles Bracelen Flood, *Grant and Sherman: The Friendship That Won the Civil War* (New York: Harper Perennial, 2005), p. 124.

18. OR, Series I, Vol. X, Part I, p. 679.

19. *New York Times*, June 2, 1862.

20. R. W. Johnson, p. 192.

21. Constantin Grebner, *"We Were the Ninth": A History of the Ninth Regiment, Ohio Volunteer Infantry April 17, 1861 to June 7, 1864*, Translated and Edited by Frederic Trautmann (Kent, OH: Kent State University Press, 1987), p. 103.

22. Lee, p. 65.

23. Ambrose, p. 54.

24. Foote, pp. 385–386.

25. Thayer, p. 200.

26. Ambrose, p. 61.

27. Frank J. Welcher, *The Union Army 1861–1865: The Western Theater*, vol. 3 (Bloomington: Indiana University Press, 1993), p. 627.

28. Cozzens, *General John Pope*, p. 76.

29. Foote, pp. 542–543.

30. *New York Times*, July 25, 1862.

Chapter 9

1. *The War of the Rebellion*, Official Records (Hereafter cited as OR), Series I, Vol. XVI, Part II, p. 212.

2. *Boston Transcript*, June 13, 1903. Article by Col. Horace N. Fisher.

3. OR, Series I, Vol. XVI, Part II, p. 217.

4. Ibid., p. 317.

5. Anson McCook, *Memoirs*, Unpublished (Columbus: Ohio Historical Society), p. 155.

6. OR, Series I, Vol. XVI, Part II, p. 281.

7. Ibid., p. 227.

8. Ibid., p. 266.

9. OR, Series I, Vol. XVI, Part I, p. 5.

10. Ibid., p. 18.

11. OR, Series I, Vol. XVI, Part II, p. 489.

12. Roy Morris Jr., *Sheridan: The Life & Wars of General Phil Sheridan* (New York: Vintage, 1992), pp. 82–83.

13. Earl J. Hess, *Banners to the Breeze: The Kentucky Campaign, Corinth and Stones River* (Lincoln: University of Nebraska Press, 2000), p. 22.

14. OR, Series I, Vol. XVI, Part I, p. 88.

15. *Boston Transcript*, June 13, 1903.

16. William W. Freehling, *The South vs. the South: How Anti-Confederate Southerners Shaped the Course of the Civil War* (New York: Oxford University Press, 2001), pp. 59–60.

17. Charles Bracelen Flood, *Grant and Sherman: The Friendship That Won the Civil War* (New York: Harper Perennial, 2005), p. 18.

18. Hess, *Banners to the Breeze*, p. 73.

19. Henry M. Cist, *The Army of the Cumberland* (New York: Charles Scribner's Sons, 1882), p. 68.

20. Dan Lee, *Kentuckian in Blue: A Biography of Major General Lovell Harrison Rousseau* (Jefferson, NC: McFarland, 2010), p. 79.

21. Cist, p. 60.

22. McCook, p. 136.

23. Lee, p. 81.

24. Nathaniel Cheairs Hughes Jr. and Gordon D. Whitney, *Jefferson Davis in Blue: The Life of Sherman's Relentless Warrior* (Baton Rouge: Louisiana State University Press, 2002), pp. 101–117.

Chapter 10

1. *The War of the Rebellion*, Official Records (Hereafter cited as OR), Series I, Vol. XVI, Part II, p. 564.

2. Earl J. Hess, *Banners to the Breeze: The Kentucky Campaign, Corinth and Stones River* (Lincoln: University of Nebraska Press, 2000), p. 80.

3. P. H. Sheridan, *Personal Memoirs of P. H. Sheridan*, vol. 1 (New York: Charles Webster, 1888), p 194.

4. OR, Series I, Vol. XVI, Part I, p. 1083.

5. Sheridan, p. 196.

6. *Cincinnati Weekly Gazette*, July 1, 1863.

7. John Beatty, *The Citizen Soldier or Memoirs of a Volunteer* (Cincinnati: Wilstach Baldwin, 1879), p. 178.

8. OR, Series I, Vol. XVI, Part I, pp. 1040–1041.

9. Library of Congress, Manuscript Reading Room (Hereafter cited as LOC), McCook Family Papers, Article in the *Steubenville, Ohio Weekly Gazette*, date unknown.

10. Anson McCook, *Memoirs*, Unpublished (Columbus: Ohio Historical Society), p. 194.

11. OR, Series I, Vol. XVI, Part I, p. 1042.

12. Ibid., p. 240.

13. Ibid., pp. 240–241.

14. Constantin Grebner, "*We Were The Ninth*": *A History of the Ninth Regiment, Ohio Volunteer Infantry, April 17, 1861 to June 7, 1864*, Translated and Edited by Frederic Trautmann (Kent, OH: Kent State University Press, 1987), p. 115.

15. OR, Series I, Vol. XVI, Part I, pp. 1038–1044.

16. Ibid., p. 1087.

17. Thomas B. Buell, *The Warrior Generals in the Civil War* (New York: Three Rivers Press, 1997), p. 186

18. Sheridan, p. 200.

19. Paul M. Angle, ed., *Three Years in the Army of the Cumberland: The Letters and Diary of Major James A. Connolly* (Bloomington: Indiana University Press, 1987), p. 25.

20. Grebner, p. 116.

21. Whitelaw Reid, *Ohio in the War: Her Statesmen, Her Generals and Soldiers*, vol. 1 (New York: Moore, Wilstach & Baldwin, 1868), p. 807.

22. Gerald J. Prokopowicz, *All for the Regiment: The Army of the Ohio, 1861–1862* (Chapel Hill: University of North Carolina Press, 2001), pp. 181–184.

23. McCook, pp. 180–181.

24. Louis M. Starr, *Bohemian Brigade: Civil War Newsmen in Action*, 1954 (Madison: University of Wisconsin Press, 1987), p. 161.

25. Beatty, p. 183.

26. LOC, McCook Family Papers, letter George W. McCook to Martha L. McCook, November 2, 1862.

27. OR, Series I, Vol. XVI, Part I, pp. 100–107.

28. Ibid., p. 124.

29. Ibid., p. 134.

30. Ibid., p. 714.

31. McCook, p. 154.

32. Prokopowicz, p. 124.

33. OR, Series I, Vol. XVI, Part I, pp. 10–11.

34. *Cincinnati Weekly Gazette*, July 1, 1863.

35. Drew Gilpin Faust, *This Republic of Suffering: Death and the American Civil War* (New York: Knopf, 2008), p. 4.

36. Connecticut Landmarks, Hartford, letter Mary McCook to Mary Sheldon, November 2, 1862.

37. Hess, *Banners to the Breeze*, p. 108.

38. *Cincinnati Weekly Gazette*, July 1, 1863.

39. OR, Series I, Vol. XVI, Part I, p. 132.

Chapter 11

1. *The War of the Rebellion*, Official Records (Hereafter cited as OR), Series I, Vol. XVI, Part II, p. 653.

2. Peter Cozzens, *No Better Place to Die: The Battle of Stones River* (Urbana: University of Illinois Press, 1991), p. 16.

3. Benson Bobrick, *Testament: A Soldier's Story of the Civil War* (New York: Simon & Schuster, 2003), p. 120.

4. *New York Times*, December 26, 1862.

5. OR, Series I, Vol. XX, Part II, p. 121.

6. Ibid., p. 175.

7. Ibid., p. 183.

8. Connecticut Landmarks, Hartford, letter Mary McCook to Mary Sheldon, November 2, 1862.

9. Ibid., letter Catherine McCook to Mary Sheldon, December 25 1862.

10. William M. Lamers, *The Edge of Glory: A Biography of General William S. Rosecrans, USA* (Baton Rouge: Louisiana State University Press, 1999), pp. 200–201.

11. Louis M. Starr, *Bohemian Brigade: Civil War Newsmen in Action*, 1954 (Madison: University of Wisconsin Press, 1987), p. 127.

12. Harry J. Maihafer, *War of Words: Abraham Lincoln and the Civil War Press* (Washington, DC: Brassey's, 2001), pp. 74–75.

13. Ibid., p. 69.

14. Catherine Clinton and Nina Silber, ed., *Divided Houses: Gender and the Civil War* (New York: Oxford University Press, 1992), p. 80.

15. Thomas L. Krannawitter, *Vindicating Lincoln: Defending the Politics of Our Greatest President* (Lanham, MD: Rowman & Littlefield, 2008), p. 274.

16. OR, Series I, Vol. XX, Part II, pp. 222–223.

17. Ezra J. Warner, *Generals in Gray, Lives of the Confederate Commanders* (Louisiana State University Press, 1959), p. 124.

18. Library of Congress, Manuscript Reading Room, McCook Family Papers, letter Alexander M. McCook to an Unidentified Doctor, November 29, 1858.

19. OR, Series I, Vol. XX, Part II, p. 242.

20. OR, Series I, Vol. XX, Part I, p. 191.

21. Ibid., p. 252.

22. Ibid., pp. 254–255.

23. OR, Series I, Vol. XX, Part II, p. 256.

24. OR, Series I, Vol. XX, Part I, p. 254.

25. Nathaniel Cheairs Hughes Jr. and Gordon D. Whitney, *Jefferson Davis in Blue: The Life of Sherman's Relentless Warrior* (Baton Rouge: Louisiana State University Press, 2002), p. 134.

26. William Sumner Dodge, *History of the Old Second Division, Army of the Cumberland* (Chicago: Church & Goodman, 1864), pp. 256–257.

27. OR, Series I, Vol. XX, Part I, p. 255.

28. Ibid., p. 192.

29. Dodge, pp. 258–259.

30. Stanley F. Horn, *The Army of Tennessee* (Norman: University of Oklahoma Press, 1952), p. 199.

31. Ibid., p. 198.

32. Cozzens, *No Better Place to Die*, pp. 79–80.

33. Roy Morris Jr., *Sheridan: The Life &*

Wars of General Phil Sheridan (New York: Vintage, 1993), p. 105.

Chapter 12

1. *The War of the Rebellion*, Official Records (Hereafter cited as OR), Series I, Vol. XX, Part I, p. 255.

2. Richard Wheeler, *Voices of the Civil War* (New York: Thomas Y. Crowell, 1976), p. 229.

3. Henry M. Cist, *The Army of the Cumberland* (New York: Charles Scribner's Sons, 1882), pp. 102–104.

4. DeAnne Blanton and Lauren M. Cook, *They Fought Like Demons: Women Soldiers in the Civil War* (New York: Vintage, 2002), p. 11.

5. Library of Congress, Manuscript Reading Room (Hereafter cited as LOC), McCook Family Papers, *New York Journal*, August 15, 1895.

6. OR, Series I, Vol. XX, Part I, p. 683.

7. Peter Cozzens, *No Better Place to Die: The Battle of Stones River* (Urbana: University of Illinois Press, 1991), p. 116.

8. Roy Morris Jr., *Sheridan: The Life & Wars of General Phil Sheridan* (New York: Vintage, 1993), p. 109.

9. *New York Times*, January 4, 1863.

10. Ibid., January 4, 1863.

11. OR, Series I, Vol. XX, Part I, pp. 777–778.

12. John M. Palmer, *The Personal Recollections of John M. Palmer: The Story of an Earnest Life* (Cincinnati: Robert Clarke, 1901), p. 149.

13. Charles Royster, *The Destructive War: William Tecumseh Sherman, Stonewall Jackson, and the Americans* (New York: Vintage, 1993), p. 244.

14. Cozzens, *No Better Place to Die*, p. 173.

15. Ibid., p. 174.

16. Geoffrey Perret, *Lincoln's War: The Untold Story of America's Greatest President as Commander in Chief* (New York: Random House, 2004), p. 217.

17. Doris Kearns Goodwin, *Team of Rivals: The Political Genius of Abraham Lincoln* (New York: Simon & Schuster, 2006), p. 499.

18. Earl J. Hess, *Banners to the Breeze: The Kentucky Campaign, Corinth and Stones River* (Lincoln: University of Nebraska Press, 2000), p. 180.

19. Thomas L. Krannawitter, *Vindicating Lincoln: Defending the Politics of our Greatest President* (Lanham, MD: Rowman & Littlefield, 2008), p. 282.

20. LOC, McCook Family Papers, Scrap-

books, *Steubenville Weekly Gazette*, date unknown.

21. William C. Davis, *Breckinridge: Statesman, Soldier, Symbol* (Baton Rouge: Louisiana
State University Press, 1974), p. 259.

22. William C. Davis, *An Honorable Defeat:
The Last Days of the Confederate Government*
(New York: Harcourt, 2001), p. 155.

23. *New York Times*, July 24, 1861.

24. *New York Tribune*, August 7, 1861.

25. *New York Tribune*, August 1, 1861.

26. Davis, *Breckinridge*, p. 289.

27. Cozzens, p. 194.

28. John Fitch, *Annals of the Army of the
Cumberland*, 1864 (Mechanicsburg, PA: Stackpole, 2003), p. 701.

29. Earl J. Hess, *The Union Soldier in
Battle: Enduring the Ordeal of Combat*
(Lawrence: University Press of Kansas, 1997),
p. 104.

30. James M. McPherson, *Tried by War:
Abraham Lincoln as Commander in Chief* (New
York: Penguin, 2009), p. 156.

31. *New York Times*, January 4, 1863.

32. OR, Series I, Vol. XX, Part I, p. 387.

33. Ibid., p. 445.

34. Ibid., p. 185.

35. Ibid., p. 186.

36. Ibid., p. 186.

37. OR, Series I, Vol. XX, Part II, p. 306.

38. Cozzens, p. 206.

39. John Beatty, *Memoirs of a Volunteer,
1861–1863* (New York: Norton, 1946), p. 160.

40. Cist, p. 129.

41. OR, Series I, Vol. XX, Part I, pp. 253–
258.

42. Ibid., p. 198.   23

43. OR, Series I, Vol. XX, Part II, p. 59.

44. *New York Times*, January 8, 1863.

45. James H. Woodard, *Gen. A. McD. Mc-
Cook at Stone River*, A Paper Prepared and
Read Before the California Commandery of
the Military Order of the Loyal Legion of the
United States, at Los Angeles, February 22,
1892, p. 152.

46. Ibid., pp. 154–155.

47. Ibid., pp. 156–157.

48. Cist, p. 129.

49. *New York Times*, January 4, 1873.

50. Fitch, p. 77.

51. R. W. Johnson, *A Soldiers Reminiscences
in Peace and War* (Philadelphia: J. B. Lippincott, 1886), pp. 210–213.

52. Frank J. Welcher, *The Union Army 1861–
1865: The Western Theater*, vol. 2 (Bloomington: Indiana University Press, 1993), p. 811.

53. R. W. Johnson, pp. 209–210.

54. Ibid., pp. 215–216.

55. Connecticut Landmarks, Hartford, letter Anson McCook to Mary Sheldon, January
10, 1863, and letter Anson McCook to John J.
McCook, February 1, 1863.

56. *The Civil War Reader: 1862*, by the editors of the *Civil War Times* and *American Civil
War* (New York: Ibooks, 2002), p. 284.

57. OR, Series I, Vol. XX, Part II, p. 311.

58. Charles Whalen and Barbara Whalen,
*The Fighting McCooks: America's Famous Fight-
ing Family* (Bethesda, MD: Westmoreland
Press, 2006), p. 77.

59. *Dayton Daily Empire*, January 29, 1863,
and February 7, 1863.

60. Whalen and Whalen, p. 188–189; *Cincinnati Daily Times*, June 30, 1863.

61. *Cincinnati Weekly Gazette*, May 20,
1863.

Chapter 13

1. Geoffrey Perret, *Lincoln's War: The Un-
told Story of America's Greatest President as
Commander in Chief* (New York: Random
House, 2004), pp. 317–318.

2. T. Harry Williams, *Lincoln and His
Generals* (New York: Knopf, 1952), p. 248.

3. Jennifer L. Weber, *Copperheads: The
Rise and Fall of Lincoln's Opponents in the North*
(New York: Oxford University Press, 2006),
p. 95.

4. William M. Lamers, *The Edge of Glory:
A Biography of General William S. Rosecrans,
U.S.A.* (Baton Rouge: Louisiana State Univer-
sity Press, 1999), p. 267.

5. *Richmond Examiner*, in *The Dakotian*
(Yankton, DT), June 23, 1863.

6. Tonia J. Smith, "Gentlemen, You Have
Played This D----D Well," *North & South* 8,
no. 5 (September 2005): pp. 72–83.

7. *New York Times*, June 10, 1863.

8. John Fitch, *Annals of the Army of the
Cumberland*, 1864 (Mechanicsburg, PA: Stackpole, 2003), p. 78.

9. Library of Congress, Manuscript Reading Room, McCook Family Papers, letter W.
T. Sherman to Annie M. Colt, August 23,
1884.

10. Nathaniel Cheairs Hughes Jr. and Gordon E. Whitney, *Jefferson Davis in Blue: The
Life of Sherman's Relentless Warrior* (Baton
Rouge: Louisiana State University Press, 2002),
p. 157.

11. John Beatty, *The Citizen Soldier, or
Memoirs of a Volunteer* (Cincinnati: Wilstach
Baldwin, 1879), pp. 235–236.

12. Gerald J. Prokopowicz, *All for the Reg-*

iment: The Army of the Ohio, 1861–1862 (Chapel Hill: University of North Carolina Press, 2001), p. 42.

13. Peter Cozzens, *This Terrible Sound: The Battle of Chickamauga* (Urbana: University of Illinois Press, 1992), p. 10.

14. Theodore C. Blegen, ed., *The Civil War Letters of Colonel Hans Christian Heg* (Northfield, MN: Norwegian-American Historical Association, 1936), p. 234.

15. Prokopowicz, p. 42.

16. *The War of the Rebellion*, Official Records (Hereafter cited as OR), Series I, Vol. XXIII, Part I, p. 411.

17. Allan Peskin, *Garfield* (Kent, OH: Kent State University Press, 1978), p. 176.

18. Dan Lee, *Kentuckian in Blue: A Biography of Major General Lovell Harrison Rousseau* (Jefferson, NC: McFarland, 2010), p. 111.

19. OR, Series I, Vol. XXIII, Part I, p. 468.

20. OR, Series I, Vol. XXX, Part III, p. 179.

21. *The Dakotian* (Yankton, DT), May 12, 1863.

22. Steven E. Woodworth, *Jefferson Davis and His Generals: The Failure of Confederate Command in the West* (Lawrence: University Press of Kansas, 1990), p. 196.

23. A. D. Kirwan, ed., *Johnny Green of the Orphan Brigade: The Journal of a Confederate Soldier* (Lexington: University of Kentucky Press, 1956), p. 90.

24. Samuel W. Fordyce IV, ed., *An American General: The Memoirs of David Sloan Stanley* (Santa Barbara, CA: Narrative Press, 2003), p. 168.

25. Margaret Leech and Harry J. Brown, *The Garfield Orbit: The Life of President James A. Garfield* (New York: Harper & Row, 1978), p. 141.

26. Hughes and Whitney, p. 170.

27. OR, Series I, Vol. XXX, Part I, pp. 35–36.

28. Cozzens, p. 60.

29. OR, Series I, Vol. XXX, Part I, p. 54.

30. Cozzens, p. 79.

31. Harry J. Maihafer, *The General and the Journalists: Ulysses S. Grant, Horace Greeley and Charles Dana* (Washington, DC: Brassey's, 2001), p. 69.

32. Peskin, p. 201.

33. Charles Carleton Coffin, *My Days and Nights on the Battlefield* (Chicago: M. A. Donahue, 1887), p. 25.

34. Cozzens, pp. 93–94.

35. Bruce Catton, *The Centennial History of the Civil War: Never Call Retreat*, vol. 3 (Garden City: Doubleday, 1965), p. 243.

36. OR, Series I, Vol. XXX, Part III, p. 604.

37. Ibid., p. 629.

38. Cozzens, p. 88.

39. OR, Series I, Vol. XXX, Part III, p. 676.

40. Francis F. McKinney, *Education in Violence: The Life of George H. Thomas and the Army of the Cumberland* (Detroit: Wayne State University Press, 1961), p. 229.

41. OR, Series I, Vol. XXX, Part III, p. 189.

42. Ibid., p. 727.

43. OR, Series I, Vol. XXX Part I, p. 115.

Chapter 14

1. *The War of the Rebellion*, Official Records (Hereafter cited as OR), Series I, Vol. XXX, Part II, p. 66.

2. Ibid., p. 76.

3. Ibid., pp. 66–67.

4. Ibid., p. 67

5. OR, Series I, Vol. XXX, Part I, p. 488

6. Earl J. Hess, *The Union Soldier in Battle: Enduring the Ordeal of Combat* (Lawrence: University Press of Kansas, 1997), p. 73.

7. Charles A. Dana, *Recollections of the Civil War* (Lincoln: University of Nebraska Press, 1996), p. 112.

8. OR, Series I, Vol. XXX, Part III, 69.

9. Peter Cozzens, *This Terrible Sound: The Battle of Chickamauga* (Urbana: University of Illinois Press, 1992), p. 295.

10. H. J. Eckenrode and Bryan Conrad, *James Longstreet: Lee's War Horse* (Chapel Hill: University of North Carolina Press, 1936), p. 225.

11. Cozzens, p. 314.

12. Albert Kern, ed., *History of the First Regiment Ohio Volunteer Infantry in the Civil War, 1861–1865* (Dayton, OH: A. Kern, 1918), p. 20.

13. OR, Series I, Vol. XXX, Part III, pp. 74–77.

14. Cozzens, p. 363; *Cincinnati Weekly Gazette*, November 18, 1863.

15. Samuel W. Fordyce IV, ed., *An American General: The Memoirs of David Sloan Stanley* (Santa Barbara, CA: Narrative Press, 2003), p. 170.

16. OR, Series I, Vol. XXX, Part I, p. 635.

17. Ibid., p. 59.

18. Ibid., p. 193.

19. John Fitch, *Annals of the Army of the Cumberland*, 1864 (Mechanicsburg, PA: Stackpole, 2003), pp. 473–474.

20. William M. Lamers, *The Edge of Glory: A Biography of General William S. Rosecrans, USA* (Baton Rouge: Louisiana State University Press, 1999), p. 346.

21. OR, Series I, Vol. XXX, Part I, p. 490.
22. Cozzens, *This Terrible Sound*, p. 391.
23. Ibid., p. 441.
24. OR, Series I, Vol. LII, p. 453.
25. Cozzens, *This Terrible Sound*, p. 534.
26. *Cincinnati Weekly Gazette*, October 28, 1863.
27. Ibid., October 28, 1863.
28. Ibid., September 30, 1863.
29. Ibid, October 28, 1863.
30. Nathaniel Cheairs Hughes Jr. and Gordon D. Whitney, *Jefferson Davis in Blue: The Life of Sherman's Relentless Warrior* (Baton Rouge: Louisiana State University Press, 2002), p. 171.
31. *New York Times*, October 11, 1863.
32. OR, Series I, Vol. XXX, Part II, p. 144.
33. Fordyce, ed., p. 171.
34. OR, Series I, Vol. XXX, Part II, p. 194.
35. William Roscoe Thayer, *The Life and Letters of John Hay*, vol. 1 (Boston: Houghton Mifflin, 1915), pp. 200–201.
36. *Diary of Gideon Welles*, vol. 2 (New York: Norton, 1960), pp. 446–447.
37. Michael Burlingame, ed., *Lincoln Observed: Civil War Dispatches of Noah Brooks* (Baltimore, MD: Johns Hopkins University Press, 1998), p. 46.
38. The Library of Congress, Manuscript Reading Room (Hereafter cited as LOC), McCook Family Papers, letter Edwin S. Stanton to Margaret McCook, dated 1847.
39. Lamers, p. 265.
40. George Fort Milton, *The Age of Hate: Andrew Johnson and the Radicals* (New York: Coward-McCann, 1930), p. 356.
41. *Cincinnati Weekly Gazette*, November 11, 1863.
42. T. Harry Williams, *Lincoln and His Generals* (New York: Knopf, 1952), p. 284.
43. Harold M. Hyman and Benjamin P. Thomas, *Stanton: The Life and Times of Lincoln's Secretary of War* (New York: Knopf, 1962), p. 290; OR, Series I, Vol. XXX, Part I, p. 204.
44. LOC, McCook Family Papers, letter Anson G. McCook to George W. McCook, October 8, 1863.
45. OR, Series I, Vol. XXXI, Part III, p. 202.
46. Ibid., p. 911.
47. Ibid., p. 911.
48. *New York Times*, October 16, 1863.
49. OR, Series I, Vol. XXX, Part I, p. 220.
50. *Cincinnati Weekly Gazette*, January 6, 1864.
51. Emmet Crozier, *Yankee Reporters, 1861–1865* (New York: Oxford University Press, 1956), pp. 368–369.
52. William Sumner Dodge, *History of the Old Second Division: Army of the Cumberland* (Chicago: Church & Goodman, 1864), pp. 264–265.
53. John Fiske, *The Mississippi Valley in the Civil War* (Boston: Houghton Mifflin, 1900), pp. 285–286.
54. Frederick D. Williams, ed., *The Wild Life of the Army: Civil War Letters of James A. Garfield* (East Lansing: Michigan State University Press, 1964), p. 254.
55. OR, Series I, Vol. XXX, Part IV, p. 126.

Chapter 15

1. *The War of the Rebellion*, Official Records (Hereafter cited as OR), Series I, Vol. XXX, Part I, p. 930.
2. Charles C. Osborne, *Jubal: The Life and Times of General Jubal A. Early, C.S.A., Defender of the Lost Cause* (Chapel Hill, NC: Algonquin Books, 1992), p. 249.
3. Michael J. Kline, *The Baltimore Plot: The First Conspiracy to Assassinate Abraham Lincoln* (Yardley, PA: Westholme, 2008), p. 18.
4. Lloyd Lewis, *The Assassination of Lincoln: History & Myth*, 1929 (New York: MJF Books, 1994), p. 109.
5. Ezra J. Warner, *Generals in Blue: Lives of the Union Commanders* (Baton Rouge: Louisiana State University Press, 1996), p. 244.
6. Ibid., p. 63.
7. Ibid., pp. 532–533.
8. OR, Series I, Vol. XXX, Part I, p. 932.
9. Ibid., p. 933.
10. Ibid., p. 934.
11. Ibid., p. 936.
12. Ibid., p. 938.
13. Ibid., p. 939.
14. Ibid., p. 941.
15. Ibid., p. 941.
16. Ibid., p. 941.
17. Ibid., p. 944.
18. Ibid., p. 948.
19. Ibid., p. 949.
20. Ibid., p. 950.
21. Warner, pp. 115–116.
22. OR, Series I, Vol. LII, Part I, p. 299.
23. OR, Series I, Vol. XXX, Part I, p. 952.
24. Ibid., pp. 961–962.
25. William Sumner Dodge, *History of the Old Second Division, Army of the Cumberland* (Chicago: Church & Goodman, 1864), p. 269.
26. Connecticut Landmarks, letter R. Shel-

don McCook to Mary Sheldon, March 4, 1864.

27. John Fitch, *Annals of the Army of the Cumberland*, 1864 (Mechanicsburg, PA: Stackpole, 2003), p. 474.

28. OR, Series I, Vol. XXX, Part I, pp. 618–619.

29. Warner, *Generals in Blue*, pp. 100–101.

30. Ibid., p. 342.

31. Whitelaw Reid, *Ohio and the War: Her Statesmen, Her Generals and Soldiers*, vol. 1 (New York: Moore Wilstach & Baldwin, 1868), p. 806.

32. Paul Andrew Hutton, *Phil Sheridan and His Army* (Lincoln: University of Nebraska Press, 1985), p. 309.

33. OR, Series II, Vol. II, pp. 848–849.

34. OR, Series II, Vol. V, p. 1.

Chapter 16

1. *Dubuque Daily Times*, March 17, 1864.

2. Charles Royster, *The Destructive War: William Tecumseh Sherman, Stonewall Jackson and the Americans* (New York: Vintage, New York, 1993), p. 34.

3. Marc Leepson, *Desperate Engagement: How a Little-Known Civil War Battle Saved Washington, D. C., and Changed the Course of American History* (New York: Thomas Dunne Books, 2007), p. 25.

4. Frank E. Vandiver, *Jubal's Raid: General Early's Famous Attack on Washington in 1864* (Lincoln: University of Nebraska Press, 1992), p. 20.

5. W. J. Tenney, *The Military and Naval History of the Rebellion in the United States*, 1866 (Mechanicsburg, PA: Stackpole, 2003), p. 583.

6. Vandiver, p. 58.

7. Leepson, p. 55.

8. *New York Tribune*, February 12, 1864.

9. *New York Times*, July 4, 1864.

10. Leepson, p. 77.

11. *New York Times*, July 6, 1864.

12. *Cincinnati Daily Times*, July 7, 1864.

13. Vandiver, p. 94.

14. *New York Times*, July 7, 1864.

15. Ibid., July 7, 1864.

16. Ibid., July 7, 1864.

17. Ibid., July 8, 1864.

18. *Baltimore American*, in *The Evening Star*, July 6, 1864.

19. *New York Times*, July 7, 1864.

20. Ibid., July 8, 1864.

21. Ibid., July 9, 1864.

22. Charles C. Osborne, *Jubal: The Life and*

Times of General Jubal A. Early, C.S.A., Defender of the Lost Cause (Chapel Hill, NC: Algonquin Books, 1992), p. 269.

23. Vandiver, p. 100.

24. Ibid., pp. 110–118.

25. *St. Paul Daily Globe*, January 21, 1886.

26. *New York Times*, July 10, 1864.

27. Leepson, p. 142.

28. *New York Times*, July 11, 1864.

29. Leepson, p. 131.

30. *Richmond Whig* of July 14, 1864, in the *New York Times*, July 18, 1864.

31. David Detzer, *Dissonance: The Turbulent Days between Fort Sumter and Bull Run* (New York: Harcourt, 2006), p. 5.

32. Thomas Goodrich, *The Darkest Dawn: Lincoln, Booth, and the Great American Tragedy* (Bloomington: Indiana University Press, 2005), p. 23.

33. Vandiver, pp. 122–123.

34. Matthew Pinsker, *Lincoln's Sanctuary: Abraham Lincoln and the Soldiers' Home* (New York: Oxford University Press, 2003), p. 133.

35. *The Evening Star* (Washington City), July 8, 1864.

36. *New York Times*, July 11, 1864.

37. Ezra J. Warner, *Generals in Blue: Lives of the Union Commanders* (Baton Rouge: Louisiana State University Press, 1996), p. 12.

38. *Cincinnati Daily Times*, July 8, 1864.

39. *New York Tribune*, March 14, 1864.

40. Margaret Leech, *Reveille in Washington, 1860–1865* (New York: Harper Brothers, 1941), p. 336.

41. Leepson, pp. 166–167.

42. *The War of the Rebellion*, Official Record (Hereafter cited as OR), Series I, Vol. XXXII, Part III, p. 305.

43. OR, Series I, Vol. XXXIV, Part IV, p. 304.

44. *New York Times*, July 12, 1864.

45. Roy Morris Jr., *The Better Angel: Walt Whitman in the Civil War* (New York: Oxford University Press, 2000), p. 113.

46. Geoffrey Perret, *Lincoln's War: The Untold Story of America's Greatest President as Commander in Chief* (New York: Random House, 2004), p. 327.

47. *St. Paul Daily Globe*, January 21, 1886.

48. Vandiver, p. 138.

Chapter 17

1. *Diary of Gideon Welles*, vol. 1 (New York: Norton , 1960), pp. 70–71.

2. Margaret Leech, *Reveille in Washington,*

1860–1865 (New York: Harper Brothers, 1941), p. 341.

3. Matthew Pinsker, *Lincoln's Sanctuary: Abraham Lincoln and the Soldier's Home* (New York: Oxford University Press, 2003), p. 135.

4. Frank E. Vandiver, *Jubal's Raid: General Early's Famous Attack on Washington in 1864* (Lincoln: University of Nebraska Press, 1992), pp. 146–148.

5. March Leepson, *Desperate Engagement: How a Little Known Civil War Battle Saved Washington, D. C., and Changed the Course of American History* (New York: Thomas Dunne Books, 2007), p. 3

6. Doris Kearns Goodwin, *A Team of Rivals: The Political Genius of Abraham Lincoln* (New York: Simon & Schuster, 2006), p. 642.

7. *New York Times*, July 17, 1864.

8. Charles C. Osborne, *Jubal: The Life and Times of General Jubal A. Early, C.S.A., Defender of the Lost Cause* (Chapel Hill, NC: Algonquin Books, 1992), p. 285.

9. Goodwin, pp. 641–642; *Dubuque Daily Times*, July 15, 1864.

10. *Richmond Examiner*, in the *New York Times*, July 22, 1864.

11. Charles Bracelen Flood, *1864: Lincoln at the Gates of History* (New York: Simon & Schuster, 2009), p. 296.

12. Leech, p. 337.

13. Glenn H. Worthington, *Fighting for Time: The Battle That Saved Washington*, 1932 (Shippensburg, PA: White Mane, 1988), p. 188.

14. Pinsker, p. 134.

15. Flood, *1864*, p. 193.

16. Worthington, pp. 183–184.

17. Osborne, p. 378.

18. Leech, p. 340.

19. Vandiver, p. 158.

20. Worthington, p. 189.

21. Donald B. Koonce, ed., *Doctor to the Front: The Recollections of Confederate Surgeon Thomas Fanning Wood* (Knoxville: University of Tennessee Press, 2000), p. 164.

22. Vandiver, pp. 167–168. There are other versions of this story, including one by General Wright in which he states that he was the one to order the president to stand down. See Pinsker, pp. 140–142.

23. Flood, *1864*, pp. 198–199.

24. Vandiver, pp. 159–161.

25. William E. Doster, *Lincoln and Episodes of the Civil War* (New York: G. P. Putnam's Sons, 1915), p. 253.

26. Vandiver, p. 155.

27. *The Evening Star*, July 13, 1864.

28. *New York Times*, July 14, 1864.

29. Leech, p. 343.

30. *The Evening Star*, July 13, 1864.

31. Osborne, p. 283.

32. Vandiver, pp. 170–172.

33. Jubal Anderson Early, *Jubal Early's Memoirs: Autobiographical Sketch and Narrative of the War between the States* (Baltimore, MD: Nautical & Aviation, 1991), p. 393.

34. *Dubuque Daily Times*, July 15, 1864.

35. *New York Times*, July 15, 1864.

36. *Dubuque Daily Times*, July 15, 1864.

37. Leepson, p. 207.

38. *New York Times*, July 22, 1864.

39. Leepson, pp. 211–212.

40. *New York Times*, July 22, 1864.

41. *Diary of Gideon Welles*, vol. 1, p. 73.

42. *Cincinnati Daily Times*, July 20, 1864.

43. *New York Times*, July 17, 1864.

44. Vandiver, pp. 176–177.

Chapter 18

1. *The War of the Rebellion*, Official Record (Hereafter cited as OR), Series I, Vol. XLVI, Part II, pp. 307–308.

2. Ibid., p. 356.

3. OR, Series I, Vol. XLVIII, Part II, p. 44.

4. Ibid., p. 157.

5. Ibid., p. 386.

6. Ibid., p. 708.

7. Ibid., p. 754.

8. J. R. Perkins, *Trails, Rails and War: The Life of General G. M. Dodge* (Indianapolis: Bobbs-Merrill, 1929), p. 174.

9. Peter Cozzens, *General John Pope: A Life for the Nation* (Urbana: University of Illinois Press, 2000), p. 255.

10. OR, Series I, Vol. XLVIII, Part II, p. 796.

11. Ibid., p. 820.

12. Ibid., p. 1162.

13. OR, Series I, Vol. XLVIII, Part I, p. 338.

14. Perkins, pp. 182–183.

15. OR, Series I, Vol. XLVIII, Part I, p. 345.

16. Charles Royster, *The Destructive War, William Tecumseh Sherman, Stonewall Jackson and the Americans* (New York: Vintage, 1993), p. 394.

17. *The Nevada Observer*, Nevada's online state news journal, June 5, 2008 (From C. C. Goodwin, *As I Remember Them*, 1913).

18. Library of Congress, Manuscript Reading Room (Hereafter cited as LOC), McCook Family Papers, letter W. T. Sherman to Annie Colt, August 23, 1884.

19. E. R. Hagemann, ed., *Fighting Rebels and Redskins: Experiences in Army Life of Colonel George B. Sanford, 1861–1892* (Norman:

University of Oklahoma Press, 1969), pp. 71–74.

20. LOC, McCook Family Papers, letter Alexander M. McCook to Annie McCook, November 22, 1887.

21. Ibid., letter Alexander M. McCook to Annie McCook, November 25, 1887.

22. Ibid., paper entitled "Alexander McDowell McCook," undated.

23. Ibid., letter W. T. Sherman to Alexander M. McCook, July 19, 1889.

24. Hagemann, ed., p. 84.

25. LOC, McCook Family Papers, letter Alexander M. McCook to Annie McCook, September 29, 1890.

26. Ibid., letter W. T. Sherman to Alexander M. McCook, January 11, 1891.

27. McCook, Anson, *Memoirs*, Unpublished (Columbus: Ohio Historical Society), p. 170.

Chapter 19

1. Anson McCook, *Memoir*, Unpublished (Columbus: Ohio Historical Society), p. 93.

2. Library of Congress, Manuscript Reading Room (Hereafter cited as LOC), McCook Family Papers, *Steubenville (Ohio) Weekly Gazette*, date unknown.

3. *Ohio Patriot*, January 3, 1878.

4. LOC, McCook Family Papers, *Steubenville (Ohio) Weekly Gazette*, date unknown.

5. Ibid., obituary from an unidentified newspaper.

6. Ibid., *Daily Evening Telegraph*, June 12, 1903.

7. Ibid., "Alexander McD. McCook, A Brilliant Corps Commander in the Civil War," by Col. Horace N. Fischer, printed in the *Boston Transcript*, June 13, 1903.

Bibliography

Books

Ambrose, Stephen E. *Halleck: Lincoln's Chief of Staff.* Baton Rouge: Louisiana State University Press, 1990.

Angle, Paul M., ed. *Three Years in the Army of the Cumberland: The Letters and Diary of Major James A. Connolly.* Bloomington: Indiana University Press, 1987.

Army Memoirs of Lucius W. Barber, Company "D" 15th Illinois Volunteer Infantry: May 24, 1861 to September 30, 1865. Chicago: J. M. W. Jones Stationery and Printing, 1894.

Basler, Roy P., ed. *The Collected Works of Abraham Lincoln,* vol. 4, 1860–1861. New Brunswick, NJ: Rutgers University Press, 1955.

Beatty, John. *The Citizen Soldier; or, Memoirs of a Volunteer.* Cincinnati, OH: Wilstach Baldwin, 1879.

_____. *Memoirs of a Volunteer, 1861–1863.* New York: W. W. Norton, 1946.

Berry, Stephen. *House of Abraham: Lincoln & the Todds, a Family Divided by War.* Boston: Houghton Mifflin, 2007.

Beymer, William Gilmore. *Scouts and Spies of the Civil War.* 1912. Lincoln: University of Nebraska Press, 2003.

Blanton, DeAnne, and Lauren M. Cook. *They Fought Like Demons: Women Soldiers in the Civil War.* New York: Vintage, 2002.

Blegen, Theodore C., ed. *The Civil War Letters of Colonel Hans Christian Heg.* Northfield, MN: Norwegian-American Historical Association, 1936.

Bobrick, Benson. *Testament: A Soldier's Story of the Civil War.* New York: Simon & Schuster, 2003.

Botkin, B. A., ed. *A Civil War Treasury of Tales, Legends and Folklore.* New York: Random House, 1960.

Buell, Thomas B. *The Warrior Generals: Combat Leadership in the Civil War.* New York: Three Rivers Press, 1997.

Burlingame, Michael, ed. *Lincoln Observed, Civil War Dispatches of Noah Brooks.* Baltimore: Johns Hopkins University Press, 1998.

_____. *With Lincoln in the White House: Letters, Memoranda and Other Writings of John G. Nicolay, 1860–1865.* Carbondale: Southern Illinois University Press, 2000.

Catton, Bruce. *The Centennial History of the Civil War, Vol. 3, Never Call Retreat.* Garden City, NY: Doubleday, 1965.

Chadwick, Bruce. *1858: Abraham Lincoln, Jefferson Davis, Robert E. Lee, Ulysses S. Grant, and the War They Failed to See.* Naperville, IL: Sourcebooks, 2008.

Cist, Henry M. *The Army of the Cumberland.* New York: Charles Scribner's Sons, 1882.

Clinton, Catherine, and Nina Silber, ed. *Divided Houses, Gender and the Civil War.* New York: Oxford University Press, 1992.

Coffin, Charles Carleton. *My Days and Nights on the Battlefield.* Chicago: M. A. Donahue, 1887.

Conger, Arthur L. *The Rise of U. S. Grant.* 1931. New York: Da Capo Press, 1996.

Cozzens, Peter. *General John Pope: A Life for the Nation.* Urbana: University of Illinois Press, 2000.

_____. *No Better Place to Die: The Battle of*

Stones River. Urbana: University of Illinois Press, 1991.

_____. *This Terrible Sound: The Battle of Chickamauga.* Urbana: University of Illinois Press, 1992.

Crary, Catherine C., ed. *Dear Belle: Letters from a Cadet & Officer to His Sweetheart, 1858–1865.* Middleton, CT: Wesleyan University Press, 1965.

Crooks, Jr., Daniel J. *Charleston Is Burning! Two Centuries of Fire and Flames.* Charleston, SC: History Press, 2009.

Crozier, Emmet. *Yankee Reporters, 1861–1865.* New York: Oxford University Press, 1956.

Dana, Charles A. *Recollections of the Civil War: With the Leaders at Washington and in the Field in the Sixties.* 1898. Lincoln: University of Nebraska Press, 1996.

Daniel, Larry J. *Shiloh: The Battle That Changed the Civil War.* New York: Touchstone, 1997.

Davis, William C. *An Honorable Defeat: The Last Days of the Confederate Government.* New York: Harcourt, 2001.

_____. *Battle of Bull Run: A History of the First Major Campaign of the Civil War.* Garden City, NY: Doubleday, 1977.

_____. *Breckinridge: Statesman, Soldier, Symbol.* Baton Rouge: Louisiana State University Press, 1974.

Detzer, David. *Donnybrook: The Battle of Bull Run, 1861.* New York: Harcourt, 2004.

_____. *Dissonance. The Turbulent Days between Fort Sumter and Bull Run.* New York: Harcourt, 2006.

Dodge, William Sumner. *History of the Old Second Division, Army of the Cumberland, Commanders: McCook, Sill and Johnson.* Chicago: Church & Goodman, 1864.

Doster, William E. *Lincoln and Episodes of the Civil War.* New York: G. P. Putnam's Sons, 1915.

Dunkelman, Mark H. *Brothers One and All: Esprit de Corps in a Civil War Regiment.* Baton Rouge: Louisiana State University Press, 2004.

Early, Jubal Anderson. *War Memoirs: Autobiographical Sketch and Narrative of the War between the States.* Bloomington: Indiana University Press, 1960.

Eckenrode, H. J., and Bryan Conrad. *James Longstreet: Lee's War Horse.* Chapel Hill: University of North Carolina Press, 1986.

Faust, Drew Gilpin. *This Republic of Suffering: Death and the American Civil War.* New York: Knopf, 2008.

Fiske, John. *The Mississippi Valley in the Civil War.* New York: Houghton Mifflin, 1900.

Fitch, John. *Annals of the Army of the Cumberland.* 1864. Mechanicsburg, PA: Stackpole Books, 2003.

Flood, Charles Bracelen. *1864: Lincoln at the Gates of History.* New York: Simon & Schuster, 2009.

_____. *Grant and Sherman: The Friendship That Won the Civil War.* New York: Harper Perennial, 2005.

Foote, Shelby. *The Civil War: A Narrative, Fort Sumter to Perryville.* Vol. 1. New York: Vintage, 1986.

Fordyce, Samuel W., IV, ed. *An American General: The Memoirs of David Sloan Stanley.* Santa Barbara, CA: Narrative Press, 2003.

Freehling, William W. *The South vs. the South: How Anti-Confederate Southerners Shaped the Course of the Civil War.* New York: Oxford University Press, 2001.

Garrison, Webb. *Amazing Women of the Civil War: Fascinating True Stories of Women Who Made a Difference.* Nashville: Rutledge Hill Press, 1999.

_____. *Strange Battles of the Civil War.* Nashville: Cumberland House, 2001.

Goodrich, Thomas. *The Darkest Dawn: Lincoln, Booth, and the Great American Tragedy.* Bloomington: Indiana University Press, 2005.

Goodwin, Doris Kearns. *Team of Rivals: The Political Genius of Abraham Lincoln.* New York: Simon & Schuster, 2006.

Grant, U. S. *Personal Memoirs of U. S. Grant.* Vol. 1. New York: C. L. Webster, 1885–1886.

Grebner, Constantin. *"We Were the Ninth": A History of the Ninth Regiment, Ohio Volunteer Infantry, April 17, 1861 to June 7, 1864.* Translated and Edited by Frederic Trautmann. Kent, OH: Kent State University Press, 1987.

Hagemann, E. R., ed. *Fighting Rebels and Redskins, Experiences in Army Life of Colonel George B. Sanford, 1861–1892.* Norman: University of Oklahoma Press, 1969.

Hanson, Joseph Mills. *The Conquest of the Missouri: Being the Story of the Life and*

Exploits of Captain Grant Marsh. Chicago: A. C. McClurg, 1910.

Harrell, Carolyn L. *When the Bells Tolled for Lincoln: Southern Reaction to the Assassination*, Macon, GA: Mercer University Press, 1997.

Harrison, Lowell H. *The Civil War in Kentucky*. Lexington: University Press of Kentucky, 1975.

Hess, Earl J. *Banners to the Breeze: The Kentucky Campaign, Corinth and Stones River*. Lincoln: University of Nebraska Press, 2000.

_____. *The Union Soldier in Battle: Enduring the Ordeal of Combat*. Lawrence: University Press of Kansas, 1997.

Hesseltine, William B., ed. *Three Against Lincoln: Murat Halstead Reports of the Caucuses of 1860*. Baton Rouge: Louisiana State University Press, 1960.

Hirshson, Stanley P. *The White Tecumseh: A Biography of General William T. Sherman*. New York: Wiley, 1997.

Horn, Stanley F. *The Army of Tennessee: A Military History*. Norman: University of Oklahoma Press, 1952.

Howe, Henry. *A Brief Historical Sketch of the Fighting McCooks*. Proceedings of the Scotch-Irish Society of America.

_____. *Historical Collections of Ohio: An Encyclopedia of the State*. State of Ohio, 1900.

Hughes, Nathaniel Cheairs, Jr., and Gordon E. Whitney. *Jefferson Davis in Blue, the Life of Sherman's Relentless Warrior*. Baton Rouge: Louisiana State University Press, 2002.

Hutton, Paul Andrew. *Phil Sheridan and His Army*. Lincoln: University of Nebraska Press, 1985.

Hyman, Harold M., and Benjamin P. Thomas. *Stanton: The Life and Times of Lincoln's Secretary of War*. New York: Knopf, 1962.

Johnson, Mark W. *That Body of Brave Men: The U.S. Regular Infantry and the Civil War in the West*. New York: Da Capo Press, 2003.

Johnson, R. W. *A Soldier's Reminiscences in Peace and War*. Philadelphia: J. B. Lippincott, 1886.

Johnston, R. M. *Bull Run: Its Strategy and Tactics*.1913. Carlisle, PA: John Kallmann, 1996.

Kern, Albert, ed. *History of the First Regiment Ohio Volunteer Infantry in the Civil War, 1861–1865*. Dayton, OH: A. Kern, 1918.

Kirwan, A. D., ed. *Johnny Green of the Orphan Brigade: The Journal of a Confederate Soldier*. Lexington: University of Kentucky Press, 1956.

Klement, Frank L. *The Limits of Dissent: Clement L. Vallandigham & the Civil War*. Lexington: University of Kentucky Press, 1970.

Kline, Michael J. *The Baltimore Plot: The First Conspiracy to Assassinate Abraham Lincoln*. Yardley, PA: Westholme, 2008.

Koonce, Donald B., ed. *Doctor to the Front: The Recollections of Confederate Surgeon Thomas Fanning Wood, 1861–1865*. Knoxville: University of Tennessee Press, 2000.

Krannawitter, Thomas L. *Vindicating Lincoln: Defending the Politics of Our Greatest President*. Lanham, MD: Rowman & Littlefield, 2008.

Lamers, William M. *The Edge of Glory: A Biography of General William S. Rosecrans, USA*. Baton Rouge: Louisiana State University Press, 1999.

Lee, Dan. *Kentuckian in Blue: A Biography of Major General Lovell Harrison Rousseau*. Jefferson, NC: McFarland, 2010.

Leech, Margaret. *Reveille in Washington, 1860–1865*. New York: Harper & Brothers, 1941.

Leech, Margaret, and Harry J. Brown. *The Garfield Orbit: The Life of President James A. Garfield*. New York: Harper & Row, 1978.

Leepson, Marc. *Desperate Engagement: How a Little-Known Civil War Battle Saved Washington, D.C., and Changed the Course of American History*. New York: Thomas Dunne Books, 2007.

Lewis, Lloyd. *The Assassination of Lincoln: History & Myth*. 1929. New York: MJF Books, 1994.

_____. *Sherman: Fighting Prophet*. New York: Harcourt Brace, 1932.

Liddell Hart, B. H.. *Sherman: Soldier, Realist, American*. 1929. New York: Da Capo Press, 1993.

McDonald, JoAnna M. *"We Shall Meet Again": The First Battle of Manassas (Bull Run), July 18–21, 1861*. New York: Oxford University Press, 2000.

McKinney, Francis F. *Education in Violence:*

The Life of George H. Thomas and the Army of the Cumberland. Detroit: Wayne State University Press, 1961.

McPherson, James M. *Abraham Lincoln and the Second American Revolution*. New York: Oxford University Press, 1990.

_____. *Battle Cry of Freedom: The Civil War Era*. New York: Oxford University Press, 1988.

_____. *Tried by War: Abraham Lincoln as Commander in Chief*. New York: Penguin, 2009.

Maihafer, Harry J. *The General and the Journalists: Ulysses S. Grant, Horace Greeley and Charles Dana*. Washington, DC: Brassey's, 2001.

_____. *War of Words: Abraham Lincoln & the Civil War Press*. Washington, DC: Brassey's, 2001.

Martinez, Susan B. *The Psychic Life of Abraham Lincoln*. Franklin Lakes, NJ: New Page Books, 2009.

Miers, Earl Schenck. *The General Who Marched to Hell: Sherman and the Southern Campaign*. New York: Knopf, 1951.

Milton, George Fort. *The Age of Hate: Andrew Johnson and the Radicals*. New York: Coward-McCann, 1930.

Morris, Roy, Jr., *The Better Angel, Walt Whitman in the Civil War*. New York: Oxford University Press, 2000.

_____. *Sheridan: The Life & Wars of General Phil Sheridan*. New York: Crown, 1992.

Nicolay, John G. *Outbreak of the Rebellion*. 1881. New York: Da Capo Press, 1995.

Neillands, Robin. *Grant: The Man Who Won the Civil War*. London: Weidenfeld and Nicholson, 2004.

Osborne, Charles C. *Jubal: The Life and Times of General Jubal A. Early, CSA, Defender of the Lost Cause*. Chapel Hill: Algonquin Books, 1992.

Palmer, John M. *Personal Recollections of John M. Palmer: The Story of an Earnest Life*. Cincinnati, OH: Robert Clarke, 1901.

Perkins, J. R. *Trails, Rails and War: The Life of General G. M. Dodge*. Indianapolis, IN: Bobbs-Merrill, 1929.

Perret, Geoffrey. *Lincoln's War: The Untold Story of America's Greatest President as Commander in Chief*. New York: Random House, 2004.

Peskin, Allan. *Garfield: A Biography*. Kent, OH: Kent State University Press, 1978.

Pinsker, Matthew. *Lincoln's Sanctuary: Abraham Lincoln and the Soldiers' Home*. New York: Oxford University Press, 2003.

Prokopowicz, Gerald J. *All for the Regiment: The Army of the Ohio, 1861–1862*. Chapel Hill: University of North Carolina Press, 2001.

Reid, Whitelaw. *Ohio in the War: Her Statesmen, Her Generals and Soldiers*. Vol. 1. Cincinnati, OH: Moore, Wilstach & Baldwin, 1868.

Reynolds, Arlene, ed. *The Civil War Memories of Elizabeth Bacon Custer: Reconstructed From Her Diaries and Notes*. Austin: University of Texas Press, 1994.

Richards, Leonard L. *The California Gold Rush and the Coming of the Civil War*. New York: Knopf, 2007.

Roland, Charles P. *The Confederacy*. Chicago: University of Chicago Press, 1960.

Royster, Charles. *The Destructive War: William Tecumseh Sherman, Stonewall Jackson, and the Americans*. New York: Vintage, 1993.

Shea, John Gilmary, ed. *The Fallen Brave: A Biographical Memorial of the American Officers Who Have Given Their Lives for the Preservation of the Union*. New York: C. B. Richardson, 1861.

Sheridan, P. H. *Personal Memoirs of P. H. Sheridan*. Vol. 1. New York: Charles Webster, 1888.

Sherman, William T. *Memoirs of General W. T. Sherman*. New York: Library of America, 1990.

Sifakis, Stewart. *Who Was Who in the Civil War*. New York: Facts on File, 1988.

Simon, James F. *Lincoln and Chief Justice Taney, Slavery, Secession, and the President's War Powers*. New York: Simon & Schuster, 2006.

Starr, Louis M. *Bohemian Brigade: Civil War Newsmen in Action*. 1954. Madison: University of Wisconsin Press, 1987.

Sword, Wiley. *Shiloh: Bloody April*. New York: William Morrow, 1974.

Tenney, W. J. *The Military and Naval History of the Rebellion in the United States*. 1866. Mechanicsburg, PA: Stackpole Books, 2002.

Thayer, William M. *From Tannery to the White House: The Life of Ulysses S. Grant, His Boyhood, Youth, Manhood, Public and Private Life and Services.* Boston: James H. Earle, 1885.

Thayer, William Roscoe. *The Life and Letters of John Hay.* Vol. 1. Boston: Houghton Mifflin, 1915.

Tripp, C. A. *The Intimate World of Abraham Lincoln.* New York: Thunder's Mouth Press, 2005.

van der Linden, Frank. *Lincoln: The Road to War.* Golden, CO: Fulcrum Publishing, 1998.

Van Horne, Thomas B. *History of the Army of the Cumberland.* Vol. 1. Cincinnati, OH: Robert Clarke, 1875.

Vandiver, Frank E. *Jubal's Raid: General Early's Famous Attack on Washington in 1864.* Lincoln: University of Nebraska Press, 1992.

Warner, Ezra J., *Generals in Blue: Lives of the Union Commanders.* Baton Rouge: Louisiana State University Press, 1996.

_____. *Generals in Gray: Lives of the Confederate Commanders.* Baton Rouge: Louisiana State University Press, 1959.

Weber, Jennifer, L. *Copperheads: The Rise and Fall of Lincoln's Opponents in the North.* New York: Oxford University Press, 2006.

Welcher, Frank J. *The Union Army 1861–1865: The Western Theater.* Bloomington: Indiana University Press, 1993.

Whalen, Charles, and Barbara Whalen. *The Fighting McCooks: America's Famous Fighting Family.* Bethesda, MD: Westmoreland Press, 2006.

Wheeler, Richard. *A Rising Thunder: From Lincoln's Election to the Battle of Bull Run; An Eyewitness History.* New York: Harper-Collins, 1994.

_____. *Voices of the Civil War.* New York: Crowell, 1976.

White, Horace. *The Life of Lyman Trumbull.* Boston: Houghton Mifflin, 1913.

Williams, Frederick D., ed. *The Wild Life of the Army: Civil War Letters of James A. Garfield.* East Lansing: Michigan State University Press, 1964.

Williams, Harry T. *Lincoln and His Generals.* New York: Knopf, 1952.

_____. *P. G. T. Beauregard: Napoleon in Gray.* Baton Rouge: Louisiana State University Press, 1955.

Williams, Kenneth P. *Lincoln Finds a General: A Military Study of the Civil War.* Vol. 3. New York: Macmillan, 1952.

Winik, Jay. *April 1865: The Month That Saved America:* New York: HarperCollins, 2001.

Woodworth, Steven E. *Jefferson Davis and His Generals: The Failure of Confederate Command in the West.* Lawrence: University Press of Kansas, 1990.

Worthington, Glenn H. *Fighting for Time: The Battle That Saved Washington.* 1932. Shippensburg, PA: White Mane, 1988.

Newspapers

Baltimore American
Boston Transcript
Chicago Tribune
Cincinnati Daily Commercial
Cincinnati Daily Times
Cincinnati Inquirer
Cincinnati Weekly Gazette
Cleveland Herald
Daily Evening Telegraph
Daily Ohio Statesman
Daily Times (Cincinnati, OH)
Dakotian (Yankton, DT)
Dayton Daily Empire
Dubuque Daily Times
Evening Star (Washington, DC)
New York Times
New York Tribune
Ohio Patriot
Philadelphia Inquirer
Press and Dakotaian (Yankton, DT)
Richmond Examiner
Richmond Whig
St. Paul Daily Globe
Washington (DC) Star

Articles, Diaries, Encyclopedias and Magazines

American National Biography. Vol. 14. New York: Oxford University Press, 1999.

Diary of Gideon Welles. Vols. 1 & 2. New York: Norton, 1960.

McCook, Daniel. "The Second Division at

Shiloh," *Harper's New Monthly Magazine* 28 (December 1863 to May 1864).

Nevada Observer, Nevada's Online State News Journal, June 5, 2008, (from C. C. Goodwin, *As I Remember Them*, 1913).

Oden, Teresa J. "The Fighting McCooks." *Kenyon College Alumni Bulletin*, Summer/Fall 1997.

Smith, Tonia J. "Gentlemen, You Have Played This D — — D Well," *North & South* 8, no. 5 (September 2005).

Tate, Roger. "The Campaign and Battle of Mill Springs," *Blue & Gray Magazine*, February 1993.

Woodard, James H. *Gen. A. McD. McCook at Stone River*. Paper Prepared and Read before the California Commandery of the Military Order of the Loyal Legion of the United States, at Los Angeles, February 22, 1892.

Archives, Manuscripts and Reference Books

The Civil War Book of Lists. Compiled by the Editors of Combined Books, 1993.

The Civil War Reader: 1862. By the editors of the *Civil War Times* and *American Civil War*. New York: Ibooks, 2002.

Commager, Henry Steele, ed. *The Civil War Archive: A History of the Civil War in Documents*. New York: Black Dog & Leventhal, 2000.

Connecticut Landmarks, Hartford. Library of Congress, Manuscript Reading Room, McCook Family Papers.

McCook, Anson, *Memoirs*. Unpublished. Columbus: Ohio Historical Society.

The War of the Rebellion; A Compilation of the Official Records of the Union and Confederate Armies. 130 vols. Washington, D.C.: GPO, 1880–1901.

Index

Numbers in *bold italics* indicate pages with photographs.